Transmedia Applications in Literacy Fields

Jason D. DeHart
The University of Tennessee, Knoxville, USA

A volume in the Advances in Linguistics and Communication Studies (ALCS) Book Series

Published in the United States of America by
    IGI Global
    Information Science Reference (an imprint of IGI Global)
    701 E. Chocolate Avenue
    Hershey PA, USA 17033
    Tel: 717-533-8845
    Fax: 717-533-8661
    E-mail: cust@igi-global.com
    Web site: http://www.igi-global.com

Copyright © 2024 by IGI Global. All rights reserved. No part of this publication may be reproduced, stored or distributed in any form or by any means, electronic or mechanical, including photocopying, without written permission from the publisher.
Product or company names used in this set are for identification purposes only. Inclusion of the names of the products or companies does not indicate a claim of ownership by IGI Global of the trademark or registered trademark.

                Library of Congress Cataloging-in-Publication Data

CIP Data in progress

British Cataloguing in Publication Data
A Cataloguing in Publication record for this book is available from the British Library.

All work contributed to this book is new, previously-unpublished material.
The views expressed in this book are those of the authors, but not necessarily of the publisher.

For electronic access to this publication, please contact: eresources@igi-global.com.

Advances in Linguistics and Communication Studies (ALCS) Book Series

Abigail G. Scheg
Western Governors University, USA

ISSN:2372-109X
EISSN:2372-1111

MISSION

The scope of language and communication is constantly changing as society evolves, new modes of communication are developed through technological advancement, and novel words enter our lexicon as the result of cultural change. Understanding how we communicate and use language is crucial in all industries and updated research is necessary in order to promote further knowledge in this field.

The **Advances in Linguistics and Communication Studies (ALCS)** book series presents the latest research in diverse topics relating to language and communication. Interdisciplinary in its coverage, ALCS presents comprehensive research on the use of language and communication in various industries including business, education, government, and healthcare.

Coverage
- Computer-Mediated Communication
- Cross-Cultural Communication
- Forensic Linguistics
- Interpersonal Communication
- Language in the Media
- Media and Public Communications

IGI Global is currently accepting manuscripts for publication within this series. To submit a proposal for a volume in this series, please contact our Acquisition Editors at Acquisitions@igi-global.com or visit: http://www.igi-global.com/publish/.

The (ISSN) is published by IGI Global, 701 E. Chocolate Avenue, Hershey, PA 17033-1240, USA, www.igi-global.com. This series is composed of titles available for purchase individually; each title is edited to be contextually exclusive from any other title within the series. For pricing and ordering information please visit http://www.igi-global.com/book-series/advances-linguistics-communication-studies/78950. Postmaster: Send all address changes to above address. Copyright © IGI Global. All rights, including translation in other languages reserved by the publisher. No part of this series may be reproduced or used in any form or by any means – graphics, electronic, or mechanical, including photocopying, recording, taping, or information and retrieval systems – without written permission from the publisher, except for non commercial, educational use, including classroom teaching purposes. The views expressed in this series are those of the authors, but not necessarily of IGI Global.

Titles in this Series

For a list of additional titles in this series, please visit: www.igi-global.com/book-series

Public Health Communication Challenges to Minority and Indigenous Communities
Kealeboga Aiseng (Rhodes University, South Africa) and Israel A. Fadipe (Ajayi Crowther University, Nigeria)
Information Science Reference • copyright 2024 • 331pp • H/C (ISBN: 9798369306246)
• US $260.00 (our price)

Quantitative Measures and Warranty Coverage of the Risk of Misinforming
Dimitar Grozdanov Christozov (American University in Bulgaria, Bulgaria)
Information Science Reference • copyright 2024 • 354pp • H/C (ISBN: 9781668488003)
• US $220.00 (our price)

AI and Its Convergence With Communication Technologies
Badar Muneer (Mehran University of Engineering and Technology, Pakistan) Faisal Karim Shaikh (Mehran University of Engineering and Technology, Pakistan) Naeem Mahoto (Mehran University of Engineering and Technology, Pakistan) Shahnawaz Talpur (Mehran University of Engineering and Technology, Pakistan) and Jordi Garcia (Universitat Politècnica de Catalunya, Spain)
Information Science Reference • copyright 2023 • 308pp • H/C (ISBN: 9781668477021)
• US $250.00 (our price)

Combining Modern Communication Methods With Heritage Education
Lia Bassa (Budapest Metropolitan University, Hungary & Foundation for Information Society, Hungary)
Information Science Reference • copyright 2023 • 317pp • H/C (ISBN: 9781668462171)
• US $215.00 (our price)

Handbook of Research on Socio-Cultural and Linguistic Perspectives on Language and Literacy Development
Angela K. Salmon (Florida International University, USA) and Amparo Clavijo-Olarte (Universidad Distrital Francisco Jose de Caldas, Colombia)
Information Science Reference • copyright 2023 • 500pp • H/C (ISBN: 9781668450222)
• US $270.00 (our price)

701 East Chocolate Avenue, Hershey, PA 17033, USA
Tel: 717-533-8845 x100 • Fax: 717-533-8661
E-Mail: cust@igi-global.com • www.igi-global.com

Table of Contents

Preface.. xx

Chapter 1
I Am My Greatest Invention: Examining Black Girl Literacies via the Visual
Narratives of Black Girls in Marvel Comics.. 1
    Christian M. Hines, Texas State University, USA

Chapter 2
Miles to Go: Tracing Spider-Man's Puerto Rican Identity Down Many
Divergent Roads.. 28
    David E. Low, Fresno State University, USA
    René M. Rodríguez-Astacio, Fresno State University, USA
    Yamil Sárraga-López, Fresno State University, USA

Chapter 3
Social Superheroes: Interactions, Judgments, and the Superhero Mission.......... 65
    Justin Martin, Whitworth University, USA

Chapter 4
An Original Comics Team and Transmedia: The JSA and Affiliation 103
    Jason D. DeHart, The University of Tennessee, Knoxville, USA

Chapter 5
The Joker: Transmedial Concept of a Comic Book Character 117
    Vladimir Popov, Independent Researcher, Serbia

Chapter 6
Significance of Transmedia Storytelling in Higher Education: Collaborative
Learning to Increase Enrollment and Retention Among Nontraditional
Students.. 133
    Anika C. Thrower, Borough of Manhattan Community College, CUNY, USA
    Alex Evangelista, Borough of Manhattan Community College, CUNY, USA

Chapter 7
Media Literacy: A Study on Media Consumption Habits and Perceptions of
Addiction Among Students 149
    Zeynep Yurtseven Avci, Eskisehir Osmangazi University, Turkey
    Özge Misirli, Eskisehir Osmangazi University, Turkey
    Gözde Tekbaş, Eskisehir Osmangazi University, Turkey

Chapter 8
(Re)Imagining Worlds and Reality in Media 175
    Jason D. DeHart, The University of Tennessee, Knoxville, USA

Chapter 9
"What Is Your Real Name?": A Vignette on Malcolm X's 1963 City Desk
Interview 189
    Dennis Matt Stevenson, The University of Tennessee, Knoxville, USA
    Joshua L. Kenna, The University of Tennessee, Knoxville, USA

Chapter 10
Emotional Literacy through Tea Objects: A Literary Rendition 211
    Ran Xiang, The University of British Columbia, Canada

Chapter 11
On These Haunted Streets: A Photopoetic Process of Transmedia Storytelling
as Critical Multimodal Literacy 238
    Lalenja Harrington, University of North Carolina at Greensboro, USA
    Karen Cox, Independent Researcher, USA

Compilation of References 279

About the Contributors 308

Index 311

Detailed Table of Contents

Preface xx

Chapter 1
I Am My Greatest Invention: Examining Black Girl Literacies via the Visual
Narratives of Black Girls in Marvel Comics 1
    Christian M. Hines, Texas State University, USA

Drawing on scholarship that conceptualizes the learning and meaning making of Black girls through the Black Girl Literacies framework, this chapter highlights examples of literacy practices in action in Marvel graphic novels with prominent Black girl characters. This framework can be used as a pedagogical tool to examine visual texts to see what themes are emergent and what can we learn from these characters, which can inform instructional practices and approaches to teaching a diverse set of students. It can ground educators in the understanding of the subversive literacies of Black girls.

Chapter 2
Miles to Go: Tracing Spider-Man's Puerto Rican Identity Down Many
Divergent Roads 28
    David E. Low, Fresno State University, USA
    René M. Rodríguez-Astacio, Fresno State University, USA
    Yamil Sárraga-López, Fresno State University, USA

In this chapter, three critical scholars of literature, literacy, multimodality, and identity trace various iterations of Miles Morales in the decade-plus since his debut. No longer confined to serialized comic books, Miles has, as of this writing, appeared in two prose novels; several popular and well-received animated films; video games; standalone graphic novels; televised cartoon programs; a picturebook; and in the form of toys, apparel, and other licensed merchandise. The character has been written and illustrated by hundreds of creators, with various backgrounds and intentions, across these media. Each is sedimented with meaning. Throughout the chapter, we examine Miles' transmedial development, specifically through the lens of his hybrid and intersecting biracial/bicultural identities, foregrounding representations of Puerto Rican identity in particular.

Chapter 3
Social Superheroes: Interactions, Judgments, and the Superhero Mission.......... 65
Justin Martin, Whitworth University, USA

In the chapter, the author considers the implications of a constructivist approach to understanding superhero media for scholarly analyses concerning the relation between social interactions, judgments, and superhero missions. The approach, social cognitive domain theory (SCDT), grounds the development, refinement, and application of moral and nonmoral social concepts in heterogeneous social interactions and arrangements. Particularly, special attention is given to comic, television, and film portrayals of T'Challa (Black Panther), Carl Lucas (Luke Cage), and the time-traveling X-Man Lucas Bishop. Previous work explores the parallels of their narratives for understanding the ubiquity of heterogeneous social and moral judgments, as their narratives can be partly distinguished through their grounding in national, local, and societal contexts, respectively. In keeping with this work, the present chapter explores the potential of three features of social judgments for understanding superheroes along three social interactional dimensions.

Chapter 4
An Original Comics Team and Transmedia: The JSA and Affiliation 103
Jason D. DeHart, The University of Tennessee, Knoxville, USA

This chapter focuses on the origins of comics heroes and the superhero genre, with attention to the messages of early comics. The introduction of characters is presented in unique multimodal fashion as a potential invitation for fandom. The refashioning of characters is further explored as it relates to particular time periods, with attention to the ways that reflect changes in culture. The nature of comics as artifacts of literacy and culture is explored, with notes on the ways that character relationships have cycled over time.

Chapter 5
The Joker: Transmedial Concept of a Comic Book Character 117
    Vladimir Popov, Independent Researcher, Serbia

This academic paper explores the transmedia narrative of the comic book character of the Joker across various media platforms. It delves into the complex creation and evolution of the Joker, highlighting the collaborative efforts of Bob Kane, Bill Finger, and Jerry Robinson, and the character's profound impact on cultural and societal norms. By examining the Joker's transmedial storytelling, the paper underscores the character's ability to adapt and resonate across different contexts, from comics to films and beyond. It further investigates the Joker's role as a mirror to societal dynamics, embodying themes of chaos, resistance, and critique of biopolitical control. The paper concludes that the Joker's enduring appeal and multifaceted nature exemplify the transformative potential of narrative characters within the transmedial landscape, serving as agents of critique and catalysts for discourse on identity, power, and resistance.

Chapter 6
Significance of Transmedia Storytelling in Higher Education: Collaborative Learning to Increase Enrollment and Retention Among Nontraditional Students.. 133
    Anika C. Thrower, Borough of Manhattan Community College, CUNY, USA
    Alex Evangelista, Borough of Manhattan Community College, CUNY, USA

Institutions of higher learning are essential in society. In the year 2023, there were over 18 million students. Though this total is substantial, it is below par compared to past trends. Long-standing college enrollment has been a catalyst for educating individuals in their chosen fields. Education attainment over time assists people in increasing the quality of life for themselves and their families, optimal health outcomes, and higher levels of productivity in communities while opening themselves to a broader range of opportunities. Because of COVID-19, in recent years, enrollment, retention, and graduation rates have been a challenge, particularly among nontraditional college students. Ensuring mattering and providing an inclusive campus environment has been more critical than ever before. As college administration and instructors seek ways to alleviate such fluctuations, collaborative learning and transmedia are viable solutions.

Chapter 7
Media Literacy: A Study on Media Consumption Habits and Perceptions of
Addiction Among Students 149
    Zeynep Yurtseven Avci, Eskisehir Osmangazi University, Turkey
    Özge Misirli, Eskisehir Osmangazi University, Turkey
    Gözde Tekbaş, Eskisehir Osmangazi University, Turkey

Abundance of information, ease of contemporary technologies, and cheapening of technology make it easier to access the media. The influence of the media in shaping behavior and shaping society in this way, brings the importance of drawing attention to the risks in the media. Addiction is one of the common topics in the media. Considering that what is widely revealed in the media will be normalized by society after a while, it is possible to say that media literacy plays an important role in recognizing these risks and minimizing them. The aim of this study is to determine the media consumption habits of the participants and the types of addiction they noticed in the media, and to determine their perceptions of an addiction they chose with the help of metaphors. The study was conducted with 176 students who took the Media Literacy course and voluntarily participated in the study. According to the findings, although the participants came across many types of addiction in media content, the addictions they noticed the most were technology-related addictions and substance addiction.

Chapter 8
(Re)Imagining Worlds and Reality in Media 175
    Jason D. DeHart, The University of Tennessee, Knoxville, USA

This chapter makes use of textual examples and description, as well as autoethnographic case study, to examine media storytelling and envisioning reality through storytelling. Attention is given to concepts of social justice, as well as implications for practice and further research. These implications include considerations of both text and readership, as well as explorations of criticality and notions of representation. A continued call for this kind of close reading of multiple texts and types of texts is central to the chapter.

Chapter 9
"What Is Your Real Name?": A Vignette on Malcolm X's 1963 City Desk
Interview 189
> *Dennis Matt Stevenson, The University of Tennessee, Knoxville, USA*
> *Joshua L. Kenna, The University of Tennessee, Knoxville, USA*

The purpose of this chapter is to provide a vignette classroom discussion of the primary source YouTube video of Malcolm X's City Desk interview March 1963 with student reactions and teacher commentary taken from classroom experience. Malcolm X is a lynchpin for introducing divisions in Black activism concerning race, policing, and education occurring in 1963, continuing in legacy movements after 1963, and reemerging in the modern push for social justice. Malcolm X holds a place in our collective historical memory that is at the same time recognizable and often misrepresented. This goal for analyzing this specific source is to provide lesson planning of the Long Civil Rights Movement focusing on Malcolm X and his legacy through a detailed sample lesson based on the digital primary source interview of Malcolm X. The larger significance is to ensure secondary classrooms keep pace with history scholarship to illustrate distinct civil rights goals rather than presenting a monolithic Civil Rights Movement.

Chapter 10
Emotional Literacy through Tea Objects: A Literary Rendition 211
> *Ran Xiang, The University of British Columbia, Canada*

As an unconventional and alternative way of doing qualitative research, arts-based methodology has gained growing interest from scholars. ABR harbors a great variety of approaches, including visual arts (photography, painting), performance art (music, ethno-drama), and literary genres (fiction, creative non-fiction, autobiography). Creative non-fiction is a genre of writing that uses literary techniques to create factually accurate narratives. It differs from fiction in that writers cannot make up or alter facts, but they can capture them in much more dramatic ways. In this chapter, the author employs literary writing techniques in the creative non-fiction writeup of her experience visiting three rare tea objects exhibitions in Japan. This chapter serves as a literary application in the field of emotional literacy, exploring how objects can elicit affective responses from human beings and the knowledge produced in the body.

Chapter 11
On These Haunted Streets: A Photopoetic Process of Transmedia Storytelling as Critical Multimodal Literacy 238
Lalenja Harrington, University of North Carolina at Greensboro, USA
Karen Cox, Independent Researcher, USA

This chapter outlines the development of a collaborative transmedia storytelling process by the authors, whose visual and poetic work is articulated here within the framework of critical multimodal literacy (CML). The authors were tasked to help bring forward the stories of black musicians involved in the opera Omar, and in doing so discovered an artistic process that was strengthened by the intersection of their critical approaches. Chronicling their engagement with Omar provided them with a uniquely situated opportunity to describe their individual meaning making processes, and then discuss how consideration of each other's process impacted our storytelling. The authors do this through sharing specific story examples from the oral history project. Engagement with black artistic presence in opera also allowed them to explore our shared focus on anchoring this work within a socio-political context that supports the naming/transformation of inequities; helping to illustrate how this work is situated within the framework of CML and reflects a transmedia process of layered storytelling.

Compilation of References 279

About the Contributors 308

Index 311

Foreword

WHAT IS BATMAN? EPISTEMOLOGICAL PATHWAYS FOR TRANSMEDIALITY IN POSTDIGITAL TIMES

The field of literacy research has drastically evolved since 2020, and especially since the impetus of transmedia studies in the mid-2000s. The COVID-19 pandemic has generated permanent change in the ways we live on the daily and consume media. These global conditions have changed research fields in significant manners. Sociomaterial entanglements (Sheridan et al., 2020), that is, the quantum forces at play between humans, nonhumans, and more-than-humans, can be partly held responsible for this global shift. The COVID-19 lockdowns, implemented internationally, represent a notorious example of how sociomaterial entanglements have drastically impacted how youth consume media, engage in literacy-laden compositions, and are themselves constantly entangled in worldly matters and meanings (Lemieux, 2024).

Inherited from social semiotics (New London Group, 1996), multimodal research and narratology, transmediality became popular in educational studies with the work of ltieracu researcher Henry Jenkins (2003, 2006). The definitions of transmediality have since evolved. At the turn of the 21st Century, literacy research was concerned with comprehending, interpreting, reacting to, and appreciating semiotic signs across multimedia platforms. Combined with one or multiple narrative arcs, these semiotic signs where negociated across discourses, platforms, users, and media. The focus, then, was on understanding how semiotic signs were catalysts for creating meaning-making for readers, viewers, gamers, and media consumers. Comprehension and interpretation were unidirectional in that these procedural meaning-making practices made by humans (e.g., youths and adolescents) occured in reaction to nonhuman objects (e.g., a comic book, a film adaptation, a platform-based fanfiction). Later, with the appearance of transmedia storytelling (Jenkins, 2003) and the emergence of fandoms (Jenkins, 2006), representations of transmedia characters were studied in the same fashion as narrative storyworlds. That is, the notions of fidelity and adaptation have been seriously studied not only by narratology and literacy researchers, but also by fans interested in how these manifested across platform and media. This trend of research and inquiry was particularly active in the 2010s until the COVID-19 pandemic. Indeed, the global pandemic instigated a shift in literacy studies from object-focused analyses (e.g., investigating the notion of fidelity in transmedia narratives) to research that is concerned with dynamisms and relationalities (Sheridan et al., 2020) across platforms, materials, and media.

Now and more extensively, a large number of literacy scholars, amongst other researchers, are no longer referring to pre- and post-pandemic times and are now developing, instead, new conceptual frameworks that anchor postdigitality (Lamb, 2023). This can take place in gaming (Ehret et al., 2023) and seek to document sociomaterial relationalities as they emerge on different social media platforms (Ehret, 2024, Lemieux et al., 2022; Low et al., 2023) and in informal learning spaces such as makerspaces (Lemieux, 2024; Rowsell & McLean, 2021). These important epistemological shifts reflect the drastic and documented increase of social media use during the pandemic, as reported internationally, have reframed literacy practices accordingly. With humans (i.e., adolescents, youths, adults) producing daily media on more-than-human, algorithmic-based social media platforms (e.g., Instagram, TikTok, Snapchat) and in nonhuman spaces (e.g., a coffee shop, an office, a living room, a bus or a train), the field of literacy (or, rather, literacies) research ultimately takes the pulse of these fleeting, yet tangible dynamisms that emerge on the daily, whether these happen on conscious or unconscious levels or at an individual or collective scale. Conversely, from rapidly changing postdigital innovations to pivotal consumerism changes since the pandemic, children and adolescents have adapted to the ways in which they interact with different media across platforms.

In literacy studies, algorithmic platforms automatically generate multimedia texts that shape how users, youth included, interact and intra-act with content (Low et al., 2023). In the Canadian context in the last three years, for instance, 90% of youths between the age of 7 to 17 owned their own cellphones and data plans: they used these tools to be active on at least one social media platform (Media Technology Monitor Junior, 2021). What is more, these interactions with media, especially social media, were not isolated literacy events: 37% of these youths were multitaskers and interacted with either other websites or watched television simultaneously (Media Technology Monitor Junior, 2021). And while this population is more likely to consume multimodal content, that is, videos and images, than publish such content, these consumerism tendencies point to a change in how literacy is enacted, understood, digested, and ultimately produced. The Canadian Broadcasting Corporation Media Technology Monitor's latest 2024 report points to even more, unsurprising yet drastic, changes in youths' digital habits. Indeed, in terms of social media use, 80% of Canadian youths use Snapchat daily and in terms of assistive technology, 25% of adolescents use artificial intelligence tools monthly (Canadian Broadcasting Corporation, 2024). These tendencies can also be observed all across the United States. Recent data from the Pew Research Centre also reported how social media's big four (TikTok, Snapchat, Instagram and YouTube) continue to be amongst the most used platforms by adolescents aged 13-17 daily (Anderson et al., 2023). This study also demonstrated that 95% of teens own a smartphone, and half of them report using going online 'almost constantly'. These progressive transformations of digital habits naturally translate into a heightened interest, in users, for the hybridity of social media, assistive technologies, traditional offline technologies (e.g., television, radio), and monomodal literacies (e.g., written advertisements) as part of daily literacy practices—some used more than others for either entertainment or functionality.

What this means for transmediality studies is that representations of transmedia characters (Lemieux, 2019) as well as narrative storyworlds exist across these platforms and youths as well as adults can easily access, consume and interact with these imaginary territories in ways that make literacy considerably less static and realistically more dynamic. What is more, consumers and users modulate, forge, and transform transmedia characters and narrative storyworlds within fan communities and blog-based fanfictions (Jenkins, 2006). With the advent of daily social media consumption and composition, these fan communities produce transmedia narratives across social media platforms. In other words, social networks constitute perfect repertoires for fandoms and researchers have widely documented these sites as public terrains for storyworld engagement and consumption (Stein, 2016). Particular symbols, hashtags more specifically, in algorithmic cultures allows fans and users to streamline searches on these platforms and look for particular information, people, and interests. For instance, #InstaPoetry (Lemieux et al., 2022), #BookTok (Low et al., 2023), and #BookTube (Ehret et al., 2018) are all hashtags that call for movement, mobilize hybrid participatory cultures, and contribute to media convergence. This concentration of information and sense-making of narrative universes happens dynamically instead of through specific transmedia storylines or characters that can be present in more static ways (e.g., through print-based or television-based comics).

With these technological and media-oriented relational habits, there needs to be collective consciousness on the ways in which these dispositions shape our understandings of literacies at home, in schools, and in-between these spaces. Then, these reflections need to also shed light on the pivotal role that transmediality occupies within the field of literacy as it mirrors the dynamic passages and voyages between these fleeting spaces. No longer can literacies research dismiss the ever shifting, entangled, messy realities of adolescents who are evolving in a world in which the notion of the "digital" is a thing of the past. Where the postdigital anchors sociomaterial dynamisms, it also challenges in questions traditional ideas that were first put forward in social semiotics as traditionnally understood in the scientific literature on teaching and learning language (New London Group, 1996). In this book on transmedia literacy, it is important to keep in mind that while the translation from one media to another (and from one platform to another) still provokes pivotal questions for educational research, there is a number of epistemological perspectives that are growing in the body of postdigital theory related to literacy studies. These need to be accounted for in research studies and beyond.

There is concrete scientific evidence that semiotic-oriented platforms are useful for meaningful literacy teaching and learning with youths and adolescents. This is undeniable. In addition, transmedial texts (Lemieux, 2023) and transmedial characters (Lemieux, 2019) exist across media and platforms: their presence is made possible by fandoms and permeate fanfictions. These texts and characters mirror a number of lived realities and situations across platforms. For example, Batman can be a cultimination or an agglomeration of multiple representations in a reader-viewer's horizon of expectations and experiences of reading comics, viewing films and playing games where Batman is involved. Batman can be a result of reconstituted fragments of *Batman and Robin* (the comics from a specific period), Ben Affleck, Robert Pattinson and Christian Bale, all at the same time. Or, one can steal, consciously or inconsciously, attributes of Affleck and Bale to reconstitute their own Batman in their mind, paired maybe with mental images of *Batman Returns* (1992 movie) and *Batman: Arkham Asylum* (2009 videogame). In parallel, these realities have the potential to both anchor and provoke diverse representations of otherwise heteronormative and white already present in collective imaginaries (Thomas, 2019). There is notable potential for discussions around social justice and what non-normative representations of whiteness and toxic masculinity can look like in a postdigital age.

This progressive work can take place within classrooms. Specifically, one of the ways to redress this is through teaching and learning methods inside the classroom and beyond. Indeed, analytical film-based teaching methods (DeHart, 2022), critical graphic novel pedagogy (DeHart, 2021), critical race comics teaching (Hollman, 2021), as well as critical social justice-oriented literacies in popular culture using Netflix (Toliver, 2018) are all methods and strategies that push us to consider transmediality in ways that question the white, heterosexual hegemony in transmedial character representations and storyworlds. These examinations can happen when we start interrogating *why* certain characters present specific features (especially those of dominant cultures), and how these can be dismantled and throught about differently to mirror, for example, historically marginalized people (think, for example, queer and BIPOC people). These critical, affective positionalities (Lemieux, 2024), may take place in affirmative, relational and inquiry-based work between people, representations, artefacts such as movies, comics, books, videogames) and transmedia narratives.

In short and in my view, transmediality can be defined as the entangled, relational actions of understanding, interpreting, and reacting to texts and characters across media and platforms. Social justice matters naturally emerge as it calls forth representational as well as more-than representational work in these dynamics. I have also explained how the social, entangled, and relational coconstructions of a transmedial narrative universe is determined by humans, nonhumans, and more-than-humans over time. Through this evolution of transmedial narratives across space and time, both characters and storyworlds become porous terrains of meaning negociation, done in light of different intersecting identities. Readers, viewers, and gamers live through these transmedial stories and really extend the original work of Louise Rosenblatt (1978) on the transactional theory of reading. For example, transmediality in classroom applications and related work on small stories (Rowsell et al., 2018) has laid the ground for how children perceive and interact with narrative storyworlds across platforms and media, speaking to the messiness and inter-reliability of interpretive and comprehensive processes. I would refer to these more-than literacy events as sociomaterial loopings—they evolve with each reading as one discovers new character versions and engages in novel story arcs across media and platforms, hopefully with a critical eye taught in classrooms and beyond.

This book on transmediality is divided in three sections and the twelve chapters cover a lineage of seminal traditions in transmedia studies as it related to literacy studies in educational settings with an international outlook. All chapters speak to transmediality within narrative storyworlds and beyond, anchoring and dismantling both local and global networks as they emerve in transmedial storyworlds. These constitutions to the field of literacies undeniably propose new avenues in studying how transmediality take place across contexts worldwide but also in a postdigital world.

Amélie Lemieux
The University of Montreal, Canada

REFERENCES

Anderson, M., Faviero, M. & Gottfried, J. (2023, December 11). *Teens, social media and technology 2023*. Pew Research. Pewresearch.org/internet/2023/12/11/teens-social-media-and-technology-2023/

Canadian Broadcasting Corporation. (2024, April 30). *MTM Jr. Releases its 2024 data on Canadian kids' media and technology habits*. CBC. cbc.radio-canada.ca/en/media-centre/mtm-jr-2024-kids-media-and-technology-habits/

DeHart, J. (2021). It's about Superman, but it's more than that: A graphic novel pedagogy in middle years classrooms. *Literacy Learning: The Middle Years*, 29(1), 47–52.

DeHart, J. (2022). *Affordances of film for literacy instruction*. IGI Global. 10.4018/978-1-7998-9136-9

Ehret, C. (2024). Critical literacies in algorithmic cultures. *Literacy*, 58(2), 157–166. 10.1111/lit.12363

Ehret, C., Boegel, J., & Manuel-Nekouei, R. (2018). The role of affect in adolescents' online literacies: Participatory pressurs in BookTube culture. *Journal of Adolescent & Adult Literacy*, 62(2), 151–161. 10.1002/jaal.881

Ehret, C., Mannard, E., & Curwood, J. S. (2022). How young adult videogames materialize senses of self through ludonarrative affects: Understanding identity and embodiment through sociomaterial analysis. *Learning, Media and Technology*, 47(3), 341–354. 10.1080/17439884.2022.2066125

Hollman, D. L. (2021). Critical race comics: Centering black subjectivities and teaching racial literacy. *Journal of Curriculum and Pedagogy*, 18(2), 119–133. 10.1080/15505170.2021.1932642

Jenkins, H. (2003, January 15). Transmedia storytelling. *MIT Technology Review*. https://www.technologyreview.com/2003/01/15/234540/transmedia-storytelling/

Jenkins, H. (2006). *Fans, bloggers, and gamers*. New York University Press.

Lamb, J. (2023). Sociomateriality, postdigital thinking, and learning spaces research. In Jandrić, P., MacKenzie, A., & Knox, J. (Eds.), *Constructing postdigital research* (pp. 154–169). Springer. 10.1007/978-3-031-35411-3_6

Lemieux, A. (2019). Dismantling *X-Men Apocalypse*: The spaces between transmedia storytelling and transmedia characters. In E. Deprêtre & G. A. Duarte (Eds.). *Transmédialité, bande dessinée et adaptation* (p. 245-256). Presses universitaires Blaise-Pascal.

Lemieux, A. (2023). À l'aube de la transmédialité: de l'oeuvre antérieure comme péritexte. In E. Deprêtre & G. A. Duarte (Eds.). *Péritexte et transmédialité* (p. 154-169). Presses universitaires Blaise-Pascal.

Lemieux, A. (2024). "Back then it was only men who worked in these kind of fields": Observing little sparks through the prism of affect and gender in maker literacies research. [OnlineFirst]. *Reading Research Quarterly*, 1–16.

Low, B., Ehret, C. & Hagh, A. (2023). Algorithmic imaginings and critical digital literacy on #BookTok. *New Media & Society* (OnlineFirst).

Media Technology Monitor/MTM Junior. (2021). *Staying connected: Youth and social media*. MTM.

New London Group. (1996). A pedagogy of multiliteracies: Designing social futures. *Harvard Educational Review*, 66(1), 60–93. 10.17763/haer.66.1.17370n67v22j160u

Rosenblatt, L. M. (1978). *The reader, the text, the poem: The transactional theory of the literary work*. Southern Illinois University Press.

Rowsell, J., Lemieux, A., Swartz, L., Burkitt, J., & Turcotte, M. (2018). The stuff that heroes are made of: Elastic, sticky, messy literacies in children's transmedial cultures. *Language Arts*, 96(1), 7–20. 10.58680/la201829745

Rowsell, J., & McLean, C. (2021). *Maker literacies and maker identities in the digital age: Learning and playing through modes and media*. Routledge.

Sheridan, M. P., Lemieux, A., Do Nascimento, A., & Arnseth, H. C. (2020). Intra-active entanglements: What posthuman and new materialist frameworks can offer the learning sciences. *British Journal of Educational Technology*, 51(4), 1277–1291. 10.1111/bjet.12928

Stein, L. E. (2016). Fandom and the transtext. In Derby Kurtz, B., & Bourdaa, M. (Eds.), *The rise of transtexts: Challenges and opportunities* (pp. 71–89). Routledge.

Thomas, E. E. (2019). *The Dark Fantastic: Race and imagination from Harry Potter to the Hunger Games*. New York University Press.

Toliver, S. R. (2018). Unlocking the Cage: Empowering literacy representations in Netflix' *Luke Cage* series. *Journal of Adolescent & Adult Literacy*, 61(6), 621–630. 10.1002/jaal.721

Preface

As a researcher, scholar and educator for eighteen years who has been actively engaged in qualitative analysis since 2015, I note the ways that storytelling trends have changed over time, including the changes that have occurred in platforms and tools made available to readers and composers. Transformations among story types and media platforms have been prolific in my tenure as a teacher, and these changes make for fascinating work in terms of scholarship. I also note the ways storytelling across media has shaped me as a reader and human being. Jenkins (2008) noted the movement of storytelling across media, leading to the formalized notion of transmedia storytelling. Jenkins (2008) further demonstrated the possibilities for branding that occur through this approach to narrative. Such moves in text and creation even link to notions of identity for readers/viewers (Esteban-Guitart & Gee, 2024).

As a comics reader, film viewer, and child who engaged with storytelling with action figures and video games, I know the ways stories and characters link together from a first-hand perspective. It is always illuminating to step back from my personal experiences and hear the descriptions of scholars who examine such practices. This kind of playful sense-making allows me to consider the steps I have taken in my journey as a scholar, teacher, and literacy-centered individual, and further allows me to think about how characters have shaped me. The integration of characters and notions of fandom have been traced further to link with other aspects of cultural identity, like faith and spirituality (Hodge, 2023).

This book features a range of scholars who speak to the ways stories can be told and the ways that literacy can be practiced across media. I am fascinated by both the theories that inform this use of storytelling across media, as well as the pedagogical processes and particular texts that teachers and researchers choose. From film to comics, and from the digital to physical, the scholars who have agreed to be part of this work note a world of words and work that democratizes language and demonstrates a variety of literacy connections.

I next offer a brief glimpse at what each authors offer in each of the chapters that have been collected in this volume.

Preface

A ROADMAP OF THE BOOK

Dr. Christian Hines leads the collection with the first chapter, entitled "I Am My Greatest Invention: Examining Black Girl Literacies via the Visual Narratives of Black Girls in Marvel Comics." Dr. Hines begins from the Black Girl Literacies framework and analyzes the literacy practices evident in Marvel graphic novels with prominent Black girl characters, including emphasis on titles like *Moon Girl and Devil Dinosaur* and characters like Shuri. Dr. Hines offers a framework in this chapter that has utility for educators and researchers, offering further implications for instructional practices that connect with a wide range of students. This chapter author speaks about the ways that readers can engage with comics and media characters, including explorations of identity/identities.

Following this chapter, Dr. David E. Low and Dr. René M. Rodríguez-Astacio offer chapter two, "Miles to Go: Tracing Spider-Man's Puerto Rican Identity Down Many Divergent Roads," in which they explore the attributes and heritage of Miles Morales across a variety of forms. The authors examine the character Miles Morales through previous work in an afterschool Comics Club with a group of Black and Latiné students in grades 4-8) in an afterschool Comics Club. This initial work, which has been explored in publication, leads to the conversation presented in this chapter. Dr. Low sums up some of the exchanges that took place around texts with Miles Morales, including questions of heroism and identity. This work points to the value of representation in texts and across media. From prose comics to animation, and including a variety of games, Miles Morales has been a figure at the forefront of culture in the past few years. Dr. Rodríguez-Astacio draws on his positionality as a Boricua scholar, in particular, to share insights into representations of Miles's Puerta Rican identity across media.

In chapter three, entitled "Social Interactions, Judgments, and the Superhero Mission: A Brief Exploration of Black Panther, Luke Cage, and Bishop," Dr. Justin Martin examines the popular appeal of superhero media across forms of storytelling through a constructivist approach. Martin points to fan-created videos that explore superhero stories and the culture of fandom that surrounds these stories, including elements of nostalgia and questions which continue to present fascinating possibilities for storytelling. From presence to ontology, as well as including explorations of moral codes and contexts, Martin explores the implications of comics storytelling choices on the social landscape. Martin further examines how these characters inform ideas of morality and diversity. This work is philosophical, textual, and roots out the architecture of characters whose presence in comics has been known to me for some time but whose identities and possibilities, as well as their thoughtful interlinking in this chapter, lead to fruitful next steps in my thinking.

Preface

In chapter four, the editor offers "An Original Comics Team and Transmedia: The JSA and Affiliation." This work allowed me to explore the original appearance of the Justice Society of America, as published in DC Comics, and trace the development of the characters and storyline across time and cultural factors. In terms of pedagogical considerations, I offer a look at the ways the team speaks to belonging and a sense of affiliation, and I link this idea to popular culture and to notions of fandom and popularity that align with larger constructs within literacy. While I have examined individual characters and their impact on readers in previous work, this is my first attempt to grapple with a comics team of characters. This chapter points to the communal nature of reading and literacy engagement both textually and pedagogically. This team is an assemblage of characters who have their own unique histories and, both individually and corporately, link with my affinity for comics and superhero storytelling.

Scholar and comics creator Vladimir Popov explores "The Joker: Transmedial Concept of a Comic Book Character" in chapter five. This chapter focuses on the transfixing character who has stood as a dominant figure of anarchy and chaos in the Batman narratives for decades. Popov explores the character's depiction across media, from comics to film, and comments on the ways that the character has changed to suit the needs of the story. This is both a character and story structure that is near to my heart as a reader, and I am pleased to include work from a scholar who is also involved in comics creation in this volume.

In chapter six, Dr. Anika C. Thrower and Dr. Alex Evangelista offer a consideration of the "Significance of Transmedia Storytelling in Higher Education: Collaborative Learning, to Increase Enrollment and Retention, among Nontraditional Students." The authors explore the essential nature of academic spaces and notes the ways that higher education trends have changed since the COVID-19 pandemic. They note the challenges that have been part of academic culture in these times, including concerns about graduation rates and retention. Aligning with my passion for using media to connect students across space and time, the findings in this chapter point to transmedia as a robust possible solution for enriching experiences of higher learning.

The author team of Zeynep Yurtseven Avcı, Eskisehir Osmangazi, Özge Mısırlı, and Gözde Tekbaş co-present their research in chapter seven, "Media Literacy A Study on Media Consumption Habits and Perceptions of Addiction Among Students." These authors comment on the accessibility of media content and the ways that media impacts behaviors, including potential risks. In a study that included 176 students, these scholars explore the notion of addiction related to media, including its social normalization and prevalence. This chapter speaks to the importance of ethics and boundaries when it comes to media, as well as the implications of misuse of media on a personal level.

Preface

In chapter eight, I return to the collection of voices with "(Re)Imagining Worlds and Reality in Media." This chapter is an opportunity to point to the ways that texts can help us rethink what we have come to accept as true for social justice-oriented implications. I use autoethnographic case study methods as well as textual description and analysis to consider how texts like graphic novels and film help readers/viewers reconsider what is possible in their worlds and link to futures which are speculative and progressive in terms of literacy practices.

Dennis Stevenson and Joshua Kenna present chapter nine, "What is Your Real Name?": A Vignette on Malcolm X's 1963 City Desk Interview." The authors speak directly to the pedagogical possibilities of transmedia storytelling through a classroom vignette. This work with students involved a YouTube video of Malcolm X's 1963 "City Desk" interview, and the authors include both their insights as well as student responses in describing the way the interview was used for instruction. Stevenson and Kenna examine the legacy of Malcolm X and features a lesson that readers can use as both a springboard into further research and practice. Stevenson has worked with me on a previous edited collection focused on the use of film in classrooms, and I was eager to work with this scholar again to share thoughts about how film and media work in developing classroom discourse.

Ran Xiang presents chapter ten, "Emotional Literacy through Tea Objects: A Literary Rendition" featuring artistic methods for research inquiry. While a number of creative methods exist for engaging in research, Xiang explores creative non-fiction, allowing for play with reality in a chapter that tethers this methodology with artifactual experiences – in this case, encountering tea objects during travel. This author expands on language and literacy through physical media while playing with possibilities for alternative research methods.

Dr. Lalenja Harrington and collaborator Karen Cox combine their efforts to co-construct chapter eleven, "On These Haunted Streets: A Photopoetic Process of Transmedia Storytelling as Critical Multimodal Literacy." As the title indicates, this chapter employs a number of fascinating elements in a mosaic of collaborative transmedia storytelling process. Harrington and Cox use visuals and poetry to share a vision of multimodal literacy (CML). This work focuses on the opera Omar and the ways these co-researchers engaged artfully to reflection on critical processes and storytelling. The authors note beautifully in the abstract, "Engagement with black artistic presence in opera also allowed us to explore our shared focus on anchoring our work within a socio-political context that supports the naming/transformation of inequities; helping us to illustrate how our work is situated within the framework of CML and reflects a transmedia process of layered storytelling." This chapter is both visual and word-based and leads into the final chapter of the collection.

HOPEFUL STEPS IN STORYTELLING

As a scholar and teacher, it is always my hope that voices are centralized and that new ways of composing, sharing, and appreciating narratives are stimulated by the work I share. Transmedia storytelling is an aspect of my literacy history that has greatly informed my pedagogy and shaped my research trajectory.

Throughout this book, it is my hope as an editor that I present contributed chapters which explore resonant themes across contexts. One of the major threads of my work has been the intentional disruption of assumptions and layers/levels of power related to texts which have been falsely deemed simplistic. Honoring texts that are important to students can often feel like honoring the student themselves; acknowledging the value of voices and stories aligns with honoring the storytellers who speak into our lives. Stories can be told with paper and pencil, printing, digital forms and platforms, fabric – even fine porcelain.

Communication is always changing, and storytelling as a practice is now supported by tools which did not exist years, even months, prior to this publication. This is a process of discovering voices as new avenues come to be.

May the conversation indeed continue as scholars discover the impact of storytelling across cultures, and as classroom spaces are enriched by this knowledge-sharing.

Jason D. DeHart
The University of Tennessee, Knoxville, USA

REFERENCES

Buckingham, D., Manzoli, G., & Farinacci, E. (2021). Media education in the digital age: An interview with David Buckingham. *Sociologia della Comunicazione*, 62(2), 17–32. 10.3280/SC2021-062002

Esteban-Guitart, M., & Gee, J. (2024). Learning as life project (s). *Learning: Research and Practice*, 10(1), 93–102.

Hodge, M. (2023). Faith and Fandom: Pop Culture Villainy in Twenty-First-Century Spirituality. *The International Journal of Religion and Spirituality in Society*, 14(3), 1–23. 10.18848/2154-8633/CGP/v14i03/1-23

Jenkins, H. (2008). *Convergence culture: Where old and new media collide*. NYU Press.

Kuby, C. R., & Rowsell, J. (2022). Magic(al)ing in a time of COVID-19: Becoming literacies and new inquiry practices. *International Studies in Sociology of Education*, 31(1-2), 231–260.

Chapter 1
I Am My Greatest Invention:
Examining Black Girl Literacies via the Visual Narratives of Black Girls in Marvel Comics

Christian M. Hines
Texas State University, USA

ABSTRACT

Drawing on scholarship that conceptualizes the learning and meaning making of Black girls through the Black Girl Literacies framework, this chapter highlights examples of literacy practices in action in Marvel graphic novels with prominent Black girl characters. This framework can be used as a pedagogical tool to examine visual texts to see what themes are emergent and what can we learn from these characters, which can inform instructional practices and approaches to teaching a diverse set of students. It can ground educators in the understanding of the subversive literacies of Black girls.

INTRODUCTION

Renowned novelist Walter Dean Myers (2014) stated that "books transmit values. They explore our common humanity." Storytelling is a pathway to make sense of the world, to understand the construction of ideologies within society. But if the books that are being consumed mostly illustrate dominant white narratives, whose values are being transmitted? And where does this position marginalized readers and students? How can educators ensure that the values and lives that are being

DOI: 10.4018/979-8-3693-3302-0.ch001

examined in the classroom are inclusive of a variety of voices? The use of literature and media should lend itself to more than educational or entertainment exchanges and supplements. The texts presented should lead to discussion; those discussions should lead to thinking and interrogation that ultimately promotes tangible action that focuses on the disruption of systems of oppression and enacting change. Change can come in various forms; divergent mindsets, equitable policies, liberating pedagogical practices, transformative schooling, etc. Texts—diverse text sets—can be a disruption to white supremacy, ableism, homophobia, racism, etc., and what is considered to be the "standard" ways of knowing. Authentic representation matters in all media forms. Including varied multimodal texts also transcends merely being immersed with words on paper. Having students engage in varied transmedia and digital texts creates opportunities to develop and extend their visual and media literacies in the classroom and across digital spaces.

Within this chapter, I highlight the ways teachers can use diverse narratives that give prominence to Black girl voices, literacies, and experiences, to support the multifaceted learning and literacy practices of Black girls in the classroom. Narratives that center the experiences of Black girls can be amplified through a variety of mediums such as books, music, movies, poetry, and for this specific work, I highlight how those narratives are transmediated in comics and graphic novels. I advocate for the use of comics and graphic novels and varied media that prioritizes the narratives of Black girls as a tool to challenge anti-Blackness in the classroom and as an avenue to reflect the ingenuity of Black girls both real and fictional (Hines, 2021). Promoting the ways that visual texts can be useful to create curricular opportunities to develop critical literacies for Black girls and all students.

COMICS AND GRAPHIC NOVELS IN THE CLASSROOM

Reading is a participatory activity where the reader engages with the text and through that participation, they make connections and infer meaning that can have an impact on their perception of the world around them (Freire, 1983; Rosenblatt, 1978). When presenting literature in the classroom, teachers can integrate texts that promote engaging in critical literacy. Critical literacy is "focused on the uses of literacy for social justice in marginalized and disenfranchised communities," (Moore & Begoray, 2017, p. 173). Educators can promote critical literacy in the classroom using comics and graphic novels to cultivate a space that encourages discussion and promotes socioemotional learning. Comic books and graphic novels provide both visual and textual images that require the reader to interact with the text on multiple levels. When reading comics and graphic novels the reader has to construct and infer meaning as they move panel to panel and page to page, "reading comic books requires an active, though largely subconscious, participation on the part of the reader," (Versaci, 2001, p. 63). These texts offer a process of multilevel visual analysis from panel to panel by examining images, text placement, font and sizing, color palette choices, body language, facial expressions, gutter-positioning and the effects of the perspective of multiple characters, spatial interpretation, and sequential events.

Within my teaching experience I have seen the effects of utilizing multiliteracies in the classroom. Even in school libraries it is noted that comics and graphic novels are the most circulated and checked out books amongst young people (Botzakis, Savitz, & Low, 2017). Educators can work on extending the learning process of using comics in the classroom by facilitating discussion, incorporating activities that allow for deeper exploration, and transformation of the visual text. These texts are not just beneficial to students, they can be positioned in teacher education and professional development to support teachers in understanding phases of adolescence, increasing knowledge around special education, addressing marginalizing views of communities of color (Low, 2017b), and developing culturally responsive English pedagogies.

Graphic novels can be utilized as tools to enact multiliteracies to analyze visual stories. Students live in a visual world. It is beneficial to continue to bring in multimodal/pictorial texts to continually expand on students' conceptualizations of what is considered literacy. Visual literacy works as an embodied practice (Snowber, 2012; Wissman et al., 2015), and as a sensory literacy (Parker, 2021). The tension between the words and images can invoke a myriad of emotions and can transform their literacy practices and the ways in which they engage in educational spaces through this, and other types of arts-based education. What students see on the pages allows them to think of time, space, and form in non-linear ways (Barry, 2019; Low, 2017a; McCloud, 1994; Parker 2021, Sousanis, 2015; Yang, 2008). Visual literacy is an active process that has been employed in the classroom via a variety of visual teaching strategies (Bishop & Counihan, 2018; Bolling, 2020; Chisolm & Whitmore, 2018; Dawson; 2018; Low, 2012; Rowsell, McLean & Hamilton, 2012; Thomsen; 2018) such as concept maps, collages, flow charts, word webs, and plot roller coasters. In these instances, we as educators can promote aligning text and images in ways that work in partnership with each other to foster comprehension. Comic literacies–another form of visual literacy–abide by cultural and multimodal practices, they illuminate the ways that comics and graphic novels are also sociocultural artifacts that allow the reader to examine intentions, audience, gender, race, power, etc. (Beach, Castek, & Scott, 2017). Comics are a form of visual storytelling and languaging that hold intellectual economy and have impressionistic value.

BLACK GIRLS IN EDUCATIONAL SPACES

To be a Black girl in this society is to be both hyper-visible and invisible. To be othered or seen as loud, fast, or aggressive (Evans-Winters & Esposito, 2010; Fordham, 1993; Morris, 2007). There is an inordinate number of disparities that Black girls have to navigate within educational spaces; racism via anti-Blackness (Epstein et al., 2017), and under representation in curriculum and academic programs (Collins et al., 2019). These practices create points of contention in the classroom and beyond where Black girls' needs as adolescents and emerging scholars are not being met, leaving them susceptible to inadequate education and othering in academic spaces (Morris, 2018).

Often instead of honoring the resilience, spiritedness, and ingenuity of Black girls, educators may try to reform or assimilate their identities into a more palatable i.e., white design (Morris, 2007). Educational spaces can be volatile for Black girls, via adultification and age compression (Epstein et al., 2017; Love, 2019) which has Black girls seen as less innocent and more adult than their white counterparts, this can result in higher disciplinary actions and Black girls being pushed out (Morris, 2018) of the public-school space. This punitive treatment can be viewed as vehement and in monstrous ways that racialized actions appear in their schooling often come in the form of exclusive curriculum, Eurocentric pedagogical standards, and excessive disciplinary actions. Black girls are also pushed to the margins or erased from conversations that encompass the educational and literacy pursuits and representation of Black and Brown youth. I posit for educators to create and cultivate educational spaces that affirm Black girls, that pushes them to engage in literacy practices that are impactful and meaningful to them, which includes diverse texts that celebrates Black girlhood (Hines & Menefee, 2022). As a Black woman I understand the importance of belonging in a space where you can be yourself and be surrounded by people who believe in you and empower you to succeed. Black girls deserve to be seen, humanized, and aware of the many ways that their lives and experiences can present a mosaic of beauty, sisterhood, and community for people who look like them.

BLACK GIRL REPRESENTATION IN COMICS AND GRAPHIC NOVELS

Within a predominantly white educational system it is important that children and young adults see themselves within the pages of the literature they are reading and the curricula they are learning. Having characters that reflect students' diverse cultural and ethnic backgrounds can aid in their racial development and challenge stereotypes. Often when Blackness is made visible through literature it is through a white lens and can be seen as a form of literary Blackface (Magoon, 2020). What is usually absent in teaching contexts is the critique of understanding the whiteness of power and privilege (Schieble, 2012). An entryway to examine the text being selected is applying critical lenses to interrogate if it explores social, cultural, and political constructs surrounding Blackness. I use the term *Black* instead of *African American* because I seek to include representations of Black across the diaspora as well as multiple intersectional identities. Readers can engage in a variety of perspectives of Black kids that fall in love, have adventures, etc., across multiple genres. Providing access to these narratives presents means to enact advocacy and enhance agency of students along with encouraging literacy development. Being pro-black during times where inclusion is being challenged is a necessary stance to take in classrooms. As these educational spaces are the sites where conceptions and ideas of language, languaging, and literacy formations take shape. This work is essential for providing equity and access to the Black community and communities of color, but also for forging ahead to collectively build new and equitable institutions that are consistent and are sustainable to Black girls. Black youth are often othered or seen as monsters, in text and media (Magoon, 2020) and those perceptions could be attributed to reasons that society does not openly value their childhood. That implicit bias of black youth not being seen as "innocent" could also influence the types of texts that are brought into various learning spaces.

Comics as a medium have historically been positioned to examine societal norms and the archetype of mankind (Smyth, 2022). Superhero narratives do not deviate from this function, these stories become historical and cultural artifacts that reflect the times of when they were produced (Cook & Frey, 2017; Soriano, 2021). When we read, we construct knowledge about society and societal norms. When we discuss collectively what we've read, we are able to make sense of those constructions, build upon them, and/or have them challenged. However, the stories that are presented as mainstream and acceptable in those texts inherently still relay a different message, that white heroes are the right kind of heroes. With this lack of diversity in texts, students of color, especially Black girls rarely see themselves within these stories. White students would also benefit from engaging with these narratives as representation of a pluralistic society (Thein et al., 2007). It's important that students see themselves not only in texts but as superheroes, specifically as youth of color who create change within their communities. Using critical literacy while reading diverse comics and graphic novels allows the reader to question how the character of color is being represented in the story and if that representation is accurate and authentic. McGrath (2007) posits that racial stereotyping exists when depictions of characters reinforce negative and biased traits of minorities that can be found across media platforms. These visual depictions can enhance the understanding of culture and ethnicities when done with intentionality and care. Jimenez (2018) explicates that it is more than simply filling the pages with characters of color, those characters should be authentic and fleshed out and written by people with similar lived experiences.

For a subculture of a medium that is almost a century old, characters of color did not appear on the scene until much later, Black superheroes did not appear in comics until the late 1960s. Black characters are often regulated to the sidelines, or when positioned as main characters, their stories are usually one-offs with no continued serialization. They can also be positioned as tokenized place holders (Hosein & Clement, 2017; Whaley, 2016) that only promote surface level diversity (Singer, 2002; Wanzo, 2015). Many superheroines when included in stories often fall victim to overly sexual depictions in print and onscreen and can be written as static one-dimensional characters (Aldama, 2020; Brown, 2013; Dallacqua & Low, 2019; Gibson, 2018; Ndalianis, 2020). These depictions can be attributed to the creators that are developing the stories portrayed in the panels.

Arguably the most popular Black superheroine is Ororo Munroe better known as Storm from Marvel's *X-Men*. Storm, although popular in her notoriety in her beginning iterations portrayed a few problematic stereotypes, she was oversexualized in her illustrations and perpetuated the strong Black women trope. Marvel over the years has made strides to increase the diversity of their characters and the authors writing their stories. A recent initiative in 2012 that was created to increase readership, Marvel began producing a cast of younger and more diverse heroes. This push for inclusiveness currently features three young Black girl characters that have been added to Marvel's expansive superhero roster. Princess Shuri–sister of the Black Panther, Riri Williams, alias Ironheart and Lunella Lafayette alias Moon Girl. The beauty of these three characters lies not within them possessing physical superhuman strength or supernatural powers, but instead their true power is their genius, intellect, and their capacity to create and build new futures.

Shuri was originally created in 2005 as an auxiliary character and then promoted to a reoccurring main character. Shuri's first solo series was written in 2018 following the success of the *Black Panther* motion picture. This series was penned by famed African-futurist novelist Nnedi Okorafor. Riri Williams debuted as Ironheart originally in 2016 and was created by Brian Michael Bendis as a predecessor to Iron Man. After receiving criticism in regard to portrayals of adultification and stereotypes of a Black girl, the series was continued by Chicago writer and professor Eve L. Ewing. *Moon Girl and Devil Dinosaur* starring Lunella Lafayette debuted in 2015 and was co-written by white writers Brandon Montclare and Amy Reeder, however she is illustrated by Afro-Brazilian artist Natacha Bustos who drew Lunella to inspire young girls of color (Alfonseca, 2020). Natacha drew Lunella to have the nuances of a Black girl, from her darker skin tone to her textured hair illustrations.

Each one of these characters is an engineer and scientist that creates platforms to use their inventions to better the community and society at large. The narratives of these Black girls are not limited to just graphic novels. Their stories have been depicted across mediums; Both Riri and Shuri appear in the Marvel Cinematic Universe in *Black Panther* and *Black Panther: Wakanda Forever*. Lunella's story has been adapted for the small screen as she stars in her own Disney and Disney+ television series: *Moon Girl and Devil Dinosaur* as well as headlining her own picture book *Moon Girl and Devil Dinosaur: Hair Today, Gone Tomorrow*. It is vital that the stories of the brilliant Black girls are transmediated across platforms. This works to provide examples to young Black girls that their stories and experiences are valid and belong in mainstream media.

To work towards antiracist and equitable schooling spaces I interrogate the racial and social positionings as they appear in the texts of these selected Marvel comic series. I focus on the versions of these heroines that were written by Black women in their current iterations. It is in this vein I seek to highlight that the authenticity of these characters are more prevalent as the creators were intentional in addressing the intersectionality of Black girlhood.

BLACK GIRL LITERACIES

Muhammad and Haddix (2016) in an extensive review of comprehensive research on Black girls and their varied intersectional literacy practices contend that those practices are; multiple, tied to identities, historical, collaborative, intellectual, and political/critical (p. 325). Black girls construct meaning over a variety of ways through arts, books, community, critical thinking, and media, etc., and it is salient that educators consider these literacies as they are constructing and implementing pedagogical and instructional practices. There is an increasingly progressive body of literature centralizing the study of Black Girl Literacies and the multiple ways that Black girls utilize their varied literacy practices and asserts how educators can purposefully develop more equitable and antiracist teaching practices.

Kelly (2020) in her work on Black girls' literacies as subversive liberatory acts, used a Black Feminist methodology to research how the critical consciousness of Black girls was developed as a tool of resistance as they navigated a predominantly white school space filled with racially oppressive school structures. McArthur (2016) explored the ways educators can use Critical Media Literacy for Black girls to enact ways of knowing and engaging in social activism. Critical Media literacy is utilized as a way to connect Black girls back to the curriculum and create a classroom space that provides opportunities to challenge racist, sexist and problematic media narratives and for Black girls to become critical readers of the world through media narratives, "critical media literacy is transformative for Black girls because it is not simply an exercise in reading and writing; it is a mode through which Black girls learn how to push back and (re)write who they are" (p. 368). Price-Dennis (2016) highlights how Black girls can use digital spaces and technological capabilities to explore society and enact agency. These digital pedagogies advance literacies across modalities. This allows Black girls to become more than consumers of mass media texts but also producers of text via the understanding of historical and contemporary social issues. Price-Dennis also notes that there is a need for more literature both qualitative and quantitative that focuses on the need and impact of digital literacies for Black girls. Toliver (2020) illustrates the communal and collaborative approaches that Black girls exhibit to conceptualize learning and meaning making in her study on a middle school book club. From conversations that surrounded the read-aloud of a shared novel, Toliver was able to see how together Black girls deliberate, construct knowledge, connect and negotiate identity and girlhood. Young et al. (2018) emphasize the political/critical of Black girls' literacies by the resistant stance that a group of elementary school Black girls took when critiquing fairy tales that display traditionally all white characters. The students read *Goldilocks and the Three Bears* and considered how the story could have been altered had Goldilocks been a Black girl. From there they brainstormed how a more inclusive story would have been authentic and garnered more appeal as representative literature.

Within my work I position the Black Girl Literacies framework to highlight the ways that comics and graphic novels that feature Black girl protagonists can: (1) aid in the construction of identity development, (2) illustrate the impacts of heroism in the form of community engagement, and (3) promote the importance of learning and meaning making within varied historical contexts. Through these texts we as educators can move away from deficit based views of Black girls and consider how their reading experiences can impact how they engage with the world.

METHODOLOGY

Critical Race Theory (CRT) as a framework has been used to interrogate race in graphic novels (Moeller & Becnel, 2018). Counter-storytelling as a tenant of Critical Race Theory interrogates the positioning and depiction of race within narratives. Counter-storytelling aligned with Critical Content Analysis of visual images (Short, 2019) examines how power is depicted and operational in visual texts. Counter-storytelling aids in evaluating stories about people of color and homing in on instances of authenticity or distortions that may arise in the narrative. This methodology has a duality within graphic novels as the narrative can be examined both visually and textually. Also utilizing counter-storytelling as a critical lens can aid in developing students' racial literacies. This specific set of graphic novels discussed in this chapter, can be used to delve into reading experiences of what it is like for Black girls to navigate everyday nuances of coming to age along with the intersection of race to explore topics like Black duality or double consciousness (Du Bois, 2014; Morris, 2021). These stories challenge the notion of Blackness only being seen as a monolith and provides breadth to how identity is established for Black girls during pubescence, "for teens of color and for indigenous teens, coming of age is integrally tied to the process of racial and ethnic identity formation" (Hughes-Haskell, 2013, p. 218).

I selected Marvel narratives due to the prominence of their heroes across popular culture. The chosen texts were ongoing iterations of already established young heroines, however they are currently being written by Black women (see table 1); *Ironheart: Meant to Fly* by Eve L. Ewing, *Moon Girl and Devil Dinosaur: Menace on Wheels* by Jordan Ifueko, *Moon Girl and Devil Dinosaur: Wreck and Roll* by Stephanie Williams, *Shuri: Wakanda Forever* by Nnedi Okorafor, and *Shuri and T'Challa: Into the Heartlands* by Roseanne A. Brown. Across the texts I read, analyzed, and coded for instances of the characters engaging in meaning making that exemplify characterizations of Black Girl Literacies. I read for examples of varied literacy practices and how those practices were being influenced. The purpose was to consider how these literacies are enacted and how those practices can be cultivated in everyday classrooms and educational spaces. I also incorporated counter-storytelling as a methodology (Solòrzano & Yosso, 2002) within the context of Critical Race Content Analysis (Pere Huber et al., 2020) to highlight the racialized contexts that these characters exist in. They are more than their superhero mantles. They are Black girls that are navigating life and creating resources and dreaming beyond limits (Hines, 2021). They are complex and beautiful and reflective of their families and communities and can be used to provide affirmation of innovative Black girls being represented in multimodal texts.

Table 1. Selected Black girl graphic novels

Author and Title	Grade Level	Description
Browne, R.A. (2022) *Into the Heartlands*. Graphix	5-8	Shuri and her brother T'Challa are constantly at odds. But when a mysterious virus invades Wakanda and puts their nation in jeopardy, the two must journey to a faraway land to locate a cure and discover an unknown history that may change everything they know about their family and Wakanda.

continued on following page

Table 1. Continued

Author and Title	Grade Level	Description
Ewing, E.L. (2020) *Ironheart: Meant to Fly*. Marvel	9-12	Riri Williams is back as Ironheart with a new suit and a new mission. When a childhood friend goes missing, Riri returns home to solve the mystery which she finds is connected to something far more sinister than she ever anticipated.
Ifueko, J. (2023) *Moon Girl and Devil Dinosaur: Menace on Wheels*. Marvel	5-8	Super genius Lunella Lafayette has gathered other inhuman kids like her and created a roller derby team as a cover for her secret superhero duties. However trouble arises when a friend turned foe divulges a plan to control the minds of those Lunella loves the most.
Okorafor, N. (2020) *Shuri: Wakanda Forever*. Marvel	9-12	T'Challa, the Black Panther has gone missing in space, and it is up to his genius scientist sister Princess Shuri to locate him and bring him back. Shuri must solve the mystery of her missing brother while balancing the duties of her nation and protecting Wakanda from new threats.
Williams, S. (2024). *Moon Girl and Devil Dinosaur: Wreck and Roll*. Graphix	5-8	Lunella Lafayette and her best friend Casey spend their evenings recording superhero adventures and working at her family owned roller rink. But strange burglaries have been happening in Lunella's neighborhood and it is up to Moon Girl and her trusty sidekick Devil Dinosaur to unmask who or what is behind it.

Analysis of Black Girl Literacy Practices

Alterity and Identity Construction

Across the text each girl has been exhibited from a young age their natural genius and possess a natural affinity for science and engineering. Thus, they create, critically think, problem solve, tinker, and innovate to figure out issues. Being aware of their genius at a critically developmental age, Riri, Shuri, and Lunella understand from the onset that they are different from the everyday people they encounter. Their inner monologue often belies the otherness they feel. Their intellectual identity is who they are and who they have been socialized to be. Yet they use their genius to aid the communities that surround them. Their perceptions are influenced by the way people react to them and the boundaries that are placed on them. Shuri and Riri excelled in their studies to the point they were schooled with other students who were far older than them. Lunella, though she stood out academically she was ostracized for the ways in which her performance showed up in the classroom. These parallels can be said of Black girls who are treated differently and are not always afforded positive encouragement.

The opening scene in the Ironheart graphic novel depicts Riri soaring through the air in her Ironheart suit. She makes her way across different continents and tells the story of how as a Black girl, growing up in contentious parts of Chicago (see Figure

I Am My Greatest Invention

1), she shouldn't be where she is, a fifteen year old enrolled at Massachusetts Institute of Technology (M.I.T.). She expounds on the background story of her stepfather and best friend succumbing to gun violence and in the wake of her pain she tries to make sense of why she was the only one left standing. That pain is what began her journey as Ironheart, as she wished to protect others from harm. She considers all the ways she wishes to be alone to have the space to figure out life, but yet she has responsibilities that she must attend to. These opening panels allude to the identity markers of Riri. She is shielded and protected in her Ironheart suit and yet on the inside is the real her who is a young vulnerable yet incredibly gifted girl still navigating the course of adolescence. The suit she adorns is an intricate part of her identity formation. Her original design was reverse engineered and replicated to be a duplicate of Iron Man's technical armor. When that suit was destroyed she created her own sleek aerodynamic suit to represent herself as a hero and not a shadow of Iron man. In both iterations of the suit, she harnessed her genius to gather the tools and parts needed to conceptualize armor that would help her protect those in need.

Figure 1. Image from Ironheart: Meant to Fly, 2018 by Eve L. Ewing ©Marvel. All rights reserved

Shuri has a similar opening monologue where she recaps all of the events that have brought her to the current moment of her life, which include her temporarily taking on the mantle of Black panther and visiting the Wakanda memory plan where she was imbued with the knowledge and powers of her ancestors. Shuri finds freedom in soaring through Wakanda's skies in a pair of wings that she engineered in her lab. She contemplates the duties and responsibilities that are placed on her as a royal teenage princess and finds solace when she is in the air clearing her mind. Metaphorically both Riri and Shuri need spaces to stretch their wings and focus on the things that bring them joy to understand who they are outside of the labels placed on them. In the same way, Black girls in the classroom are piecing together their identities and are influenced by the expectations of society.

In the graphic novel *Into the Heartlands*, Shuri is positioned differently as she is of a younger age in this novel as it is geared towards middle grades. Even though she is young in age, she has a passion for environmental activism locally and globally (see Figure 2). She is respected for her genius yet she is often boxed out of important decisions because of her age. Shuri is very self assured and knowledgeable. She works with older scientists to develop technology that would be revolutionary in Wakanda, yet she is still working on the kinks in them. Because of her youthfulness her identity is developed in trying to prove herself beyond the shadow of her brother and the appearance of inexperience due to youthfulness. To that end she embarks on a quest to find a cure for a virus that is plaguing Wakandans. Her resourcefulness and persistence aided her in her adventure, and it is her extraordinary capabilities combined with help of T'Challa that makes her successful in her endeavor. Her belief that she is more than the opinion of a few paired with familial support fostered Shuri's intellectual confidence.

I Am My Greatest Invention

Figure 2. Image from Into the Heartlands, *2022 by Roseanne A. Brown ©Graphix. All rights reserved*

    Lunella's identity construction is formulated differently than Shuri and Riri. Lunella often builds her gadgets in secrecy. She has a lab that she has created under her middle school and she tests out her inventions during high risk situations. Although Lunella's parents are aware that she is academically gifted, they often encourage her to pace herself and lean into the normalities of her childhood. This leaves Lunella feeling misunderstood and often isolated. Those feelings cause her to turn inwards to her science and giftedness to find belonging in the creation of her projects. She tells herself that she is her own greatest invention, and with that statement she formulates her identity within the bounds of her intellect and ingenuity.

    Familial connections contribute to a large part of each girl's identity. Riri's relationship with her mother Ronnie grounds her in a world that views her intellect and engineering as a commodity. While away at M.I.T and engaging in her superhero activities. Ronnie continuously checks in on Riri, when noticing Riri isolating herself from her classmates, Ronnie recruits a neighborhood friend Xavier to call Riri, thus establishing an age appropriate friendship and also encouraging Riri to go to therapy with her to work through her trauma. It is in these mother daughter moments where Riri is affirmed and empowered. Her mother understands the weight her daughter carries but still creates a homespace for her to exist as an average teenager. This visual depiction allows for the examination of considering the intersectionality of Black girls of having to be student, daughter, warrior, hero, friend, and still needing areas to just be. This can invoke considerations of what type of educational spaces are teachers cultivating for Black girls.

This type of space cultivation is also illustrated in the *Moon Girl: Menace on Wheels story*. Lunella's parents continually push Lunella to enjoy being a young girl and do mundane kid things despite being a superhero. They have chats with her that the world is different for her as a Black girl and that they love and support who she is, not what she can do for the world. The visual illustrations of the family dynamic of each character can disrupt stereotype notions of damaged and othered Black families. Each girl comes from a home that is firmly rooted in love, care, and support. Their families may not agree with the decisions these young heroines make, but they support them and trust that they will do the right thing.

Moon Girl: Menace on Wheels is also explicit in its conversations surrounding the marginalization of Black girls, but also highlighting the value in empowering Black girls and identity development through the bonds of sisterhood. This is a story specifically crafted around the narrative of Black girls and their hair. One of the members of Lunella's roller derby team is a Black girl named Tasha. Tasha consistently challenges Lunella on accepting herself which includes the outward representation of her hair. Tasha is criticized by both her team mate Olivia and her mother on her natural locs and the preference for straighter, more white presenting hair. The illustrations of Tasha throughout the narrative have her moving through a series of versatile natural hairstyles; from a twist out, cornrow braids, two strand twists and Senegalese braids. These choices are intentional and meant to convey authentic portrayals of a Black girl being her complete self. The opening panel shows Lunella and her friend on the bleachers in a skating rink. On the wall is a painting that says Boogie Down Roller Rink and a dark skinned Black woman with an afro on skates is majestically drawn (see Figure 3). Immediately beneath the mural stands Lunella standing proud with her fist in the air and rocking her afro puff ponytail. Right next to her standing two bleachers below is Tasha wearing a twist out style. The positioning of these characters indicate to the reader that these two characters will be taking center stage. The main contention of the narrative is the makeover that straightens Black girls hair to make them more acceptable. When Tasha falls victim to the "sparkle makeover" not only is her hair straightened, but it turns blonde. She now has captured the attention and adoration of online fans. Once she has changed back she solemnly remarks how the censored version of her was the crowd favorite unlike the real her. Lunella and her friends assure her they like the natural and real Tasha all along and that version is the better one.

I Am My Greatest Invention

Figure 3. Image from Moon Girl and Devil Dinosaur: Menace on Wheels, 2023 by Jordan Ifueko ©Marvel. All rights reserved

The story is robust with Black cultural references and stylistic choices that intentionally play homage to the beauty and ingenuity of Black girls. Unpacking the layers of this text allows the reader an opportunity to engage in the nuances of a particular tradition of Black girlhood. From illustrations of bonnets, hairstyles, conversations around respectability politics, this text alone presents nuanced representations of the lived experiences of Black girls and can create a space for Black girls reading this story to be seen and valued. Discussions can be centered on the ways that Blackness has had to thrive past the challenges and restraints of assimilation. Black girls can consider their self-hood and discuss the varied ways they navigate throughout society. Bringing these stories into the classroom, educators can consider the identity negotiations that can be constructed from engaging with visuals that provide affirming representation of the cultural aspects of Black girlhood. Promoting identity development in the classroom for Black girls looks like discussions and activities where they can interrogate their identities. They can create zines, bring in an assortment of digital texts such as music, videos, or create their own multimodal narratives that allot for expression of who they are. Creating original works that showcase the intersectionalities of their identities and positioning them as creative reader responses that disrupts hegemonic ideas that surround Black girlhood.

Advancing Historical Herstories

Across the texts there are multiple references to famous real world Black women who have made impacts across history. The opening panels of Ironheart depict Riri soaring through the sky quoting from Maya Angelou's poem *Still I Rise*. Riri's previous aspirations were to be an astronaut and there is a poster of Mae Jemison on her wall. Lunella often makes correlation in her personal thoughts to women such as Katherine Johnson the first Black woman mathematician that worked for NASA and Octavia Butler famed science fiction writer. It is through these references that the reader is exposed to impactful Black women who may be unfamiliar to them. Having students reading and learning from Black women scholars, inviting Black women speakers in the classroom, creating book clubs to exchange texts, and in turn bringing these texts into the classroom and pairing them with projects that center the women mentioned allows Black girls to connect to the curriculum and provides them a space where they can be represented and valued.

The Shuri graphic novels also provide avenues to attend to Black girls historical literacies. In both graphic novels Shuri leans into the wisdom and information provided by her ancestors to guide her decisions. *Into the Heartlands*, young Shuri uses a Wakandan children's tale to access clues that can direct her to coordinates and information that can lead her to the cure. This information is provided through old journal jottings of a famed woman Wakandan scientist N'Yami. Throughout her journey Shuri interacts with visions of her older self and with the scientist N'Yami as guideposts when she is most vulnerable. She and T'Challa also encounter one of their ancestors Bashenga, the original Black Panther who explains a pivotal moment in Wakandan history. Through their travels they learn about the context of their home and politics and why certain tribes have been exiled. It is with this knowledge the siblings take a sociopolitical stance to right a wrong and work for equitable inclusion of the exiled tribe to change the trajectory of the nation from their secretive past. Being exposed to a history that was hidden from them allowed them a change to a decision that was beneficial to all. Although the Shuri stories are rife with the history surrounding the warriors and heroes of the fictional nation of Wakanda, these same strategies can be replicated in the classroom.

Providing Black girls with the chance to research and design projects that center important historical figures in their lives allows them to have autonomy and take ownership of their learning while creating space to build their self-efficacy by taking pride in their cultural heritage. Critical texts that centralize the knowledge and scholarship of Black women are essential to the classroom. It provides an opportunity to acknowledge the contributions that Black women have made to society that often go overlooked. These texts can serve as mediums to restore and connect to erased histories, herstories, and literacies.

Collaborative Community Engagement

The stories highlight how Riri, Shuri, and Lunella understand that they alone can not save the world and fix all of their community issues. They are often joined by local friends and allies in the form of other popular Marvel superheroes. Riri interacts with some of the more famed icons such as Ironman, Miles Morales, and Dr. Strange. But her most consistent collaborative support is from her neighbor and friend Xavier. Likewise, from Shuri, she works alongside Ironman, Storm, Rocket, Groot, Miles Morales, and Ms. Marvel. However, her Wakandan friend Muti is her constant aid and strategist. It is these intimate relationships where both characters can let their guard down and work in tandem to develop tangible solutions. That vulnerability creates space to exchange ideas and build off of collective thinking. Riri's construction of her autonomous artificial intelligence in the form and image of her best friend Natalie is another prominent example of fusing her skills with her need for community. Natalie is based off of the coding and analytics of memories and interactions that Riri accumulated with Natalie when she was alive. Her A.I. also is configured around Riri's behavioral patterns, thoughts, actions, and dreams. It is from this endeavor that the A.I. takes on the unintended form of the person that had the most influence on Riri becoming who she is, her former best friend. The A.I. intuitively adapts to Riri's actions and reactions, just as a real friend might. Natalie (in the form of A.I.) and Xavier promote the advantages of collaboration and perspective taking. They often provide Riri with additional context or nuance to consider when undertaking issues. They affirm and validate her when she is feeling insecure, and they suit up to join her in battle when needed. For Riri, her heroism is tied to giving back and helping others. Early on in her story she departs the halls of M.I.T and returns home to Chicago. While there she discovers a childhood friend Daija is missing. With the help of her mother and her friend Xavier, she discovers her missing friend and a plot that involves the labor exploitation of underage children. Riri works to free the children that are being used. Riri then creates a lab for the children where they can learn and have a place to go and be themselves. She understands the importance of nurturing genius and providing safe spaces and she gives that back to the next generation.

Lunella offers the same form of a safe space for kids that have been outcast by creating her roller derby team. She understands the need for community with people that share similar experiences to her. At first the team is a guise for her to do her heroism undercover, but with the prodding and gentle interference of her teammates, they quickly illustrate for Lunella the benefits of friendship and working together. Lunella initially resists because she does not want to put her friends in danger, eventually she relents and it is through their teamwork and Lunella's inventions that they are able to save the day.

Each text is also heavily STEM focused and it is the intellect and inventions of each girl that aid them in their super hero quest. Riri collaborates with Nadia Van Dyne alias The Wasp and they trade ideas on improving their labs that are specifically designed for girls who want to be scientists and engineers. Nadia seeks out Riri to learn from her on what is working well in her lab. This is juxtaposed with the Dean of M.I.T. who only uses Riri and her inventions for profit and sees providing her with lab space as ownership of her technology and her ideas. It is the comparison of these two dynamics that readers can examine the ways that whiteness can be positioned as allyship and partnership or the ways in which it can be viewed as colonization and suppression of ideas and knowledge. Lunella interweaves aspects of Black culture within her coding schematics. When she is working to deactivate the sparkle makeover chemicals in Tasha's hair she creates tiny mechanical robots which she refers to as "M.O.O.N bugs" which stands for "microscopic object oriented nanobots". She creates protocols that are named Black hairstyles and hair care processes (see figure 4) combining the essence of who she is with her technology to save the day.

I Am My Greatest Invention

Figure 4. Image from Moon Girl and Devil Dinosaur: Menace on Wheels, 2023 by Jordan Ifueko ©Marvel. All rights reserved

    Riri, Lunella, and Shuri are also collaborative and communal with each other. Across their different stories each girl comes in contact with each other. Both Riri and Lunella take different trips to Wakanda where they both meet and collaborate with Princess Shuri. Both Riri and Shuri become mentors and surrogate sisters to Lunella. The exchange of ideas and the empowering dynamic of sisterhood across the diaspora illustrates that three girl geniuses from three different backgrounds find commonality and home within each other. Lunella is exposed to new technological advances. And Riri and Shuri team up on a joint mission to protect Wakanda.

Opportunities for activities that advances Black girls communal literacy learning could be students considering the various small businesses, organizations, and/or affinity groups in their communities that they can align with for creating resources for a local social justice issue. Students can design their ideal after school program, who would be the audience, what would be the focus, and what they would do. Educators can use these texts to have Black girls explore project based learning to become involved in the democratic processes of their local communities much like Riri, Shuri, and Lunella. The panels are filled with ways that each girl makes meaning, understands changing perspectives, and considers new opportunities when working alongside different people and with each other. These literacy practices can engage students to consider the experiences of Black girls in the contemporary, fantasy, and the supernatural in literature. For instance, which visual mediums or pop culture works do students experience today that present Black girls and Black bodies as heroes and warriors? Which visual or mediated narrative forms and structures invite students into the storytelling process? How can visual texts promote the teaching and learning of literary elements such as allusion, characterization, imagery, and symbolism, among others?

Implications for Teachers

In a current political landscape that seeks to erase the history and identities of Black and marginalized folks, it is imperative that educators be intentional in enacting and embodying culturally responsive practices. Creating space for Black girls in the classroom by having them engage in visual trans-mediated texts that illustrate their lived experiences can aid in creating a transformative learning experience. Educators can understand that even though these characters are fiction, the challenges and experiences that are illustrated within the panels are very real. These and similar texts can be used to interrogate beliefs and biases that may be held about Black girls. Educators must first understand the educational oppression and discrimination that Black girls face, but also honor the ingenuity that they bring into the classroom and create space for it to be developed further. These visual texts also are examples of including narratives that are not rooted in oppression and enslavement. But including texts that are full, robust, authentic representations of the lived experiences of Black girls and the Black community. It is important to note that every reading experience is different, and readers may not make the same connections as I did, however these stories do provide an entryway for exploring the nuanced ingenuity of Black girlhood.

Bringing in or creating curriculum materials that honor Black ways of being, learning, and meaning making, and having students, especially Black girls be immersed with texts and resources that are written by Black authors and originated

I Am My Greatest Invention

by Black content creators creates spaces for literacy development. I have provided a suggested list of graphic texts that explores the multiplicities of Black girlhood (see Table 2). Affirming the literacy practices of Black girls is taking into account the vastness of Black girlhood. It is more than just surface level representative texts, but it is the care and intentionality of selecting texts that consider the cultural positioning and belief systems of Black girls. It's giving students access to texts across mediums such as film, television, music, social media etc., that interrogates images of family, community, multiple ways of learning. A robust, authentic variety of texts that advocate for critical media literacy and invokes decoding skills and criticality.

Table 2. Suggested graphic novels about Black girls

Author and Title	Grade Level	Themes and Topics
Bagley, J. (2023). *Duel*. Simon & Schuster Books for Young Readers.	5-8	● Coming of Age ● Family ● Sisterhood
Christmas, J. (2022). *Swim Team*. HarperAlley.	5-8	● Black History ● Family ● Friendship
Couvson, M. (2023). *Charisma's Turn: A Graphic Novel*. The New Press.	9-12	● Coming of Age ● Family ● Self-esteem
Johnson, V. (2020) *Twins*. Graphix.	5-8	● Blended Family ● Coming of Age ● Self-discovery
McKinney, L.L. (2021). *Nubia: Real One*. DC Comics.	9-12	● Activism ● Family ● Friendship
Miller, S. (2023). *Curlfriends: New in Town*. Little Brown Ink.	5-8	● Fitting In ● Friendship ● Sisterhood
Montague, L. (2022). *Maybe an Artist: A Graphic Memoir*. Random House Studio.	9-12	● Coming of Age ● Memoir ● Self-discovery

continued on following page

Table 2. Continued

Author and Title	Grade Level	Themes and Topics
Okorafor, N. & Jennings, J. (2022). *After the Rain: A Graphic Novel*. Harry N. Abrams.	9-12	● African Folklore ● Family ● Self-discovery
Ortega, C. (2022). *Frizzy*. First Second.	5-8	● Family ● Hair Love ● Self-esteem
Rowser, J. (2022). *Wash Day Diaries*. Chronicle Books.	9-12	● Hair Love ● Self-care ● Sisterhood

Utilizing Black Girl Literacy (BGL) framework alongside visual narratives in the classroom centers Black literacies and voices in texts, art, media, etc., and provides students a foundation to develop their sociopolitical consciousness and critique the historical and contemporary positioning of Black people within the structural dynamics of society. Thus, reading visual and any multimodal text from the perspective of BGL lens can be a tool for counter storytelling and disrupts monolithic and negative narratives about Black women and girls while holding space for the multiple, multifaceted, and complex identities of Black girls. Cultivating classroom spaces that affirm Black girls and Blackness can help all students to identify injustices, confront racism, and work collaboratively towards social change.

CONCLUSION

Black girls deserved to be represented in their curriculum, literature, and beyond. Educators can work intentionally and strategically to honor and affirm the Black girls they will inevitably come in contact with and create spaces to cultivate deep learning to enact criticality. The texts that we as educators place in front of students whether informational or literary should always be an intentional practice in equity that not only affirms identities but invites inquiry into dismantling ongoing systems of oppression. Students, especially Black students deserve to be seen within the context of literature inside and outside of the classroom. Graphic novels depicting the experiences of Black girls can be tools to shape students' voices, positions, and power. These texts should include visual texts that encapsulates various examples of Black girl literacies and showcase that yes Black girls are magic, but they are also fun, flawed, carefree, and full of ingenuity. Books that are representative of intersectional experiences of Black girls.

REFERENCES

Aldama, F. L. (2020). Gender and sexuality in comics. In Aldama, F. L. (Ed.), *The Routledge Companion to Gender and Sexuality in Comic Book Studies* (1st ed., pp. 1–12). Routledge. 10.4324/9780429264276-1

Alfonseca, K. (2020). This Afro-Latina comic book artist uses her characters as a voice for outsiders. *HuffPost.* https://www.huffpost.com/entry/latinx-comic-book-artist-natacha-bustos-marvel_n_5f696408c5b655acbc6ee48d

Barry, L. (2019). *Making comics.* Drawn Quarterly.

Beach, R., Castek, J., & Scott, J. (2017). Acquiring Processes for Responding to and Creating Multimodal Digital Productions. In Hinchman, K. A., & Appleman, D. A. (Eds.), *Adolescent literacies: A handbook of practice-based research* (pp. 292–309). Guilford Publications.

Bishop, R., & Counihan, E. (2018). Beyond the page: New literacies in the twenty first century. *Voices from the Middle*, 25(4), 39–44. 10.58680/vm201829628

Bolling, B. (2020). Transmedia superheroes, multimodal composition, and digital literacy. In Kirtley, S. E., Garcia, A., & Carlson, P. E. (Eds.), *With Great Power Comes Great Pedagogy* (pp. 117–134). University of Mississippi Press. 10.2307/j.ctvx5w9g0.14

Botzakis, S., Savitz, R., & Low, D. E. (2017). Adolescents reading graphic novels and comics: What we know from research. In Hinchman, K. A., & Applemann, D. A. (Eds.), *Adolescent Literacies: A Handbook of Practice-Based Research* (pp. 310–322). The Guilford Press.

Brown, J. A. (2013). Panthers and vixens: Black superheroines, sexuality, and stereotypes in contemporary comic books. In Howard, S. C., & Jackson, R. L.II, (Eds.), *Black Comics: Politics of Race and Representation* (pp. 133–150). Bloomsbury.

Chisolm, J. S., & Whitmore, K. F. (2018). Visual learning analysis: Using digital photography to analyze middle level students' social-emotional learning and engagement. *Voices from the Middle*, 25(4), 34–38. 10.58680/vm201829627

Collins, K. H., Joseph, N. M., & Ford, D. Y. (2020). Missing in action: Gifted Black girls in science, technology, engineering, and mathematics. *Gifted Child Today*, 43(1), 55–63. 10.1177/1076217519880593

Cook, M. P., & Frey, R. (2017). Using superheroes to visually and critically analyze comics, stereotypes, and society. *SANE Journal: Sequential Art Narrative in Education*, 2(2), 1.

Dallacqua, A. K., & Low, D. E. (2019). I never think of the girls": Critical gender inquiry with superheroes. *English Journal*, 108(5), 76–84. 10.58680/ej201930128

Dawson, C. M. (2018). Visual thinking strategies in the English classroom: Empowering students to interpret unfamiliar texts. *Voices from the Middle*, 26(1), 44–48. 10.58680/vm201829774

Du Bois, W. E. B. (2014). *The souls of Black folk*. (Unabridged Edition). Dover Publications Incorporated.

Epstein, R., Blake, J., & González, T. (2017). Girlhood interrupted: The erasure of Black girls' childhood. SSRN *Electronic Journal*. Crossref, 10.2139/ssrn.3000695

Evans-Winters, V. E., & Esposito, J. (2010). Other people's daughters: Critical race feminism and Black girls education. *Educational Foundations*, (Winter-Spring), 11–24.

Fordham, S. (1993). "Those loud Black girls": (Black) women, silence, and gender "passing" in the academy. *Anthropology & Education Quarterly*, 24(1), 3–32. 10.1525/aeq.1993.24.1.05x1736t

Freire, P. (1983). The importance of the act of reading. *Journal of Education*, 165(1), 5–11. 10.1177/002205748316500103

Gibson, M. (2018). Let's hear it for the girls! Representation of girlhood, feminism, and activism in comics and graphic novels. *Mai, Feminism and Visual Culture*, 1(1), 1–13.

Hines, C. (2021). My brain is all the super-power I need': Examining Black girls in STEM and schooling spaces in Marvel comics. *Research on Diversity in Youth Literature*, 4(1), 9.

Hines, C. M., & Menefee, D. L. (2022). # BlackGirlLiteratureMatters: Exploring the multiplicities of Black girlhood. *English Journal*, 111(3), 67–74. 10.58680/ej202231570

Hosein, S., & Clement, R. (2017). The proverbial and image hangover: A discussion between Comics Researchers. *The Word Hoard*, 6, 35–43.

Huber, P. (2020). Theorizing a Critical Race Content Analysis for Children's Literature about People of Color. *Urban Education*, 1–25.

Hughes-Hassell, S. (2013). Multicultural young adult literature as a form of counter-storytelling. *The Library Quarterly: Information, Community. Policy*, 83(3), 212–228.

Jiménez, L. M. (2018). PoC, LGBTQ, and Gender: The intersectionality of America Chavez. *Journal of Lesbian Studies*, 22(4), 435–445. 10.1080/10894160.2018.14 4950129727592

Kelly, L. L. (2020). Exploring Black girls' subversive literacies as acts of freedom. *Journal of Literacy Research*, 52(4), 456–481. 10.1177/1086296X20966367

Love, B. (2019). *We want to do more than survive: Abolitionist teaching and the pursuit of educational freedom*. Beacon Press.

Low, D. (2012). Spaces invested with content: Crossing the gaps in comics with readers in schools. *Children's Literature in Education*, 43(4), 368–385. 10.1007/s10583-012-9172-5

Low, D. (2017a). Students contesting "colormuteness" through critical inquiries into comics. *English Journal*, 106(4), 19–28. 10.58680/ej201729013

Low, D. (2017b). Waiting for Spider-Man: Representations of urban school 'reform' in Marvel comics' Miles Morales series. In Abate, M. A., & Tarbox, G. A. (Eds.), *Graphic Novels for Children and Young Adults: A Collection of Critical Essays* (pp. 278–297). UP of Mississippi. 10.2307/j.ctv5jxmqd.22

Magoon, K. (2020, June 17). Our modern minstrelsy. *The Horn Book*. https://www.hbook.com/story/our-modern-minstrelsy

McArthur, S. A. (2016). Black girls and critical media literacy for social activism. *English Education*, 48(4), 362–379. 10.58680/ee201628672

McCloud, S. (1994). *Understanding comics: The invisible art*. William Morrow.

McGrath, K. (2007). Gender, race, and Latina identity: An examination of Marvel Comics' amazing fantasy and arana. *Atlantic Journal of Communication*, 15(4), 268–283. 10.1080/15456870701483599

Moeller, R. A., & Becnel, K. (2018). Drawing diversity: Representations of race in graphic novels for young adults. *School Library Research*, 21, 1–17.

Moore, A., & Begoray, D. (2017). "The last block of ice": Trauma literature in the high school classroom. *Journal of Adolescent & Adult Literacy*, 61(2), 173–181. 10.1002/jaal.674

Morris, B. (2021). YA author: The Black duality sandwich. *Voices from the Middle*, 28(3), 12–13. 10.58680/vm202131173

Morris, E. (2007). "Ladies" or "loudies"? Perceptions and experiences of Black girls in classrooms. *Youth & Society*, 38(4), 490–515. 10.1177/0044118X06296778

Morris, M. (2018). *Pushout: The criminalization of Black girls in schools*. New Press.

Muhammad, G., & Haddix, M. (2016). Centering Black girl literacies: A review of literature on the multiple ways of knowing Black girls. *English Education*, 48(4), 229–336. 10.58680/ee201628670

Myers, W. (2014, March 15). Where Are the People of Color in Children's Books? *New York Times*. https://www.nytimes.com/2014/03/16/opinion/sunday/where-are-the-people-of-color-in-childrens-books.html

Ndalianis, A. (2020). Female fans, female creators, and female superheroes: The semiotics of changing gender dynamics. In Aldama, F. L. (Ed.), *The Routledge Companion to Gender and Sexuality in Comic Book Studies* (1st ed., pp. 310–328). Routledge. 10.4324/9780429264276-27

Parker, M. (2021). *Teaching Artfully*. Clover Press.

Price-Dennis, D. (2016). Developing Curriculum to Support Black Girls' Literacies in Digital Spaces. *English Education*, 48(4), 337–361. 10.58680/ee201628671

Rosenblatt, L. (1978). *The reader the text the poem: The transactional theory of the literary work*. Southern Illinois Press.

Rowsell, J., McLean, C., & Hamilton, M. (2012). Visual literacy as a classroom approach. *Journal of Adolescent & Adult Literacy*, 55(5), 444–447. 10.1002/JAAL.00053

Schieble, M. (2012). Critical Conversations on Whiteness With Young Adult Literature. *Journal of Adolescent & Adult Literacy*, 56(3), 212–221. 10.1002/JAAL.00130

Short, K. G. (2019). Critical Content Analysis of Visual Images. In Johnson, H., Mathis, J., & Short, K. G. (Eds.), *Critical Content Analysis of Visual Images in Books for Young People: Reading Images* (1st ed., pp. 3–22). Routledge. 10.4324/9780429426469-1

Singer, M. (2002). "Black Skins" and White Masks: Comic Books and the Secret of Race. *African American Review*, 36(1), 107–118. 10.2307/2903369

Smyth, T. (2022). *Teaching with Comics and Graphic Novels*. Taylor & Francis. 10.4324/9781003291671

Snowber, C. N. (2012). Dancing a curriculum of hope: Cultivating passion as an embodied inquiry. *Journal of Curriculum Theorizing*, 28(2).

Solórzano, D. G., & Yosso, T. J. (2002). Critical Race Methodology: Counter-Storytelling as an Analytical Framework for Education Research. *Qualitative Inquiry*, 8(1), 23–44. 10.1177/107780040200800103

Soriano, R. N. B. (2021). The World's Hero: God's and Archetypes in the Myth of Superman. *International Journal of Language and Literary Studies*, 3(2), 262–276. 10.36892/ijlls.v3i2.582

Sousanis, N. (2015). *Unflattening*. Harvard University Press.

Thein, A. H., Beach, R., & Parks, D. (2007). Perspective-taking as transformative practice in teaching multicultural literature to white students. *English Journal*, 97(2), 54–60. 10.58680/ej20076247

Thomsen, J. (2018). Comics, Collage, and Other Things with Crayons: The Power of Composing with Image. *English Journal*, 107(3), 54–61. 10.58680/ej201829467

Versaci, R. (2001). How comic books can change the way our students see literature: One teacher's perspective. *English Journal*, 91(2), 61–67.

Wanzo, R. (2015). It's a Hero? Black Comics and Satirizing Subjection. In Gateward, F., & Jennings, J. (Eds.), *The Blacker the ink: Constructions of black identity in comics and sequential art* (pp. 314–332). Rutgers University Press. 10.2307/j.ctt1hd186b.19

Whaley, D. (2016). *Black Women in Sequence: Re-inking Comics, Graphic Novels, and Anime*. University of Washington Press.

Wissman, K. K., Staples, J. M., Vasudevan, L., & Nichols, R. E. (2015). Cultivating research pedagogies with adolescents: Created spaces, engaged participation, and embodied inquiry. *Anthropology & Education Quarterly*, 46(2), 186–197. 10.1111/aeq.12098

Yang, G. (2008). Graphic novels in the classroom. *Language Arts*, 85(3), 185–192. 10.58680/la20086181

Young, J. L., Foster, M. D., & Hines, D. (2018). Even Cinderella is White: (Re)Centering Black girls' voices as literacies of resistance. *English Journal*, 107(6), 102–108. 10.58680/ej201829719

Chapter 2
Miles to Go:
Tracing Spider-Man's Puerto Rican Identity Down Many Divergent Roads

David E. Low
https://orcid.org/0000-0001-7999-5001
Fresno State University, USA

René M. Rodríguez-Astacio
https://orcid.org/0000-0001-9071-7619
Fresno State University, USA

Yamil Sárraga-López
Fresno State University, USA

ABSTRACT

In this chapter, three critical scholars of literature, literacy, multimodality, and identity trace various iterations of Miles Morales in the decade-plus since his debut. No longer confined to serialized comic books, Miles has, as of this writing, appeared in two prose novels; several popular and well-received animated films; video games; standalone graphic novels; televised cartoon programs; a picturebook; and in the form of toys, apparel, and other licensed merchandise. The character has been written and illustrated by hundreds of creators, with various backgrounds and intentions, across these media. Each is sedimented with meaning. Throughout the chapter, we examine Miles' transmedial development, specifically through the lens of his hybrid and intersecting biracial/bicultural identities, foregrounding representations of Puerto Rican identity in particular.

DOI: 10.4018/979-8-3693-3302-0.ch002

Miles to Go

INTRODUCTION

One of David's prominent memories of Miles Morales, Spider-Man, came early in the character's existence. Back in 2012, David – a white educator and literacy researcher – was working with a group of mostly Black and Latiné students (grades 4-8) in an afterschool Comics Club in South Philadelphia (see Low, 2015; Low & Campano, 2016), and provided copies of Miles' first comic book series, *Ultimate Comics: Spider-Man*. These comics led to many memorable exchanges among the students, including the following, which occurred when Kyrie glanced at Raman's comic and noticed Miles Morales for the first time.

Kyrie: *Wait! Spider-Man's not Black!*
Raman: *He is.*
Alexi: *That's the Ultimate Spider-Man!*
Kyrie: *No, the Amazing Spider-Man was white.*
Alexi: *The Amazing Spider-Man died!*
Kyrie: *Yeah? But there can't be another Spider-Man 'cause he ain't turned Black!*
Alma: *Read the story, will you?*
Raman: *He died and then this kid, Miles Morales, he actually got bit by the spider, which gave him, like . . . it gave him the same powers as—*
Kyrie: *Abilities, you mean?*
Raman: *Yes. The same abilities as the original Spider-Man, but he also gained more abilities—*
Alexi: *He can turn invisible.*
Raman: *—Like invisibility and venom shot.*
Kyrie: *So is that what the new Spider-Man is now? The Black guy? Honestly, I've never seen a Black superhero.*

Later, David asked the group of students which actor they imagined playing Miles in what was, at that point, only a hypothetical movie adaptation. In unison, multiple Black boys exclaimed: "ME!" It was a powerful moment—children who in 2012 were not used to seeing characters that looked like them in superhero films, felt a strong affinity for Miles (e.g., Klepek, 2017; Low, 2017a). They could now envision themselves as part of a cinematic universe they loved dearly. At the same time, David came to question why none of the Latiné students had joined in the chorus of "ME!" and seemed to feel less directly represented within Miles' identity umbrella. Wasn't Miles Latiné too?

Miles Gonzalo Morales has functioned as something of a cipher for Black urban boyhood since the character's debut (Low, 2017b). When introduced in 2011's *Ultimate Fallout* #4, by white comics creators Brian Michael Bendis and Sara Pichelli, the comics world took note, especially once Miles took on the mantle of Spider-Man in Marvel's "Ultimate" line of comic books. Academics and the popular press alike expressed interest in a character alternately referred to as the "Black Spider-Man" (Fu, 2015; McWilliams, 2013) and the "nonwhite Spider-Man" (Riesman, 2014; see an aggregate of media responses at Newton, 2011). However, Blackness (or *non-whiteness*) was not Miles' only racial or ethnic identity. Miles has an African American father (the bafflingly named Jefferson Davis) and a Latina mother, Rio Morales, from whom he takes his surname. Otherwise, he would be Miles Davis. This background was evident from Miles' earliest appearances on the page and none of it was added retroactively. The character's biracialism and Puerto Rican heritage were simply sublimated by his Black identity in those early years, reflecting a superhero publishing landscape that has had difficulties representing complexly intersectional lives with simultaneity (Chan, 2022; Deman, 2023; Gill, 2016). As a biracial teenager with superpowers, we argue that Miles' identity was never either-or, but both-and.

In this chapter, we – three critical scholars of literature, literacy, multimodality, and identity – trace various iterations of Miles Morales in the decade-plus since his debut. No longer confined to serialized comic books, Miles has, as of this writing, appeared in two prose novels; several popular and well-received animated films; video games; standalone graphic novels; televised cartoon programs; a picturebook; and in the form of toys, apparel, and other licensed merchandise. The character has been written and illustrated by hundreds of creators, with various backgrounds and intentions, across these media. Each is sedimented with meaning. In the sections ahead, we examine Miles' transmedial development, specifically through the lens of his hybrid and intersecting biracial/bicultural identities, foregrounding representations of Puerto Rican identity in particular.

THEORETICAL AND METHODOLOGICAL GROUNDING FOR READING ACROSS MEDIA

Locating Ourselves in the Research

René's first encounter with Miles Morales occurred in 2011 when rumors of a new Spider-Man first hit social media via a Puerto Rican newspaper article (*El Nuevo Dia*, 2011). The article announced that the new Spider-Man would be Afro-Latino and have Morales as their last name. As a Puerto Rican living in Puerto Rico, René immediately took interest in the social media response. While comments responding to Miles' forthcoming debut were a mixed bag, many of them were negative, ranging from support at having a superhero of Latiné descent to total disappointment over Peter Parker's eventual demise in *Ultimate Spider-Man*. [These responses mirrored a larger U.S. media response (see Newton, 2011), and included some shockingly bad takes. For example, *LA Weekly* referred to Miles as Spider-Man's "PC replacement" and wrote, "Apparently, *half-human, half-spider* wasn't diverse/culturally cutting-edge enough for Marvel Comics' most revered superhero" (Wilson, 2011, n.p.).]

Some commenters on *El Nuevo Dia* posted that it was about time that we got our own Black and Hispanic superhero and that Peter needed a break from being a superhero. Those who shared the same last name as the character offered that the Morales are the good ones. The news was also met with criticism and baffling anti-Black rhetoric, with comments about how a new Black and Hispanic Spider-Man stained the race, a classic example of racism in Latin American culture. The general consensus was that Marvel was running out of ideas instead of exploring existing Puerto Rican characters, such as Cecilia Pérez in *X-Men*. Other users poked at the news with zesty and saucy humor, while connoisseurs of Marvel Comics provided examples of other times Marvel had given characters the mantle of Spider-Man, such as Miguel O'Hara. All of these comments inspired René's emerging scholarship and teaching. René first introduced Miles Morales into his university courses in Spring 2022, when he opened the semester with Jason Reynolds' *Miles Morales: Spider-Man*, a young adult novel. Based on students' strong responses, René continues to teach Spider-Man as part of a conversation about what counts as a literary text in secondary ELA classrooms.

Much like René's, Yamil's first encounter with Miles Morales was guided by early rumors in Puerto Rican media publications about a new character replacing Peter Parker as Spider-Man in the early 2010s. At the time, Yamil's interactions with comics were fairly limited, as accessibility to comics was not common in most municipalities in Puerto Rico due to a lack of brick-and-mortar comic book stores. However, Yamil had significant familiarity with comic book heroes through his media consumption of superhero movies and TV shows, with Spider-Man being one of the most easily recognizable characters in the Marvel pantheon. Having a common nationality with the character definitely guided Yamil's early interest in Miles, especially as the character was further developed and his role in the comics universe defined. During his early years as an educator in Puerto Rican postsecondary institutions, Yamil used comics in literary development courses as a medium for exploring genres in textual analysis. Most of his students were language learners and benefited from texts that highlighted their interests regarding language, culture, and the socioeconomic and racial issues portrayed in Miles Morales comics.

Unlike René and Yamil, David does not recall hearing about Miles until after the character debuted, when he brought *Ultimate Comics: Spider-Man* comic books to his students in South Philly. As an English educator, David has often turned to comics as a medium for students to take up a range of literacies and modalities, and to have fun doing so. Moreover, as a critical educator, David has invited students to think critically about intersectional representations of race, class, gender, and culture in comics and related media, and to draw from their own identities and lived experiences (Low, 2017a). For reasons that we will get into in the pages ahead, Miles Morales provides vast potential for critical transmedial examinations across any number of axes.

Modal Affordances for Adapting and Representing Intersectional Identities

Linda Hutcheon (2006) argued that "all media have an underlying commonality with respect to their role in the process of adaptation, and all genres reveal information about how adaptation functions" (paraphrased in Kinney, 2013, p. 7). Media analysts, it follows, can examine how textual issues extend across a range of media, comparatively analyze those media, and "tease out the theoretical implications from multiple textual examples" (Hutcheon, 2006, p. ix). As a character that originated in comic books before moving into other media, we take great interest in the functions, possibilities, and limitations of Miles' transmedial adaptations.

In the sections ahead, we closely examine Miles Morales, a character that is younger than most comic book icons, both in terms of his age in the story (eleven to eighteen) and how long he has existed. Superman has been around since 1938. Batman, Wonder Woman, and Captain America were introduced shortly after. Spider-Man, Iron Man, Thor, and the X-Men came on the scene in the early 1960s. Miles is that rare 21st century creation that has made a sizable mark in a corporate landscape governed by bankable intellectual property. Because of Miles' relative newness, storytellers across mediums have fewer comic book stories at their disposal to adapt. While the superhero genre remains constant from medium to medium, Miles' adapters have created new stories, tones, and versions of the character for their adaptations.

One of the goals of our chapter is to explore the affordances of various media for representing intersectional identities and narratives within the superhero genre. Ahead, we turn to a number of transmedial stories to ascertain which mediums have tended to foreground or deemphasize Miles' cultural complexity and hybridity. We aim not to be deterministic in our analysis. By highlighting media and modality, we nevertheless try not to strip creators of agency in making character-based or tonal decisions. To that end, we discuss the identities of creators who have worked on the Miles Morales character and examine concepts including representation, identity, authenticity, conflation, erasure, and the importance of OwnVoices representation.

We also think it important to note that we are not media/communications scholars. In our multimodal textual interpretations of Miles Morales, we have not focused on things like typography or the composition of a shot as our units of analysis. Rather, we were more concerned with cultural representations through image and language, writ large. We are literature and literacy scholars who followed Miles outward from his comic book origins. Our analysis was literary, multimodal, and situated within our own identities as critical educators, as consumers of superhero texts, and in the case of René and Yamil, as Puerto Ricans.

Critical Content Analysis of Transmedia Texts

As a research triad, we selected critical content analysis as a shared methodology for reading across a range of multimodal, transmedia adaptations. Critical content analysis provides a well-established framework for "closely examin[ing] plotlines, characterization, and assumptions" in literature, and by extension, other narrative media-texts (Johnson, Mathis, & Short, 2017, p. vii). The methodology allows researchers to make "valid inferences from texts to the contexts of their uses" (Krippendorff, 2003, p. 18). As researchers, we drew inferences from numerous Spider-Man texts to "make sense of something outside of the text" (Short, 2017, p. 4), that *something* being the construction of hybrid and intersectional superhero identities (e.g., Dallacqua & Low, 2021; Gill, 2016).

The underlying principle of critical content analysis is that all texts and media are created from particular perspectives (Arizpe & Styles, 2016; Botelho & Rudman, 2009) and contain messages, both overt and unintended, that can be interrogated (Low et al., 2021; Vasquez, 2010). Critical content analysis seeks to investigate how authors' and media creators' perspectives might be internalized by readers and viewers. It does this by posing questions such as: 'Whose story is told? From whose point of view? Who/what is included and who/what is excluded? What aspects of a character are moved into the foreground or background? Which characters have a voice? Which have the power to act versus to be acted upon?' (Martínez-Roldán, 2013; Johnson & Gasiewicz, 2017; Rodríguez & Vickery, 2020). As researchers, we approached this methodology by posing identity-related questions about the underlying messages transmitted in Spider-Man media-texts to audiences about what being Puerto Rican looks and sounds like in a biracial/bicultural superhero like Miles Morales.

Upon selecting lenses through which to examine Miles' transmedia appearances, we performed close readings and viewings, documenting patterns and themes, and "developing these into a focused set of categories to report findings" (Short, 2017, p. 12). Our categories were populated with evidence from across the media-texts we located, as well as by our interpretations of that evidence, and theories interwoven into those interpretations. Now, without further ado, we invite you into a situated critical reading of our transmedia data corpus, which consisted of comic books, prose novels, films, video games, graphic novels, cartoon shorts, picturebooks, and licensed merchandise.

CRITICAL ANALYSIS OF OUR TRANSMEDIA DATA CORPUS

Birthed in a Panel: Miles' Comic Book Origin Story

A mere seven years before swinging into theaters and winning the Oscar for best animated feature, Miles Morales was introduced by Marvel Comics in the fourth issue of a 2011 miniseries, *Ultimate Fallout*. (If you are interested in purchasing a copy in mint condition now, be prepared to spend a thousand dollars.) From there, Miles quickly gained traction, becoming a contemporary fan-favorite. That was no small feat, considering mainstream comic books tend to feature bankable characters introduced in the 1940s-80s that already possess brand recognition. Nevertheless, Miles made an immediate impact on readers, and readers of color in particular.

Later in 2011, Miles began headlining his first solo series, *Ultimate Comics Spider-Man,* which ran for 28 issues before receiving a title change in 2014 to *Miles Morales: Ultimate Spider-Man,* which itself ran for 12 issues. These storylines took place in Marvel's "Ultimate Universe" (2000-2016), in a parallel reality from Marvel's established "Earth-616" universe (1961-). That all changed in 2016 when Miles was transported over into Marvel's mainstream continuity. For the first time, Miles could interact with tentpole characters, including Earth-616 Peter Parker and Tony Stark. Miles' mother, who had been killed in the Ultimate Universe, was miraculously revived. Miles also, for the first time, starred in a comic book whose title included no qualifier—it was just called *Spider-Man* and ran for 28 issues. (See Vin's helpful reading guide on *The Cosmic Circus*, n.d.)

One remarkable thing about Miles' first six years in publication is that he was written almost exclusively by his co-creator, Brian Michael Bendis. Bendis, a white author who has written prolifically for both Marvel and DC, explained in a 2014 interview that his goal in creating Miles and Miles' family was to "write people outside of my own experience" in a way that readers would "recognize as the world around [them]" (Riesman, 2014, n.p.). Considering that most creators employed by major publishers to write comic books in the 2010s (and before...and since) were white, it was necessary to write outside one's own experience if character diversification was a goal. Many of Marvel's and DC's Black and Brown superheroes were created by white men, including Black Panther, Black Lightning, Storm, Luke Cage, John Stewart (Green Lantern), Falcon, Ironheart, America Chavez, Blue Beetle, and Sunspot. Calls for more inclusive hiring practices in the comics industry (both on the creative side and the editorial side) have been ongoing for decades (Rodríguez-Astacio, Hines, & Miller, 2024).

While diversification is a worthy goal, a likely pitfall of Bendis' way of thinking is that writing characters outside of his experience resulted in confusing ideological and cultural (mis)representations and omissions. (We're looking at you, "Jefferson

Davis.") At times, Bendis' portrayal of Miles, his Afro-Latiné family, and their life in Brooklyn included bewildering content that overlaid middle class white cultural norms and languaging practices onto characters of color. When Miles' mother cooked, she prepared "meatloaf and mashed potatoes and peas," rather than authentic Puerto Rican cuisine (Jimenez, 2016, n.p.). Rio and Miles never spoke Spanish, nor did Miles have any Puerto Rican friends (Mills, 2023; Santos Jr., 2021).

Sometimes, Bendis and Pichelli's Miles comics relied on negative stereotypes of communities of color. One such example occurred in *Ultimate Comics Spider-Man* #1 (2011), when Miles and his family attended a charter school lottery to help him rise above the limitations of his neighborhood, which was presented in pathological terms—a place of urban blight that needed to be escaped (Low, 2017b). The school lottery scene was presented without irony or critique; rather, after securing a spot at the exclusive Brooklyn Visions Academy, Rio proclaimed to Miles: "You have a chance. Oh, my God, you have a chance" (Bendis & Pichelli, 2011, p. 12). This scene was later juxtaposed against Miles wondering if he was predisposed to criminal activity like his Uncle Aaron; a negative and pernicious stereotype about Black boys and criminality. Overall, Bendis and Pichelli did not include abundant depictions of community wealth in their Miles Morales comics, nor the robust multilingualism or multicultural pride one would expect to see in Brooklyn.

In another example, taken from *Spider-Man* #2 (2016), Bendis wrote Miles as a character that seemed to champion colorblindness. In a three-page sequence full of metacommentary, Miles watched a vlogger run play-by-play on Miles' earlier fight with a supervillain, which had been caught on film. In the melee, Miles' costume was ripped, revealing his brown skin underneath. The excited vlogger reported: "The new Spider-Man is brown. He's a kid of color! This is huge! Is he African American? Is he Indian? Hispanic? I don't know. But he is def color, so exciting!" Miles was not happy about this: "Uh… And she cares why?" When his best friend Ganke asked him why the video bothered him, Miles responded: "I don't know. Because who cares?" Their conversation continued:

Miles: *I don't want that.*
Ganke: *Want what?*
Miles: *The qualification.*
Ganke: *You're losing me.*
Miles: *I don't want to be the Black Spider-Man. I want to be Spider-Man.*
Ganke: *Okay, poof, you're Spider-Man.*
Miles: *First of all, I am half Hispanic.*
Ganke: *So go tell* [the vlogger].

While Miles' perspective is understandable, it is more reflective of Bendis' ideology as a white writer than it is in line with how Miles would later be portrayed in other media—as a character who embraced his biracial and bicultural heritage and his community affiliation. It's also somewhat shocking that Miles wouldn't understand why representation matters.

There was significant backlash to the sequence (Abad-Santos, 2016; Riesman, 2018). The comics critic J.A. Micheline (2016) wrote on social media: "[H]eads up white writers: don't write characters of color whose take is 'I don't want to be defined by my race.' ... Even if that is a feeling that some/many PoC have, think for a fucking second about the power dynamics involved in you doing that" (n.p.). These sorts of head-scratching characterizations of Miles and his family were not uncommon during Bendis' six-year run, which complicated, but did not necessarily diminish, fans' love for the character.

David Betancourt, a biracial (Black and Puerto Rican) journalist, wrote in 2018 that:

> *In all the years I've been reading comic books, I identify with Marvel's biracial Spider-Man more than any other character. Miles Morales…not only is a pop culture representation of my youth, but the type of hero that before his creation in 2011 existed only in my imagination… I spent my whole life reading comics where the main superhero never looked like me, let alone shared my exact racial makeup (n.p.).*

Clearly, Miles' identity – his *identities* – mattered to readers, adults and children alike (Klepek, 2017). So why didn't identity matter more to Bendis? And when Bendis was writing the character, why didn't identity matter more to Miles? It was only during an interview with Betancourt that Bendis confirmed that Miles' mother, Rio, was Puerto Rican. Previously, Rio had simply been characterized as "Latino" and Miles as "half Latino." This lack of cultural specificity withheld from Miles authentic storytelling possibilities. "I still love the character, don't get me wrong," explained Anthony Otero, who, like Miles and Betancourt, is Black and Puerto Rican, "but it's the way he's written that I'm not a fan of" (in Riesman, 2018, n.p.).

We do not mean to be hypercritical of Bendis' lengthy run as Miles Morales' writer. In Miles, Bendis co-created an important new character that inspired countless readers. Just as significantly, the character was laden with storytelling potential that would be realized once other writers – both in comics and other media – were able to have a turn. In 2017, Bendis announced he would be leaving Marvel Comics to write exclusively for DC, the "Distinguished Competition." This opened the door to new writers taking on Miles, with mixed results. 2018 saw the launch of a new comic book title, *Miles Morales: Spider-Man,* which ran for 42 issues before being relaunched (with the same title) in 2022 with a new #1. The series was helmed by writer Saladin Ahmed, the first author of color to write a Miles title. Ahmed's first storyline dealt with the detainment of immigrant children and felt ripped from the headlines. In terms of explicitly Puerto Rican content, the comics still tended to prioritize a sort-of pan-Latinidad over specific Boricua representation.

As Riesman (2018) argued at the end of Bendis' run, there is a "paradox at the heart of Miles Morales… Put simply, Miles is the rare character who is largely beloved for his potential more than for his existing stories, especially when it comes to the matter of race" (n.p.). Incidentally, Jason Reynolds' prose novel and Sony's animated *Into the Spider-Verse* film were both in the pipeline in 2017-18, and fans would see Miles' biracial/bicultural representation continue to evolve outside of comics—notably, by including more direct portrayals of his then-dormant Puerto Rican identity.

Miles Morales: Spider-Man and *Miles Morales: Suspended*: Miles as a Blatino Adolescent in Young Adult Novels

Announced at San Diego Comic Con in 2017, Disney/Marvel would publish a series of young adult novels based on Miles Morales. Following the trend of adapting superheroes with origins in comic books into young adult prose novels (Miller, Hines, & Rodríguez-Astacio, 2022), Disney/Marvel enlisted Jason Reynolds, a renowned children's and young adult writer. In 2017's *Miles Morales: Spider-Man*, Jason Reynolds, who is Black, introduced Miles Morales to the novel's readers as being just your average adolescent. A Blatino student attending Brooklyn Visions Academy, the novel centers Miles' experiences as a young man on a scholarship, juggling the many responsibilities that come with maintaining financial aid while grappling with not-so-micro aggressions from his racist history teacher, Mr. Chamberlain. Miles is also struggling with the recent death of his Uncle Aaron. Distressed and questioning his superhero identity, Miles' powers are on the fritz; he is haunted by nightmares and his "Spidey sense" is broken. Thus, Reynolds' novel explores how Miles Morales navigates the expectations set on him as both an adolescent, as a person of color facing racism, and as a superhero who is part of larger intersecting communities.

An essential aspect of this novel is how Reynolds forefronts Miles Morales as an adolescent with a foot in multiple worlds. The domestic, school, and communal spaces that Miles inhabits are the predominant settings of the novel, as opposed to high-flying superheroic settings. This provides a more grounded and nuanced understanding of Miles' identity vis-a-vis other people in his life. For example, in the novel, readers are first introduced to Miles Morales in his home, after he has been suspended from school. (Miles was punished for leaving the classroom after his history teacher, Mr. Chamberlain, denied Miles a bathroom break.) Miles' mom, Rio Morales, stands by the kitchen window, fanning out smoke and frying chicharrones de pollo for Sunday dinner as she declares, "Because I swear, if you get suspended again for something like this, it's gonna be you I'm fanning out of the window" (p. 1). The opening scene brings into focus Miles and his family's weekend rituals. As explained in Reynolds' prose:

Sunday dinner at Miles's house was a tradition. Throughout the week Miles was away, staying on campus at the Brooklyn Visions Academy, and on Saturday, well... even Miles's parents knew that there wasn't a sixteen-year-old in all of Brooklyn who wanted to spend Saturday evening with his folks. But Sunday was perfect for an early family meal. A lazy day for everyone. As a matter of fact, besides his mother making him get up for early morning mass, Miles typically had the rest of the day free to loaf around and watch old sci-fi movies with his dad in the afternoon and pray his mother was making his favorite for dinner—pasteles (p. 6).

One aspect this passage immediately highlights is Miles' ethnic identity from his mother's side through a traditional Puerto Rican dish, pasteles. This savory food, a masa made of green bananas with meat filling and wrapped in plantain leaves, alludes to Miles' unmistakable Puerto Ricanness, or as the islanders call it, mancha de plátano, a term derived from a Luis Llorenz Torres poem.

Miles' bicultural heritage is further supported by other aspects represented in the Morales household, for example, when "Miles set the chicken, the [yellow] rice, and the greens on the table" (p. 5). Another instance depicts Miles finding his parents dancing salsa as he comes home from school:

Miles climbed the stairs to his house, pizza and rose in hand. He could hear music coming from the other side of the door. He jiggled the key just right to unlock it, and was met by his mother and father in the living room, dancing hand in hand. Horns, cowbell, timbales, and conga drums blaring through the speakers. Salsa. The Fania All-Stars (p. 172).

In this scene, Rio and Jeff tease Miles about finally spilling the salsa on his crush, which alludes to the story of how his parents met after a spilled salsa incident. Rio invites Miles to dance and reminds him, "You remember this, Miles. We danced all the time when you were little" (p. 172). The scene is also peppered with Spanish, as the salsa song Miles and Rio dance to is sung by Celia Cruz, "Yo soy un hombre sincero, de donde crece la Palma" (p. 173). Rio instructs Miles how to dance with sazón: "Less culo, more waistline. Hip. Hip. Let your body do what it wants. It's telling you how it wants to move" (p. 174). It is through these private moments in the Morales home that Miles embodies his heritage and makes visible to readers his identity as a half-African American and half-Puerto Rican adolescent.

Miles to Go

In contrast, Miles' Puerto Ricanness is absent in scenes depicting his school community and curriculum. In most instances throughout the novel, Miles is racialized as Black. The book "open[s] conversations about contemporary manifestations of racism" (Worlds & Miller, 2019, p. 43), but does not necessarily engender conversations about Miles' intersectional Blatino identity. It is as if Miles is forced to shed his Puerto Rican heritage outside of the home. Representations of Miles' Boricua identity continued to be relegated to domestic spaces in Reynolds' follow-up novel. In 2023, Athenaeum published a standalone sequel titled *Miles Morales: Suspended*. This novel continues documenting Miles' everyday life attending Brooklyn Visions Academy following the aftermath of freeing his racist history teacher, Mr. Chamberlain, from the clutches of the Warden, a 400-year-old mind-controlling entity who compelled adults into maintaining institutionalized racism in spaces inhabited by adolescents. Upon returning to school, Miles discovers that his teacher is still a racist asshole (Miles' words, not ours, although we agree with this assertion) toward BIPOC students. Miles and his friends stage a walkout in Mr. Chamberlain's classroom, which lands Miles, to no one's surprise, in detention once again.

This multimodal novel is told through verse, from Miles' perspective (yes, Spider-Man is a poet!), prose from a third-person narrator, and sporadic illustrations that weave the conversation of censorship in educational spaces through a newfound enemy. The novel's villain – termites – metaphorically infest and threaten the school's foundation and students' access to a just education. As in Reynolds' previous novel, Miles' Boricua identity receives limited exposition, as the novel takes place during a whole day of detention at school. When Miles is introduced in the novel's opening pages, at home, his biraciality is again tied to his parents. In the poem "Home," Miles writes:

My mother
keeps a bodega
hanging off her shoulder.
And I swear my pop's
the chin-up champ.
I'm from them.
I'm from there.
That's my Brooklyn,
and I'm Miles
away from home (p. 10).

As explained in the prose following the poem, "Home" braids Miles' racial and ethnic identities, reclaiming Miles' hybridity as "Boricua and Black and Brooklyn as hell" (p. 11).

Overall, *Miles Morales: Suspended* "can be positioned...to teach about contemporary attacks on Black literature through book bans" (Miller, Hines, & Rodríguez-Astacio, in press), although we can simultaneously recognize a joint erasure of Puerto Rican identity and history in classrooms throughout the United States. When Reynolds was asked in 2017 if he had any intent in describing the realities lived by Afro-Puerto Rican males for his audience to understand their lived experiences, the author responded:

Not necessarily. I think it's more important than trying to get people to understand, I just wanted to authentically serve the story. This is who Miles is. Black, Puerto Rican, Brooklynite, with a family who has a complicated past. I didn't make that up, Marvel did. So what I had to do was really show what all those elements mean. It would've been lazy and disingenuous to take the information given, and pretend it holds no bearing on who Miles is and how he maneuvers through the world (Abercrombie, 2017).

In trying to capture the authentic cultural and social realities of Miles, Reynolds rejected the colorblind approach of Bendis in the comic books as well as a reductive pan-Latin lens. Reynolds recognized Miles' biracial identity, even if the story required stuffing it into constrained narrative spaces.

Importantly, Reynolds' version of Miles Morales would impact the general public's knowledge of the character, especially through subsequent movie and video game releases. Similarly, Miles' Boricua heritage and history across transnational borders would continue to be explored in standalone graphic novels and picturebooks (Campbell, 2021), even if they have not yet touched upon the possibility of Miles being part of the Nuyorican diaspora, although Reynolds refers to Miles as a Brooklynite. We examine these transmedia texts in the following sections.

Miles' Spider-Versal Appeal: Sony's Animated Films and the Making of a Cultural Icon

Miles Morales' pop cultural reach expanded dramatically when *Spider-Man: Into the Spider-Verse* (Persichetti, Ramsey, & Rothman) hit theaters in 2018. Artistically, the film surpassed nearly all expectations, innovating a new style of animation, fleshing out the still-fledgling character and his family in compelling and culturally-specific ways, and turning a 327% profit in the process. The film won Best Animated Feature at the 91st Academy Awards and has been widely praised for its aesthetics, its mix of humor and pathos, and its authentic representations of complex characters. Moreover, the film, the first in a planned trilogy, took Bendis' Miles character and turned him into a cultural icon. The film and its sequels are not part of the Marvel Cinematic Universe, but they do acknowledge that Miles Morales exists in a shared multiverse.

While there have been critiques of *Into the Spider-Verse* – chiefly, that it was animated and not live-action (Betancourt, 2018) – most responses to the film were glowing. The film received accolades from reviewers and fans alike, earning it a 94% fresh rating on Rotten Tomatoes. Other than its high-flying action, comedic pacing, and emotional depth, a large part of the film's success owed to how well it handled the multicultural specificity of Miles and his community. The film's multilingualism (Miles and Rio – voiced by Luna Lauren Vélez – speak to one another in English and unsubtitled Spanish) and non-superficial references to hip hop culture (graffiti, fashion, rapping, and knowledge) made the characters, and their Brooklyn milieu, feel authentically lived in and not at all pandering.

Throughout the movie, and its 2023 sequel *Spider-Man: Across the Spider-Verse* (Dos Santos, Powers, & Thompson), Miles struggles with his identity and what is expected of him as a superhero with responsibilities to his bicultural family and larger community. Thus, in spite of the fact that Miles' voice actor, Shameik Moore, is not of Latiné heritage, the films did much to correct misrepresentations and omissions of Miles' Puerto Ricanness rampant in other media (Gomez, 2018; Molina-Guzmán, 2021). For many fans of Miles, it is the films' version of the character – red hoodie pulled over his Spider-Man mask, and a pair of Jordan 1s – that has become the definitive Miles. As Richard Newby (2018) argued, "it's not just superheroics that make *Into the Spider-Verse* work. It's culture" (n.p.).

"For some children," wrote Jada Gomez (2018), "their first vision of Spider-Man will be an image of a Black and Puerto Rican teen, saving the world – and even alternate universes – in a hoodie and limited edition kicks. That's some badass, powerful imagery… It would have been easy for the film to to simply use Miles as a diversity prop, but its attention to the Nuyorican experience provides representation that is completely refreshing" (n.p.). Indeed. Throughout *Into the Spider-Verse* and *Across the Spider-Verse,* viewers are treated to details that highlight Miles' cultural and psychological complexity without sacrificing humor or fun.

In the opening scenes of 2018's *Into the Spider-Verse,* we are introduced to Peter Parker as the legendary Spider-Man. He is not only a superhero but has become a brand. After this quick introduction to an at-once familiar friendly neighborhood Spider-Man, Peter confidently stresses "…the only thing standing between this city and oblivion, is me. There's only one Spider-Man and you're looking at him." The next scene transitions to Miles in his bedroom, finishing a fresh stack of sticker graffiti while blasting Post Malone's "Sunflower" through his headphones. As Miles sings along to the music and flubs the lyrics, we hear Rio ("Miles! Miles, papá, time for school!") and Jeff call after their son to get ready for school. An empty green suitcase waits for Miles to finish packing clothes for school, and we can spy a patch of the Puerto Rican flag stitched onto the suitcase's side. This first look at Miles immediately informs viewers there is another Spider-Man entering the spotlight and he's different from Peter Parker. He is a biracial adolescent enmeshed in graffiti and hip hop culture. According to Newby (2018), "*Into the Spider-Verse* isn't just the next great leap in superhero movies because of its introduction of the comic book multiverse, but because it treats [B]lack and Latino heritage as a key piece of a superhero identity, and that's just as important as any spider symbol" (Newby, 2018, n.p.). As the new symbol of the community, we catch glimpses of Miles walking through the neighborhood on his way to school, greeting friends and neighbors in both English and Spanish, all while tagging buildings and signs with his sticker graffiti. This sequence taps us into the vibrant flow of the diverse Brooklyn community Miles belongs to.

Following in the footsteps of Marvel's *Black Panther* (Coogler, 2018), *Into the Spider-Verse* is also accompanied by a robust original soundtrack that anchors the world of Miles Morales and his community via hip-hop and reggaeton culture. In essence, it captures the music that Miles the adolescent would listen to, and yet, as Williams (2018) put it, "[t]he most impressive part is how the compilation hangs together as its own separate body of work" (n.p.). Spring Aspers, Head of Music for Sony's Motion Picture Group described the Post Malone track as "anthemic, but also heartfelt — the perfect soundtrack for Miles to discover the Spider-Man inside himself" (*Variety* Staff, 2018). The audience gets to jam to the track along with Miles in the opening scenes, creating an access point to Miles' headspace as he grows into his newfound powers and responsibilities. Miles also listens to the track in moments of deep reflection, the album working as an anchor to his roots. Another track that speaks to Miles' heritage is "Familia" by Nicki Minaj and Anuel AA feat. Bantu. Anuel AA, a reggaetonero from Puerto Rico, sings in Spanish how family and loyalty comes above all else. Thus, the original soundtrack as a paratext becomes an artifact representative of urban spaces and adolescent life. "*Spider-Man: Into the Spider-Verse,*" writes Gomez (2018), "isn't one of the best Spidey films in the franchise because of Miles' ethnicity. It's enriched by it, thanks to the Nuyorican nuance…But most importantly, and poignantly, it gives a new generation of Spider-Man aficionados a hero they can relate to on so many incredible levels" (n.p.). And in a nod to David's Latiné students from 2012, who did not imagine themselves playing the role of Miles, Gomez describes her own experience in the movie theater in 2018: "I watched young Latinx grade schoolers climb into their seats next to their parents to root for a Spider-Man who looked like them... [T]hey're all grasping that an Afro-Latinx superhero can now be a norm for them" (n.p.).

After receiving numerous accolades, fans wondered whether the next entry in the series, 2023's *Across the Spider-Verse,* could possibly live up to the high standards of the first film or whether it would suffer a sophomore slump. If we can surmise anything from Rotten Tomatoes ratings, the sequel maintained pace, receiving an identical critical score as its predecessor. *Across the Spider-Verse* expands on themes and concepts introduced in the first film, and does so in imaginative ways. Importantly, the sequel does not give short shrift to Miles' or his community's identities. Rather, in many cases, it amplifies them. Set in a shared multiverse of parallel realities called the Spider-Verse, Miles ventures into this maelstrom as he, and a team of Spider-people, pursue Spot, a supervillain that threatens the very fiber of the Spider-Verse.

In developing a story in which Miles is away from home, the team at Sony made sure to remind audiences where Miles' roots lie. Interviewing Phil Lord, one of the writers and producers of both *Spider-Verse* films, Vanessa Diaz (2023), a self-described New Yor-Rican and Cuban blogger, initiated the following exchange:

Diaz: This film showcases Miles' Puerto Rican culture and mother more than in the last film, which I greatly appreciated. I wondered if that was something that the team [was] more mindful of wanting to include when making this second film?

Lord: It was a big ambition of our directors to include. They wanted to show the neighborhood barbecue and watch all the flavors of Miles' neighborhood in Brooklyn come together. The barbecue has a little bit of Jeff's family that are there, and there's a little bit of his side of the Caribbean influence, because his family has some Caribbean heritage. It's a little mix of everything, and also, if you go down Avenue De Puerto Rico in Brooklyn, [there are] Mexican bakeries, which is why Miles goes to a Mexican bakery to get the cake. There is a lot of fine detail in that, which is to say there is no monolithic culture anywhere! (n.p.).

Well said. It is the films' attention to cultural specificity and complexity, and the pains they take not to be reductive, that makes them so profound.

When we first meet Miles in *Across the Spider-Verse*, he is in the midst of battling a new villain of the week, Spot, and texting with his parents while they wait for him at his school for a meeting with a college counselor. Miles narrates how he has grown into his role as Spider-Man in a reel that is reminiscent of Peter's introduction from *Into the Spider-Verse*. Despite his highs and lows, we quickly find out Miles is stretched thin and burdened by having to keep his superhero identity a secret from his parents. He wonders about the possibility of his parents accepting the news.

Miles' new responsibilities and anxieties affect his school performance. During the meeting with the school counselor, Rio and Jeff discover Miles is keeping good grades but he has been absent from Spanish class (6 times!) and is on track to earn a B. When Miles' mother yells at him for getting a B in Spanish class, she then *snaps* in Spanish. You can even see the Puerto Rican flag when she snaps her fingers at Miles, while he replies "Cálmate mami. Eso is not my fault!" Rio is disappointed and even questions Miles' use of Spanglish while Jeff declares "Takes after his uncle."

The scene, although hilarious, is a reminder of the pressures Miles experiences as a male, middle-class Afro-Boricua adolescent, and adds nuance to Latiné representation by highlighting intersections in the form of meeting expectations of his Puerto Rican heritage, being an exemplary and responsible student, translanguaging, and keeping out of the shadows of his Uncle Aaron's life of thievery. Miles Morales, a half-assed Puerto Rican and delinquent losing his scholarship? Unthinkable! But even teenage superheroes do lead complicated and alienating lives.

Much like its predecessor, *Across the Spider-Verse* also played with the theme of subverting expectations and narratives imposed on minorities. In an article published in *The New Yorker*, Jay Caspian Kang (2023) noted:

> *When Miles attends a meeting with his parents with a college counselor at his school, the counselor suggests that Miles, who wants to study physics at Princeton, write an essay playing up his status as a bootstrapping immigrant from a proud but impoverished family. Miles's parents seem confused by the request. His mother, Rio, points out that she is from Puerto Rico, which is part of the United States. His father, Jefferson, says they own a floor of a building in Brooklyn, implying that they aren't exactly poor. This is a funny and heartening scene that reminds the viewer that minorities are not a monolith, and allows the movie a little self-applause—a golf clap, more than anything—for defying the Hollywood impulses that might otherwise turn a Brooklyn-born character named Miles Morales into Bernardo from "West Side Story" (n.p.).*

Since his earliest appearances, Miles has been carrying the burden to champion diversity not only within the confines of his story but also as a cultural icon. Thus, it makes sense the film serves as a meeting ground for metacommentary on the kinds of pigeon-holing multi-ethnic people face.

In all, both films feel almost miraculous in terms of how well they are able to honor, with depth and complexity, the competing forces that beat at the heart of Miles' character while maintaining the exhilarating and humorous tone fans expect from a *Spider-Man* story. We end this section agreeing with Richard Newby's (2018) sentiments, which we would extend to refer to both of the *Spider-Verse* films: "Miles Morales is better presented in [these films] than he ever has been before. That's not a slight against Bendis, who consulted on the film[s], or any of the other writers who have told Miles' story. Rather it's an awareness that a diverse team of filmmakers, writers, and animators brought out aspects of Miles that are immediately recognizable for kids of color. *Into the Spider-Verse* [and *Across the Spider-Verse*] doesn't change Miles Morales, it elevates him" (n.p.).

Miles to Go

Into the Gamerverse? Miles as a Playable Video Game Character

An important medium in which Miles' story has been further explored and expanded is video games. While Miles appeared in several other games (e.g., *Marvel's Ultimate Alliance 3* and *Lego Marvel Super Heroes 2*), his identity and narrative complexity did not come into play until 2018's *Marvel's Spider-Man* for the PlayStation 4. The widely acclaimed game, developed by Insomniac Games and published by Sony Interactive Entertainment, anchors its narrative in Peter Parker's Spider-Man as part of a jointly created Gamerverse. This multimedia storyscape includes tie-ins to other games as well as comics and books.

Although Miles is not the main protagonist of *Marvel's Spider-Man,* he is introduced as a key character in Peter Parker's story through the latter's connection to Miles' father, NYPD Officer Jefferson Davis. At this point in the game's storyline, Miles does not have superpowers. Nevertheless, he is thrown into the action during an attack orchestrated by Mayor Norman Osborne's office. During the attack, Miles' father, Jefferson Davis, is killed by one of the games' villains, Negative Man. This is followed by one of the few playable scenes in which players control Miles during the events of the attack and its immediate aftermath. Most of Miles' narrative in the first game involves his feelings of loss, grief, and impotence in the face of a city that buckles under criminality. However, under his mother Rio Morales' guidance, and Peter's mentorship, Miles finds ways to help his community by volunteering in a shelter for the homeless with Peter's Aunt May. Over the duration of the first game, Miles the civilian gets to explore ways in which he can serve his community and advocate for others, demonstrating that his call to serve goes beyond being a superhero. The game ends with Miles being bit by a spider and obtaining powers similar to Peter's. In a demonstration of trust and camaraderie, Miles confides in Peter about his powers only to learn that Peter is Spider-Man.

While the first game in the video game series did not explore much of Miles' Blatino identity, it did open the door for Miles to become a major protagonist in the game series, with the second entry, *Spider-Man: Miles Morales* (Insomniac Games, 2020) handing Miles the main protagonist role in the absence of Peter Parker. The link between the first and second games in the series is also explored in the tie-in novel, *Marvel's Spider-Man Miles Morales: Wings of Fury* (2020) by YA author Brittney Morris. The supplemental novel (sold separately) begins shortly after the events of the first game, with Miles leaving Brooklyn to move with his abuela to Spanish Harlem following his father's death. Miles struggles to find his place in this new community, one that feels both familiar and strange. In Spanish Harlem, Miles' Puerto Rican roots are explored through his abuelita, who welcomes Miles and Rio with food (tostones, even though Miles was craving pizza) and Puerto Rican warmth. In this new community, Miles is faced not only with his cultural roots but also with the role his Blatino identity plays in his life as a superhero.

While Miles' Puerto Rican cultural heritage doesn't play a significant role in advancing the Gamerverse's story, it is his race that pushes important narrative events. An early event in Morris' tie-in novel puts Miles at odds with the police in response to racial profiling and overt racism. As Miles expresses, following his encounter with the police, "I'm supposed to be a superhero, but can I really be if I'm seen as a villain because of the color of my skin?" (p. 30). Throughout the novel, Miles confronts his identity as Spider-Man, wondering what his role is in a city that already has a Spider-Man. However, by the end of the novel, and in the face of a crisis that threatens the city, he comments, "I realize that for the longest time I've been wondering what kind of Spider-Man I'm going to be. Wondering if my best is good enough. And I realize, whether it is or isn't 'enough', it's all I've got" (p. 130).

The second, shorter entry in the series of video games, which serves as a stand-alone link between numbered PlayStation 4 Spider-Man entries, is the unnumbered *Spider-Man: Miles Morales* (Insomniac Games, 2020). In the game, Miles finds himself the sole protector of New York City, as Peter is busy accompanying MJ Watson on a trip to Zymkaria due to events linked to the first game. In this second game, players continue to explore some of the themes introduced in Morris' novel, such as Miles' racial and cultural identity, his connection to his community, and his role as a superhero of color. Miles clearly values his Puerto Rican heritage, as the game subtly illustrates. Some of Miles' sketches of possible spider-suits made the Puerto Rican flag central to their design.

Early events in the game also place his Latino identity at the forefront of the narrative, with players, piloting Miles, exploring his grandmother's house (now his house as his grandmother has moved to Puerto Rico following the events of the first game). Through interactions with the environment, players get to view iconic trappings of Puerto Rican culture. For example, Miles' bedroom has several decorations that link to his Puerto Rican identity, including a small Puerto Rican flag with gold fringes, commonly observed used as a decoration for those of Puerto Rican heritage. He also has a coqui figure, a small frog native to Puerto Rico that is often considered a symbol of the archipelago. As players explore the house, it is evident that Miles' Puerto Rican identity is critical to his new environment, be it through his abuela's decorations or his mother's cooking.

The game begins at Noche Buena or Christmas Eve, which is often celebrated in Latiné communities with families getting together to enjoy food. The game portrays typical Puerto Rican cuisine, such as arroz con gandules (rice and peas), pasteles (a traditional dish similar to a Mexican tamal but often made with green bananas), potato salad, empanadillas (fried empanadas), tembleque (a coconut-based dessert with a jell-o like texture), and dulce de coco (coconut candy bars). The house is festooned with Puerto Rican imagery including vejigante masks (typical carnival masks in Puerto Rican culture which also inspired the hero El Vejigante, who made a single appearance in a 2010 issue of *Fantastic Four*), paintings representing many aspects of Puerto Rican culture, miniature casitas shown on the walls, and the pava (a straw hat made of palm leaves often worn by jíbaros, iconic Puerto Rican farming figures). Franzese (2020) writes, "Even the way Miles and his mother say 'te quiero' to each other felt like I was witnessing myself in a video game because it carries the same weight I, and many other Puerto Ricans, use to express our love to our parents" (n.p.). All of these details provide a strong sense of authenticity to Miles' Puerto Rican heritage, one that perhaps was not as evident in other portrayals of his family in other media (Franzese, 2020; Lugo, 2021). As Centeno (2023) writes, "It's the little details that make Miles the true Spider-Man of Harlem" (n.p.).

The major plot of *Spider-Man: Miles Morales* involves the conflict between a criminal organization called the Underground and a major energy conglomerate from Marvel Comics, Roxxon, who are each vying for control of a new energy source, Nuform. It is this conflict that guides the game's narrative, with the Harlem community at the intersection of the events. It is in Miles' relationship with his community that the game triumphs in its representations by having Miles get to know and interact with his new community, building relationships with people such as a bodega owner, a barber, and a restauranteur. It is this sense of community that allows Miles to feel connected to his Latiné roots. As Mills (2022) explains, "The game allows players to explore the ways in which Miles Morales' superpowers and Afro-Puerto Rican identity re-shapes Spider-Man's relation to themes of power and responsibility." In fact, as the narrative continues, Miles questions the purpose of his powers and who he gets to protect. The relationship with the Spanish Harlem community is even more integral to the game's plot as it reaches its conclusion, with Miles discovering his friend Phin is the leader of the Underground and the villain known as the "Tinkerer." In the game's concluding moments, after absorbing a major dose of Nuform, and following Phin's sacrifice to save the community from an explosion, Miles collapses in front a group of people from his neighborhood. His face showing, it is at this moment that his community rallies behind a superhero that represents them, saying, "He's our Spider-Man." We couldn't have said it better ourselves.

The second numbered entry of the game series, *Marvel's Spider-Man 2* (Insomniac Games, 2023), places the spotlight on both Peter and Miles as they share a storyline that has them face new and recurring villains. Early in the game narrative, we see a contrast of two heroes faced with their superhero powers and the responsibilities they entail. While Peter is fired from his short stint as a teacher at Brooklyn Visions after an encounter with Sandman, Miles faces lost opportunities due to his role as Spider-Man vis-a-vis friends who are leading normal lives. Miles sees his superhero path as one mirroring Peter's, replete with troubles leading a normal life. Miles' looming college application essay serves as a constant reminder of his goals outside of superheroing. One point of difference between the Spider-Men that is particularly poignant in the first few chapters of the game is Miles' support system. The game highlights his family relationships and friendships with Ganke and and Haley.

Exploring Miles' living space in the game presents a clear shift in how his heritage is represented. Now that his abuela's stuff has been sent to her in Puerto Rico, following the events of Miles solo game entry, the house is a lot more subdued in its displays of Puerto Rican culture. Gone are the decorations that represented Miles' Puerto Rican heritage, with a major exception being a singular Puerto Rican flag covering a portion of the apartment's entryway hallway. The flag caused a critical response after the game's release, as designers confused the Cuban flag with the Puerto Rican flag—both flags having the same design with inverted colors. This was not a difficult mistake to make. As the poet Lola Rodríguez de Tió (1893) wrote, "Cuba y Puerto Rico son de un pájaro las dos alas" (n.p.) and share some common heritage as Caribbean islands. Game developers quickly addressed the mistake, sending an update that replaced the flag.

While gamers pointed out the flag mistake on social media, they also praised the game's representation of Puerto Rican culture. While some of the more evident cultural iconography was gone from the apartment, it remained a center of his link with his community. In fact, when looking outside the window of Miles' room, gamers see a tagged "El Barrio" sign, with Miles-as-Spider-Man added into the mural. The image is emblematic of Miles embracing his community and the Boricua aspects of his identity.

Miles' major storyline in *Marvel's Spider-Man 2* is centered around Mister Negative's escape from Rikers Prison. Miles' connection to Mister Negative as the one responsible for the death of his father guides a significant part of Miles' inner conflict as he finds difficulty in reconciling his role as a student, hero, and friend with his need for justice and vengeance. Nevertheless, a significant part of Miles' side missions finds him helping his community, including Harlem's Cultural Center, retrieve stolen instruments for a fundraising gala. In fact, within the gala players have the opportunity to review some of the instruments' history, accurate to the real-life histories of famous composers and performers. In this game, as well as those that came before it, Miles as a playable character has a significantly stronger connection to our real world through his link to the community, making the character extremely interesting to explore in its multiple facets and representations.

Miles to Go

After Shocks and *Stranger Tides*: **Miles Explores his Roots in Marvel/Graphix's Standalone Graphic Novels**

In the spring of 2021, Marvel took steps to expand its elementary school-aged readership by launching a line of original graphic novels aimed at middle grades readers. In partnership with Scholastic, Marvel established a new imprint to be sold outside of specialty comic book shops. With both Marvel's and Scholastic's logos on the spine, these titles would be carried in chain bookstores and even retailers like Wal-Mart. They would also be spotlighted to millions of children attending Scholastic Book Fairs at school. Unlike episodic comics, Marvel/Graphix titles featured standalone stories, occurring outside the established continuity of Marvel's Earth-616 universe.

As important as how the books were sold was the content within them. Marvel/Graphix titles emphasized diverse, culturally authentic characters and creative teams. To the degree that the line was overtly intended to bring in middle grades readers, it seemed equally invested in welcoming a more ethnically- and gender-diverse readership. With the massive sales of non-superhero comics created by Raina Telgemeier, Jeff Smith, and Kazu Kibuishi in the 2010s, Scholastic had demonstrated that there was a viable market for middle-grade comics that did not feature widely known, white, male 'legacy' characters (Botzakis et al., 2017; Kisner, 2024). Marvel/Graphix's books aimed to capture that zeitgeist and showcased newer Marvel heroes that had been introduced or popularized in the previous decade, i.e., Miles Morales, Kamala Khan, Shuri, and Doreen Green. (Note: Many of these characters, including Miles, also appeared in the illustrated *Avengers Assembly* series of novels for middle-grade readers, which we do not review in this chapter.)

One of the early offerings in the Marvel/Graphix line was *Miles Morales: Shock Waves* (Reynolds & Leon, 2021). In this graphic novel, Miles is portrayed as a biracial young adult being raised in Brooklyn by his parents. Both Miles' and his mother Rio's Puerto Ricanness are highlighted throughout the text, through language (Spanish appears frequently) and actual plot. In one of the graphic novel's plotlines, Miles raises funds for Puerto Rico after relatives on the island lose their home in an earthquake. Eventually, Miles uncovers a conspiracy when he learns that a wealthy American industrialist-philanthropist, Harrison Snow, is only providing financial aid to Puerto Rico to strip-mine the island's wealth.

The earthquakes presented at the outset of the graphic novel are reminiscent of real-life natural disasters that have massively disrupted the lives of Puerto Rico's residents in recent years, including Hurricane Maria in 2017, shock waves in 2020, and Hurricane Fiona in 2022. Such context is crucial for appreciating what Justin A. Reynolds (an African American author committed to propagating Black Boy Joy; no relation to Jason Reynolds, who wrote the Miles Morales prose novels discussed above) and Pablo Leon (a Guatemalan author-illustrator whose work spotlights Latiné culture) were trying to accomplish. In *Shock Waves*, Miles' Puerto Rican heritage – as well as his diasporic identity – play a front-and-center role in the narrative. Miles wrestles with his relationship to the island from which his mother, and numerous other family members, hail. In developing the villain Harrison Snow, Reynolds and Leon's text asks readers to consider historical acts of colonial violence that have occurred, and that continue to occur, against Puerto Ricans (Rodríguez-Astacio & Low, 2023). Toward the end of the graphic novel, Miles connects the pillaging of the island to his own Boricuan heritage, saying "Snow might be using the earthquake aftermath to strip-mine the island that raised Mom. The land where our family still lives. Where Mom's heart beats" (p. 91). In this graphic novel, the stakes are both personal and political.

Throughout *Shock Waves*, Rio shares memories and pictures with Miles of growing up on the island. Miles tells her: "I love your stories, Mom. It's like I'm there on the island with you" (p. 107). Elsewhere, Rio connects her experiences to the contemporary geopolitical concern that, as Puerto Rico continues to be pummeled by disasters, folks on the mainland will lose interest and abandon empathy. "That's what I'm afraid will happen…that people will grow tired and bored. That the earthquake will be old news and it'll be years before Puerto Rico recovers" (p. 53). This book is steeped in generational memory.

All told, Miles' Puerto Rican identity plays a pivotal role in *Shock Waves*. Miles keeps a postcard his abuela sent him from El Yunque National Forest, creates street art featuring the Puerto Rican flag, and gives a speech ending with the lines "I love you, Mom. And we love you, Puerto Rico! WE LOVE YOU, PUERTO RICO!" (p. 112). As cliché as it is to write, the island serves as a character in its own right.

In contrast, Reynolds and Leon's follow-up graphic novel, *Miles Morales: Stranger Tides,* released in 2022, is less directly concerned with Puerto Rico and the diaspora. The book's scope is larger and less familial: "This isn't a Brooklyn thing. Or even a New York City thing. We're talking about saving the whole world" (p. 26). The narrative revolves around a villain who uses a video game to freeze onlookers in a permanent state of hibernation. (One of them is Miles' Uncle Aaron.) In terms of locating specific Latiné content, readers must turn to the illustrations, where the Puerto Rican flag appears in the background of four panels (pp. 31, 38, 82, and 83), and to characters' discussions of food. On page 27, Jefferson prepares a snack for Miles and his friend Ganke:

Jefferson: *Eat up, fellas. Don't be shy. The platanos are almost ready.*
Rio: *Someone say platanos?*
Miles: *Mom.*
Rio: *Mijo.*

While less overt than in *Shock Waves*, these subtextual linguistic and alimentary cues from *Stranger Tides* nevertheless remind readers that Miles' Boricuan identity is a part of his character.

Read together, Reynolds & Leon's two graphic novels multimodally highlight – through image, linguistic markers, major plot points, and symbolic content – Miles' roots in Puerto Rico and the ways his Latiné heritage impacts his everyday life as a biracial/bicultural teen superhero living in the diaspora. As the books' illustrator, Pablo Leon, explained (in Chan, 2022):

> *I've made it my mission to bring a spotlight on Latinos, our culture, our indigenous representation, our roots, and our very real problems. Much of my work has been mostly about generational memory… It was important to me to portray Miles' Afro-Latino side because it's one that's often sidelined and not nearly explored as much, and I think it's just as important to his character development. And when [Shock Waves] came out, reading about kids devouring the book and feeling seen, feeling that they could relate to Miles' struggles, it made me feel good, knowing we did a good job (n.p.).*

Leon's words serve as a fitting epigraph to this section.

Amazing Friends and *Through a Hero's Eyes*: Miles' Appearances in Media Intended for Young Children

It is difficult in the 2020s to spend much time in spaces frequented by children and not encounter Miles Morales. The character appears on t-shirts, backpacks, Halloween costumes—you name it—typically in full superhero garb (i.e., with mask on). On a visit to an amusement park in February 2024, David was pleasantly agog over just how many young children were festooned in Miles gear. A decade-plus after being nowhere, Miles was everywhere. Clearly, in the character's second decade of existence, he had caught on with young children, despite his appearances in comic books, prose and graphic novels, films, and games having mostly targeted teen and adult audiences.

Some children surely came to know Miles through the television show *Spidey and his Amazing Friends* (Marvel Studios Animation, 2021-). The Disney Junior program focuses on the heroic adventures of Miles (Spin), Gwen (Ghost Spider), and Peter (Spidey), who are portrayed as children themselves. While amusing and lighthearted, the characterization of all three heroes is thin. Viewers learn little about the characters' lives in the eleven-minute cartoon segments, which highlight wholesome and humorous stories about teamwork. There are notable exceptions, to be sure: Miles/Spin – voiced by Jakari Fraser – enjoys pistachio ice cream, he paints, and his mother, Rio, is an ER doctor. As far as Miles' Puerto Rican identity is concerned, one episode – Season 2's "Halted Holiday" (Harzan & Bachynski, 2022) – features explicit Boricua content. In episode S2.E8, viewers meet Gloria Morales, Miles' grandmother (voiced by Sophia Ramos), who is visiting New York from Puerto Rico for Thanksgiving. Miles' and Gwen's families are celebrating the holiday at Peter's house, and Miles' abuela Gloria is taking a cab from the airport to meet them. When her taxi becomes stuck in traffic caused by the villainous Doc Ock, the three heroes snap into action.

While the plot of "Halted Holiday" is preposterous (Doc Ock erects force fields in NYC's tunnels to steal passengers' Thanksgiving desserts), it is riddled with meaningful linguistic and symbolic Latiné content. Early in the episode, we hear Rio speaking to her mother on the phone: "Hola mamí, que pasa?" She later calls Miles "mijo" and all three children "niños." Meanwhile, Miles shows his friends a family portrait he painted, telling them, "Abuela Gloria is the best. I made her this painting to take home to Puerto Rico. When she looks at it, she'll remember how much I love her." Viewers learn that Gloria is bringing a homemade flan – a custard dessert of Spanish origin, made in the Puerto Rican style – to Thanksgiving and that it is Miles' favorite. When we meet Gloria in an obstructed traffic tunnel, she is represented as robustly bilingual, and often translanguages (e.g., "I hope you all get home to your familias in time for dinner" and "Ay mijo, que bueno, I love it"). When all three spider-heroes are later imprisoned in a force field by Doc Ock, it is Abuela Gloria who saves the day, tossing her flan in the villain's face and seizing her force field generator. (Don't worry, Gloria brought a spare flan.) The plot of the episode is decidedly silly, but its casual multilingualism and mentions of Puerto Rico may nevertheless enable some children, who rarely encounter such representations in early childhood superhero programming, to feel seen.

As of this writing, *Spidey and his Amazing Friends* has aired three seasons on Disney Junior. [Note: Another show featuring roughly the same characters, *Marvel's Spider-Man,* ran for three seasons (2017-2020) on Disney XD. The show targeted preteens and referred to Miles' character as Spy-D and Kid Arachnid. Also, Miles (voiced by Nadji Jeter) lived in Manhattan and his father Jefferson was revealed to be the villain Swarm. Miles' mother Rio and uncle Aaron did not seem to exist at all in the narrative. In spite of these interesting departures, we are not reviewing *Marvel's Spider-Man* in this chapter due to its absence of Latiné content.] Many of *Spidey and his Amazing Friends'* storylines have been directly adapted into Disney Books that are faithful to their source material. The only other explicit Latiné content we discovered in our viewings occurred in the six additional episodes in which Rio Morales appears (S1.E6, S1.E12, S2.E1, S2.E11, S2.E12, S3.E1). While she is not as central to the plotlines of these episodes as Abuela Gloria in "Halted Holiday," the character, voiced by Gabrielle Ruiz, brings bilingualism (English and Spanish) into the show. Further, she provides Miles opportunities to express his own bilingualism, which do not appear otherwise.

David, René, and Yamil were not sure if *Spidey and his Amazing Friends* (and its associated books and merchandise) accounted for Miles' vast popularity with young children. While the show is fast paced, lighthearted, and aesthetically pleasing, its characterizations are underwhelming. Aside from consuming content meant for older audiences, which young children absolutely do, we wondered about other media featuring Miles that were specifically intended for an early childhood audience. How did they portray Miles? As luck would have it, Disney Books released an original picturebook in late 2023 titled *Miles Morales Spider-Man: Through a Hero's Eyes*. This standalone book was unrelated to the Disney Books adaptations of the cartoon show. While still too new to ascertain its influence, we were curious to see if *Through a Hero's Eyes* delved deeper into the character than Spin's appearances on *Spidey and his Amazing Friends*. Would the book highlight aspects of Miles' Latiné identity beyond flan and Spanish-language sobriquets?

Written by Denene Millner and illustrated by Mónica Paola Rodríguez, the picturebook explicitly explores Miles' aspirations as an artist in connection to his Puerto Rican heritage and his Nuyorican identity. Before the official text of the picturebook begins, readers encounter declarations from the book's creators. Millner, a Black author from Long Island, dedicated the book to "children who tell the stories and sing the songs of their ancestors' tongue, knowing that this land and that land, too, are both home." Meanwhile, Rodríguez, an illustrator from San Juan (a rare Puerto Rican creator hired to work with the Miles character), dedicated her work to "all the Borinqueños, pa'que tu lo sepas!" (*to all the Puerto Ricans, so that you know!*). Prior to the narrative even beginning, the book's creators have stated their commitment to preserving generational memory, lifting the transnational diasporic spirit, and centering Puerto Rican identity. Then we get into the text proper.

In *Through a Hero's Eyes,* Miles is portrayed as a preteen Brooklynite—already a superhero (we get none of his origin story), and a burgeoning artist. He loves to draw and, patrolling the city as Spider-Man, watches muralists painting buildings with great admiration. One of those muralists is Mr. Arty, a fellow Puerto Rican, who Miles recognizes as a patron of Cutz's Swag Shop where they both get their hair cut. The barbershop features heavily in Millner's narrative, occupying four of the book's nineteen openings. (Note: In unpaginated picturebooks, two-page spreads are known as openings.) It is within the barbershop that readers are introduced to several characters as well as a great deal of Afro-Latiné content. Black and Puerto Rican art, culture, and language seem to drip off the page. While not explicitly mentioned in the book's narration, we also see a mural of Arturo Alfonso Schomburg in the background of opening 3. Schomburg was an historian of African and Puerto

Rican descent, and the namesake of New York's Schomburg Center for Research in Black Culture.

In openings 6 and 7, Cutz's patrons are talking about a new Jean-Michel Basquiat exhibit:

Cutz: *All you need to know is that Basquiat is THE man.*

Mojo: *Basquiat is okay, but he's no Romare Bearden! …*

Mr. Arty: *Art is more than pretty pictures. It's a celebration of culture and life and the artists who make it. Barely anyone knows that Basquiat has puertorriqueño running in his veins.*

Miles: *My mami taught me that same thing. Basquiat is one of my favorite artists.*

This conversation leads into opening 8, where "Before long, the whole shop is buzzing with small facts and big truths about Puerto Rican culture." Patrons speak of Puerto Rico's beautiful beaches and the quality of mofongo (a dish made of mashed fried plantains) on the island and in Brooklyn. In addition to the picturebook's paragraph-length expositions, there are interesting visual cues, such as Cutz emanating a speech balloon with only the Puerto Rican flag in it. One unnamed patron's speech balloon simply contains "¡Boricua!" Another patron offers the apt summation: "Look around you. Puerto Rico is everywhere." Miles is overwhelmed with emotion.

The omniscient narrator informs readers that "Miles's mom is puertorriqueña, and she's taught him all about her culture—his culture. But he's never heard anyone talk about Puerto Rico and art the way Mr. Arty does" (opening 8). Much of the remainder of the picturebook concerns Miles building a friendship with Mr. Arty, whom he tells: "I'm half-Puerto Rican, like Basquiat, and I like to draw. I want to be an artist someday" (opening 9). Some of their exploits together (with Rio in tow) involve dancing bomba with master bomberos (opening 14), dining at Mr. Arty's favorite restaurant where they eat "mofongo with pork, the national Puerto Rican dish… It's sweet, savory, warm, and tastes like home" (opening 14), and collaborating on a mural that features the Brooklyn bridge, bomberos, drums, and the Puerto Rican flag (opening 17). Miles' crime-fighting adventures as Spider-Man play a tertiary role in this story about cultural belonging in the diaspora and the role artists play in uplifting the community. Insofar as there is *any* superhero content, it is Miles grappling with how he can learn more about art when he's so busy being Spider-Man (opening 11).

Ultimately, the book's message, delivered by Mr. Arty, is that our lives are not an either-or. It's not that Miles can be *only* an artist or *only* Spider-Man. He can be both. It is an important transnational metaphor, pertaining to the feeling that one is neither here nor there but always in between (Ghiso & Low, 2013). Miles voices this feeling in opening 16, asking Mr. Arty: "What if you're not sure where your place is?"—a common refrain among those living in a diaspora. The answers to

Miles' questions come to him through his artmaking and super-heroics. "I'm puertorriqueño and an artist. It is my calling, and I carry it in my heart" (opening 16). And: "Like Puerto Rico, like Brooklyn, Miles must hold Spider-Man in his heart, ALWAYS" (opening 19).

In contrast to *Spidey and his Amazing Friends*, *Through a Hero's Eyes* shows us that early childhood media need not be superficial in their representations of culture, language, and identity. While written for an audience of young children, the themes of *Through a Hero's Eyes* are deep and resonant, touching upon intergenerational immigrant trauma, the arts as a form of cultural remembrance, and the importance of creating community within the diaspora. By weaving explicit Boricua visual, textual, and symbolic content throughout, Millner and Rodríguez provide fans of Miles Morales one of the deepest representations of his character as a biracial teen grappling with a swath of intersecting identities, and being pulled in various directions. And miraculously, they did so in a picturebook that can be appreciated, on multiple levels, by the youngest of Spider-Man fans. It is no mere coincidence that having an OwnVoices creative team gave readers the deepest opportunity yet to celebrate the vibrancy of Miles' Puerto Rican heritage.

Miles as Merchandise: Is There Room for Cultura in Toys, Apparel, and Product Packaging?

This section may be the shortest, as it deals with non-narrative texts, but that does not make these texts insignificant. In the 2020s, as Miles Morales has become a pop culture icon, the character has appeared on increasing arrays of licensed merchandise and apparel. Rarely, if ever, is the character's Puerto Rican identity on display. As critical consumers of popular culture, we might issue a series of questions regarding Miles' appearances in this milieu. 1.) When Miles appears on a product, is his face visible or is he wearing a full Spider-Man costume with his mask on? 2.) If he speaks, does Miles ever use Spanish? 3.) If there is a description of Miles on the product's packaging, does it describe any aspects of his cultural identity/ies? 4.) Are any Puerto Rican signifiers present?

We want to be explicit in clarifying that it is not an action figure's or a backpack's job to determine the associations children have with it. Children should be able to bring their own intentions, imaginations, and identities onto a plaything or clothing item. Nor is it the responsibility of a Lego set or a box of macaroni and cheese to flesh out a character's backstory. Card and tabletop games (i.e., *Marvel Champions*) are meant to be played with more than grappled with. But… (there's always a but)… with a character as significant as Miles, in terms of both his racio-cultural representation and his ascendant popularity, it might be irresponsible for licensors to strip him of ethnic and cultural signifiers in the interest of moving as much merchandise as possible. In these products, we can see Miles' iconicity struggling against the authenticity and specificity that made him groundbreaking in the first place.

CONCLUSION: CON GRAN PODER

The goal of our critical transmedial content analysis was never to put media formats in competition with each other or to proclaim one medium superior for representing intersectional lives. Different media and genres do different things to us; they act upon us in different ways. It is important that we not analyze all story-texts as if they are attempting to achieve the same effects. Each is created for particular audiences and purposes, by particular people, and such context is important to highlight. Nevertheless, it seems odd to expect only some media formats to highlight characters' intersectional identities with nuance or particularity.

Superhero stories provide audiences the simplicity and clarity that our daily realities cannot. It can be refreshing to separate the world into good and evil, heroes and villains. But as we add stories, across media, from differently situated creators – each of whom leaves sediments of themselves in the texts they create – audiences regain some of the messiness of life in these stories—the simultaneity, the contradiction. (Does Miles live in Brooklyn, Manhattan, or Spanish Harlem? Is he eleven or sixteen? Is he called Spider-Man, Spin, or Spy-D? What is Jefferson's job? It depends on the story! The medium is part of the message!) Characters originating in comic books get built up over many years and sometimes over many decades. We should not expect them to be fully formed from inception. They are canvases to be passed from painter to painter, bearing traces of what came before—palimpsests, if you will. In Miles Morales, Bendis created a flawed but strong foundation, rife with possibilities for extension and adaptation, both within and beyond the comics medium. Subsequent creators have come in and made additions and corrections to Bendis' initial design. (From meatloaf and mashed potatoes and peas to platanos y mofongo y pasteles y tostones y flan, oh my!)

Just as our goal is not to put media formats in competition with one another, it is certainly not our goal to place Miles' Black and Puerto Rican heritages at odds. Miles' Blackness is not separate from his Latinidad. Miles is *both-and.* As Newby (2018) wrote, "the fact that Miles looks more [B]lack than Latino opens up interesting narrative possibilities and conversations. While media so often codes him as the [B]lack Spider-Man...his Puerto Rican heritage is just as important" (n.p.). As media analysts, we can focus on individual aspects of a character to see how they are brought into the foreground or background (Deman, 2023). Like actual people, characters contain multitudes, and they show us many facets of both themselves and ourselves. The intersections among Miles' Blackness and Puerto Ricanness provide important storytelling opportunities in and across different media. Throughout the Spider-Verse, there are audiences eager to explore those intersections and traverse the billowing web of connections opened up within them. Far from being a limitation, the fact that Miles is not a single-authored or single-axis character creates opportunities for many creators to leave their mark upon him. This means, of course, that some facets of his identity might be highlighted or downplayed, leading to omissions and lacunae. In this chapter we've turned a spotlight on Miles' Boricua identity, but it is not our goal, either, to make Miles all about his ethnicity. He is a dynamic character involved in many disparate stories. It is not inherently problematic for creators to focus on Miles' love of sci-fi, his poetry and art making, his school experiences, or his commitment to fighting villains, sometimes in his neighborhood community and other times across the galaxy. Just so long as creators remember that "being biracial does affect the kind of Spider-Man Miles Morales is" (Newby, 2018, n.p.).

Just as there is not one right way to be Latiné or Puerto Rican, or biracial, or from New York City, there are many ways of being Miles Morales. There are new Miles stories coming out all the time and more opportunities to flesh out his character in interesting ways. A transmedia lens is ideal for looking across and analyzing those representations with both admiration – we are fans, after all – and with criticality. In order to better showcase Miles' (and by extension, readers') richly intersectional lives, the identities that make up his character need not be seen as divergent, competing, or even crisscrossing, but as hybrid, transmedial, and multiversal in nature. "This Afro-Latino boy who would become Spider-Man is a sign of our times, a reminder of the past, and a means of hope for the future" (Newby, 2018, n.p.).

REFERENCES

Abad-Santos, A. (2016, March 7). The biggest drama in comic books right now is over Spider-Man and race. *Vox.* https://www.vox.com/2016/3/7/11173456/spider-man-miles-morales

Abercrombie, D. (2017, August 2). Miles Morales: A Spider-Man novel – An interview with Jason Reynolds. *Redital.* https://www.redital.com/2017/miles-morales-a-spider-man-novel-an-interview-with-jason-reynolds/

Arizpe, E., & Styles, M. (2016). *Children reading picturebooks: Interpreting visual texts* (2nd ed.). Routledge.

Bendis, B. M. (Writer), & Pichelli, S. (Illustrator). (2011). *Ultimate Comics Spider-Man* #1. Marvel Comics.

Bendis, B. M. (Writer), & Pichelli, S. (Illustrator). (2016). *Spider-Man* #2. Marvel Comics.

Betancourt, D. (2018, December 13). Miles Morales is a Spider-Man who's biracial like me. So why wasn't I more excited for his movie? *The Washington Post.* https://www.washingtonpost.com/arts-entertainment/2018/12/13/miles-morales-is-spider-man-whos-biracial-like-me-so-why-wasnt-i-more-excited-his-movie/

Botelho, M. J., & Rudman, M. K. (2009). *Critical multicultural analysis of children's literature: Mirrors, windows, and doors.* Routledge. 10.4324/9780203885208

Botzakis, S., Savitz, R., & Low, D. E. (2017). Adolescents reading graphic novels and comics: What we know from research. In Hinchman, K. A., & Appleman, D. A. (Eds.), *Adolescent Literacies: A Handbook of Practice-based Research* (pp. 310–322). The Guilford Press.

Campbell, E. (2021). In conversation…*Miles Morales: Spider-Man* and *Miles Morales: Shock waves.Journal of Children's Literature*, 47(2), 92–94.

Casale-Hardin, M. A. (2015, Jun 15). "Mejorar la raza": An example of racism in Latino culture. *Huffpost.* https://www.huffpost.com/entry/mejorar-la-raza-an-exampl_b_7558892

Cavna, M. (2011, August 4). Miles Morales and me: Why the new biracial Spider-Man matters. *The Washington Post.* www.washingtonpost.com/blogs/comic-riffs/post/miles-morales-and-me-why-the-new-biracial-spider-man-matters/2011/08/04/gIQABzlGuI_blog.html

Centeno, A. (2023, October 6). What *Spider-Man: Miles Morales* gets right about cultura and the authentic Puerto Rican experience. *IGN.* https://www.ign.com/articles/spider-man-miles-morales-cultura-authentic-puerto-rican-experience

Chan, G. (2022, November 7). Jumping into multiple story worlds with author and illustrator Pablo Leon. *Forbes.* https://www.forbes.com/sites/goldiechan/2022/11/07/jumping-into-multiple-story-worlds-with-pablo-leon/?sh=78cf7f1d6b18

Christmas [Cartoon short]. In H. Wilcox (Executive Producer), *Spidey and his Amazing Friends.* Disney Junior; Marvel Studios Animation.

Coogler, R. (Director). (2018). *Black panther* [Film]. Marvel Pictures.

Dallacqua, A. K., & Low, D. E. (2021). Cupcakes and beefcakes: Students' readings of gender in superhero texts. *Gender and Education*, 33(1), 68–85. 10.1080/09540253.2019.1633460

Deman, J. A. (2023). *The Claremont run: Subverting gender in the X-Men.* University of Texas Press.

Diaz, V. (2023). Chris Miller & Phil Lord chat about Puerto Rican culture in *Spider-Man: Across the Spider-Verse! Brite & Bubbly.* https://briteandbubbly.com/chris-miller-phil-lord-interview-spider-man/#:~:text=This%20film%20actively%20shows%20more,characters%20in%20a%20superhero%20film

Dos Santos, J., Powers, K., & Thompson, J. K. (Directors). (2023). *Spider-Man: Across the Spider-Verse* [Film]. Columbia Pictures, Marvel Entertainment, & Sony Pictures Animation.

El Nuevo Dia. (2011) Tras la muerte de Peter Parker, el heredero del traje de Spiderman, será Miles Morales, un joven de origen hispano. [Link to news article by El Nuevo Día] [Status Post]. *El Nuevo Dia.* https://www.facebook.com/100064912923247/posts/226486017394289/

Franzese, T. (2020, December 15). Why we love *Spider-Man: Miles Morales. Inverse.* https://www.inverse.com/gaming/spider-man-miles-morales-ps5-harlem-diversity-inclusion

Fu, A. (2015). Fear of a black Spider-Man: Racebending and the colour-line in superhero (re)casting. *Journal of Graphic Novels & Comics*, 6(3), 269–283. 10.1080/21504857.2014.994647

Ghiso, M. P., & Low, D. E. (2013). Students using multimodal literacies to surface micronarratives of United States immigration. *Literacy*, 47(1), 26–34. 10.1111/j.1741-4369.2012.00678.x

Gill, V. S. (2016). "Everybody else gets to be normal": Using intersectionality and Ms. Marvel to challenge "normal" identity. *The ALAN Review*, 44(1), 68–78.

Gomez, J. (2018, December 12). Miles Morales in 'Into The Spider-Verse' is the Afro-Latinx representation we were missing — and not just because he's a superhero. *Bustle.* https://www.bustle.com/p/miles-morales-in-into-the-spider-verse-is-the-afro-latinx-representation-we-were-missing-not-just-because-hes-a-superhero-14947742

Harzan, A. (Writer), & Bachynski, D. (Director). (2022). Halted holiday / Merry Spidey.

Hutcheon, L. A. (2006). *A theory of adaptation*. Routledge. 10.4324/9780203957721

Insomniac Games (2018). *Marvel's Spider-Man* (PlayStation 4 version) [Video game]. Sony Interactive Entertainment.

Insomniac Games (2020). *Spider-Man: Miles Morales* (PlayStation 4 version) [Video game]. Sony Interactive Entertainment.

Insomniac Games (2023). *Marvel's Spider-Man 2* (PlayStation 4 version) [Video game]. Sony Interactive Entertainment.

Jimenez, A. (2016, April 5). Miles from representation: On needing more from Bendis's Spider-Man. *The Middle Spaces.* https://themiddlespaces.com/2016/04/05/miles-from-representation/

Johnson, H., & Gasiewicz, B. (2017). Examining displaced youth and immigrant status through critical multicultural analysis. In Johnson, H., Mathis, J., & Short, K. G. (Eds.), *Critical content analysis of children's and young adult literature: Reframing perspective* (pp. 28–43). Routledge.

Johnson, H., Mathis, J., & Short, K. G. (Eds.). (2017). *Critical content analysis of children's and young adult literature: Reframing perspective*. Routledge.

Kang, J. C. (2023, June 6). The Post-racial vision of "Across the Spider-Verse". *The New Yorker.* https://www.newyorker.com/news/our-columnists/the-post-racial-vision-of-across-the-spider-verse

Kinney, M. E. (2013). Linda Hutcheon's *a theory of adaptation*. *Critical Voices. The University of Guelph Book Review Project*, 3(3), 7–15.

Kisner, J. (2024, February 6). The magic of Raina is real. *The Atlantic.* https://www.theatlantic.com/magazine/archive/2024/03/raina-telgemeier-cartoonist-smile-guts-books/677180/

Klepek, P. (2017, July 7). Why Miles Morales, the first Black/Latino Spider-Man, means so much to people. *Vice*.https://www.vice.com/en/article/gybyq3/why-miles-morales-the-first-black-spider-man-means-so-much-to-people

Krippendorff, K. (2003). Content analysis: An introduction to its methodology. *Sage (Atlanta, Ga.)*.

Low, D. E. (2015). *Comics as a medium for inquiry: Urban students (re-)designing critical social worlds*. [Unpublished doctoral dissertation. University of Pennsylvania, Philadelphia, PA].

Low, D. E. (2017a). Students contesting "colormuteness" through critical inquiries into comics. *English Journal*, 106(4), 19–28. 10.58680/ej201729013

Low, D. E. (2017b). Waiting for Spider-Man: Representations of urban school "reform" in Marvel Comics' Miles Morales series. In Tarbox, G. A., & Abate, M. A. (Eds.), *Graphic novels for children and young adults: A collection of critical essays* (pp. 278–297). University Press of Mississippi. 10.2307/j.ctv5jxmqd.22

Low, D. E., & Campano, G. (2016). Multiliteracies, the arts, and postcolonial agency. In Campano, G., Ghiso, M. P., & Welch, B. J. (Eds.), *Partnering with immigrant communities: Action through literacy* (pp. 92–102). Teachers College Press.

Low, D. E., Lyngfelt, A., Thomas, A. A., & Vasquez, V. M. (2022). Critical literacy and contemporary literatures. In Pandya, J. Z., Mora, R. A., Alford, J., Golden, N. A., & deRoock, R. S. (Eds.), *The critical literacies handbook* (pp. 308–316). Routledge. 10.4324/9781003023425-36

Lugo, J. (2021). *Puerto Rican culture references in* Marvel's Spider-Man: Miles Morales - JJ's first 20. [Video]. YouTube.https://www.youtube.com/watch?v=ri2mzQWCkIE

Martínez-Roldán, C. M. (2013). The representation of Latinos and the use of Spanish: A critical content analysis of Skippyjon Jones. *Journal of Children's Literature*, 39(1), 5–14.

McWilliams, O. C. (2013). Who is afraid of a Black Spider(-Man)?" *Transformative Works and Cultures,* 13. https://journal.transformativeworks.org/index.php/twc/article/view/455/355

Micheline, J. A. [@elevenafter]. (2016). [Tweet]. Twitter.

Miller, H. C., Hines, C. M., & Rodríguez-Astacio, R. M. (2022). With great power comes…youth empowerment? A critical content analysis of Marvel's superhero young adult literature. *The ALAN Review*, 50(1), 33–44.

Miller, H. C., Hines, C. M., & Rodríguez-Astacio, R. M. (2022). *Teaching Miles Morales: Suspended* to resist erasure in a time of book bans. *English Journal*.

Millner, D., & Rodríguez, M. P. (2023). *Miles Morales Spider-Man: Through a Hero's Eyes*. Disney Books.

Mills, R. M. (2022). A post-soul Spider-Man: The remixed heroics of Miles Morales. *The Black Scholar*, 1(52), 41–52. 10.1080/00064246.2022.2007345

Mills, R. M. (2023, June 1). 'Across the Spider-Verse' and the Latino legacy of Spider-Man. *The Conversation*. https://theconversation.com/across-the-spider-verse-and-the-latino-legacy-of-spider-man-205892

Molina-Guzmán, I. (2021). *Into the Spider-Verse* and the commodified (re)imagining of Afro-Rican visibility. In Dagbovie-Mullins, S. A., & Berlatsky, E. L. (Eds.), *Mixed-race superheroes*. Rutgers University Press. 10.36019/9781978814639-012

Morris, B. (2020). *Marvel's Spider-Man Miles Morales: Wings of fury*. Titan Books.

Newby, R. (2018, December 12). 'Into the Spider-Verse' and the importance of a biracial Spider-Man. *The Hollywood Reporter*. https://www.hollywoodreporter.com/movies/movie-news/why-spider-man-spider-verse-is-important-fans-color-1168367/

Newton, M. (2011, August 4). How the media reacted to news of a non-white Spider-Man. *Forbes*. https://www.forbes.com/sites/matthewnewton/2011/08/04/how-the-media-reacted-to-news-of-a-non-white-spider-man/?sh=9dcb94a4f612

Persichetti, B., Ramsey, P., & Rothman, R. (Directors). (2018). *Spider-Man: Into the Spider-Verse* [Film]. Columbia Pictures, Marvel Entertainment, & Sony Pictures Animation.

Reynolds, J. (2017). *Miles Morales: Spider-Man*. Marvel.

Reynolds, J. (2023). *Miles Morales: Suspended*. Atheneum.

Reynolds, J. A., & Leon, P. (2021). *Miles Morales: Shock waves*. Marvel/Graphix.

Reynolds, J. A., & Leon, P. (2022). *Miles Morales: Stranger tides*. Marvel/Graphix.

Riesman, A. (2014, May 1). Comics Legend Brian Michael Bendis on *Guardians of the Galaxy*, Sexism, and Making a Nonwhite Spider-Man. *Vulture*. https://www.vulture.com/2014/04/comics-brian-michael-bendis-spider-man-guardians-x-men.html

Riesman, A. (2018, December 14). Is Miles Morales finally getting his due as Spider-Man? *Vulture*. https://www.vulture.com/2018/12/miles-morales-of-into-the-spider-verse-the-race-problem.html

Rodríguez, N. N., & Vickery, A. E. (2020). Much bigger than a hamburger: Disrupting problematic picturebook depictions of the Civil Rights movement. *International Journal of Multicultural Education*, 21(2), 109–128. https://ijme-journal.org/index.php/ijme/article/view/2243/1371. 10.18251/ijme.v22i2.2243

Rodríguez-Astacio, R. M., Hines, C. M., & Miller, H. C. (2024). Criticality and the cowl: Teaching Black superhero narratives with DC graphic novels for young adults. *The ALAN Review*, 51(2), 11–19.

Rodríguez-Astacio, R. M., & Low, D. E. (2023). Using superhero graphic novels to foreground transitions in our teaching with upper elementary and middle grades readers. *The Reading Teacher*, 76(5), 640–645. 10.1002/trtr.2189

Rodríguez de Tió, L. (1893). A Cuba. *Ciudad Seva*. https://ciudadseva.com/texto/cuba-y-puerto-rico-son-de-un-pajaro-las-dos-alas/

Santos, J. J.Jr. (2021). Talented tensions and revisions: The narrative double consciousness of Miles Morales. In Dagbovie-Mullins, S. A., & Berlatsky, E. L. (Eds.), *Mixed-race superheroes*. Rutgers University Press. 10.36019/9781978814639-010

Short, K. G. (2017). Critical content analysis as a research methodology. In Johnson, H., Mathis, J., & Short, K. G. (Eds.), *Critical content analysis of children's and young adult literature: Reframing perspective* (pp. 1–15). Routledge.

Variety Staff. (2018). Post Malone and Swae Lee drop new song 'Sunflower' from 'Spider-Man' soundtrack". *Variety*. https://variety.com/2018/music/news/post-malone-swae-lee-sunflower-spider-man-soundtrack-1202984388/

Vasquez, V. (2010). *Getting beyond "I like the book": Creating space for critical literacy in K-6 classrooms* (2nd ed.). International Reading Association.

Vin. (n.d.). Spider-Man Miles Morales reading guide. *Cosmic Circus*. https://thecosmiccircus.com/spider-man-miles-morales-reading-guide/

Williams, A. (2018). The '*Spider-Man: Into The Spider-Verse*' soundtrack is exactly what Black superhero music should be. *Uproxx*. https://uproxx.com/music/spider-man-into-the-spider-verse-soundtrack-review/

Wilson, S. (2011, August 2). Miles Morales: Spider-Man's PC new replacement is half-Black, half-Latino. *LA Weekly*. https://www.laweekly.com/miles-morales-spider-mans-pc-new-replacement-is-half-black-half-latino/

Wolk, D. (2021). *All of the Marvels: A journey to the ends of the biggest story ever told*. Penguin.

Worlds, M., & Miller, H. C. (2019). *Miles Morales: Spider-Man* and reimagining the canon for racial justice. *English Journal*, 108(4), 43–50. 10.58680/ej201930049

Chapter 3
Social Superheroes:
Interactions, Judgments, and the Superhero Mission

Justin Martin
https://orcid.org/0000-0003-0698-0049
Whitworth University, USA

ABSTRACT

In the chapter, the author considers the implications of a constructivist approach to understanding superhero media for scholarly analyses concerning the relation between social interactions, judgments, and superhero missions. The approach, social cognitive domain theory (SCDT), grounds the development, refinement, and application of moral and nonmoral social concepts in heterogeneous social interactions and arrangements. Particularly, special attention is given to comic, television, and film portrayals of T'Challa (Black Panther), Carl Lucas (Luke Cage), and the time-traveling X-Man Lucas Bishop. Previous work explores the parallels of their narratives for understanding the ubiquity of heterogeneous social and moral judgments, as their narratives can be partly distinguished through their grounding in national, local, and societal contexts, respectively. In keeping with this work, the present chapter explores the potential of three features of social judgments for understanding superheroes along three social interactional dimensions.

SOCIAL SUPERHEROES

As evidenced by its box-office success, transmedia appeal, frequent revisions, scholarly attention, and the incorporation of its iconography and mythology into political activities, superhero media has and continues to permeate American culture and civic imagination (Burke, 2020; Jenkins, 2020; Martin, 2023b; Miczo,

DOI: 10.4018/979-8-3693-3302-0.ch003

2016; Philips, 2022; Wandtke, 2012). It is also a genre that deeply resonates with fans, as evidenced by both the myriad discussions they have around the motives and methods of superheroes' actions, and perspectives concerning the relevance of superhero media for their own understandings of justice (Phillips & Strobl, 2013). Scholars further argue that part of the genre's cultural appeal is due to the dual ability of its narratives to simultaneously *contribute* to the reinforcement of certain beliefs, values, norms, and understandings of a social, moral, or political nature and *challenge* them (Curtis, 2016; Philips, 2022). As a cultural phenomenon, superhero narratives are inherently social in the sense that at times they serve as allegories or representations of certain real world social, moral, and political concerns, contribute to them, explore possibilities for new forms of social interaction and organization, or some combination thereof (Curtis, 2016, 2023; Jenkins, 2020; Phillips & Strobl, 2013). Thus, their popularity and ubiquity throughout society, broadly construed, is at least partly attributable to the ability of their narratives to penetrate aspects of our social reality.

This form of social embeddedness characteristic of their superhero missions occurs against the backdrop of navigating the trust citizens put in them (Phillips & Strobl, 2013), and is broadly consistent with Wright's (2021) view of the purpose of morality within social groups. She contends that when people come together and agree to live socially, they co-create structures whose purpose is to inform and regulate the beliefs, values, and behaviors important for conformity or peaceful coexistence between individuals (and sub-groups) within the larger group. In this context, the purpose of morality is to provide conceptual boundaries individuals within the group can rely on to adjudicate between two broad categories of deviant or divergent beliefs, where deviance/divergence refers to beliefs that are (currently) outside of the community's accepted norms. One category includes instances where such deviance is *harmful* to the group and thus should not be allowed to enter and animate activity within the group, such as beliefs propagating oppression, exploitation, and human rights abuses. The other category includes instances when deviance is *warranted* and thus beneficial to the group on the grounds of moral (and by extension, social) progress, as assessed by say, more fair and humane treatment between persons. When morality-governed structures are functioning well, they successfully *regulate divergence* by both protecting the group from harmful beliefs, behaviors, etc., and promoting diverse perspectives that can benefit the group in the present and/or future.

Similarly, Miczo (2016) conceives of superheroes as having dual social functions. On the one hand, they use their abilities for moral or ethical ends, helping, protecting, and preserving the welfare and dignity of others. At the same time, they preserve an important social space, known as the public sphere, where people within communities and societies doing life together can gather, literally and figuratively, to discuss, debate, and deliberate on substantive matters. In her analysis of superheroes' debates concerning the merits of registering with the government during the *Civil War* storyline (Millar & McNiven, 2006-2007), Wood (2016) examines their reasoning through Kohlberg's (1971/1981, 1980) constructivist approach to moral development, noting how the rationales on both sides were consistent with *conventional* and *postconventional* moral reasoning, with appeals to either social relationships (conventional), communal or societal order (conventional), or principles undergirding the fabric of a society of equals (postconventional). The story centers around the societal response to an event involving a reckless superhero battle near a school that resulted in hundreds of kids being killed. The backlash led to the passing of the Superhero Registration Act (SRA), and superheroes were divided on whether to register with the government in accordance with the act or refuse and become outlaws. The story thus represents one of the more notable stories in superhero comics where the physical clashes between the opposing superhero camps were proxies for or reflected their articulated perspectives on the merits of governmental authority and the laws created to maintain it.

Thus, one way to view superhero narratives in terms of their social, civic, or societal relevance is in terms of how many of their actions, inactions, and the principles they defend and sometimes reconsider or violate, reflect tensions in their dual responsibilities. Their responsibilities to protect and preserve both those aspects of their world's social fabric (1) considered worth *keeping as is* and (2) considered flexible in a manner that leaves open possibilities concerning how things *can or should be*. Although not focused on the morality-society relationship, it is worth noting Wandtke (2012)'s observation of the many ways thematic and character-relevant features of superhero comics are revised in some respects yet reproduced in others. Broadly speaking, this suggests, in keeping with previous analyses (Martin, 2021, 2023a, 2023b, 2024; Martin et al., 2023), that people's understanding of superheroes, their treatment of others, and how they are treated, may have implications for the meanings people attribute to how they themselves are treated and treat others.

Superhero Missions: Similar, Yet Different

The essay contains two parts. Part one sketches out some main ideas from a constructivist approach to the development of moral and nonmoral social concepts, Social Cognitive Domain Theory (SCDT; Nucci & Itlen-Gee, 2021; Smetana et al., 2014; Smetana & Yoo, 2022; Turiel, 1983, 1998; Turiel et al., 1987), with specific attention given to its emphasis on the relationship between social interactions, conceptual understandings, and the heterogeneity of moral judgments. This relationship means that human social life is sometimes multifaceted, sometimes ambiguous, and often complex. This complexity is evident in three interrelated aspects of this construction process informing the content and contours of people's judgments about and concerning relations with others. These are the *distinctions* people make between various social interactions in accordance with certain definitional criteria, *coordination* of competing considerations in multifaceted social interactions, and *informational assumptions* sometimes underlying people's judgements of social interactions (Killen, 2018; Nucci et al., 2017; Smetana et al., 2014; Smetana & Yoo, 2022; Turiel, 1983, 2002; Turiel et al., 1987; Wainryb, 2004). Each is discussed in the context of SCDT more broadly followed by illustrative examples from the narratives of Black Panther, Luke Cage, and Bishop in accordance with their particular social arrangements.

To elucidate these ideas within the context of superhero narratives, the chapter explores some recent scholarship on superheroes and how their missions (1) can be analyzed through the lens of SCDT on the one hand, and (2) occur against the backdrop of varying social contexts or arrangements relevant to an interrogation of morally relevant decisions on the other. This portion of the chapter draws on the comic worlds of Black Panther, Luke Cage, and Lucas Bishop, and contends their superhero missions, in part, are characterized by different approaches to the relationship between social arrangements, social interaction, and morally relevant judgments. Black Panther's mission occurs within a monarchy-based social arrangement. Luke Cage's mission takes place within a local neighborhood. Lastly, Lucas Bishop's superhero mission is formed by his experiences growing up in a future dystopian society. Disciplinary explorations into their narratives give considerable attention to the social contexts in which their superhero missions are developed and refined and suggest the two (the superhero and their social ecology) are intricately linked. The chapter concludes by briefly exploring the potential for superhero media to serve as stimuli for pedagogical and research activities aimed at interrogating the relationship between social interactions and judgments within a superhero context.

By exploring similarities and differences across their respective narratives, the chapter accentuates how superheroes dynamically relate to their social contexts. Two similarities germane to the present analyses are the narrative emphases on the relationship between morality and legality and the distinction between legitimate and illegitimate uses of power. In Black Panther narratives, the social context is national and involves a superhero who is also a king of a sovereign nation. He must balance his superhero mission with an overlly political one: using the power of the state to govern Wakandans the best way he sees fit in accordance with tradition. In Luke Cage narratives, the social context is more local and, despite times when he is involved in local politics, events focus mainly on what it means for a superhero to represent everyday people in Harlem. He performs his superhero mission while also maintaining the essence of what holds communities together: trust and shared obligations. In Bishop narratives, the social context is societal, specifically when it comes to between group relations between humans and mutants. His superhero mission is balanced along two dimensions: his (1) role as a law enforcement officer and (2) time-traveling across different social arrangements—one of which is dystopian.

As explored throughout the chapter, these differences in social context—national, local, and societal—contribute to relevant thematic differences animating the tenor of their narratives. The author contends that these differences in social arrangements afford opportunities for scholarly and pedagogical analyses. Black Panther's struggles to balance his superhero and political responsibilities highlight how political decisions can yield implications that affect people in robust and varied ways (e.g., as in the case of say, what the nation should do with vibranium). Luke Cage's narratives, with their prioritization of trust and shared obligations, often accentuate the problem of corruption—which, at its core, is a violation of both. Bishop's narratives, through superhero-law enforcement and future society-present society comparisons, highlight the robust asymmetry between societal and moral considerations that can exist within dystopian social arrangements. Specifically, this gap pertains to the difference between societal authorities treating mutants as ends versus as means.

Although beyond the scope of the present analysis, it is worth noting the significance of these superheroes when it comes to the lack of and veridical portrayals of black superheroes. Indeed, this significance has been examined by many scholars (e.g., Fawaz, 2016; Lund, 2015; McMillen, 2020; Nama, 2011), and indirectly influenced the present analysis. In full disclosure, these are among the author's favorite characters because of the author's ability to identify with various aspects of their experiences along racial or cultural lines. However, this influence notwithstanding, the present analysis is not focused on their racial significance, but their significance via specific applications of the superhero mission within unique social contexts. Thus, the analysis assumes that, in addition to being black superheroes whose actions should thus be understood at least in part along racial lines, their broader cultural relevance also stems from the ways that their morally relevant missions are formed, carried out, and elaborated as superheroes who just happen to be black.

SUPERHEROES, SOVEREIGNTY, AND SCDT

Superheroes are generally defined as prosocial and ethical agents who use their powers in the service of others (Coogan, 2006; Miczo, 2016) and often break the law doing so (Curtis, 2016; Phillips & Strobl, 2013). As much as superheroes work to uphold law and order and alongside the interests of their governments, they also disobey their governments when they believe it is in the best interests of human or societal welfare. Thus, a common theme within superhero narratives concerns the relationship between legality and morality, as superheroes occupy liminal spaces between these conceptual borders, sometimes working within society's legal apparatus and at times operating outside of it (Martin, 2023a, Martin et al., 2023). Similarly, Curtis (2016, 2023) argues that the notion of sovereignty, which includes interrelated concepts such as law, authority, hierarchy, and legitimacy, is germane to a well-rounded understanding of superhero mythology. Two characteristics of superhero sovereignty—the notion that superheroes at times act like the state—include the abilities to legitimately use violence to maintain social order and determine which situations or threats necessitate and therefore justify said violence. If superheroes embody, elucidate, and challenge notions of sovereignty, they do so by highlighting tensions between the promise of building a sensible, ordered world through properly harnessed power on the one hand and the threat of destroying said world through chaos and annihilation on the other.

Across the superhero narratives discussed in the chapter, questions of sovereignty are both ever-present and contextualized due to the nature of social arrangements characterizing the superheroes' respective missions. Whether the threats come from outside or within Wakanda's borders, Black Panther's actions, both as a superhero and a politician, engender questions related to the (il)legitimate use of violence and/or power. For instance, how many times should Black Panther be able to leave Wakanda for superhero missions (e.g., as say, a member of the Avengers), yet maintain the same authority as king when he returns? In the case of Luke Cage, such sovereignty is localized where questions often center around why *he* can choose when to work alongside law enforcement and outside of law enforcement, yet other Harlem residents cannot. What gives him the authority to make these decisions when, in nearly every other facet aside from his superpowers, he acts as a JAG ("just a guy")? In Bishop narratives, the questions are not so much centered around his ability to act as sovereign as they are around what happens when human sovereign authority puts "all its weight" into dehumanizing mutants. In this way, Bishop's ability to time-travel serves as a context for comparing different perspectives on how governmental authority should be used in societies where humans and mutants attempt to co-exist.

Broadly speaking, these conceptions of superheroes, centered on the relationship between what is right and what is legal and questions of superhero sovereignty, parallel two classes of social interactions SCDT contends are distinguished using definitional criteria based on the actions' features. One class of interactions is generally focused on group cohesion, organization, and functioning, and is usually understood by appealing to concepts related to rules, norms, social expectations, authority, hierarchy, custom, and tradition. These acts belong to the *conventional* or *societal* (henceforth used interchangeably) domain of social interaction and judgment. Examples include forms of greeting in social interaction, and following the authority dictates of and rules established by teachers, parents, bosses, and institutions. The other class of interactions, by contrast, is generally focused on the treatment of persons consonant with their inherent dignity and are usually understood by appealing to concepts related to harm/welfare, fairness/justice, civil liberties, and human rights. These acts belong to the *moral* domain of social interaction and judgment, with examples including hitting, stealing from, and violating the civil or human rights of others (Smetana et al. 2014; Smetana & Yoo, 2022; Turiel, 1983; Turiel, et al., 1987). Both kinds of interactions are important to and ubiquitous throughout societies.

Definitionally, judgments and actions in the moral domain are understood to differ from those in the societal domain because the former are construed as generalizable, not contingent on the existence of authority dictates, laws, or rules, and laws or rules prohibiting acts in question can or should not be altered. Judgments and actions in the societal domain, by contrast, are generally understood to be contextual as opposed to generalizable (in the institutional or geographical sense), contingent upon the existence of authority dictates, laws, or rules, and laws or rules prohibiting acts in question can be altered. Acts in both domains are generally considered to be impersonal, either due to the importance of group cohesion, functioning, and organization (societal) or the primacy of treating persons as ends and not means (moral). Generally, most would probably agree that whether to obey a nation's laws (societal) and tell the truth (moral) in everyday interactions should not be a matter of personal discretion. In other words, it would be hard to live with others if from day-to-day it was unclear if those people frequently interacted with would adhere to laws and tell the truth about matters of substance.

From the perspective of SCDT, superheroes' actions often prioritize the moral domain, as they use their abilities to protect and preserve the welfare and dignity of persons, and work to achieve justice for them when they have been victimized. These morally-relevant actions and accompanying symbolism (e.g., reflected in their speeches, costume, insignia, physical stature, and spatial positioning) further suggest that they are acting in accordance with and represent generally held principles whose importance is not reducible to, or dependent upon authority dictates, laws, rules, popular opinion, or personal preference (Curtis, 2016; Jenkins, 2020; Martin, 2021, 2023a, 2023b, 2024; Miczo, 2016; Peters, 2020; Wandtke, 2012). This prioritization of SCDT-consistent definitional criteria is in line with the common understanding of superheroes as selfless, inspiring moral exemplars.

Superheroes, by and large, orient their actions towards preserving the welfare of those whom criminals and/or supervillains wish to harm. In doing so, they often inflict harm on would-be perpetrators. And when they are unable to prevent harm to others, they seek justice for the victims. Although superhero narratives are open to varying interpretations (Curtis, 2016; Martin, 2023), it is possible, suggests SCDT, to view this orientation–given its robustness and consistency across narratives–through the prism of the moral domain which is qualitatively different from the societal domain. For instance, their heroic acts often happen without the sanction of legitimate authorities and include various violations of due process rights afforded under the law (authority, law, or rule non-contingency). Moreover, these actions often extend beyond local contexts, national borders, or the planet earth (generalizability). Lastly, their frequent justifications for their actions and appeals for governments, institutions, and citizens to aspire to be better suggest they believe that the principles their actions seek to uphold–e.g., prevention of harm to innocent persons and holding wrongdoers accountable–govern actions that are not matters of personal preference (impersonality) and should be safeguarded by laws, the existence and enforcement of which should not be up for debate (inalterability). Some examples of these conceptual distinctions throughout the narratives of Black Panther, Luke Cage, and Bishop are included below, but they are explored more extensively elsewhere (Martin, 2019, 2021, 2023a, 2024; Martin et al., 2023). In their own way, these narratives substantively engage with questions about how to balance moral and societal considerations while trying to do life together.

Black Panther, Wakanda, and Second-Order Phenomena

Black Panther's visibility in *Captain America: Civil War* (2016) and *Black Panther* (2018) contributed to increased scholarly attention, with analyses of both Black Panther and Wakanda conducted across multiple disciplines. Myron et al. (2023) contends that part of the first solo film's appeal was its ability to create multiple ways of understanding the world (e.g., sociological, psychological, historical, religious, futuristic). Jordan and Kim (2019) analyze Black Panther narratives from the perspective of cognitive psychology, exploring how T'Challa's concepts of persons, groups, and their interrelations inform both his superhero mission and leadership within the Wakandan monarchy. Conversely, Hicks (2019) examines various Wakandans through the lens of cultural development, drawing parallels between the characters' actions–and what they suggest about their understanding of the relationship between discrimination, oppression, and identity–and the characterization of stages of identity development.

Other scholarship also centers Wakandan society. Bein and Lewis (2022) interrogate various perspectives on justice (retributive, reparative, restorative, and transformative) in terms of the optimal path forward for Wakanda, while Boudreaux (2022) interrogates the relationship between tradition, justice, and societal functioning amidst efforts to carve out said path. Curtis (2021) examines *Black Panther* (2018) using the features of sovereign authority and its implications for thinking about the legal, universal justice, and human rights themes articulated and defended by T'Challa and Killmonger, both when T'Challa was king and when Killmonger briefly held the mantle. Collectively, these analyses highlight how Wakandans attempt to address injustice by appealing to or emphasizing the significance of (1) individual and structural forms of accountability, (2) balancing the maintenance of tradition and movement toward more just social relations, and (3) universal human rights, specifically in terms of resource allocation. Thus, Wakandan society plays a significant role in Black Panther's superhero mission.

These issues, broadly speaking, pertain to matters broadly understood by SCDT as belonging to the societal (e.g., law, authority, and tradition) and moral (e.g., harm, justice, and human rights) domains of social interaction and judgment. And while Black Panther's dual roles as superhero and king often serve to accentuate the primacy of these issues in superhero narratives, they characterize major narrative events of many superheroes (Curtis, 2016; Martin, 2023a; Martin et al., 2023; Peters, 2020; Phillips & Strobl, 2013; White, 2019). As Bainbridge (2020) notes, neither superheroes nor supervillains are bound by the laws, rules, or authority of the state. And while both superheroes and supervillains tend to emerge under societal conditions where the state's authority, laws, and rules are insufficient for maintaining social order, it is usually the state's inability to protect citizens from the latter that animates the actions of the former.

Wakandan society as a whole and its monarchy-based government are important features to consider when trying to understand the motives and meaning of his actions as both king and superhero. Along these lines, one affordance these sets of social arrangements provide relates to the moral-societal domain relationship. Specifically, actions in one domain often implicate considerations in the other, since he defends and thus represents moral principles related to relations between persons and the interests of the Nation–chief of which is the maintenance of societal cohesion, order, and tradition. SCDT refers to these types of social interactions as *second-order combinations*, where an act generally falls within one domain, yet the surrounding features of the social interaction or situation can lead to implications relevant to another domain (Smetana, 1983; Turiel, 1983). As Martin (2021) notes, the central conflict in *Black Panther* (2018) could be viewed in this way, as the decision to alter laws and policies concerning the sharing of vibranium (societal) can have implications for the harm and welfare of others (moral). In other words, variations concerning who has access to vibranium and how that access was granted (e.g., say, through sharing or stealing) can lead to variations in the extent to which it is used to preserve or destroy life, uphold or violate human rights, etc.

The remarks of Queen Ramonda, now leader of Wakanda, to the United Nations at the beginning of the second film, *Black: Panther: Wakanda Forever* (2022), further illustrates this idea of the "vibranium question" being understood as a second-order phenomenon:

It has always been our policy to never trade vibranium under any circumstance. Not because of the dangerous potential of vibranium, but because of the dangerous potential of you.

Similarly, when she first meets Namor, he explains the dilemma he and his nation are facing because of the events at the end of *Black Panther* (2018):

Your son exposed the power of vibranium to the world. In response, other nations have begun searching the planet for it. His choice has compromised us.

Albeit from a different perspective, Namor also appeals to a societal-moral combination, as T'Challa's decision as king to alter their policy concerning vibranium had implications for the safety of Namor and his people. Martin and colleagues (2023) similarly argue that aspects of the core conflict in the comic event *A Nation Under Our Feet* (*ANUOF*; Coates & Stelfreeze, 2016-2018) can be understood as second-order phenomena. At the heart of the conflict is whether T'Challa is still fit to lead Wakanda, and by extension, if this institutional arrangement in the form of a prolonged monarchy is in Wakanda's best interest. Throughout the 12-issue series, T'Challa tries to prevent radical factions within Wakanda from destroying it while trying to chart a new path forward for the nation that takes the criticisms of him and the monarchy seriously. The series ends with various Wakandan stakeholders meeting to discuss the best way forward and T'Challa forming a council to create a new constitution that alters the monarchy.

In at least two respects, events from the series can be construed as societal-moral phenomena. For instance, one could argue that his willingness to alter the constitution was partially informed by the view that certain governmental actions or policies, if heavily unfavored by citizens, can lead to violence and loss of life. Another societal-moral combination is suggested by his discussion with Aneka, a former member of the government security force, Dora Milaje, who broke the law in rebellion against the government:

If I pardon you, what else have I pardoned in a future unseen?...Your freedom would be the death of Wakanda. - T'Challa (Black Panther #12, 2017, p. 6)

If this death is literal and not (just) figurative, it appears he views his decision to either use his authority to hold her accountable or pardon her as having implications for the welfare of other Wakandans.

Social Superheroes

Luke Cage, Harlem, and the Problem of Corruption

Scholars argue that some key features of Luke Cage's superhero narrative include his dynamic relationship with Harlem, the moral complexities of the characters, and his multifaceted or nuanced approach to the use of violence (Derry et al., 2017; Martin, 2023a; Mack, 2020). This dynamism and complexity extend to the relationship between the narratives and the reader/viewer, as he performs his superhero mission alongside multifaceted characters who encourage readers/viewers to reconsider their judgments and underlying assumptions concerning right and wrong, and the substantive influences on a person's harmful or unjust actions (Mack, 2020). Whereas previous analyses examine these themes along economic, gender, and/or racial dimensions (Mack, 2020; Martinez, 2022; McMillen, 2020; Nama, 2011; Philips, 2022), a humanistic or universalist approach reveals Luke Cage's superhero mission as one of many contexts through which one can reflect on the application of moral and nonmoral social concepts scholars suggest are generally shared amongst people across the globe (e.g., Atari et al., 2023; Graham et al., 2013; Haidt & Joseph, 2007; Helwig, 2006; Killen & Smetana, 2015; Turiel, 1983, 2002; Turiel et al., 1987; Wainryb, 2006; Yoo & Smetana, 2022). In this sense, superheroes like Luke Cage have much in common with their non-powered neighbors.

In addition to second order phenomena concerning the societal and moral domains, social arrangements common within superhero narratives often portray these domains in conflict. According to SCDT, these and other domain conflicts are ubiquitous throughout and important for mature sociomoral development (e.g., Helwig, 2006; Killen & Smetana, 2015). Martin (2023a) argues that Luke Cage narratives frequently interrogate the relationship between law and morality against a backdrop that sees Luke Cage influencing and being influenced by residents of Harlem on the one hand while navigating corruption on the other. Considering SCDT's view that morality and legality can be distinguished in accordance with definitional criteria, the role of corruption in Luke Cage narratives can serve as a reminder of this distinction through illustrating what happens when these criteria are exaggerated to immoral ends. For instance, Luke Cage received his powers while being incarcerated for a crime he did not commit but was framed for (*Hero for Hire #1*, 1972; Goodwin & Tuska, pp. 7-13), and corrupt police officers and politicians inform much of his superhero mission in the *Luke Cage* television series (Coker, 2016-2018; Martin, 2023a). Luke Cage narratives thus center questions around the (morally) legitimate and illegitimate uses of power, and the importance of always remembering the difference.

In *Luke Cage: Gang War* #1 (Barnes & Bachs, 2023), this conflict between the societal and moral domains—exemplified through Luke's struggles to challenge the corruption of specific public officials while preserving the legitimacy of public institutions—is explored after the passing of former mayor Wilson Fisk's (i.e., Kingpin's) Anti-Vigilante Act (AVA). Under AVA, superheroes are deemed vigilantes and civilians are prohibited from getting involved in crime-related matters, such as intervening to try to stop a robbery. Once Luke, now Mayor of New York, decides to go against AVA and start recruiting fellow vigilantes to join him to help protect the city from a new threat, he is aware that he may need to earn their trust again seeing he is now a politician (*Luke Cage: Gang War* #1, Barnes & Bachs, 2023, p. 29). In *Luke Cage: Gang War* #2 (Barnes & Bachs, 2023, p. 7), his wife, fellow superhero and vigilante Jessica Jones, upon learning of his decision to go against AVA, jokes that a public official breaking the law is not original. Thus, as both a politician and vigilante, he is aware of the potential challenges he may face in his efforts to help the city given the all-too-familiar alliance between public officials and corruption.

Even when Luke Cage leaves Harlem, as when he travels to New Orleans to investigate human experimentation, police corruption factors into the story (*Luke Cage* #3, 2017, Walker & Blake II, p. 10). Fearing that evidence might lead to his culpability, the wealthy Cyril Morgan phones a contact in local law enforcement to see if something can be done to keep him in the clear. Once he learns his contact does not have jurisdiction, he mentions he will reach out to his FBI contacts. It is important to keep in mind that such corruption can be of an institutional or individual nature. Concerning the latter, it is possible to view some of his interactions with fellow New York vigilantes the Punisher (*Civil War* #5, p. 17; Millar & McNiven, 2006) and Daredevil (*Shadowland* #1, p. 18; Diggle & Tan, 2010) as suggestive of a belief in the dangers of being corrupted by personal desires or vendettas. In the former, he refers to Punisher as a "nut job" and is open to handing him over to the cops. In the latter, he tries to encourage Daredevil to change course once he sees him taking a more authoritarian approach to his superhero mission by establishing himself as judge, jury, and executioner in Hell's Kitchen.

One important feature of Luke Cage narratives is that he navigates the relationship between the moral and legal, whether through his attempts to address corruption or other criminal activity, with the influence of the community. His substantive commitment to community, articulated during his speech honoring a beloved community member, involves working with both law enforcement and criminals if he deems it necessary to achieve justice–even if there are substantive disagreements along the way (*Luke Cage*, "Just to Get a Rep;" "Suckas Need Bodyguards;" "The Creator;" "Soliloquy of Chaos;" "They Reminisce Over You;" "Can't Front on Me;" Coker, 2016, 2018). Martin (2023a) suggests this reciprocal and mutually influential relationship between Luke Cage and Harlem informs his superhero mission in many ways. One concerns his views on when to use violence himself and prevent others from using it. The other is through community members encouraging him to reflect on the implications of his actions and inaction for both his superhero mission and the welfare of Harlem.

In addition to exploring Luke Cage's view on the relationship between law and morality through a different social arrangement as a politician, *Luke Cage: Gang War* #1 (Barnes & Bachs, 2023) also highlights the importance of the community for his superhero mission. Frustrated with AVA precluding him from going after dangerous criminals (p. 11) and no longer having a pulse on the community (p. 13), he decides to become a vigilante again. This means visiting everyday people throughout the city to reconnect and understand the conditions affecting their lives. For example, he visits a scientist in Queens to learn amount the bullets the criminals used in a recent event (p. 15) and a seamstress in the Bronx to make his new vigilante costume (p. 18). These interactions reinforce how Luke Cage's superhero mission in general and his navigation of the morality-legality conflict in particular are rooted in his relationship to his community.

Bishop, Dystopia, and Moral-Societal Asymmetries

Unlike Black Panther and Luke Cage, there is a lack of scholarship on Lucas Bishop, save for the occasional mention as a marginal character in the analysis of another character's narrative journey. An exception is Lund's (2015) analysis interrogating the implications of some of his portrayals for thinking about the relationship between poverty, crime, and the carceral state. The present analysis, based on a conception of superheroes as inherently social (Curtis, 2016; Jenkins, 2020; Martin, 2023b; Martin et al., 2023; Miczo, 2016; Phillips & Strobl, 2013), alludes to similar sociological phenomena. Centering developmental psychology focuses on the broader social conditions informing Bishop's superhero journey, analyzed in the context of the potential relationship between dystopian social arrangements and the decisions he makes concerning the societal (e.g., law, authority) and moral (e.g., harm, fairness) domains.

Whereas Black Panther and Luke Cage narratives primarily focus on present social arrangements Bishop narratives explore the application of societal and moral considerations to social arrangements in a dystopian future. Given the level of immorality toward mutants on behalf of the state characteristic of these arrangements, Bishop's actions often accentuate the definitional criteria people tend to use to distinguish between matters of society and matters of morality—such as (non)generalizability, rule or authority-(in)dependence, and (in)alterability (Smetana et al. 2014; Smetana & Yoo, 2022; Turiel, 1983; Turiel, et al., 1987). For instance, narrative events within Bishop's dystopian future often include the arbitrary treatment of mutants in a manner that bears on human rights, such as the stripping of due process rights, the right to consent to medical procedures, and the right to life

(Martin, 2024). Therefore, mutants live in a constant state of precarity, vulnerability, and fear (*Lives and Times of Lucas Bishop* #1 and #2, Swierczynski & Stroman, 2009; *X-Men* #206, Carey & Bachalo, 2007; X-Factor #26, David & Eaton, 2007; *XMTAS*, "Days of Future Past," Houston, 1993; *Wolverine and the X-Men; WATXM*, "Future X", Filippi, 2009). A state that animates Bishop's actions regardless of the time period he currently lives in. These abuses make salient the characteristics of moral acts (e.g., as generalizable, independent of authority, etc.) and serve as reminders of how, as articulated by SCDT, social relations within the moral and societal domains are fundamentally different.

Bishop's superhero journey includes time operating both as a law enforcement officer charged with maintaining law and order and a rebel risking his life for human rights (Martin, 2024; *X-Men: The Animated Series*; *XMTAS*, "Days of Future Past," Houston, 1993; "One Man's Worth," Houston, 1995; *X-Men: Legends* #5 and #6, Portacio, Haberlin, & Prianto, 2023). Although in many ways the same can be said about other superheroes who at times work for the government and at times against it, Bishop narratives are unique in that this navigation occurs against the backdrop of a particularly exaggerated moral-societal asymmetry in two respects. One is the dystopian nature of the social arrangements allows for the exploration and interrogation of the inverse relationship between coerced societal regulation and human rights violations. Second, this gap between upholding and disregarding human rights is further heightened by time-travel, as readers and viewers witness the stark contrasts between present and future societies. This ability to frequently compare radically different societies and their implications for the (im)moral treatment of persons affords readers and viewers the opportunity to explore how abstract concepts like human rights, law, authority, and society interact across very disparate social configurations. Configurations that, as Martin (2024) suggests, inform his morally relevant actions.

As someone with experience working as an agent of the state, Bishop's superhero mission is consistent with many others who take it upon themselves to protect people when the government deems itself incapable of doing so (Bainbridge, 2020). And if fictional governmental and legal apparatuses share features of those in the real world, these two features of Bishop narratives, collectively, reflect another affordance of the genre: providing some insight into the ways real-world governments, acting as sovereign authorities and with the law as their instrument, legitimize various forms of violence against persons to maintain social order (Curtis, 2016). Albeit within different social arrangements, Bishop's narratives, like those of Black Panther and Luke Cage, often address questions about the legitimate and illegitimate uses of power.

COORDINATION

According to SCDT, the complexity of social life is not only due to heterogeneous social interactions that inform diverse understandings, evaluations, and applications for relevant social concepts. Social life is also complex because on many occasions, interactions are multifaceted in the sense that multiple concepts or considerations–either within the same domain or between different domains–conflict (Turiel, 1983). During these situations, as for instance, when a harm consideration conflicts with a justice consideration (within-domain) or a harm issue conflicts with a legal issue (between domain), figuring out the (most) appropriate course of action may involve a process known as *coordination*. Competing considerations are weighed against each other before arriving at a decision that resolves any ambiguities or difficulties that may arise. This ability is evident in older children and increases throughout adolescence (Helwig & Jasiobedska, 2001; Helwig & Kim, 1999; Nucci et al., 2017; Turiel & Nucci, 2018), suggesting that by the time most superheroes commit to their superhero missions, they can weigh multiple considerations when navigating ethical or moral dilemmas (Martin, 2024). To the extent conceptual distinctions people make between various social interactions help explain some of the *what* of social judgments involving and relations between persons, coordination helps explain the *how* when social situations include multiple or competing elements.

Black Panther

As noted, the actions of superheroes are open to interpretation (Curtis, 2016). Nonetheless, considering the morally laden nature of their narratives and the frequent dilemmas they find themselves in during their pursuit of justice, it is reasonable to view superhero narratives as a useful context for a general understanding of the process of coordination. In *Black Panther* #12 (Coates & Steelfreeze, 2017), T'Challa's discussion with Aneka concerning the implications of not holding her accountable for her vigilantism and disregard of Wakandan law, is suggestive in this regard. Two potential considerations relevant for the present analysis are justice and social order. If his desire to pardon her (p. 5) is rooted in a principle of justice such that he thinks she broke the law for the right reasons, he seems to appeal to the effect his actions may have on Wakanda if their system of law no longer has the regulatory authority necessary for maintaining social order.

T'Challa's discussion with Wakandan teacher and philosopher Changamire–in which Changamire calls him a hero and not a king (p. 13) can also be read through the lens of coordination. Specifically, the mentioning of T'Challa as a *hero* when he seeks Changamire's counsel as a *king* to assist him in quelling the violence and restoring societal order suggests that T'Challa is weighing moral and societal considerations and his inability to arrive at a resolution brings him to Changamire. Even though these discussions in comics and television often lack the details of coordination processes present in moral development research (e.g., Nucci et al., 2017), they nevertheless highlight considerations characters are weighing or at least accounting for when trying to determine the best way forward. Moreover, these interactions, as with his interaction with Aneka concerning accountability (*Black Panther* #12, Coates & Stelfreeze, 2017, pp. 5-6), point to a core element of Black Panther narratives, which is the exploration of the moral implications of societal (i.e., based on law, tradition, and/or authority) decisions.

Luke Cage

For Luke Cage, the contexts suggestive of coordination often relate to his connection to Harlem. Thus, storylines often wrestle with the question of "What does, or should Harlem stand for?" and provide opportunities to explore competing considerations characteristic of coordinated reasoning. As with the discussion of Black Panther, the presence of these competing considerations within superhero narratives has implications for thinking about the process of coordination even in the absence of clear evidence of Luke Cage engaging in such a process. What is important is whether his articulation of his position appeals to multiple concerns or considerations.

These appeals are common in the *Everyman* story, which centers around a health professional with an ability to share people's afflictions with others. Angry with the amount of injustice in Harlem and the widening gap between the haves and have nots–a gap which in her view is often associated with harmful or unjust outcomes for the poor–she decides to target various wealthy people in Harlem she believes are exploiting poor residents. Characteristic of Luke Cage narratives in general, the narrative conflicts are not limited to her personal vendetta against the rich and wealthy. She also convinces many other Harlemites to join her cause, and thus Luke Cage must both defend the community from the Everyman while also trying to persuade members of the community to not adopt her approach to rectifying injustices. In *Luke Cage* #3 (Chapter 5, Del Col & Lindsay, 2018, p. 9) he appeals to Harlemites he encounter on the street seeking out rich people to harm. Later (Chapter 6, p. 4), he tries to reason with Everyman by arguing that her actions are making Harlem worse not better. After Everyman is no longer a threat, Luke Cage broadcasts a live cell phone video where he appeals to Harlem to stop destroying the city and each other because that's not who they are)

Social Superheroes

Yeah, the Everyman had noble intentions. She was one of us. But now she's playing God. It's not right....This isn't us. This isn't Harlem. - Luke Cage #3: Chapter 6 (Del Col & Lindsay, 2018, p. 13)

This appeal is more important considering that at the time, he thought he was going to die soon due to CTE. This notion that a community entails interpersonal obligations on behalf of its members to each other, is consistent with a similar appeal to Harlem he gives to the police department in the last episode of *Luke Cage*'s first season ("You Know My Steeze;" Coker, 2016). In it, he speaks of the importance of those with the ability to do more to do so to preserve the community's way of life. Likewise for the appeal he makes to both cops and vigilantes at the end of the *Gang War* series. After the police join the vigilantes and they defeat the robots, Luke Cage expects the captain to arrest him and the other vigilantes for violating AVA. Once the captain explains why he will break the law himself and not arrest him (#4, Barnes & Bachs, 2024, p. 18), Luke Cage stresses the importance of working together for the welfare of the city:

If New York is going to survive, to be the place we live and love, it's going to take good people coming together. - p. 20

This appeal can be seen through the prism of competing moral and societal considerations, where the struggle or dilemma is between advocating for the fair or just treatment of persons (moral) while also maintaining social order and a sense of community unity (societal). It can also be construed as competing moral considerations, where one may consider the merits of advocating for justice in ways that include harming others. Collectively, these appeals, as well as interactions with Harlemites who vary in their perspectives on the law, highlight the relationally dynamic nature of Luke Cage's superhero mission (Martin, 2023a). A mission that often positions the community itself as an integral partner in his efforts to provide justice for and preserve the livelihood and dignity of its residents. This partnership also extends to situations where Luke Cage is vulnerable, uncertain, and scared. When he learns he does not have CTE but there is a non-negligible risk of developing it given his superhero activity (his ability protects his body better than his brain), he seeks community assistance in the form of a support group (*Luke Cage* #3, Chapter 5, Del Col & Lindsay, 2018, p. 18). In more ways than one, Luke Cage *is* Harlem.

Bishop

Considering Bishop's unique experiences as both an agent of and rebel against the state throughout his narrative history (Martin, 2024), it is worth pondering the nature of his experiences that appear to inform his reconsidering of and shifting perspectives concerning the state. Or, put another way, what role do his relevant social interactions and arrangements play in his decisions concerning the morality-society relationship? One category of social interactions is implied in *X-Men: Legends* #5 (Portacio, Haberlin, & Prianto, 2023, p. 5) when he recalls his earlier thinking at the start of his job as a member of the Xavier's Security Enforcers (X.S.E.). His job was to apprehend criminal mutants. He soon realized, however, that the job was not as straightforward as he initially assumed. Violent, dangerous mutants were kept in a place called The Pool, and the potential threats were kept in a place called The Settlement. That interacting with mutants who differ in their status as actual versus potential threats might lead to him questioning the teleology of his duties is supported by the question that serves as the last text on the page (Portacio, Haberlin, & Prianto, 2023, p. 5):

But were they really all the criminals they led us to believe?

Amidst this questioning, he continued to focus on his mission and follow the dictates of his superior, although he admits that the question lingered (Portacio, Haberlin, & Prianto, 2023, p. 6):

But the straws kept sneakily piling up on my back...until one friggin' broke it.

The cause for the break was an assignment to terminate five rogue mutants who Bishop believed was in possession of many weapons and were likely planning a major attack. Once he realized that the intel was wrong and the mutant, who was trying to protect his family (who were not mutants), was not a criminal, he tries to convince the mutant to still come with him and trust him to figure out what he believes to be a misunderstanding. As his appeal to reason seem to be working, sentinels arrive and kill the mutant and his family. In anger, he uses his power to destroy one of the sentinels. Later, when Bishop confronts his boss, the warden, about the use of sentinels—as he was told sentinels would no longer be used in the apprehension of mutants—he is reminded of his place in the hierarchy as his concerns were not taken seriously. Deciding to take matters into his own hands and accept the consequences for disobeying authority when he does, he devises a plan to free the innocent mutants and families and give them a chance to start over at a new life (*X-Men: Legends* #5, Portacio et al., 2023, pp. 6-12; *X-Men: Legends* #6, p. 7).

Social Superheroes

In terms of the societal-moral asymmetry characteristic of Bishop narratives, these events are important because (1) how the mutant and his family were treated and (2) the ease in which Bishop's concerns were discarded point to the arbitrary treatment of mutants that bear on their human rights (Martin, 2024). In this case, however, it was a mutant, acting as an agent of the state, who was responsible for the subjugation of fellow mutants. The warden's treatment of Bishop echoes his treatment by the authority apparatus in "Days of Future Past" (*XMTAS*, Houston, 1993) where he also served as an agent of the state in his dystopian future. After apprehending a group of mutants, he discovers that he has fulfilled his captured mutant quota and is now disposable. He is immediately arrested and imprisoned like the mutants he just apprehended. To further illustrate this inverse relationship between the increasing use of authoritarian means of social control and the violation of human rights and dignity, Bishop learns those five innocent people were essentially killed over *money*. The family was the last holdout in an area targeted for a neighborhood redevelopment project, and the warden used his authority over Bishop and the sentinels to clear the way for a potentially profitable project (*X-Men: Legends* #5, Portacio et al., 2023, p. 11).

These events highlight the heterogeneity or flexibility of Bishop's thinking around moral and societal matters, as his varied experiences trying to maintain social order in a dystopian society inform his decisions about when to work with and against the state. To the extent he is interacting with violent mutants threatening the social order, he agrees with the goals of the state to maintain public safety (*X-Men: Legends* #5, Portacio et al., 2023, p. 13). But the threat assessment must be clear, unless he has no problems criticizing and trying to alter his society for the sake of preserving human rights and dignity.

Bishop's experiences point to multiple considerations bearing on the moral and societal domains that could reasonably factor into coordinated reasoning around dilemmas characteristic of his job as an X.S.E. officer. For instance, it is worth considering whether his questions surrounding mutant criminality were informed or accompanied by attempts to weigh his beliefs in the importance of maintaining social order and public safety with his belief in the fair and just treatment of persons. And how might his attempts to weigh these considerations be influenced by the information about the mutants in question his boss chooses and does not choose to disclose? Similarly, as a law enforcement officer, and as evidenced by his desire to still have the mutant come with him back to the prison to sort things out and seek an explanation from the warden about the reinstitution of sentinels, he values hierarchy and authority. He even admits to using it for the purposes of freeing the innocent prisoners and the families when he uses his authority as the higher-ranking officer to convince his friends and fellow officers, Malcolm and Randall, to help him (*X-Men: Legends* #5, Portacio et al., 2023, p. 18). Thus, at times he may have also been weighing the merits and implications of disobeying and obeying authority for both his own welfare (i.e., what could happen to him if/when he gets caught) and the welfare of the innocent prisoners.

Informational Assumptions

If domain distinctions parallel the *what* of judging and understanding social interactions and coordination the *how*, then the beliefs people hold about the world and their place in it provides insight into the *backdrop* against which these judgments and understandings are applied across varying situations. These worldview beliefs, or informational assumptions about reality, can be *physical*, *social*, or *psychological* in nature, and can influence how certain moral acts are judged and understood in certain contexts (Wainryb, 2004; Wainryb & Turiel, 1993). Some superheroes, for example, believe in a higher power and that humans possess souls, and this belief about the nature of physical reality can constrain their actions–as in the case of superheroes who refuse to kill due to religious convictions (Clark, 2020). Others, in contrast, may hold specific views about the psychological constitution of persons–such as their inability to change or be rehabilitated through the justice system–and these views may give them license to kill without remorse (Henderson, 2017; Phillips, 2022). And if sometimes superheroes work to alter or destroy certain institutions, it is possible that these efforts are informed by beliefs about the corruptibility of the institution or the moral or civic promise of a different institution–i.e., assumptions about social reality.

Black Panther

From this perspective, superheroes' relationships with their social contexts can be informed by specific beliefs they have about their physical, psychological, and social words. For Black Panther, an important element to the narratives that has yet to be discussed concerns his beliefs about the physical word. Within Wakandan religion, death is viewed as a transition into an afterlife, and does not mark the end of substantive interaction and communication. The city of the dead, Necropolis, is a place T'Challa often goes to seek counsel from the ancestors when weighing difficult decisions (*New Avengers* #18, Hickman & Schiti, 2014, pp. 3-9; *Black Panther* #11, Coates & Sprouse, 2017, pp. 1-2, 20-23). In *New Avengers*, Black Panther is the leader of the team, and they are contemplating whether to destroy another planet in order to save their own. In *Black Panther* #11, he is dealing with a violent revolution instigated by those who question his legitimacy as king as well the legitimacy of the monarchy itself. The advisory function of these interactions was also featured in

Social Superheroes

Black Panther (2018) and *Black Panther: Wakanda Forever* (2022), where serious questions about Wakanda's past, present, and future were being debated.

Despite the varying reasons for communing with the ancestors, their interactions, just as dynamic and animated as with the living, point to how beliefs related to an afterlife can inform their decisions. As T'Challa struggled with the moral implications of destroying a planet, he expressed his concerns with the ancestors. While understanding his dilemma, they were unanimous in their advice: do whatever it takes to save Wakanda and its people. Eventually he is convinced, as the interaction ends with him telling them he will do what needs to be done. When the time comes to make the decision, he appears ready. When he asks Reed Richards (i.e., Mr. Fantastic), who could not bring himself to use the device to destroy the other world, he is shown with the ancestors behind him–implying his decision to do the unthinkable is substantively informed by his belief in the existence and importance of an afterlife (*New Avengers* #21, Hickman & Schiti, 2014, p. 15). Although he ultimately decides to defy his ancestors by refusing to destroy the other planet, it is apparent through his (1) struggling with the decision, (2) mentioning that he wants to do it but cannot, and (3) deceased father disowning him, that who he is as a king is significantly influenced by his afterlife beliefs (pp. 17). Given the importance of the afterlife in Wakandan society, it is also likely that conceptions of the afterlife inform their approach to the sharing of Vibranium in *Black Panther* (2018) and *Black Panther: Wakanda Forever* (2022) given that arguments on both sides often appealed to what is best for the future of Wakanda.

Luke Cage

Given the primacy of corrupt social arrangements in Luke Cage narratives, Luke Cage's superhero mission is particularly suggestive of beliefs related to social reality, as he often articulates a certain view or vision for what the community of Harlem is and could (or should) be, and the important role individuals play within that community. As Martin (2023a) describes, these beliefs often center around the nature of street-level and organized crime, their impact on the community, and the insufficiency of law enforcement across the two seasons of *Luke Cage* (2016-2018). As noted above, assumptions about corrupt institutions, or at least corrupt individuals representing institutions, is common within Luke Cage narratives. Unsurprisingly, so is mistrust of institutions and individuals working within them. How, one might ask, does his views about institutional corruption and mistrust inform his approach to being a superhero? It is possible that his decisions to work ***alongside***, ***inside***, and ***outside*** governmental institutions are at least partially informed by his beliefs about the corruptibility of institutions. In terms of working alongside law enforcement, Luke Cage has no problem doing so when he determines he can trust the people he is working with. This is the case with the FBI agent in *Everyman* (Chapter 5, Del Col & Lindsay, 2018, pp. 14-15), the police captain in *Gang War #4* (Barnes & Bachs, 2024, pp. 18-20), and detective Misty Knight throughout the *Luke Cage* television series. Maybe there are times where, despite being distrustful of an institution, he carves out specific contexts in which he can work with good people within those institutions. This view is consistent with the premise behind *Gang War*, as he initially wants to make a difference from the inside. This decision to work inside a government institution may have been easier to make since he would be the mayor and would presumably have more decision-making authority to institute substantive changes. But once we felt he would be unable to fulfill his self-instituted obligation to protect New York, he violates AVA and resumes his superhero mission as a vigilante.

There is one constant amidst his willingness to serve the people of Harlem–and, as mayor, New York–across different social arrangements: his commitment to his conception of a community that includes its members working together to preserve and maintain each other's dignity and livelihood. Therefore, if social reality beliefs, particularly concerning corruption and community, inform his superhero mission, they may do so by contributing to the belief that although institutions and individuals within them are sometimes corrupt, corruption is not a fixed characteristic. And whether he thinks the situation requires him to work alongside, inside, or outside of governmental institutions to fulfill his obligations to others and remind them of their obligations to each other, these actions presuppose a malleable view of corruption. People, and therefore the institutions they build and run, can change. Consistent with this view, it is reasonable to wonder how much Luke Cage's beliefs about institutions informed his decision to resist the Superhero Registration Act (SRA) when superheroes were legally mandated to register with the government (*Civil War #4*, Millar & McNiven, 2006, p. 16).

Bishop

Considering both (1) Bishop's experiences with institutions–from being born and raised in dehumanizing mutant camps, escaping the camp as a youth, and working as an X.S.E. officer charged with policing mutants–and (2) the potential influences these may have had on his developing moral understanding (Martin, 2024), it is likely that his decision to work towards the betterment of mutants is at least partially informed by his beliefs about social behavior. While Martin focuses on his dystopian future, his beliefs about the nature of social and psychological reality may also be informed by present social interactions and arrangements. One such arrangement is when the X-Men were nearing extinction, and the Office of National Emergency (O.N.E.) was responsible for keeping the remaining 198 mutants safe at the Xavier Institute for

Social Superheroes

Higher Learning. Although not dystopian, these social arrangements, as told in *Civil War: X-Men* (Hine & Paquette, 2006), contain many of the same elements Martin (2024) contends are important to understanding Bishop's orientation toward moral and societal concepts as well as their interrelations. For instance, Bishop works with sentinels to police mutants (*Civil War: X-Men* #1, Hine & Paquette, 2006, p. 15), references the future he is trying to prevent as justification for his actions (*Civil War: X-Men* #1, p. 14; *Civil War: X-Men* #3, Hine & Paquette, 2006, p. 18), and centers concerns over mutant rights in the context of being perceived as threats (*Civil War: X-Men* #1, pp. 1, 5; *Civil War: X-Men* #2, Hine & Paquette, 2006, p. 16; *Civil War: X-Men* #3, p. 11; *Civil War: X-Men* #4, Hine & Paquette, 2006, p. 21). Thus, the story affords opportunities to examine potential factors influencing his decisions within the societal-moral asymmetry characteristic of his narratives.

Before he traveled to the X-Men's past in *Uncanny X-Men* #282 (Portacio & Byrne, 1991), he assumed upon becoming an X.S.E. officer that if mutants police themselves, social relations between officers and prisoners would be better than if policed by humans (*X-Men: Legends* #5, Portacio et al., 2023, p. 5). Although he soon learned that mutants can dehumanize fellow mutants, his belief in the value of mutants regulating their own behavior traveled with him to the past. During an attempt by mutants Domino and Shatterstar to break out the remaining mutants so they did not have to live under O.N.E.'s authority that turned into a violent riot, Bishop and Cyclops disagree on how things should have been handled. Believing that people would have been killed if the fighting continued, Cyclops let Domino, Shatterstar, and the remaining mutants (including the rioters) go free (*Civil War: X-Men* #1, Hine & Paquette, 2006, p. 13). Through the lens of informational assumptions, the nature of Bishop's disagreement with Cyclops's decision (*Civil War: X-Men* #1, Hine & Paquette, 2006, p. 14) is particularly informative (emphasis from Hines):

> *That's why mutants* **must** *police themselves. Otherwise, there's* **chaos**. *And you know what follows* **chaos**? *This [pointing to the "M" branded on his face]....You have no idea what* **real** *oppression is.*

In light of the human rights abuses he witnessed and experienced growing up in a future where mutants were considered disposable threats and his varied experiences policing mutants (*X-Men: Legends* #5-6, Portacio et al., 2023; *Civil War: X-Men* #1, Hine & Paquette, 2006, p. 16), this response suggests that many of Bishop's actions are informed by his belief in the relationship between distrust and chaos (and by extension, trust, and order). In other words, when people fear those they interact with, they tend to distrust them. This distrust can lead to chaos in the form of dehumanization, violence, and overall social disorder. This was the formula that helped define both his childhood and adulthood, and the formula he tries to prevent when he gets the chance (Martin, 2024).

When done correctly, Bishop appears to surmise, mutants policing mutants can engender trust, leading to humane treatment, preservation of human welfare and dignity, and overall social order. This view, coupled with his belief that people can be good or bad but not monsters (*Civil War: X-Men* #4, Hine & Paquette, 2006, p. 22) suggests that under social arrangements where the societal-moral asymmetry is particularly wide, people will likely resort to treating others inhumanely either to survive, save others, or both. To the extent he believes this is a feature and not a bug of the human experience, he also appears to believe that societies whose social orders are characterized by trust and humane treatment stand the best chance to prevent these forms of inhumane treatment from manifesting. Moreover, in contrast to Luke Cage, it is worth considering what role his beliefs about the relationship between distrust and chaos play in his decision to support the SRA and help the government arrest superheroes who refuse to do so (*Civil War* #3, Millar & McNiven, 2006, p. 6).

IMPLICATIONS

Given the broad consistency in the features of superhero narratives that afford opportunities for the interrogation of social and moral concepts (Martin, 2023b), the above-mentioned aspects of social arrangements–second order phenomena, corruption, and social order-human rights asymmetries–are often portrayed in other superhero narratives. These three superheroes were chosen largely due to their importance in my own scholarship concerning the relationship between moral and societal concepts through a constructivist lens. The constructivist emphasis on social interaction, meaning making, and thought heterogeneity contributes significantly to my intellectual interests in analyzing superheroes whose societies and communities are considered central to their missions. Constructivist analyses of Black Panther, Luke Cage, and Bishop help reveal some of the ways superheroes, despite their consistent motivations and frequent predictability (e.g., in terms of the motivations of many of their villains, use of violence, etc.), are both socially responsive to and adaptive within their differing social contexts. They are embedded in varied social interactions and relationships–an embeddedness that has implications for both pedagogy and scholarship.

What follows is a brief exploration of how second order phenomena, corruption, and social order-human rights asymmetries can potentially be useful stimuli for research and pedagogical activities. In relation to these efforts, the tables below include examples of moral and societal conflicts (Table 1) and potential learning activities and/or research stimuli (Table 2). They can be used in conjunction with the examples referenced in this discussion or serve as bases for other learning and research activities. The learning activities described below could be assessed in myriad ways depending upon comfort, expertise, and objective. Examples include, but are not limited to, written assignments, podcasts, group presentations, structured debates, team-teaching, think-pair-share discussions, examinations (written or verbal), and class polling followed by critical discussions of the results. The same goes for research activities, with some examples including content analyses, focus groups, individual interviews (both open-ended and semi-structured), likert-scale surveys, and think-alouds were participants' thought processes around designing and/or altering social arrangements are verbalized, transcribed, and analyzed.

Black Panther

In *Black Panther* #12 (Coates & Steelfreeze, 2017, pp. 15, 17-18), T'Challa ushers in a new political era for Wakanda by forming a council to create a more democratic form of government. The goal is for every region in Wakanda to work together to create a new government elected by Wakandans. When his mother reminds him that he must remain king because it is the will of their god, he responds by saying while he remains king, he refuses to be a tyrant. Consistent with the SCDT emphasis on domain distinctions, it is worth noting that when T'Challa and Shuri are discussing the role of the Wakandan ancestors in the moral perspective of Wakandan kings and the political configurations they enforce and maintain, they appear to conceptually distinguish the societal and moral domains. Shuri separated tradition from morality and T'Challa separated creed from morality. Although we will not know for certain if they were relying on the definitional criteria mentioned above when making these distinctions, SCDT suggests that conceptual distinctions are part-and-parcel of social relations.

College educators can have students interrogate this decision via coordination and informational assumptions. Through activities focused on reflecting on and articulating competing considerations and exploring the beliefs underlying those considerations, students can demonstrate and learn skills in oral communication, written communication, and critical thinking–skills that are relevant across multiple disciplines. Using events like these and others as stimuli, for example, activities can incorporate aspects of social science disciplines such as political science, sociology, and psychology and humanities disciplines such as English, history, and philosophy. As an analog, researchers can use similar hypothetical vignettes to investigate adults' (college students' and others') perceptions and beliefs concerning superheroes as politicians. Studies can manipulate both the type of political configuration or system of government by which the superhero is held accountable and the nature of the threats they are facing to their nation to explore potential associations between their understanding of superheroes and the political arrangements animating their actions.

Luke Cage

Pedagogical and research activities involving Luke Cage can center on his attempts to protect and preserve the dignity of "the community" amid the ubiquity of corrupt institutions or corrupt individuals using institutions for their own ends. *Gang War* offers some useful material in this regard, as the more common vigilante superhero tale is told alongside a less common tale of a vigilante turned mayor. The existence of AVA further complicates his mission as it draws a clearer line between what civilians can and cannot do in crime-related matters. Or, put another way, it more clearly establishes the social hierarchy when it comes to responding to crime, with superheroes prohibited from challenging law enforcement's monopoly on the use of violence in the service of law and order.

In *Luke Cage: Gang War* #3 (Barnes & Bachs, 2024, p. 6), Luke Cage tells a cop to stand back, and he will handle the attack. When the cop reminds him of AVA, he tells the cop that he does not care, and he is welcome to arrest him when this is over. Using this and/or similar events, educators can have students interrogate his approach to AVA as both mayor and vigilante via coordination and informational assumptions. For instance, are the reasons he gives and the suggested coordinating of competing considerations that may inform his actions consistent with the reasons he gives for others *not* to take matters into their own hands (*Luke Cage* #3, Chapter 6, Del Col & Lindsay, 2018, pp. 4, 13)? What factors into his determination that some citizens e.g., Iron First, Jessica Jones) can act as vigilantes but others cannot? Are having a superpower and good intentions the only criteria? In line with Martin's (2023a) emphasis on the reciprocal nature of Luke Cage's relationship to Harlem, activities can allow students to understand, defend, and criticize responses to "the fact of Luke Cage" from various stakeholders (e.g., local government, education, law enforcement, private business, etc.). Stakeholder analyses can focus on Harlem if the main themes of the activity are centered on vigilantism, or New York more broadly if students are examining vigilantism in the context of AVA and Luke being Mayor.

One way these themes can be examined in a research context is with hypothetical scenarios assessing adults' understandings of the relationship between morality and legality in the context of vigilantism. Such assessments can be made via a focus on real-world vigilantism as well as a focus on superhero vigilantism. Further, scenarios could vary systematically by the nature of the institutional corruption characteristic of the hypothetical city or community.

Social Superheroes

Bishop

With or without the narrative affordances of time-travel, Bishop's social interactions can also serve as a basis of educational and research activities. In keeping with Martin's (2024) suggestions, the focus of these activities could center the asymmetry between societal and moral goals common within his narratives and its implications for human rights. Without incorporating time-travel, potential activities based on his experiences in the past can examine his motivations and justifications for policing mutants. Specifically, students can explore the ending of *Civil War: X-Men* #4 (Hine & Paquette, 2006, p. 21), where O.N.E. offers him a job working with them to protect the remaining mutants in a less oppressive–and thus, more humane–manner. As he responds by saying he will think about it, students can identify and interrogate the pros and cons of accepting the offer, given the normal tensions that exist between mutants and humans. They can also consider whether there are other possible social arrangements that may be mutually beneficial to humans and mutants. If instead the focus is on his dystopian future, then similar activities can be created around his decision in *X-Men Legends*: #6 (Portacio et al., 2023, p. 2) to free a dangerous villain, Fitzroy, to help him break out innocent prisoners. As with the first example, students can analyze the pros and cons of such a decision while also exploring the possibility of alternative social arrangements.

If incorporating time-traveling, then other types of comparison-based activities are made available. One type particularly germane to the present chapter is a comparison of the society he comes from and the society he currently lives in concerning (in) humane treatment of mutants and (the lack of) respect for mutant rights. Using the two previously mentioned comics, for example, students can conduct an in-depth comparison of the features of both societies concerning human-mutant relations, and explore their own criteria to determine at what point can a society with a clear societal-moral asymmetry be considered *dystopian*? Put another way, is the fact that both past and future governments are oppressing mutants and restricting their daily activities enough to describe those social arrangements as dystopian, or do other features need to be present? As with Black Panther and Luke Cage, these themes can also inform empirical studies of adults' judgments and understandings around law, morality, superheroes, and vigilantism. For Bishop specifically, studies can draw on the features of the past and future societies in which he worked for or at least with the state in some law enforcement capacity to explore how adults conceive of the relationship between social order and human rights, and their boundary conditions for determining (morally) acceptable and unacceptable levels or forms of asymmetry.

In keeping with previous scholarship on the use of superhero narratives to explore social science concepts (Strong, et al., 2023; Strong et al., 2023), these implications, by no means exhaustive, provide opportunities for educators and researchers to incorporate events common within these superheroes' narratives into their classrooms and "labs", respectively. Whether through focusing on the wide-reaching implications of certain actions (Black Panther), institutional corruption (Luke Cage), or asymmetries in the relationship between social order and human rights (Bishop), educators and researchers can gain insight into how popular culture figures like superheroes are understood and interrogated. They can also provide insight into potential consistencies and inconsistencies concerning the application of societal and moral concepts people use to understand their own social worlds and those of superheroes.

Table 1. Sample moral and societal conflicts by superhero

Superhero	Conflict	Potential Moral Consideration(s)	Potential Societal Consideration(s)
Black Panther	Considering whether to change Wakandan law in efforts to address humanitarian crises (e.g., poverty, disease, famine, war).	Preserving and safeguarding human welfare and dignity, compromising the safety of Wakandans, etc.	Creating new legal precedents and traditions, maintaining social order if changes are considered unpopular by many Wakandans, the use of authority to enforce the new law, etc.
Luke Cage	Refusing to turn over a criminal or supervillain out of suspicion they will not be held accountable due to police corruption.	Protecting citizens from harm by keeping the criminal off the streets, providing a sense of accountability or justice for victims, violation of due process (and potential human) rights by going rogue, etc.	Breaking the law, probability of new laws to outlaw vigilantes, maintaining social order once citizens find out the criminal was not handed over to proper authorities, etc.
Bishop	As a law enforcement officer tasked with capturing and detaining dangerous mutants, considering whether to disobey the government's command to torture mutants in order to obtain information on a dangerous mutant.	Physical harm, denial of due process (and human) rights, etc.	Following chain of command, maintaining order and efficiency within law enforcement (e.g., other officers following suit can lead to disorder) and broader society (e.g., fear of a dangerous mutant on the loose can lead to disorder by disrupting everyday activities, etc.).

continued on following page

Social Superheroes

Table 2. Continued
Table 2. Potential learning activities and/or research stimuli

Activity	Description	Example	Goal
Alternative Path	Alter act; explore interdisciplinary implications for varying social arrangements.	Instead of Bishop using Fitzroy to try and break out mutants falsely imprisoned, he instead succeeds in overthrowing the prison warden and takes over the prison himself.	Encourage students to apply various social science theories and concepts (e.g., sociology, psychology, political science) to interrogate the implications of his decision for understanding the relationship between authority, social order, and human rights.
Origin Story	Vary contextual situations by the presence or absence of origin story information.	T'Challa's path to becoming Black Panther and king of Wakanda can be altered to where, in the eyes of Wakandan law and tradition, he obtained both statuses illegitimately.	By having students/respondents evaluate various moral actions taken by T'Challa as Black Panther and explain those evaluations using justifications, teachers/researchers can identify some of the criteria used to determine the acceptability of superheroes' actions and the extent to which varying significant life events informing their superhero missions lead to different evaluations and justifications.
Can Superheroes Change?	Indicate whether superheroes can do anything that would make them a villain; justify their position; then adopt the opposing view and discuss ways to strongman the opposing view using multiple disciplines.	Students are presented with various moral violations committed by Luke Cage and for each, they must determine and justify whether committing the act now makes him a villain. When discussing ways to strongman the opposing view, they are asked to consider the view from the perspective of Harlemites, the law, and other superheroes.	Students will identify and interrogate their central definitional criteria for superheroes and supervillains; they will also explore multidisciplinary and interdisciplinary approaches to analyzing Luke Cage's (in)actions and their implications for individuals and society.

*If used for experimental stimuli, the names of current superheroes (and associated characters) can be replaced with hypothetical characters with the same individual and narrative features to address concerns related to character familiarity.

CONCLUSION

As social creatures, superheroes tend to serve multiple functions within the popular imagination. These include (1) representing broad, widely understood moral principles related to welfare, justice and human rights, (2) at times defending the status quo while at times challenging it, and (3) encouraging reflection on the relation between moral and societal concepts in our own lives. Given these and related functions, it is important to consider the nature of and influences on their social interactions, as well as the backdrop conditions or social arrangements in which these interactions take place. To the extent a constructivist analysis of superhero media can elucidate key features of these social interactions and the role they may play in superheroes' societal and moral judgements, educators and scholars in psychology, sociology, anthropology, and political science can benefit from examining these interactions in more detail–both inside the classroom and the research lab. If they do, then just maybe we will learn more about ourselves in the process.

REFERENCES

Atari, M., Haidt, J., Graham, J., Koleva, S., Stevens, S. T., & Dehghani, M. (2023). Morality beyond the WEIRD: How the nomological network of morality varies across cultures. *Journal of Personality and Social Psychology*, 125(5), 1157–1188. 10.1037/pspp000047037589704

Bainbridge, J. (2020). "This land is mine!:" Understanding the function of super-villains. In Burke, L., Gordon, I., & Ndalianis, A. (Eds.), *The superhero symbol: Media, culture, and politics* (pp. 63–78). Rutgers University Press.

Bein, S., & Lewis, D. (2022). Transforming Wakanda: Justice (or not?) in Black Panther. In Pérez, E., & Brown, T. E. (Eds.), *Black Panther and philosophy: What can Wakanda offer the world?* (pp. 14–21). John Wiley & Sons. 10.1002/9781119635871.ch2

Black Panther #11 (2017). "A nation under our feet, part 10." Script: T. Coates. Art: C. Sprouse.

Black Panther #12 (2017). "A nation under our feet, part 10." Script: T. Coates. Art: B. Stelfreeze.

Boudreaux, A. (2022). Challenge day: Tradition and revolution in Wakanda. In Pérez, E., & Brown, T. E. (Eds.), *Black Panther and philosophy: What can Wakanda offer the world?* (pp. 3–13). John Wiley & Sons. 10.1002/9781119635871.ch1

Burke, L. (2020). Introduction: "Everlasting symbols.". In *L. Burke, I. Gordon, & A. Ndalianis* (pp. 1–22). Rutgers University Press.

Civil War #1-7 (2006-2007). Script: M. Millar. Art: S. McNiven.

Civil War #3 (2006). Script: M. Millar. Art: S. McNiven.

Civil War #4 (2006). Script: M. Millar. Art: S. McNiven.

Civil War #5 (2006). Script: M. Millar. Art: S. McNiven.

Civil War: X-Men #1 (2006). Script: D. Hine. Art: Y. Paquette.

Civil War: X-Men #2 (2006). Script: D. Hine. Art: Y. Paquette.

Civil War: X-Men #3 (2006). Script: D. Hine. Art: Y. Paquette.

Civil War: X-Men #4 (2006). Script: D. Hine. Art: Y. Paquette.

Clark, D. D. (2019). Matt Murdock's ill-fitting Catholic faith in Netflix's *Daredevil*. In Stevenson, G. (Ed.), *Theology and the marvel universe* (pp. 139–156).

Coker, C. H. (2016). *"Just to Get a Rep." Luke Cage. Season 1, episode 5.* Marvel. Netflix.

Coker, C. H. (2016). *"Suckas Need Bodyguards." Luke Cage. Season 1, episode 6.* Marvel. Netflix.

Coker, C. H. (2016). *"Soliloquy of Chaos." Luke Cage. Season 1, episode 12.* Marvel. Netflix.

Coker, C. H. (2016). *"You Know My Steez." Luke Cage. Season 1, episode 13.* Marvel. Netflix.

Coker, C. H. (2018). *"The Creator." Luke Cage. Season 2, episode 11.* Marvel. Netflix.

Coker, C. H. (2018). *"Can't Front on Me." Luke Cage. Season 2, episode 12.* Marvel. Netflix.

Coker, C. H. (2018). *"They Reminisce Over You." Luke Cage. Season 2, episode 13.* Marvel. Netflix.

Coogan, P. (2006). *Superhero: The secret origin of a genre.* MonkeyBrain Books.

Curtis, N. (2016). *Sovereignty and superheroes.* Manchester University Press.

Curtis, N. (2021). Two paths to the future: Radical cosmopolitanism and counter-colonial dignity in Black Panther. In White, R. T., & Ritzenhoff, K. A. (Eds.), *Afrofuturism in Black Panther: Gender, identity, and the remaking of blackness* (pp. 299–314).

Curtis, N. (2023). Superhero storytelling: The law, sovereignty and time. *Law, Culture and the Humanities*, 17438721231169162. 10.1177/17438721231169162

Derry, K. (2017). Bulletproof love: *Luke Cage* (2016) and religion. *Journal for Religion* [JRFM]. *Film and Media*, 3(1), 123–155.

Shadowland #1 (2010). Script: A. Diggle. Art: B. Tan. *Black Panther* #12 (2017). "A nation under our feet, part 10." Script: T. Coates. Art: B. Stelfreeze.

Feige, K. (Producer), Russo, A., & Russo, J. (2016). *Captain America: Civil War* [Motion Picture]. USA. Marvel.

Feige, K. (Producer), & Coogler, R. (2018). *Black Panther* [Motion Picture]. USA. Marvel.

Feige, K. (Producer), & Coogler, R. (2022). *Black Panther: Wakanda Forever* [Motion Picture]. USA. Marvel.

Filippi, N. (2009). *"Future X." Wolverine and the X-Men. Season 1, episode 9. Nicktoons.* Television.

Graham, J., Haidt, J., Koleva, S., Motyl, M., Iyer, R., Wojcik, S. P., & Ditto, P. H. (2013). Moral foundations theory: The pragmatic validity of moral pluralism. In Devine, P., & Plant, A. (Eds.), Vol. 47, pp. 55–130). Advances in experimental social psychology. Academic Press.

Haidt, J., & Joseph, C. (2007). The moral mind: How five sets of innate intuitions guide the development of many culture-specific virtues, and perhaps even modules. In Carruthers, P., Laurence, S., & Stich, S. (Eds.), *The innate mind* (Vol. 3, pp. 367–391).

Helwig, C. C. (2006). Rights, civil liberties, and democracy across cultures. In Killen, M., & Smetana, J. G. (Eds.), *Handbook of moral development* (1st ed., pp. 185–210). Psychology Press.

Helwig, C. C., & Jasiobedzka, U. (2001). The relation between law and morality: Children's reasoning about socially beneficial and unjust laws. *Child Development*, 72(5), 1382–1393. 10.1111/1467-8624.0035411699676

Helwig, C. C., & Kim, S. (1999). Children's evaluations of decision-making procedures in peer, family, and school contexts. *Child Development*, 70(2), 502–512. 10.1111/1467-8624.00036

Henderson, S. E. (2017). Daredevil: Legal (and moral?) vigilante. *Ohio State Journal of Criminal Law*, 15, 133–182.

Hicks, V. (2019). Stages of minority identity development: A juxtaposition of T'Challa and Erik Killmonger. In Langley, T., & Simmons, A. (Eds.), *Black Panther psychology: Hidden kingdoms* (pp. 36–51). Sterling Press.

Houston, L. (1993). *"Days of Future Past: Part I." X-Men: The Animated Series. Season 1, episode 11. Fox Kids.* Television.

Houston, L. (1993). *"Days of Future Past: Part II." X-Men: The Animated Series. Season 1, episode 12. Fox Kids.* Television.

Houston, L. (1995). *"One Man's Worth: Part I." X-Men: The Animated Series. Season 4, episode 1. Fox Kids.* Television.

Houston, L. (1995). *"One Man's Worth: Part II." X-Men: The Animated Series. Season 4, episode 2. Fox Kids.* Television.

Jenkins, H. (2020). What else can you do with them? In Burke, L., Gordon, I., & Ndalianis, A. (Eds.), *Superheroes and the civic imagination* (pp. 25–46). Rutgers University Press.

Jordan, J. S., & Kim, D. J. (2019). Who is the Black Panther? The self as embodied others. In Langley, T., & Simmons, A. (Eds.), *Black Panther psychology: Hidden kingdoms* (pp. 81–96). Sterling Press.

Killen, M. (2018). The origins of morality: Social equality, fairness, and justice. *Philosophical Psychology*, 31(5), 767–803. 10.1080/09515089.2018.1486612

Killen, M., & Smetana, J. G. (2015). Origins and development of morality. In Lamb, M. E. (Ed.),; 7th ed., Vol. 3, pp. 701–749). Handbook of child psychology. Wiley-Blackwell Publishing Ltd.

Kohlberg, L. (1971/1981). *The philosophy of moral Development: Moral stages and the idea of justice*. Harper & Row.

Kohlberg, L. (1980). Stages of development as a basis for education. In Munsey, B. (Ed.), *Moral development, moral education, and Kohlberg: Basic issues in philosophy, psychology, religion, and education* (pp. 15–100). Religious Education Press.

Letizia, A. (2020). *Graphic novels as pedagogy in social studies: How to draw citizenship*. Palgrave Macmillan. 10.1007/978-3-030-44252-1

Luke Cage #3 (2018). "Everyman, parts 5 & 6." Script: A. Del Col. Art:Lindsay, J..

Luke Cage #3 (2017). Script: D. Walker. Art: N. Blake II.

Luke Cage: Gang War #1 (2023). Script: R. Barnes. Art: R. Bachs.

Luke Cage: Gang War #2 (2023). Script: R. Barnes. Art: R. Bachs.

Luke Cage: Gang War #3 (2024). Script: R. Barnes. Art: R. Bachs.

Luke Cage: Gang War #4 (2024). Script: R. Barnes. Art: R. Bachs.

Lund, M. (2015). "X Marks the Spot:" Urban dystopia, slum voyeurism and failures of identity in *District X.Journal of Urban Cultural Studies*, 2(1-2), 35–55. 10.1386/jucs.2.1-2.35_1

Mack, A. D. (2020). Afrosurrealism, aristotle, and racial presence in Netflix's *Luke Cage. Dialogue. The Interdisciplinary Journal of Popular Culture and Pedagogy*, 7(2), 26–37.

Martin, J. (2023b). Superhero media as a potential context for investigating children's understanding of morally relevant events. *Libri & Liberi: Journal of Research on Children's Literature*, 12(1), 11–35. 10.21066/carcl.libri.12.1.1

Martin, J. (2024). Time-travel and teleology: Morality, society, and the life of Lucas Bishop. *REDEN.Revista Española De Estudios Norteamericanos*, 5(2), 128–153. 10.37536/reden.2024.5.2414

Martin, J. F. (2019). Growing up in Wakanda: Understanding the psychological features of social life. In Langley, T., & Simmons, A. (Eds.), *Black Panther psychology: Hidden kingdoms* (pp. 21–35). Sterling Press.

Martin, J. F. (2021). The many ways of Wakanda: Viewpoint diversity in Black Panther and its implications for civics education. *Dialogue: The Interdisciplinary Journal of Popular Culture and Pedagogy*, 8(1), 24–36.

Martin, J. F. (2023a). Harlem's superhero: Social interaction, heterogeneity of thought, and the superhero mission in Marvel's *Luke Cage. Popular Culture Review*, 34(2), 43–89. 10.1002/j.2831-865X.2023.tb00798.x

Martin, J. F., Killian, M., & Letizia, A. (2023). Comics and community: Exploring the relationship between society, education, and citizenship. In DeHart, J. D. (Ed.), *Exploring comics and graphic novels in the classroom* (pp. 203–228). IGI Global.

Martinez, M. J. (2022). Aspiration and the violence of gentrification in Marvel's *Luke Cage. Cultural Studies Critical Methodologies, 22*(2), 163-172.

McMillen, S. M. (2020). Re-envisioning black masculinity in *Luke Cage*: From blaxploitation and comic books to Netflix. *Journal of Popular Culture*, 53(2), 484–472. 10.1111/jpcu.12905

Miczo, N. (2016). *How Superheroes Model Community: Philosophically, Communicatively*. Relationally.

New Avengers #18. (2014). Script: J. Hickman. Art: V. Schiti

New Avengers #21. (2014). Script: J. Hickman. Art: V. Schiti

Nucci, L., & Ilten-Gee, R. (2021). *Moral Education for Social Justice*. Teachers College Press.

Nucci, L., Turiel, E., & Roded, A. D. (2017). Continuities and discontinuities in the development of moral judgments. *Human Development*, 60(6), 279–341. 10.1159/000484067

Peters, T. D. (2020). Daredevil as legal emblem. *Law. Technology and Humans*, 2(2), 198–226. 10.5204/lthj.1656

Philips, M. (2022). Violence in the American imaginary: Gender, race, and the politics of superheroes. *The American Political Science Review*, 116(2), 470–483. 10.1017/S0003055421000952

Phillips, N. D., & Strobl, S. (2013). *Comic book crime: Truth, justice, and the American way*. New York University Press.

Smetana, J. G. (1983). Social-cognitive development: Domain distinctions and coordinations. *Developmental Review*, 3(2), 131–147. 10.1016/0273-2297(83)90027-8

Smetana, J. G., Jambon, M., & Ball, C. (2014). The social domain approach to children's moral and social judgments. In Killen, M., & Smetana, J. G. (Eds.), *Handbook of moral development* (2nd ed., pp. 23–45). Psychology Press. 10.4324/9780203581957.ch2

Smetana, J. G., & Yoo, H. N. (2022). Development and variations in moral and social-conventional judgments: A social domain theory approach. In Killen, M., & Smetana, J. G. (Eds.), *Handbook of moral development* (3rd ed., pp. 19–36). Routledge. 10.4324/9781003047247-3

Strong, M. T., Cook, T., Belet, L., & Calarco, P. (2023). Changing the world: How comics and graphic novels can shift teaching. *Humanity & Society*, 47(2), 245–257. 10.1177/01605976231158969

Strong, M. T., Greenidge, G., & Chaplin, K. S. (2023). Afrofuturism as an instructional method. In Chin, J., & Kozimor, M. L. (Eds.), *Emerging stronger: Pedagogical lessons from the pandemic* (pp. 86–101). Routledge. 10.4324/9781003316336-12

The Lives and Times of Lucas Bishop #1 (2009). Script: D. Swierczynski. Art: L. Stroman.

The Lives and Times of Lucas Bishop #2 (2009). Script: D. Swierczynski. Art: L. Stroman.

Turiel, E. (1983). *The development of social knowledge: Morality and convention*. Cambridge University Press.

Turiel, E. (1998). The development of morality. In Damon, W. (Ed.),; 5th ed., Vol. 3, pp. 863–932). Handbook of child psychology. Wiley.

Turiel, E. (2002). *The culture of morality*. Cambridge University Press.

Turiel, E., & Banas, K. A. (2020). The development of moral and social judgments: Social contexts and processes of coordination. *Eurasian Journal of Educational Research*, 20(85), 23–44. 10.14689/ejer.2020.85.2

Turiel, E., Killen, M., & Helwig, C. C. (1987). Morality: its structure, function, and vagaries. In Kagan, J., & Lamb, S. (Eds.), *The emergence of morality in young children* (pp. 155–243).

Turiel, E., & Nucci, L. (2018). Moral development in context. In Dick, A., & Mueller, U. (Eds.), *Advancing developmental science: Philosophy, theory, and method* (pp. 95–109). Psychology Press.

Uncanny X-Men #282 (1991). Script: W. Portacio. Art: J. Byrne.

Wainryb, C. (2004). 'Is' and 'ought': Moral judgments about the world as understood. *New Directions for Child and Adolescent Development*, 103(103), 3–18. 10.1002/cd.9415112532

Wainryb, C. (2006). Moral development in culture: Diversity, tolerance, and justice. In Killen, M., & Smetana, J. G. (Eds.), *Handbook of moral development* (1st ed., pp. 211–240). Psychology Press.

Wainryb, C., & Turiel, E. (1993). Conceptual and informational features in moral decision making. *Educational Psychologist*, 28(3), 205–218. 10.1207/s15326985ep2803_2

Wandtke, T. R. (2012). *The meaning of superhero comic books*. McFarland.

White, M. D. (2019). *Batman and ethics*. John Wiley & Sons.

Wood, M. (2016). Moral decisions in Marvel's Civil War: Stages of hero development. In Langley, T. (Ed.), *Captain America vs. Iron Man: Freedom, Security, Psychology* (pp. 11–23). Sterling Press.

Wright, J. C. (2021). Morality as a regulator of divergence: Protecting against deviance while promoting diversity. *Social Cognition*, 39(1), 81–98. 10.1521/soco.2021.39.1.81

X-Factor #26 (2007). "Messiah complex, part 7." Script: P. David. Art: S. Eaton.

X-Men #206 (2007). "Messiah complex, part 9." Script: M. Cary. Art: C. Bachalo.

X-Men: Legends #5 (2023). Script: W. Portacio & B. Haberlin. Art: W. Portacio.

X-Men: Legends #6 (2023). Script: B. Haberlin & W. Portacio. Art: W. Portacio.

KEY TERMS AND DEFINITIONS

Coordination: The process of weighing multiple considerations in a given situation that resolves conflicts or ambiguities between them.

Informational Assumptions: The assumptions about "matters of fact" that people hold about the world, others, etc., that can inform their moral evaluations in a given situation.

Chapter 4
An Original Comics Team and Transmedia:
The JSA and Affiliation

Jason D. DeHart
The University of Tennessee, Knoxville, USA

ABSTRACT

This chapter focuses on the origins of comics heroes and the superhero genre, with attention to the messages of early comics. The introduction of characters is presented in unique multimodal fashion as a potential invitation for fandom. The refashioning of characters is further explored as it relates to particular time periods, with attention to the ways that reflect changes in culture. The nature of comics as artifacts of literacy and culture is explored, with notes on the ways that character relationships have cycled over time.

INTRODUCTION

Superheroes occupy a unique and even philosophical corner of reading materials in American culture (Gavaler & Goldberg, 2019). Whether capturing the vision of culture as vigilante and patriotic, joining power to power in an advance on evil forces, or whether presented through the grim and streaked artwork and storytelling of the late 1980s, comics present a visual means of thinking about zeitgeist, as well as a narrative sensibility that links with images. In the late 1930s and early 1940s, comics became a rich source of reading material and multiple characters sprang up as publishers raced to introduce the next storyline to captivate their audience. The ethos of some characters was so palpable that they were also used in public service announcements of the time. This period of publishing, which spanned from the late

DOI: 10.4018/979-8-3693-3302-0.ch004

Copyright © 2024, IGI Global. Copying or distributing in print or electronic forms without written permission of IGI Global is prohibited.

1930s to the early 1960s, has been called the Golden Age of Comics, a term coined by Lupoff (Quattro & Shelley, 2004).

From the printed form of comics and comic strips to the current age of storytelling across film, television, and digital/print comics and graphic novels, storytellers continue to revisit narrative arcs and trends, and they continue to pass the history of the characters down through approaches that either directly honor the past or work in opposition to it. With a view to the past, readers can also note the lack of diversity and representation among popular characters, as I will explore further in this chapter. During the Golden Age, not only was the comic book in its modern formulation introduced, but the narrative movement and expectations of the superhero genre were established. Muscio (2023) noted the use of comics as a means of promoting U.S. actions in World War II, as well as the ways technology and science were depicted with a loose magical nature.

The stories that revolve around what is known as the DC trinity – Superman, Batman, and Wonder Woman – take media precedence with many iterations of these characters in toys, live-action film, animation, and more. Yet, there are fascinating characters who occupy second and third tiers. The Justice Society of America (JSA) is and has been an assortment of heroic figures who have their own sometimes less obvious presence across media. Notably, Booker (2010) has pointed out that the JSA was the first published superhero team. In spite of this, while scholarship about other teams exist, a focus on the JSA is more piecemeal. From this look at a superhero team, I note possibilities for creating a classroom community where belonging is fostered, and where students can explore the texts that are most salient to them.

A JSA LITERATURE REVIEW

The Justice Society first appeared in 1940, at a time when comics had just become a fixture in American culture. This initial team featured characters who would take on a variety of incarnations over time, including the Atom, Doctor Fate, Flash, Green Lantern, Hawkman, Hourman, Sandman, and Spectre. Booker (2010) noted that, unlike the Justice League, the Justice Society has often featured characters who have not established popularity in standalone adventures before being part of the book. Linking back to my previous comment about representation, it is noteworthy that the entire lineup of characters was White and male, even with some characters' likenesses being hidden behind masks.

The trajectory of the book's publication and popularity declined after World War II, a period in which comics and superhero narratives were less popular (Booker, 2010). Even individual members of the team whose books had been launched found cancellation. The initial run of JSA. Gardner Fox and Sheldon Mayer are credited

An Original Comics Team and Transmedia

with the first run of the team that appeared in *All-Star Comics*. Notable creators who worked on the book included Carmine Infantino, Jack Kirby, Joe Simon, and Alex Toth, to name a few. The team appeared from issue three of *All-Star* up to issue fifty-seven.

As time would continue, the characters introduced in this initial lineup would travel with stories and find popularity again, and they would eventually serve a unique narrative purpose as legacy characters in the world of comics established by DC. The public's first introduction to the JSA draws upon a flat coloring style, with all eight members of the team assembled around a circular blue table. A callout below the characters lists of a roster – in this way, the cover acts as a visual hook to introduce the reader to both the visual design of the characters, at least form the waist up, as well as their nomenclature. The additional text "episodes as personally related at the first meeting of the Justice Society of America" on the cover indicates the team nature of the book and conveys the name of the team, as well as intimating a feeling of membership and kinship with the group. This image is then also used as the splash page, or first large one-panel story page, to illustrate the team and roster once more, along with the use of the word "Club" to indicate that their affiliation is a private one. A sense of invitation and belonging is shared with the audience this way, linking to the participatory nature of fandom (Guschwan, 2012).

The continuing design and affordances of the comic point to the nationalistic nature of the book. The book title is rendered in larger red script, decorated with white stars. The cover of issue forty-one is notable example of the ways that the comic was used to link to ideas of nationalism, as the subtitle "The Case of the Patriotic Crimes" appears just below the main title, with seven of the heroic characters (this time including two female heroes), descend toward an open hand that is grasping symbols of American culture and innovation. Throughout the series, primary colors of American culture and patriotism are present on covers.

REDEMPTION ACROSS SPACE AND TIME (AND WELCOMING IN THE CLASSROOM)

The disappearance of the team due to the realities of publishing and popularity was later explained through their existence in an alternative universe, marking a moment in comics that could arguably account for much of the multiversal storytelling that has taken shape in recent years in comics, from both DC Comics and Marvel Comics. This mode of storytelling allows multiple iterations of characters to exist simultaneously. For fandom, this means that stories can be part of their own directions, even apart from a singular story-thread of isolated canon. This also means that characters never truly part ways from the possibility of returning. On the industry side, such storytelling allows for the return or reappearance of characters and furthermore allows for different versions of the same characters to exist. In the case of a popular character like Batman or Superman, this can lead to an endless series of telling and retelling across a variety of story spaces. In the case of the JSA, this led to a notion of an Earth-One and Earth-Two assembly of heroes and stories that could combine when needed for a particular story.

Initial meetings of JSA characters occurred in the more popular book, *The Flash*, in the 1960s, beginning with "The Flash of Two Worlds" (1961). Eury (2005) noted that, at this time, DC Comics changed the name of the team from Justice Society to Justice League to reflect the popularity of Major League Baseball. The story of the changes in the team reflect this ebb and flow of popular opinion and interaction with fandom. Members of the original roster, including the Spectre, began to popular other corners of the DC universe, including starring in their own limited series. It should be noted that the version of The Flash, Barry Allen, that is introduced in this series is different from the Jay Garrick version of the character. Garrick is the Flash character in the JSA line-up, and is represented as a figure with blue pants, a red shirt, and a large metal disc on his head.

In the comics, he seems to be perpetually smiling. The Barry Allen rendition of the character, and later the Wally West version, is represented as a figure in a crimson body suit, head to toe with golden lightning bolts on the sides of his cowl. Likewise, the JSA version of Green Lantern is Alan Scott, a character who is later redesigned as Hal Jordan, and then other later versions of the character. Like some heroic accoutrements (e.g., a helmet, a planet of origin) which result in abilities, the use of the Green Lantern ring is an object that can be passed down and the Green Lantern affiliation is, in fact, not just a singular character status, but an invitation to a larger "corps" of Lanterns. This use of the ring as an invitation means that the Green Lantern status has even more possibilities for a naturally inclusive team of heroes than the typical hero status might.

Teachers consider the history thus far as a link to the ways that popular culture and affinity groups make community possible for readers, including readers who are part of cultural identities that have been pushed to the margin by dominant cultures (Espinoza-Zemlicka, 2020). From these readings, readers then become composers and co-constructors, fashioning belonging and identity in their own formulations through fan fiction in response (Freeman & Taylor-Ashfield, 2017). Readers have the potential to not only engage in passive observation of comics stories, but to link to communities of literacy practice gathered around a common affection for a particular character or group.

The 1970s found the return of *All Star Comics* with new characters introduced to the ranks. The Huntress and Power Girl were explored in this follow-up series, and creators like Gerry Conway, Keith Giffen, Bob Layton, and Joe Staton worked on the book. Characters continued to appear across series and as part of various team-ups until the mid-1980s when DC's *Crisis on Infinite Earths*, linking Earth-One and Earth-Two into a single story-thread. Arguably, *Crisis* would change the future path of DC Comics as event-oriented books became a mainstay throughout the 1990s and 2000s, and as the story-verse was subsequently retconned.

The JSA would return in a series of two chapters, one for eight issues and one for ten issues, in the early 1990s, then again for eighty-seven issues from 1999 until 2006. A thirty-nine issue series called *JSA: Classified* ran from 2005-2008. Fifty-four additional issues of *Justice Society of America* ran from 2007 until 2011, and the team was also featured in *JSA: All-Stars* from 2010 until 2011. Stories like this one display the elasticity and longevity of the group, and point to the commitment of fans as a form of continued storytelling in community nostalgia.

Through these various incarnations, the team has included Atom Smasher, Black Adam, Black Canary, Doctor Mid-Nite, Hawk Girl, Mister Terrific, Obsidian, Starman, Wildcat, Wonder Woman, and many others. At the time of this writing, there is both a limited series *JSA* series, as well as one focused on the Wesley Dodds/Sandman character. In terms of popularity, Wright (2003) noted the secondary status of many of the JSA team members, and pointed to their limited frame of abilities. Prominent examples of limited power include the hour-span of super powers of Hourman, the narrative demand of Dr. Mid-Nite's heroic activity after sunset, and the status of Atom as a diminutive character.

The limited scope of heroism, as well as the roles that the JSA characters often played in stories, supported their stance as secondary characters who were able to team up with more popular characters when needed. In terms of representation, while some women were introduced to the team throughout these series, there was still a noticeable lack of characters of color. The only character on the team with diverse abilities, Dr. Mid-Nite, proves to be an interesting case.

MEDIA REPRESENTATIONS OF THE TEAM

As with many characters that are found in comics, there has been a range of media representations of the JSA, from live-action television to appearances in the 2022 DC film, *Black Adam*. The story features versions of the characters Atom Smasher, Cyclone, Dr. Fate, and the titular character. They are linked to the main team through references and a brief cameo of Superman, although the continuity of the films was changed the following year.

Other merchandise, including action figures, has included representations of the characters, as well. The DC Comics imprint, Elseworlds, featured alternative takes on the characters throughout the 1990s and 2000s. These stand-alone stories recast characters in different periods and formulations, according to creative directions and with fidelity to particularly consistent aspects of characters. *JSA: The Liberty File* is one such example in which Batman is renamed The Bat, Hourman is renamed The Clock, and Doctor Mid-Nite is renamed The Owl. The series revisited the time of the original series in some regards, but explored a darker corner of the universe with more realism. The characters are in a different set of relationships and other characters appear in altered circumstances. The book resulted in two sequels, as well. What it notable about this story in terms of forming a link to the original series is that the setting is much the same and the characters, though reworked in relationships with one another, remain static in much of their design. However, the tone of this vision of the past is starker and more realistic than the sunny image of the original Golden Age storytelling approach.

The popularity and presence of the characters would only increase in media as time went by. The CW series, *Stargirl*, further explored some of the characters, casting them as a second generation, including iterations of Starman, Dr. Mid-Nite, Hourman, and Wildcat. The original team was presented as a group of mentors, shrouded in mystery, and the youthful characters were required to make sense of their calling to take up the mantle or resist the invitation to heroism. Geoff Johns famously created this version of Stargirl in honor of his sister (Dollar Bin Bandits, 2023).

In some cases, the original roster members have been presented as retired characters, as when Wildcat/Ted Grant was depicted in the CW show *Arrow*. In this example, he is taking the role of mentor for the Laurel Lance character. In the comics, Wildcat is granted a magic spell that allows him sustainability as an active hero for generations; the television depiction is not so mystical, as his aging is more evident and his role is more of a first-generation figure, passing down tradition to a successor. In narrative linking, Wildcat trained with more prominent figures in the DC universe, providing a backchannel to the larger network of characters. Wildcat's status as a human character with some unique abilities at times links him closely with the Batman character, and the two were featured in a stand-alone series that resulted in a collected team-up book (Dixon et al., 1997). Wildcat's status in live action and animation is often relegated to cameo appearances, making use of his role as a trainer – again, linking with the narrative of comics past.

Possibilities exist in terms of pedagogy in this context for students to compare media representations, engage in critical literacy work, and engage with characters at a level of criticality or empathy (DeHart, 2024). By doing so, students can engage in the full range of creative and responsive tasks, linking their experiences to characters and texts that resonate with them.

An Original Comics Team and Transmedia

SOCIAL AND CULTURAL IMPACT

Individual heroes on the team have been recast and reconsidered in intriguing ways. Notably, Dr. Fate was reintroduced in a three-volume series from 2015 until 2016 from creators Paul Levitz and Sonny Liew. This series explored the passing of the mantle to an Egyptian-American medical student, linking the mythology of the character to a more closely aligned cultural representation. The character is presented in a youthful way, including a hoodie, that is unlike to more middle-aged and seasoned depictions in other stories. In a similar narrative move, the original Wildcat experiences a loss of physical ability and is then succeeded by his goddaughter, who becomes a notable Latina superhero (Aldama, 2017). As a male character, Wildcat demonstrates some less positive characteristics, including chauvinism, and has been compared to more objectified depictions of characters like Catwoman (Lecker, 2007). In light of the flexibility of characters and narratives, Ted Grant/Wildcat's injuries were retconned later to be of less severity, allowing for him to perform a more active narrative function and as a means of continuing his established reputation as a formidable fighter.

This consideration of representation among characters it not limited to ethnicity or gender. Echevarria (2023) noted the differently-abled status of Dr Mid-Nite, a character whose blindness is an aspect of his heroic work. Echevarria (2023) contrasted this difference in ability with that of Barbara Gordon/Batgirl, who is traumatically injured and has to make use of a wheelchair for some time in comics. Dr. Mid-Night, according to Echevarria (2023) experiences diverse abilities in a more passive regard. This navigation of abilities is met with technological advancements as a means of navigation in a similar fashion to the ways Matt Murdock/Daredevil, a heroic figure in the Marvel universe, is able to use a kind of "radar vision" to not only sense the world around him, but to do so in heightened ways that exceed the senses of other characters in the book. In the case of Dr. Mid-Night, the use of technology to aid his sight seems to be more of a narrative point to limit his daytime vigilante activities. With the scientific origins of characters like this, multiple opportunities exist for not only comparing characters across media, but also exploring the science that informs stories as a means to link content areas.

ROLES AND GENERATIONS

There is a dynamic of mentorship and passing on of the mantle that is a foundation point in the JSA stories. As a secondary hero team, although they are the first in DC publishing, they occupy a story-space of narrative ancestry. In a sense, this movement toward narrative reconciliation and preservation is almost a story service to readers who have traced the development of the characters, acting as an intergenerational story type. From a larger vantage, this sharing of heroic mantle can be juxtaposed with the ways that popular stories and characters are shared from one generation to the next. In my work interviewing creators, there is often a link to a family member or friend – sometimes a grandmother, father, brother, or mother. This is a kind of literacy mentor in the reader's life, sharing books and giving insights into the world of comics and fandom. In some instances, family members even have links to people working in the comics or publishing industry, who are then able to provide additional mentorship (DeHart, 2024B). There is a sense of legacy in this use of characters, a narrative is familiar to long-time readers of the medium and comics historians, but which is only hinted as a subtle backstory for those who are uninitiated when it comes to the wider range of the story (Shapira, 2019). All of this speaks to the ethos of shared storytelling in classroom practice as a foundational notion of literacy; furthermore, this work does not only apply to early grades. Shared writing and storytelling across media contains ripe possibilities across age groups.

Linking this look at a comics series to my work in literacy, there is a sense of affiliation for the reader. As noted in another recent interview (DeHart, 2024B), an immersive sense of fandom is part of comics culture, including conventions and embodying characters through live-action roleplay. Kingston (2015) noted this participatory nature of fandom, with readers interacting with a variety of story types within the comics medium and across a range of genres. This notion of participation leads to a sense of engagement, creating the possibility for fostering a sense of belonging. Peeples et al. (2018) pointed to this phenomenon of interactive fandom, as well, and Black (2018) has noted the possibilities for engaging with characters, including the interactive nature of sharing fan fiction. This fan fiction practice can be established in online communities of affirmational interaction with other fans. Interaction and belonging, according to Black (2018), are not the only benefits of engaging in this mode of fandom. Being an online and interactive way of engaging, fan fiction contains affordances for building practice across languages, as well as in building a critical stance when it comes to media. My own work (DeHart, 2018) has drawn upon this trend and has pointed to the ways a middle-grade student used the visual narrative of Batgirl to explore and create, composing a multiple-page narrative about Batwoman and engaging in fan fiction reading. The ways in which readers take up characters, past and present, is fascinating and elastic work, and the work of including more characters that represent a range of experiences is an ongoing and pressing need to build an inclusive readership.

The characters in the JSA also frequently stem from a specific historical context. Even though their abilities and activities are fantastic, their interactions are rooted in particular periods. Wildcat, for example, originally appeared in 1942 and has

An Original Comics Team and Transmedia

a rough-and-tumble history as a character seeking employment, having come of age during the Great Depression. Grant suffers tragedy, as comics characters so often do, and is inspired by his knowledge of the Green Lantern to fashion his own costume and begin a path of reconciliation as a vigilante. In a book-within-book moment, Grant is inspired by an interaction with a youth who has engaged with Green Lantern through comics.

The political context of some stories includes the formation of the All-Star Squadron in response to an attack by Japan, with Hawkman and a character called Liberty Belle leading this team formation (Manning et al., 2021), and I have noted the positive nationalistic stance of Golden Age comics. Just as the Wildcat character encounters the mythic, Hawkman is a transplanted figure from the alternative world of Thanagar, and his helmet contains a redemptive power, similar to Dr. Fate's adornment. Hawkman is a character that has experienced death and resurrection by means of the mythological elements that are part of his vestment (Grabowski-Górniak & Polska, 2019). This aspect of the character acts on the one hand as a link to larger-than-life fantasy storytelling.

STORY CYCLES

On the more commercial side of the conversation, there is an immediate restorative link should the character need to return in one form or another. The story movement of a character meeting a demise and resurrection is hardly a new narrative device (Campbell, 2008). Likewise, Korté and Who (2019) have pointed to the narrative tradition of keeping villains alive, establishing a no-kill policy for superheroes, as a means of ensuring not only the heroes can return, but their enemies can recur as often as they wish (and as the audience demands and responds). The dual effect of this decision is that fandom can continue to engage with the same characters across a range of stories and periods, with a relative security in their ability to return when the story fits or when the demand increases; meanwhile, comics companies have a standing supply of popular characters to pull from instead of engaging in new creations. Shapira (2019) likened some of this narrative cycling for popular characters (namely in this work, Superman) as linked with myth of Sisyphus. Just like Sisyphus, Superman will awaken each morning with some new vision of himself tackling some new vision of one of his rogues gallery characters, and attempting to sustain the life of some vision of Lois Lane.

Pointing again to the intergenerational nature of comics fandom and storytelling, the members of the JSA arguably cast a vision of a bedrock of comics history. The current age of heroes, in whatever iteration they appear, have a narrative flexibility that allows them to exist across time. There is the historical vision of

Batman, embodied in some narratives a character out of time. In Tom King's run on the character, Bruce Wayne even battled an out-of-time version of his father, returned from a different dimension as a more malevolent version of the Batman character. In this way, the popularity of the character leads to their identity almost as a kind of mantle. A similar mantle is seen in the character of the Flash, in terms of the passing on of powers. The ability to move at superspeed acts as a kind of initiation into heroics, with Barry Allen later mentoring Wally West, teaching him ways of using his powers. The 2023 film version of the Flash attempts to present this narrative with alternative versions of Barry interacting with each other across multiversal timelines.

In the DC universe, there is a preexisting set of characters who can be seen as the initial narrative steps in the superhero world, existing in a pseudo-World War II context. This context, as noted, has been expanded on and explored in different ways by writers like Dan Jolley and B. Clay Moore. Additionally, characters go through various permutations over time, allowing for a Jay Garrick design to make way for Barry Allen or Wally West. The image of the character, with his large metal helmet, is a visual that links to the past, and can be found in popular media representations, as well. The redesign of Green Lanterns to accommodate for changes in time, from Alan Scott to Hal Jordan to Kyle Rayner, is a visual that wordlessly illustrates flexibility and narrative sustainability of the character(s). Alan Scott's design is still brought back to the forefront in publishing at times, as well, as has been in the case in the 2023 limited series based on the character (Sheridan et. al, 2023).

AFFILIATION

In dovetail fashion, I return to the opening commentary about the ways the first appearance of the JSA links to aspects of fandom. The first character beyond the introduction that the reader meets is Johnny Thunder – who, as it turns out, is not at the meeting. In page two panel one, the narrative box reads: "Poor Johnny Thunder has been left out of the meeting and is he sore!" (Fox et al., 1940). The message of affiliation is rendered with clarity – the JSA is a team book, the reader is invited to peek into the meeting from the cover and splash page. Now, however, upon beginning the narrative, the reader is an outsider, uninitiated and unaware of what is happening behind closed doors. Johnny's anger at this turn of events leads to him kicking a fire hydrant and stating his desire to be part of the group. The splash

An Original Comics Team and Transmedia

page has additional features, including a marble-like base and dark background, that almost make the design appear as a formal invitation.

Johnny's powers begin to take over, and he is aloft in the air, alongside Dr. Fate, who informs him that the meeting has not yet begun. In this way, the reader and character who is leading the conversation about the JSA might be seen as a "luftmensch," or a person/man whose thinking and life is in the clouds (Schwarz, 2016) – a recurring example of imagination. This is particularly salient as the reader notes what Johnny sees in the first panel on the page. It is not a closed door, and it is not a "Do Not Disturb" sign, but rather a newsstand with comics. This subtle visual move points to the desire of the reader and the larger work of literacy to invite the outsider in and to make a safe space of welcome for the newcomer.

In quick succession, the reader meets the rest of the JSA ranks, first The Flash and on through the roster. From the hotel where the team has their first meeting, the story continues across media in various incarnations – history and the publishing market has confirmed that this invitation was successful. The role of the reader as one who daydreams with purpose, then, rises above the typical disparaging nature of the term to the status of an act of engagement is desirable. The design and nature of the team book is communal, and fandom has the opportunity to respond and likely keep responding.

It the task of the literacy educator, taking in the full range of texts that storytelling communities have to offer across forms of media, to make these narratives accessible and to engage in with them alongside students. This is work of nostalgic mentorship as well as mentorship for readers, writers, composers, thinkers, and creators.

REFERENCES

Aldama, F. L. (2017). *Latinx superheroes in mainstream comics*. University of Arizona Press.

Black, R. W. (2009). Online fan fiction and critical media literacy. *Journal of Computing in Teacher Education*, 26(2), 75–80.

Booker, M. K. (Ed.). (2010). *Encyclopedia of comic books and graphic novels* [2 volumes]. Bloomsbury Publishing USA.

Campbell, J. (2008). *The hero with a thousand faces*. New World Library.

DeHart, J. D. (2018). Strategies for a safe literacy space for English language learners. *Kappa Delta Pi Record*, 54(2), 90–92. 10.1080/00228958.2018.1443681

DeHart, J. D. (2024). *Building critical literacy and empathy with graphic novels*. NCTE.

DeHart, J. D. (2024b). *Words, images, & worlds* [podcast]. https://www.youtube.com/@WordsImagesWorlds/videos

Dixon, C. (1997). *Batman/Wildcat*. DC Comics.

Dollar Bin Bandits. (2023). *Interview with Geoff Johns*. https://www.youtube.com/watch?v=KluvNlmNI0o

Echevarria, R. (2023). *Treatment of the differently abled: Representations of disability from Victorian periodicals to contemporary graphic narratives*. [Undergraduate Honors Thesis, The University of Central Florida].

Espinoza-Zemlicka, L. (2020). Fans in the gutter: People of color in comics fandom. *Pathways (Chestnut Hill, Mass.)*, 1(2), 1–12.

Eury, M. (2005). *The justice league companion*. TwoMorrows Publishing.

Fox, G. A., & Giella, J. (1961). *The Flash* (Vol. 123). DC Comics.

Freeman, M., & Taylor-Ashfield, C. (2017). 'I read comics from a feminist point of view': Conceptualizing the transmedia ethos of the Captain Marvel fan community. *Journal of Fandom Studies*, 5(3), 317–335. 10.1386/jfs.5.3.317_1

Gavaler, C., & Goldberg, N. (2019). *Superhero thought experiments: Comic book philosophy*. University of Iowa Press. 10.2307/j.ctvn5twvb

Grabowski-Górniak, P., & Polska, W. (2019). The death of the (super) hero: The duality in depictions of death in superhero narratives. *Symbolae Europaeae*, 14, 61–73.

Guschwan, M. (2012). Fandom, brandom and the limits of participatory culture. *Journal of Consumer Culture*, 12(1), 19–40. 10.1177/1469540512438154

Jolley, D. (2000). *JSA: The liberty files*. DC Comics.

Kington, C. S. (2015). Con culture: A survey of fans and fandom. *Journal of Fandom Studies*, 3(2), 211–228. 10.1386/jfs.3.2.211_1

Korté, S., & Who, H. Q. (2019). *What is the story of Wonder Woman?* Penguin.

Lecker, M. (2007). *Treacherous, deviant, and submissive: female sexuality represented in the character Catwoman* [Doctoral dissertation, Bowling Green State University].

Levitz, P., & Liew, S. (2015-2016). *Dr. Fate*. DC Comics.

Manning, M. K., Wiacek, S., Scott, M., Jones, N., & Walker, L. Q. (2021). *The DC Comics Encyclopedia New Edition*. Penguin.

Moore, B.C. (2013). *JSA Liberty Files: The whistling skull*. DC Comics. *Stargirl*.

Muscio, A. (2023). The ambiguous role of science and technology in Marvel superhero comics: From their 'Golden Age' to the present-day. *Technological Forecasting and Social Change*, 186, 122149. 10.1016/j.techfore.2022.122149

Peeples, D., Yen, J., & Weigle, P. (2018). Geeks, fandoms, and social engagement. *Child and Adolescent Psychiatric Clinics of North America*, 27(2), 247–267. 10.1016/j.chc.2017.11.00829502750

Quattro, K., & Schelly, B. (2004). *The New Ages: Rethinking Comic Book History*. Comicartville Library.

Schwarz, H. (2016). Diasporas of the Mind: Jewish and Postcolonial Writing and the Nightmare of History by Bryan Cheyette. *Philip Roth Studies*, 12(2), 105–109. 10.5703/philrothstud.12.2.0105

Shapira, T. (2019). Wrestling with legacy. In Darowski, J. (Ed.), *The Ages of The Flash: Essays on the Fastest Man Alive* (pp. 91–105). McFarland.

Sheridan, T., et al. (2023-2024). *Alan Scott: Green Lantern*. DC Comics.

Wright, B. W. (2003). *Comic book nation: The transformation of youth culture in America*. JHU Press. 10.56021/9780801865145

KEY WORDS AND DEFINITIONS

Comics: A medium comprised of images and words, and including a particular set of design elements (e.g., gutters, panels, word balloons).

Elseworlds: The DC Comics imprint that began in the 1990s in which popular characters were recast across time and in a variety of contexts.

Fandom: The individual and communal practice of engagement with particular texts and characters, as well as stories, across media, often including interactions with other fans.

Gutter: The blank space between comics panels in which inferences and movements in narrative are left to the imagination of the reader in order to link the static images together.

Multiverse: The narrative structure employed by popular comics publishers wherein multiple versions of the same character can exist simultaneously, albeit in different but connected realities.

Panel: A narrative box that contains story structure in comics. Some pages feature one panel (i.e., a "splash page), while other pages feature multiple panels.

Transmedia: The phenomenon of stories and characters being represented across forms of media (e.g., television and comics; toys and film).

Chapter 5
The Joker:
Transmedial Concept of a Comic Book Character

Vladimir Popov
https://orcid.org/0000-0002-1493-6702
Independent Researcher, Serbia

ABSTRACT

This academic paper explores the transmedia narrative of the comic book character of the Joker across various media platforms. It delves into the complex creation and evolution of the Joker, highlighting the collaborative efforts of Bob Kane, Bill Finger, and Jerry Robinson, and the character's profound impact on cultural and societal norms. By examining the Joker's transmedial storytelling, the paper underscores the character's ability to adapt and resonate across different contexts, from comics to films and beyond. It further investigates the Joker's role as a mirror to societal dynamics, embodying themes of chaos, resistance, and critique of biopolitical control. The paper concludes that the Joker's enduring appeal and multifaceted nature exemplify the transformative potential of narrative characters within the transmedial landscape, serving as agents of critique and catalysts for discourse on identity, power, and resistance.

THE EVOLUTION OF THE JOKER'S ORIGIN STORY

The Joker's origin story has varied significantly over time, while it evolved through different cultural contexts, narrative needs, and audience expectations. These variations not only enriched character's mythos but also provided insights into the shifting paradigms of storytelling within comic book and film media.

The enigmatic origin and evolution of the Joker, has always been a subject of intrigue. Created by Bill Finger, Bob Kane, and Jerry Robinson, the Joker first emerged in the inaugural issue of the Batman comic book on April 25, 1940, published by DC Comics. The character's inception and the specific contributions of its creators to its visual and narrative identity remain somewhat enigmatic to this day, with each creator asserting a distinctive claim over the character's conception and evolution (Eason, 2008). This means that the authors created the concept of the Joker character by exchanging ideas with each other, based on the inspirations of other already existing characters, which were also designed based on some other ideas, thus making the concept and artwork of the Joker quite trans-artistic from the very beginning of its development (Šuvaković, 2005). However, the 1951 *Detective Comics no. 168* introduced him as the former Red Hood, a criminal who fell into a vat of chemicals which bleached his skin, colored his hair green, and stretched his lips into a perpetual grin. Alan Moore's *The Killing Joke* from 1988 provided a more detailed and tragic backstory for the Joker, portraying him as a failed comedian who turns to crime to support his pregnant wife, only to suffer a series of catastrophic events. Moore's narrative introduced existential themes, illustrating the Joker's transformation as a response to an absurd and indifferent universe, resonant with Camus's notion of the absurd hero (Camus, 1942). This story emphasized the fragility of human psyche under extreme stress, suggesting that madness could be just one bad day away.

The Joker's affinity for offering different accounts of his origins, as seen in *The Dark Knight*, aligns with his portrayal as a figure that heavily relies on embodying chaos and unpredictability through his life. His self-professed approach to life, characterized by impulsivity and nihilism, is nicely captured in his line, "I just do… things," (Fhlainn, 2011). This narrative choice not only deepens the character's enigma but also reflects a postmodern skepticism towards fixed identities and histories. Alan Moore's *The Killing Joke* further explores this narrative ambiguity, presenting the Joker's past as a 'multiple choice' scenario, thereby destabilizing any singular understanding of his origins (Moore, 1988).

The adoption of various aliases for the Joker, such as the name Jack Napier in Tim Burton's 1989 adaptation and a new name in Todd Phillips' 2019 *Joker*, shows the power of the transmedial exploration of the character's identity. The variability of the Joker's name across narratives shows in full scope the transmedia storytelling's capacity to adapt and evolve character mythologies in response to different narrative demands and cultural contexts.

The 2019 film Joker, directed by Todd Phillips and starring Joaquin Phoenix, represents a significant evolution in the portrayal of the iconic character within the cinematic domain, offering a deep exploration into the origins and development of the Joker persona. This iteration distinguishes itself by presenting Arthur Fleck, a character grappling with social marginalization and a neurological disorder that triggers involuntary laughter, as the embodiment of the Joker. Situated within a narrative framework that critically examines the repercussions of a capitalist democratic society on individuals living on its fringes, Arthur's transformation into the Joker is shown as a manifestation of societal failure rather than a villainous ascent. On the other hand, Phillips' film provides a psychological study focused on societal neglect and mental illness, offering a social commentary on the failures of societal institutions to protect the vulnerable. This narrative draws on the theories of social constructionism, suggesting that identity and madness are constructed through social and interpersonal experiences (Berger & Luckmann, 1966).

The collaborative nature of the Joker's creation also reflects the concept of collective intelligence in transmedial storytelling, where multiple participants contribute to the development of the narrative universe (Jenkins, 2006). Despite the disputes among its creators regarding the Joker's origins, it is evident that the character's development was a collaborative effort that benefited from the inputs of Finger, Kane, and Robinson. This collective creation process has allowed the Joker to evolve into a multifaceted character with a rich narrative depth.

Moreover, the influence of external sources, such as the photograph of Conrad Veidt, highlights the intertextuality inherent in transmedial storytelling that refers to the relationship between texts and how they transform one another. The Joker's creation, inspired by Veidt's portrayal in *The Man Who Laughs*, shows us how existing texts can inform and enrich new stories, contributing to their complexity and appeal. In other words, the Joker not only reflects the collaborative efforts of his creators but also embodies the dynamic interplay between different texts and media, contributing to the richness of the Batman universe and the broader landscape of popular culture.

It can be argued that the evolution of the Joker's origin stories reflects broader societal changes and anxieties, particularly concerning the nature of evil and madness. The varied stories highlight a societal shift from viewing villainy as an inherent trait to understanding it as a complex product of social, psychological, and existential factors.

CONTRASTING THE JOKER'S EVOLVING ORIGIN WITH BATMAN'S STABLE NARRATIVE

Batman's origin story has remained remarkably consistent since his inception: as a young boy, Bruce Wayne witnesses the murder of his parents and vows to spend his life fighting crime. This narrative, embedded in *Detective Comics no. 33* from 1939, serves as a foundational myth that defines Batman's moral and existential framework. The stability of Batman's origin story contrasts sharply with the mutable and often ambiguous origins of the Joker, offering a rich area for analysis regarding the implications of these narrative choices. Batman's stable origin story aligns with Jungian theories of archetypes, particularly the hero archetype, which involves a journey that begins with a personal loss and transforms the individual into a figure of justice (Jung, 1959). Batman's consistent narrative reinforces his role as a symbol of order and justice, contrasting with the Joker's representation of chaos and moral ambiguity. This relation showcases the thematic depth of their rivalry, presenting an everlasting battle between order and chaos.

The constancy of Batman's origin story has several implications. First, it establishes a clear moral foundation, positioning Batman as a character with unwavering principles. Unlike the Joker, whose fluctuating backstories invite empathy or repulsions by turns, Batman's fixed origin story offers a stable moral compass for the audiences (Eco, 1972). This stability is crucial in a genre where complexity often blurs the lines between heroism and villainy. Furthermore, Batman's unchanging origin story reflects societal values that emphasize the importance of personal tragedy in defining identity and purpose. In cultural terms, Batman presents the ideal of turning personal grief into a catalyst for improvement and societal contribution. This narrative choice resonates with the American ethos of individualism and redemption, potentially explaining the enduring appeal of Batman's character across different cultural landscapes (Bellah, 1985). In contrast, the Joker's evolving origin stories reflect a postmodern fascination with ambiguity and the complexities of identity. Each version of his backstory—from the Red Hood to the failed comedian and beyond—serves to destabilize the audience's understanding of his character, challenging them to reconsider their perceptions of morality and sanity, like Lyotard mentions in his postmodern condition (Lyotard, 1984). This fluidity allows the Joker to embody contemporary anxieties about the unpredictability and inherent chaos of modern life.

In other words, contrasting narrative stability of Batman and the fluidity of the Joker's origins significantly enhance the thematic and psychological complexity of their stories.

The Joker

THE JOKER'S PORTRAYAL IN COMIC BOOKS

Originating in the Golden Age of American comics, the Joker was initially intended to be a short-lived character, appearing in just one or two issues of Batman (webarchive, 2021). However, editorial decisions, particularly by Whitney Ellsworth, significantly extended his presence, leading to appearances in nine of the first twelve Batman episodes (Eason, 2008). Initially portrayed as a psychopath, the Joker's character underwent a notable transformation in 1942 when DC Comics' editorial team reimagined him as a prankster. This shift aimed to make the character more palatable to a younger audience, reflecting broader societal and cultural trends of the time.

The transition into the Silver Age of American comics marked a significant turning point in the portrayal of the Joker, against the backdrop of declining comic book popularity in America since 1954 (Reynolds, 1994). The criticism of comics, as voiced by German-American psychiatrist Frederic Wertham, who contended that mass media, and comics in particular, contributed to rising delinquency, violence, and even homosexuality among teenagers, played a crucial role in altering public perception and consumption of comic books (Webster, 1981). The backlash from parents, coupled with instances of public comic book burnings and the regulations enforced by the American Association of Comic Magazines, necessitated another transformation in the Joker's character. DC Comics editors redefined the Joker as a comedic and humorous figure, devoid of his previously murderous intent (Cohen, 2008). By 1964, this transformation had led to a significant decline in the Joker's popularity, resulting in his removal from monthly publications (Eason, 2008).

The shifting portrayal of the Joker, from a psychopathic villain to a harmless prankster, mirrors broader societal concerns and the comic industry's responses to cultural and regulatory pressures. The character's adaptations highlight the dynamic interplay between creators, audience expectations, and societal values, underscoring the fluidity of narrative characters in transmedial contexts. Moreover, the Joker's evolution reflects Jenkins' notion of "narrative architecture," where characters and stories are not fixed but are continually reshaped by their interactions with audiences and their cultural contexts (Jenkins, 2006). Furthermore, the Joker's character development can be situated within broader discussions of media effects and moral panics, as illustrated by the reactions to Frederic Wertham's criticisms. The comic book industry's self-regulation, through the creation of less controversial characters, demonstrates the impact of societal concerns on media production and the complex relationship between media creators and their audiences.

The resurgence of the Joker during the Bronze Age of American comics marks a pivotal moment in the character's evolution, reflecting broader shifts in the comic book industry and American culture. Screenwriter Dennis O'Neill and illustrator Neal

Adams played instrumental roles in this revival by returning the Joker to his roots as an impulsive psychopath in 1973 (Eason, 2008), thus reinvigorating interest in the character. O'Neill's exploration of the Joker's origins and insanity (rocketllama, 2009), coupled with Adams' redesign of the character's physical appearance to a gaunter and more sinister figure, redefined the Joker for a new generation (Phillips, 2008). This period also witnessed the collaborative efforts of screenwriter Steve Englehart and illustrator Marshall Rogers in 1977-78, further expanding the Joker's persona and visual design. Their contributions would significantly influence Tim Burton's 1989 film adaptation of Batman, setting a precedent for the character's portrayal in various media (Eason, 2008).

A central theme in the Joker's comic book appearances is his representation of chaos and anarchy that challenges Batman's order and control. This theme is vividly portrayed in *The Killing Joke* (Moore, 1988), where the Joker's actions are driven by his philosophy that "one bad day" is enough to drive anyone to madness. This graphic novel explores deeper psychological motivations of the Joker, setting a standard for his character complexity in later narratives. Moore's narrative suggests that the Joker's anarchism serves as a mirror to the absurdity and unpredictability of life, a theme that resonates deeply with existentialist philosophy (Camus, 1942).

The 1990s and 2000s saw the Joker's character delve into darker territories, with a marked increase in psychological complexity. A seminal work from this period is, for example, *Arkham Asylum: A Serious House on Serious Earth* (Morrison, 1989), which presents the Joker not only as a villain in the story, but as a deeply disturbed individual, as well. Morrison's portrayal of The Joker in this story was deeply influenced by psychoanalytic theories, particularly those concerning the formation of identity and the Jungian concept of the shadow self, reflecting the darker impulses within all individuals (Jung, 1953).

Another recurring theme is the Joker's duality with Batman, which has been one of the most prominent focal points in understanding both characters over the years. The graphic novel *Batman: The Man Who Laughs* (Brubaker, 2005) revisits the Joker's origin in parallel to Batman's, emphasizing that both characters were born out of personal tragedies. This narrative explores the philosophical questioning of how trauma can lead to vastly different outcomes—heroism, or villainy. This duality is often framed within the context of Nietzschean philosophy as well, where Batman and the Joker represent opposing moral aesthetics, one adhering to a moral code and the other absurd nihilism (Nietzsche, 1886).

It can be argued further that the Joker's enduring appeal in comic books stems from his ability to embody extreme philosophical and psychological themes that challenge both the protagonist and the audience's moral compasses. His complex relationship with Batman provides audiences a complex and dynamic frame of reference to explore themes of trauma, morality, and personal identity within both the characters and themselves.

THE JOKER'S CHARACTER IN FILM ADAPTATIONS

The Joker's transition from comic books to films has allowed for a rich exploration of his character through various cinematic interpretations, each reflecting different societal contexts and filmmaking styles. This examination focuses on key film adaptations, noting the significant differences and constants in his portrayal, which highlight broader cinematic and psychological theories.

In the 1966 film *Batman*, played by Cesar Romero, the Joker character is depicted with a campy and playful demeanor, reflecting the pop art movement and a more satirical approach to superheroes typical of the era (Sabin, 1996). This portrayal aligns with the theories of Susan Sontag on camp as "love of the unnatural: of artifice and exaggeration" (Sontag, 1964), which suggests that such a style celebrates the absurdity and theatricality inherent in the comic book medium.

Jack Nicholson's portrayal in Tim Burton's *Batman* from 1989 marked a significant shift towards a darker and more serious Joker. Burton's gothic aesthetic and emphasis on psychological complexity introduced a version of the Joker that is both a flamboyant criminal mastermind and a deeply disturbed individual. This adaptation resonates with the Freudian concept of the uncanny, where the familiar is made disturbingly strange and unsettling (Freud, 1919), thus enhancing the Joker's menacing qualities while maintaining his comic undertones.

Heath Ledger's interpretation in Christopher Nolan's *The Dark Knight* from 2008 is widely regarded as a seminal depiction, bringing intense psychopathological dimensions to the character. This portrayal that dives into themes of anarchy, terror, and the abyss of the human psyche, significantly is influenced by existentialist philosophy. Ledger's Joker is a force of nature that disrupts social order, that, it can be argued, embodies Nietzsche's concept of the *Übermensch*, which operates beyond conventional morality (Nietzsche, 1883).

The most recent major film portrayal by Joaquin Phoenix in Todd Phillips' *Joker* from 2019 shifts focus from the grandiose criminal aspect to an intense, character-driven study of societal neglect and mental illness. This film portrays this version of the Joker's character with a focal point on critique of social systems. The concept of the Joker as a biopolitical apparatus also intersects with Michel Foucault's notions of biopower and governmentality, wherein power is exercised over populations through an array of governmental techniques and procedures aimed at regulating social bodies and managing life (Foucault, 1978). In other words, Phoenix's portrayal brings a raw, unsettling realism to the character, emphasizing the impact of societal structures on individual psychopathology.

The evolution of the Joker's portrayal in films reflects changing societal norms and anxieties about morality, chaos, and the human psyche, and each actor and director brought a unique vision to the character, influenced by contemporary cultural and psychological theories, which allows the Joker to remain a relevant and compelling figure in popular culture.

THE JOKER'S REPRESENTATION IN OTHER MEDIA FORMS

The Joker's portrayal extends beyond the realms of comic books and films into video games and animation as well, where his character continues to evolve, adapt, and engage with new audiences. Video games offer a unique interactive experience, allowing players to engage directly with the character of the Joker. Notably, in the *Batman: Arkham Asylum* series, the Joker is portrayed not just as Batman's adversary but as an omnipresent force influencing the game's narrative and player decisions (Rocksteady Studios, 2009-2016). The concept of agency in video games, as discussed by Jannet Murray (Murray, 1997), suggests that this medium allows for a deeper exploration of character's motivation and player-character relationships, giving the Joker a platform to manipulate both characters within the game and the players themselves.

Furthermore, in *Batman: Arkham Asylum* and its sequels, the Joker's strategies and actions can be directly countered or supported by the player, creating a dynamic narrative that emphasizes the character's chaotic nature. This interactivity is aligned with Manovich's theory of the language of new media, which posits that digital environments transform narrative structures and user engagement (Manovich, 2001).

Animation is another form of media that provides a versatile medium for exploring the Joker's theatricality and psychological complexity. In animated series like *Batman: The Animated Series* (Timm & Radomski, 1992-1995), the Joker is both a comical and menacing figure, showcasing his dual nature in a format accessible to both younger audiences and adult viewers. The flexibility of animation allows for exaggerated expressions and actions that highlight the Joker's maniacal behaviors and elaborate schemes. Bakhtin's concept of the carnivalesque, which celebrates subversive and alternative voices in literature, can be applied to understand the Joker's appeal in animation (Bakhtin, 1965). His portrayal often disrupts the established order, embodying the spirit of carnival through his chaotic actions and disdain for societal norms.

The Joker

In other words, the Joker's adaptability to video games and animation is not merely a testament to his complexity as a character but also an indicator of the shifting paradigms in narrative consumption and audience engagement in digital and animated media. The interactive nature of these video games in general enhances the depth of his character by allowing players to explore his psychological attributes firsthand, while animation leverages visual storytelling to highlight his iconic status.

LITERACY IN COMICS AND THE JOKER'S NARRATIVE IMPACT

The concept of literacy in comics extends beyond basic textual understanding to include the decoding of visual language and complex narrative structures. The Joker's portrayal across various media—especially in comics—offers a unique case study for exploring this broader definition of literacy. This discussion contextualizes the findings of the Joker's multifaceted character within the scope of comic literacy, emphasizing how his portrayals challenge and redefine traditional narratives.

Scott McCloud's *Understanding Comics* (McCloud, 1993) provides a foundational framework for analyzing how comics communicate through a combination of visual and textual elements. McCloud discusses how the integration of words and images in comics creates a unique language that requires a specific form of literacy. The Joker's narratives often exploit this language, utilizing visual cues, textual ambiguity, and the interplay between the two to engage readers in a deeper interpretative process. The Joker's character consistently challenges traditional narrative structures and moral binaries often found in comic books. Unlike typical villain archetypes, the Joker operates within a moral grey area, often embodying a philosophy that questions societal norms and ethics. This complexity engages readers in a critical analysis of morality and justice, pushing the boundaries of traditional comic book storytelling.

For example, in *The Killing Joke* (Moore, 1988), the Joker's attempt to drive Commissioner Gordon insane by exposing him to extreme violence challenges the notion of resilience and the inherent goodness assumed of heroes in comics. This narrative invite reader to question the stability of morality and the impact of trauma, enriching the reader's literary and psychological engagement with the text. The Joker's adaptability also reflects changes in sociocultural narratives over time. As societal issues evolve, so too does the Joker's character, often mirroring or satirizing contemporary concerns. This adaptability not only demonstrates the Joker's relevance across different eras but also highlights the role of comics as a medium for social commentary. The Joker's enduring appeal suggests a collective fascination with exploring themes of chaos, order, and morality through a familiar yet unpredictable character.

It can be argued that the Joker's engagement with complex narrative structures and challenging traditional narratives enhances comic literacy among readers. His character acts as a catalyst for deeper literary and cultural discussions, encouraging readers to engage with and interpret comics at a more sophisticated level.

LITERACY IN COMICS AND THE JOKER'S TRANSMEDIAL NARRATIVE

The Joker's presence across various media platforms provides an excellent opportunity to examine how complex storytelling and character development in comics can enhance literacy. This section delves into the ways in which the Joker's transmedia narrative promotes a deeper level of literacy among audiences, through the lenses of narrative theory, psychology, and media studies. The Joker's character is renowned for its depth and complexity, which challenges readers and viewers to engage with the content on multiple levels. According to narrative theorist Jerome Bruner (Bruner, 1986), engaging with complex narratives enhances the reader's capacity to construct reality and understand diverse perspectives. The Joker's stories often involve intricate plots, moral ambiguities, and philosophical questions that require readers to employ higher-order thinking skills.

In *The Killing Joke* story (Moore, 1988), the narrative structure itself—interweaving the present actions with flashbacks and possible hallucinations—demands a sophisticated level of narrative literacy. Readers must navigate through these layers of reality and non-reality. This reading action as a form of mental exercise enhances their ability to interpret complex texts and images simultaneously. The development of the Joker's character over time exemplifies how dynamic and evolving character arcs can maintain reader engagement and promote literacy. The transformation from a mere villain to a deeply troubled individual with a backstory invites readers to explore themes of psychology and human behavior through engagement with their identity and the self. This engagement is not just passive consumption but an active interpretation and synthesis of the information presented.

Visual literacy plays a crucial role in understanding comics, and the Joker's portrayal utilizes this to its full extent. McCloud (1993) emphasizes the importance of interpreting visual cues in comics, which range from panel transitions to color usage and framing. The Joker's varied appearances, from his sinister smile to the chaotic environments he often inhabits, are meticulously designed to convey psychological depth and emotional states, encouraging readers to develop skills in visual analysis and interpretation. The Joker's narrative also reflects societal issues and critiques, promoting media literacy by encouraging audiences to analyze and critique the role of media in shaping perceptions and attitudes. It can be argued that

The Joker

the Joker's transmedia narrative significantly contributes to enhancing narrative and visual literacy by engaging audiences with complex storylines, sophisticated character development, and reflective societal critiques. This engagement not only promotes a deeper understanding of the content but also encourages critical thinking and discussion among its audiences.

The interaction between a media text and its audience is fundamental in shaping both the narrative itself and its interpretation. In the case of the Joker, the audience's engagement across various media platforms—comics, films, video games, and animation—plays a critical role in both the evolution of his character and the thematic complexity of his stories. This section explores how audience responses and participatory culture have influenced the Joker's transmedia narrative. According to Stuart Hall (Hall, 1997), media texts are encoded by their creators with intended meanings, but it is the audience that decodes these messages, sometimes aligning with and at other times diverging from intended interpretations. This encoding and decoding process highlights the active role of the audience in constructing meaning, which is particularly evident in the varied receptions to different portrayals of the Joker.

Henry Jenkins' concept of participatory culture explores further this dynamic, suggesting that audiences are not merely consumers but also creators of content, engaging with and responding to media in ways that can influence its direction and interpretation (Jenkins, 2006). In the context of the Joker, fan reactions, discussions, and even fan-created content contribute to the ongoing development of his character across different media.

The varied reactions to different film portrayals of the Joker illustrate how audience perceptions can influence media representations. For instance, the dark and chaotic Joker in *The Dark Knight* (Nolan, 2008) resonated with contemporary audiences' anxieties about terrorism and societal breakdown, leading to widespread acclaim and further dark, complex portrayals of characters in superhero films. Conversely, the more controversial depiction in *Joker* (Phillips, 2019) sparked intense debate about mental health and violence in society, demonstrating how audience reactions can provoke discussions that extend beyond the film itself. In comic books, the Joker's evolution has also been partially guided by audience reception. Storylines that resonated strongly with readers, such as the tragic elements introduced in *The Killing Joke* (Moore, 1988), have often been revisited and expanded in later issues and adaptations. Reader feedback through letters, online forums, and social media has influenced writers' and artists' approaches to the character, encouraging more sophisticated and layered narratives.

It can be argued that the Joker's character serves as a reflection of societal and individual anxieties, with audience engagement playing a crucial role in shaping his narrative across media. The feedback mechanisms inherent in fan culture and media consumption ensure that the Joker continuously evolves in response to changing societal contexts and audience expectations.

The use of comic books and transmedia storytelling as educational tools has garnered significant attention, with the Joker's narrative providing a rich case study. This section explores the educational potential of these media, emphasizing how they can be used to develop critical thinking, cultural awareness, and complex literacy skills. Lev Vygotsky's theories on the educational potential of storytelling and narrative play (Vygotsky, 1978) suggest that stories are fundamental to cognitive development. Comics and transmedia storytelling extend this concept by offering multimodal narratives that combine visual, textual, and sometimes interactive elements, which can enhance learning and engagement. The complexity of these narratives, particularly in characters like the Joker, requires audiences to engage in higher-order thinking that involves analysis, synthesis, and evaluation.

Comics have been recognized for their role in developing literacy skills, particularly in reluctant readers. They offer a blend of visual and textual storytelling that can be more accessible than traditional texts, while still challenging readers to interpret narrative nuances (McCloud, 1993). The Joker's story arcs, often rich with complex themes and moral questions, provide material for discussions about ethics, psychology, and social issues, making them useful for educational settings.

Transmedia storytelling, where a single-story spans multiple media platform, offers unique educational opportunities. Jenkins (2006) highlights how transmedia storytelling can foster learning through layering information and perspectives across different media, enhancing engagement and comprehension. The Joker's narratives across comics, films, and video games invite audiences to connect dots and form a holistic understanding of the character and his motivations, practicing skills that are valuable in both academic and real-world contexts.

In other words, engaging with transmedia narratives like Joker's, for example is, can significantly enhance literacy and learning outcomes with audiences. This engagement not only improves traditional literacy skills but also develops critical media literacy, ethical reasoning, and cultural awareness among learners.

THE JOKER'S TRANSMEDIAL JOURNEY AND SOCIETAL REFLECTIONS

The Joker's evolution across various media—comics, films, video games, and animation—provides a compelling lens through which to examine changes in societal attitudes and values over time. His character serves as an example for cultural anxieties, moral dilemmas, and shifts in the collective psyche, reflecting broader societal trends through the nuances of his portrayals. Media theorists like Marshall

The Joker

McLuhan have argued that media are not just channels of information but also cultural artifacts that shape and reflect societal norms and values (McLuhan, 1964) The Joker, as a transmedia character, embodies McLuhan's idea of the medium as the message, where his portrayals across different platforms highlight distinct aspects of society at various times.

From his early comic appearances as a straightforward villain to more nuanced portrayals in films like *The Dark Knight* and *Joker*, the evolution of the Joker's character coincides with significant societal changes. During periods of relative stability, the Joker often appears more cartoonish and less threatening, whereas times of social unrest or complexity see him depicted with greater psychological depth and moral ambiguity. This correlation suggests that the Joker acts as a narrative device to explore and respond to contemporary societal fears and tensions. For instance, the anarchic Joker of Christopher Nolan's *The Dark Knight* reflects post-9/11 anxieties about terrorism and societal breakdown, while Todd Phillips' *Joker* mirrors contemporary concerns regarding mental health and socioeconomic disparities (Peacock, 2019). These films use the Joker to question and critique societal norms, using his chaos as a contrast to expose the failures and cracks within societal structures.

The showcasing of mental health issues in *Joker* (2019) offers a clear example of how the character's transmedia journey reflects changing societal attitudes. Once stigmatized and oversimplified, mental health and illness are increasingly recognized in media as complex issues deserving empathy and understanding. The film's sympathetic portrayal of Arthur Fleck's descent into the Joker persona challenged audiences to consider the societal factors contributing to mental health struggles, aligning with growing advocacy for mental health awareness and reform.

It can be argued that the Joker's shifting characterizations across media platforms are directly influenced by changing societal norms, values, and anxieties. His character offers a unique opportunity to engage with and critique these changes, providing a space for audiences to explore uncomfortable or controversial issues through a familiar yet unsettling figure.

CONCLUSION

Exploration of the Joker as a transmedia character, enabled us to delve into his complex portrayals across comics, film, video games, and animation. Each medium has contributed uniquely to the development of his character, reflecting and influencing societal attitudes and values over time. The Joker's evolution from a mere antagonist to a symbol of chaos and critique of societal norms exemplifies the dynamic potential of transmedia storytelling to deepen character complexity and engage diverse audiences. I tried to showcase how the Joker's narrative in comics introduces themes of chaos and psychological depth, while film adaptations explore his sociopathy within varied societal contexts. Video games offer interactive experiences of his malevolent tactics, and animation reaches diverse demographics, broadening his impact. Each media portrayal invites audiences to reconsider morality, identity, and the human psyche, showcasing the Joker's role as both a narrative and cultural figure.

The exploration of the Joker also sheds light on the broader theme of literacy in comics. This form of literacy is not merely about reading and understanding text but involves interpreting complex narratives and visual languages that comics uniquely offer. The Joker's multifaceted character challenges readers and viewers to engage with sophisticated themes and encourages a deeper reading experience that transcends traditional literary forms.

The educational potential of comics and transmedia storytelling is significant, as evidenced by the Joker's use in discussing complex psychological, ethical, and societal issues. This engagement enhances critical thinking and interpretative skills, illustrating how comics can be potent tools for education and cultural critique.

In conclusion, the Joker's transmedia journey not only enriches his character but also highlights the evolving capabilities of comics and related media to engage with and reflect upon complex societal issues. His narrative across media platforms demonstrates the profound impact of storytelling in shaping cultural discourse and individual perception. As comics and transmedia continue to evolve, their potential to influence education, culture, and society remains a promising area for continued research and application.

REFERENCES

Bakhtin, M. (1965). *Rabelais and His World*. Indiana University Press, 15-16.

Bellah, R., Madsen, R., Sullivan, W. M., Swidler, A., & Tipton, S. M. (1985). *Habits of the Heart: Individualism and Commitment in American Life*. University of California Press, 14.

Berger, P. L., & Luckmann, T. (1966). *The Social Construction of Reality: A Treatise in the Sociology of Knowledge*. Anchor Books, 118-119.

Brubaker, E. (2005). *Batman: The Man Who Laughs*. DC Comics.

Bruner, J. (1986). *Actual Minds, Possible Worlds*. Harvard University Press, 88. 10.4159/9780674029019

Camus, A. (1942). *The Myth of Sisyphus*. Gallimard, 108.

Eason, B. (2008). *DARK KNIGHT FLASHBACK: THE JOKER, PART 1*. Comic Book Resources. https://www.cbr.com/dark-knight-flashback-the-joker-part-i/.

Eason, B. (2008). *DARK KNIGHT FLASHBACK: THE JOKER, PART 2*. Comic Book Resources. https://www.cbr.com/dark-knight-flashback-the-joker-pt-ii/

Eason, R. (2008). The Birth of the Joker: The Men Behind the Clown. *Gotham Chronicles*, 12(3), 45–59.

Eco, U., & Chilton, N. (1972). The Myth of Superman. *Diacritics*, 2(1), 14–22. 10.2307/464920

Fhlainn, S. N. (2011). The Dark Knight: Heath Ledger's Joker, Anarchy, and Chaos in Gotham. *The Journal of Popular Film and Television*, 39(2), 82–83.

Foucault, M. (1978). *The History of Sexuality: An Introduction* (Vol. I). Random House.

Freud, S. (1919). *The Uncanny*. Imago Publishing.

Hall, S. (1997). *Representation: Cultural Representations and Signifying Practices*. Sage Publications.

Jenkins, H. (2006). Fans, Bloggers, and Gamers: Exploring Participatory Culture. New York University Press.

Jenkins, H. (2006). *Convergence Culture: Where Old and New Media Collide*. NYU Press, 5-6.

Jung, C. G. (1959). Archetypes and the Collective Unconscious. Princeton University Press. 117.

Lyotard, J.-F. (1984). The Postmodern Condition: A Report on Knowledge. University of Minnesota Press, 36.

Manovich, L. (2001). *The Language of New Media.* MIT Press, 91.

McCloud, S. (1993). *Understanding Comics: The Invisible Art.* Harper Perennial.

McLuhan, M. (1964). *Understanding Media: The Extensions of Man.* McGraw-Hill, 19–20.

Moore, A. (1988). *The Killing Joke.* DC Comics.

Morrison, G. (1989). *Arkham Asylum: A Serious House on Serious Earth.* DC Comics.

Murray, J. H. (1997). *Hamlet on the Holodeck: The Future of Narrative in Cyberspace.* The Free Press, 55.

Nietzsche, F. (1883). *Thus Spoke Zarathustra.* Ernst Schmeitzner, 26.

Nietzsche, F. (1886). Beyond Good and Evil. Random House.

Nolan, C. (Director). (2008). *The Dark Knight.* Warner Bros. Pictures.

Peacock, S. (2019). Joker: A Serious Study of the Clown Prince of Crime. University of Mississippi Press.

Phillips, T. (Director). (2019). *Joker.* Warner Bros. Pictures.

Rocksteady Studios. (2009-2016). *Batman: Arkham series.* Warner Bros. Interactive Entertainment.

Sabin, R. (1996). *Comics, Comix & Graphic Novels: A History of Comic Art.* Phaidon Press, 61.

Sontag, S. (1964). *Against Interpretation and other Essays.* Farrar, Straus and Giroux.

Šuvaković, M. (2005). *Pojmovnik suvremene umetnosti.* Horetzky, Zagreb, Vlees & Beton.

Timm, B., & Radomski, E. (Creators). (1992-1995). *Batman: The Animated Series.* Warner Bros. Animation.

Vygotsky, L. (1978). Mind in Society: The Development of Higher Psychological Processes. Harvard University Press, 80.

Chapter 6
Significance of Transmedia Storytelling in Higher Education:
Collaborative Learning to Increase Enrollment and Retention Among Nontraditional Students

Anika C. Thrower
Borough of Manhattan Community College, CUNY, USA

Alex Evangelista
Borough of Manhattan Community College, CUNY, USA

ABSTRACT

Institutions of higher learning are essential in society. In the year 2023, there were over 18 million students. Though this total is substantial, it is below par compared to past trends. Long-standing college enrollment has been a catalyst for educating individuals in their chosen fields. Education attainment over time assists people in increasing the quality of life for themselves and their families, optimal health outcomes, and higher levels of productivity in communities while opening themselves to a broader range of opportunities. Because of COVID-19, in recent years, enrollment, retention, and graduation rates have been a challenge, particularly among nontraditional college students. Ensuring mattering and providing an inclusive campus environment has been more critical than ever before. As college administration and instructors seek ways to alleviate such fluctuations, collaborative learning and transmedia are viable solutions.

DOI: 10.4018/979-8-3693-3302-0.ch006

Copyright © 2024, IGI Global. Copying or distributing in print or electronic forms without written permission of IGI Global is prohibited.

INTRODUCTION

Because of COVID-19, institutions of higher education have experienced marked ebbs and flows in enrollment, retention, and graduation rates. In 2010, Students enrolled in community colleges around the United States were at eleven million. These institutions experienced a dramatic drop to 6.7 million for the 2021-2022 academic year (National Center for Education Statistics, 2024). Since then, community colleges have begun to see more promising rates, though unpredictable fluctuations could be an issue for some time. These instabilities are especially concerning in vulnerable populations such as nontraditional and, many times, minority college students. To remain relevance, college and universities need to undergo significant transformations and initiatives to engage students while attracting new students. Of particular concern is enticing while maintaining nontraditional college student enrollment. As institutions seek solutions, collaborative learning has emerged as a critical pedagogical tool yielding successful results. Concurrently, transmedia storytelling, known for its multi-platform narrative approach, has gained traction. This chapter delves into exploring the intersection of collaborative learning and transmedia narratives. Together, such applications may assist in reinvigorating student interest and engagement through responsive pedological approaches in the higher education landscape. More importantly, it promises to increase enrollment, retention, and graduation rates among vulnerable populations.

NONTRADITIONAL COLLEGE STUDENTS AND HEALTH

A traditional college student is usually seen as a younger adult who has newly received a diploma from secondary school and is moving to higher education. At the same time, nontraditional students often elect to enroll in a college beyond what is seen as the typical age and later in life. This could be because of various reasons. A nontraditional college student has the following attributes: 25 years of age and older, a part-time student, a full-time job, from a single-parent home, and possesses a GED or high school completion certificate. Additional attributes include likely not residing on campus, enrollment in nondegree programming, and likely to belong to a marginalized population (National Center for Education Statistics, n.d.). Nontraditional students, who are often minorities, experience various issues on and off the college campus, including dealing with microaggressions, financial funding sources, and addressing competing priorities and matters. Mattering for the college student means feeling like their presence and contribution to the campus environment is valued and welcomed. Candidly, higher education attainment is associated with improved health outcomes.

The Center for Disease Control and Prevention (CDC, 2024a) expressed that individuals from ethnic minority groups experience a plethora of preventable morbidity and mortality outcomes along with disability compared with their counterparts being non-Hispanic White people. Research shows minority populations experience higher rates of illness and death across a wide range of health conditions, including diabetes, hypertension, obesity, asthma, and heart disease, than their White counterparts (CDC, 2024b). Sadly, non-Hispanic/Black Americans are on the trajectory to die four years earlier than White Americans.

This is especially concerning as research indicates associations between decreased educational attainment rates in minority populations and lower socioeconomic status (Thrower et al., 2024). Education provides an opportunity for economic comfort, leading to lessened morbidity and mortality. Health disparities are more pronounced in minority populations. The Center for Disease Control and Prevention asserts inequalities in education is a long standing determinate of health gaps (Alder, 1994; CDC, 2024c; CDC 2012; Marmont et al. 1997 & Marmont & Shipley 1996,) and poor health outcomes (Thrower, 2013). Furthermore, higher education attainment increases the likelihood of processing and understanding wellness concepts. The intersection between education and health leads students to incorporate such models as the six dimensions of health into their lives. These dimensions include social, physical, environmental, intellectual, spiritual, and emotional health. Attentive to such models makes individuals likelier to make better health decisions for themselves and their families, thus increasing opportunities for higher quality of life. In fall 2020, 640,000 fewer students were enrolled in U.S. colleges and universities than in the previous year (NCES, 2021). Many of these students belonged to minority populations. A catalyst for COVID-19 has been colleges taking a closer look at enrollment, retention, and graduation rates.

TONY'S LIFE AS A NONTRADITIONAL STUDENT

The impact of falling off the sofa woke Tony out of his sleep. Startled by his teenage twin sons bickering again, his book, laptop, and cell phone spilled onto the floor. At 44 years old, he has been a single father for the last five years. For Tony, things can sometimes be challenging without a reliable support system. A new stress wave seeped in when Tony thought things were improving in his household. His adrenaline rushes as he moves swiftly towards his boys' shared bedroom and notes the time on the wall clock down the hall. It's the third day he forgot to set his alarm. This sets him back, especially on Thursdays, his 8:00 am Environmental

Statistics class. Exhaling, he had exactly 33 minutes to make it to the train station, starting him on his journey through the New York boroughs and onto campus in Manhattan. After hurryingly settling his kids' feud, he had only 20 minutes left to make his train. At this time, he needed to brew his coffee, pack his food for the day, take a quick shower, and dash out the door.

Done!

With 4 minutes to spare, he grabs his bookbag and dashes out the door. To Tony's delight, he made it to his bus but left his coffee and lunch on the kitchen counter. His rumbling stomach reminded him that today was his long day. He won't leave campus until 3:30 pm to go straight to his night job without eating. Feeling exhausted from his late night of school work and hunger pains, he pulled out his notebook and started to review class notes on the train.

Later, around noon, he eavesdrops on younger students in a student lounge area. While eating fresh pizza, they discuss their nagging parents' cutting allowances and their dating dilemmas. As he overhears the dialogue, he thinks, "Shit, wait until real life sets in, and you got to figure out how you're going to eat!". Outside of his noisy stomach pains, he sits quietly, trying to figure out how to eat on the cheap. In a moment of being overwhelmed, partly because of his growling stomach, he wonders why he even started college at his age. "Tony, how stupid can you be!" he unknowingly says aloud, garnering the attention and side eyes of the younger students nearby. "Creepy old head," one of them loudly whispers. Embarrassed, he gathers his things and walks toward his class. Tony's mind wonders as he remembers when his life started to get complicated.

As an A student in high school, he wishes he would have only gone to college earlier. But when his mother got diagnosed with terminal cancer, he had to work to support her and his younger sister. At this point, Tony is determined to honor his mother's dying wish, to attend college and make something of himself.

Sometimes, honoring his mother's wishes has been challenging despite his best efforts. Today is one of those days. Snapping himself back into reality, he starts his regiment of prep talk before entering his last class of the day. Regardless of his best efforts, these talks on days like this often turn into negative self-talk, such as, "Why can't I just be normal." Tony is growing weary of the odd looks and snide comments from his professors and fellow students. They make him feel like an outsider. In class, Tony is left out of small group discussions. His raised hand goes unnoticed, or the instructors call upon him as an afterthought. He feels devalued by his instructors and students alike. During breaks, informal conversations often happen around him like he is invisible. Sometimes, he wishes he were; why bother!

He feels like he is fighting an uphill battle by returning to school. Among his circle of friends, he is always the butt of the joke as they insinuate he is going to college to try to recapture his youth. His peers, many of whom are childhood friends,

Significance of Transmedia Storytelling in Higher Education

have never attended college. The classes he needs are only offered during the day, which means he must work nights. This routine is riddled with issues, including leaving his teenage sons to fend for themselves in their seedy neighborhood. His mind wonders further. If he was not attending classes, he could be around more for his boys, pick up additional shifts to catch up on bills, and have a social life. The few times Tony expressed his inadequacies and overwhelming feelings to people who care, they tell him life will get easier.

Inaudibly, he scoffs, "when"?

TARGETED APPROACHES TO INCREASE ENROLLMENT, RETENTION AND GRADUATION RATES

The tides are changing. According to the National Student Clearinghouse Research Center (2024), the tides are changing as undergraduate enrollment grew 1.2 percent in fall 2023 compared to 2022, with approximately 176,000 students enrolled in American colleges. With most increases being seen among older students. Likewise, certificate programs offered through vocational institutions have increased enrollment by 1.8 percent in fall 2023 and 15.6 percent above pre-pandemic levels (Insider Higher Ed, 2024). Colleges and vocational institutions have taken note and desire to move away from operating under traditional models to attract. Post-COVID-19, administration and faculty alike have become more attuned to seeking solutions. In order to speak to the call of action continuing to see increases in enrollment, retention, and graduation rates, institutions must actively compile an arsenal of specialized services while creating a more inclusive environment. As a result, institutions offer courses after hours and on weekends, diversify staff, and offer certificates and micro-credits rather than standard degrees. The college has allotted targeted funding for campus outreach campaigns and social events, leveraging campus resources and offering first-year experience programming. Also, they are restructuring policies and offering courses in creative modalities that have the probability of building learning between both traditional and nontraditional learners. Since nontraditional students often have unique needs, their plights to attain higher education must be recognized (Thrower et al. 2024).

Furthermore, administration boards anticipate that department faculty will assist. Strategic plans include revisiting responsive instructional pedagogy approaches, especially with nontraditional learners in mind. Such initiatives answer the call for broader approaches and methods to appeal to the wide range of student needs and fluctuating college enrollment rates.

COLLABORATIVE LEARNING

The concept of collaborative learning, with its roots in seminal literature spanning organizational research, social psychology, and education (Warneken et al., 2011), has evolved significantly over the past 50 years. This evolution, particularly in the last three decades, has led to a plethora of theories and associated studies. However, due to its diverse origins and historical perspectives, arriving at a precise definition has been a challenge, especially among experts from different fields.

Collaborative learning has been a staple in the American educational landscape for almost half a century, with educators incorporating its techniques across subjects and grade levels. When implemented effectively, collaboration proves to be a potent teaching tool. Some theorists define collaboration as students mutually agreeing to work together to understand a concept or solve a problem (Vassigh et al., 2014). It can range from simple, brief exercises in small groups to managing extensive projects or programs. Others offer more elaborate definitions, emphasizing equal partnership and unified effort among participants (Seel et al., 2017). They stress collaboration involves engaging with the entire project rather than just within individual components.

Contrary to oversimplified views, collaboration extends beyond task completion; it involves buy-in from teachers (Evangelista & Thrower 2023a & 2023b) and active commitment from learners with class materials pointed towards specific goals (Kang et al., 2012). It emphasizes group creation, where each member contributes to collective learning and understanding. Most theorists agree that collaboration fosters a collective identification, understanding, and solution process, enabling more profound engagement with material than solitary learning. Such applications have been quite helpful during COVID-19. In the pandemic's wake, renewed opportunities have arisen for colleges to engage students and encourage degree attainment. These opportunities present challenges for some educational facilities moving into new and uncharted online environments (Evangelista & Thrower 2023a & 2023b). Outside of the routine in-person offerings, institutions offer flexible classes, including accelerated and late-start courses.

The collaborative process incorporates interactive qualities such as mutual reference, communal goals, reciprocal communication, and ongoing negotiation (Laurillard, 2013a). It allows for the construction of shared meanings among participants and involves the identification and reorganization of collective knowledge. Essential elements include abstract problem understanding, iterative interpretation, and the application of rigorous evidence standards (Lai, 2011).

Collaboration requires shared meaning among participants actively engaged in a process, product, or event, facilitating interpersonal relationships and task completion (Laurillard, 2013b). It requires coordination and synchronous activity in a shared space, whether physical or virtual (Robinson et al., 2017). Shared awareness and understanding facilitate the construction of new ideas and products through interactions with others (Graham & Jones, 2019).

Collaboration transcends cooperation, encompassing mutual engagement toward a communal task (Laurillard, 2013b). Such mutual learning is vital for both traditional and nontraditional students as it provides knowledge sharing and learning opportunities. While cooperation may involve task assignments and resource sharing, true collaboration entails a collective effort based on mutual engagement and shared goals.

NAVIGATING COLLABORATIVE LEARNING: STRATEGIES, CHALLENGES, AND THEORIES

When considering pedagogies for collaborative learning, navigating potential pitfalls that may arise within groups is essential. Sometimes, collaboration can devolve into mere cooperation or even independent, uncoordinated efforts, notably if the group needs more cohesion and structure. Students may perceive demands for task specialization negatively, leading to imbalances in activity levels and added stress, ultimately compromising the quality of collaboration and satisfaction with outcomes.

To foster effective collaboration, instructors should address potential issues openly and encourage the development of necessary skills among students. Lee (2012) distinguishes between collaboration and cooperation, emphasizing that collaboration involves sharing physical and intellectual resources and aligning goals, responsibilities, values, beliefs, and attitudes from the outset. This comprehensive sharing leads to synergy, resulting in new, superior-quality outcomes.

Research on collaboration spans various levels, from interpersonal to inter-organizational. While much attention has been given to intergroup and inter-organizational collaborations, factors influencing collaborative actions in online and physical settings have been identified, including context, support, tasks, interaction processes, teams, and individuals, along with overarching factors. Leadership and followership dynamics are crucial in organizational collaborations, where relationship-building activities like cooperation, courage, honesty, and support facilitate agreement and collaboration.

At the interpersonal level, group activities can be categorized into projects, tasks, and steps, each contributing uniquely to the collaborative effort. Projects define the mission, tasks support project completion, and steps ensure proper execution of tasks. Despite the wealth of research, there remains a significant gap in the form of a unified theory for effective collaboration in educational settings. This gap necessitates the consideration of personal, interpersonal, and intragroup factors in the context of collaborative learning.

Colbry et al. (2014) made a significant contribution to the field by developing a grounded theory of collaboration. Their theory, known as Collaborative Theory (CT), identifies two broad categories of collaborative behaviors: Individual First and Team First. Individual First encompasses themes like turn-taking and status-seeking, while Team First involves influencing others, organizing work, and building group cohesion (Colbry et al. 2014). This theory provides valuable insights into effective collaboration by recognizing the interplay between individual agency and team dynamics, thereby guiding the understanding and implementation of collaborative pedagogies.

COLLABORATION IN TEAMWORK AND TEAM BUILDING

Collaboration serves as a critical component for effective teamwork and team building. Research has shown that successful teams often depend on personality traits, values, abilities, and the collaborative skills of individual team members. These factors shape the attitudes, behaviors, and cognitive states that influence whether a team achieves its goals (Wier, 2018). McEwan et al. (2017) found positive and significant medium-sized effects of teamwork interventions on teamwork and overall team performance. In the workplace, effective collaboration has been found to reduce burnout, lower stress, and increase positive feelings towards tasks. A Deloitte study (2023) found that among employees who collaborate in the workplace, 73% do better work, and 60% are found to more innovative.

In a study by DePrada, (2022) entitled *Teamwork skills in higher education: is university training contributing to their mastery?"* the mastery of teamwork skills among university students and its relation to certain socio-academic variables was examined. The study found significant gender differences, with female students outperforming their male counterparts in most teamwork skills, except for leadership abilities. The study also found that students' skills improved as they progressed in their studies, particularly those related to adaptability and decision-making (DePrada, 2022)

The Four Pillars of Peer Assessment for Collaborative Teamwork in Higher Education (Sridharan, McKay & Boud, 2023) highlights the power of combining two intertwined models of peer learning, namely peer assessment/feedback and collaborative team-based learning, to prepare graduates for the world of work and encourage acceptable social behaviors.

Significance of Transmedia Storytelling in Higher Education

Finally, (Saghafian, O'Neill, 2018), document the teamwork experiences of students in both traditional face-to-face and online programs in higher education The study suggests that the teamwork experiences of students in each modality have been documented primarily through evaluative research conducted over short spans of time and limited by a priori frameworks.

These studies provide valuable insights into the role of teamwork in education and how it can be effectively integrated into teaching and learning practices. Hence, demonstrating the significance of individual contributions, team dynamics such as collaboration, and socio-academic variables in effective collaboration. They also underscore the need for continuous research and development to further enhance teamwork skills in such ways that are inclusive of nontraditional students.

HARNESSING THE SYNERGY OF COLLABORATIVE LEARNING AND TRANSMEDIA NARRATIVES IN EDUCATION

Collaborative learning and transmedia narratives represent two dynamic approaches that have gained traction in modern educational settings. These methodologies not only enhance traditional teaching practices but also foster a more engaging and inclusive learning environment. The symbiotic relationship between collaborative learning and transmedia narratives, stressing their combined potential to revolutionize education.

Transmedia narratives represent a dynamic approach that has gained traction in modern educational settings. These methodologies not only enhance traditional teaching practices but also foster a more engaging and inclusive learning environment (Amon, 2019). Transmedia narratives in education can be understood in three ways: as a literacy necessary to actively evolve in this movement of participatory culture; as the product resulting from that sequential enhancement resulting from different analogical and digital media, conveyed by a narrative; and, lastly, as a strategy that explores that narrative that is developed in different means to achieve concrete didactic objectives (Gonzalez, 2019).

Recent research has shown promising outcomes in higher education when merging transmedia narratives with collaborative learning. Students interacting with transmedia narratives often exhibit enhanced critical thinking, creativity, and motivation (Hovious, et. al, 2021). Moreover, the integration of transmedia narratives into curricula enables educators to create immersive educational experiences that prompt students to engage more deeply with the material (Palioura and Dimoulas, 2022). Such holds great promise in assisting instiutions of higher education in addressing enrollment, retention and graduation rates among its students, especially those deemed as nontraditional.

Collaborative learning transcends the boundaries of conventional classroom settings by fostering critical thinking, communication, and teamwork skills among students. Various expressions of collaborative learning in higher education, such as group projects, peer review, online discussion forums, and problem-based learning, have been recognized for their efficacy in promoting student engagement and achievement (Ghodsi & Laal, 2012; Liu & Carless, 2006; Gao et al., 2013; Savery, 2015). These methods not only prepare students for the collaborative demands of the workforce but also nurture a culture of continuous improvement and mutual support within other areas of their lives.

Transmedia narratives offer a diverse and immersive approach to presenting educational content across multiple platforms, including texts, videos, and interactive media. By accommodating various learning preferences, transmedia narratives make education more accessible, engaging and captivating, allowing students to explore concepts from multiple perspectives (Scolari, 2018). Integrating transmedia narratives into curricula enables educators to create immersive educational experiences that prompt students to engage deeply with the material.

However, as with all new and innovative strategies, the effective integration of transmedia narratives into educational contexts requires faculty to possess proficiency in new media literacy. Training initiatives aimed at equipping educators with the necessary skills to conceive and execute transmedia-driven collaborative projects can significantly enhance educational quality and learner engagement (Jenkins et al., 2016).

The merging of transmedia narratives with collaborative learning has shown promising outcomes in higher education. Students interacting with transmedia narratives often exhibit enhanced critical thinking, creativity, and motivation, while educators trained in transmedia storytelling express increased confidence in facilitating collaborative learning experiences (Fleming, 2015).

Despite its numerous benefits, collaborative learning also presents challenges that educators must address. Uneven participation, conflict resolution, and assessment complexity are among the hurdles that require careful navigation (Burdett, 2003; Johnson & Johnson, 2009; Oakley et al., 2004). However, these challenges can be mitigated through structured approaches and effective teaching strategies.

Transmedia storytelling ignites learners intellectual health. Such a serves as a catalyst for collaborative learning by enhancing student engagement, promoting diverse perspectives, and incorporating interactive elements into the learning process (Scolari, 2018; Jenkins, 2006; Pratten, 2015). Several interactive storytelling platforms, such as Skyword, Infogram, Storyboard That, Storybird, and Shorthand, facilitate collaborative learning experiences through transmedia narratives.

Significance of Transmedia Storytelling in Higher Education

Case studies, such as Professor Emily Thompson's Multiverse Classroom and the Smithsonian Institute's interactive history lessons, exemplify the effective integration of transmedia storytelling and collaborative learning in education (Jenkins et al., 2016; Squire & Dikkers, 2016). These initiatives demonstrate how leveraging technology and multimedia platforms can enhance student learning experiences and promote active engagement.

To maximize the benefits of integrating transmedia narratives and collaborative learning, educators should align transmedia content with learning objectives, promote active engagement, provide support and guidance, and encourage creativity and expression (Beach et al., 2016; Freeman et al., 2017; Ash & Kellner, 2016; Fleming, 2015). By adopting best practices and embracing innovative pedagogical approaches, educators can harness the synergistic potential of collaborative learning and transmedia narratives to create transformative educational experiences particularly for the nontraditional college student.

CONCLUSION AND CONSIDERATIONS FOR FUTURE RESEARCHERS

Integrating collaborative learning and transmedia narratives in education presents a transformative approach to teaching and learning. It also has the potential to engage students while preparing them for the collaborative demands of the world around them. However, the effective integration of these methodologies at the college level is a continuous process that requires unwavering administration and faculty dedication to research and development.

Future studies could focus on developing effective strategies for integrating transmedia narratives into various educational contexts and exploring the impact of these strategies on student engagement, learning outcomes, and improving the nontraditional student experience. Additionally, research could also investigate how collaborative learning can be further enhanced through transmedia narratives, particularly in fostering critical thinking, creativity, and problem-solving skills among students.

In conclusion, the synergy of collaborative learning and transmedia narratives holds excellent potential for revolutionizing education and addressing the demands of enrollment, retention, and graduation rates. By embracing these innovative pedagogical approaches, higher education institutions can create transformative educational experiences that engage students and prepare them for what will come to life post-college.

REFERENCES

Amon, B. T. (2019). Transmedia narratives in education: The potentials of multisensory emotional arousal in teaching and learning contexts. *Narrative Transmedia*, 1-26.

Ash, K., & Kellner, D. (2016). *Teaching in the Multimodal World: Digital Tools for New Literacies*. Routledge.

Beach, R., Anson, C. M., Breuch, L. K., & Swiss, T. (2016). *Teaching writing using blogs, wikis, and other digital tools*. Teachers College Press.

Burdett, J. (2003). Overcoming challenges in collaborative learning. *Educational Leadership*, 61(1), 64–68.

Carless, D., & Liu, N. F. (2006). Peer feedback: The learning element of peer assessment. *Teaching in Higher Education*, 11(3), 279–290. 10.1080/13562510600680582

Center for Disease Control and Prevention. (2012). *Higher education and income levels keys to better health, according to annual report on nation's health*. CDC. https://www.cdc.gov/media/releases/2012/p0516_higher_education.html

Center for Disease Control and Prevention. (2024a). *Minority Health*. CDC. https://www.cdc.gov/minorityhealth/index.html

Center for Disease Control and Prevention. (2024b). *Racism and Health*. CDC. https://www.cdc.gov/minorityhealth/racism-disparities/index.html

Center for Disease Control and Prevention. (2024c). *Health Disparities*. CDC. https://www.cdc.gov/healthyyouth/disparities/index.htm

Colbry, S., Hurwitz, M., & Adair, R. (2014). Collaboration theory. *Journal of Leadership Education*, 13(4), 63–75. https://www.emerald.com/insight/content/doi/10.12806/V13/I4/C8/full/html. 10.12806/V13/I4/C8

Deloitte. (2023). *Delivering on the promise of Digital Collaboration*. Deloitte. https://www.deloitte.com/au/en/services/consulting/blogs/delivering-on-promise-digital-collaboration.html

DePrada, J. (2022). Teamwork skills in higher education: Is university training contributing to their mastery? *The Journal of Higher Education*, 47(3), 321–336.

Evangelista, A., & Thrower, A. (2022). Collaborative Online Learning Experiences Among Health Educators. *NERA Conference Proceedings 2022*. Digital Commons. https://digitalcommons.lib.uconn.edu/nera-2022/8

Evangelista, A., & Thrower, A. (2023a). Online Collaboration: The influence of faculty characteristics, training & presentation mode. *Journal of Education & Practice.* https://www.iiste.org/Journals/index.php/JEP/article/viewFile/61775/63764

Evangelista, A., & Thrower, A. (2023b). Rethinking the online environment through collaborative learning. *Open Scholarship of Teaching and Learning*, 2(3). 10.56230/osotl.70

Fleming, L. (2015). *Worlds of Making: Best Practices for Establishing a Makerspace for Your School.* Corwin Press.

Freeman, S., Eddy, S. L., McDonough, M., Smith, M. K., Okoroafor, N., Jordt, H., & Wenderoth, M. P. (2017). Active learning increases student performance in science, engineering, and mathematics. *Proceedings of the National Academy of Sciences of the United States of America*, 111(23), 8410–8415. 10.1073/pnas.131903011124821756

Gao, F., Luo, T., & Zhang, K. (2013). Tweeting for learning: A critical analysis of research on microblogging in education published in 2008-2011. *British Journal of Educational Technology*, 44(3), 783–801.

Ghodsi, S. M., & Laal, M. (2012). Benefits of collaborative learning. *Procedia: Social and Behavioral Sciences*, 31, 486–490. 10.1016/j.sbspro.2011.12.091

Graham, C., & Jones, N. (2019). Impact of a social network messaging app on team cohesiveness and quality of completed team projects in an undergraduate team project. *Journal of Educational Technology Systems*, 47(4), 539–553. 10.1177/0047239518821937

Hovious, A., Shinas, V. H., & Harper, I. (2021). The compelling nature of transmedia storytelling: Empowering twenty-first-century readers and writers through multimodality. Technology. *Knowledge and Learning*, 26(1), 215–229. 10.1007/s10758-020-09437-7

Inside Higher Ed. (2024). *Enrollments Rise After Pandemic-Related Declines.* Inside Higher Ed. https://www.insidehighered.com/news/students/retention/2024/01/24/enrollment-rising-first-time-pandemic

Jenkins, H. (2006). *Convergence Culture: Where Old and New Media Collide.* New York University Press.

Jenkins, H., Ito, M., & Boyd, D. (2016). *Participatory Culture in a Networked Era: A Conversation on Youth, Learning, Commerce, and Politics.* Polity Press.

Johnson, D. W., & Johnson, R. T. (2009). An Educational Psychology Success Story: Social Interdependence Theory and Cooperative Learning. *Educational Researcher*, 38(5), 365–379. 10.3102/0013189X09339057

Kang, M., Yoon, S., Yoo, Y. R., Lim, H., & Kim, M. (2012). Investigating the Predictive Power of Metacognition and Perceived Interaction on Web-Based Collaborative Learning Outcomes. *World Conference on Educational Media and Technology*, Denver, Colorado, USA.

Laal, M., & Ghodsi, S. M. (2012). Benefits of collaborative learning. *Procedia: Social and Behavioral Sciences*, 31, 486–490. 10.1016/j.sbspro.2011.12.091

Lai, E. R. (2011). *Collaboration: A literature review*. Pearson. https://images.pearsonassessments.com/images/tmrs/Collaboration-Review.pdf

Laurillard, D. (2013a). *Teaching as a design science: Building pedagogical patterns for learning and technology*. Routledge. 10.4324/9780203125083

Laurillard, D. (2013b). *Rethinking university teaching: A conversational framework for the effective use of learning technologies* (2nd ed.). Routledge. 10.4324/9781315012940

Lee, H. J., & Baek, E. (2012). Facilitating deep learning in a learning community. *International Journal of Technology and Human Interaction*, 8(1), 1–13. 10.4018/jthi.2012010101

Liu, N. F., & Carless, D. (2006). Peer feedback: The learning element of peer assessment. *Teaching in Higher Education*, 11(3), 279–290. 10.1080/13562510600680582

Marmot, M., Ryff, C. D., Bumpass, L. L., Shipley, M., & Marks, N. F. (1997). Social inequalities in health: Next questions and converging evidence. *Social Science & Medicine (1982)*, 44(6), 901–910. 10.1016/S0277-9536(96)00194-3

Marmot, M. G., & Shipley, M. J. (1996). Do socioeconomic differences in mortality persist after retirement? 25-year follow-up of civil servants from the first Whitehall study. *BMJ (Clinical Research Ed.)*, 313(7066), 1177–1180. 10.1136/bmj.313.7066.11778916748

McEwan, D., Ruissen, G. R., Eys, M. A., Zumbo, B. D., & Beauchamp, M. R. (2017). The effectiveness of teamwork training on teamwork behaviors and team performance: A systematic review and meta-analysis of controlled interventions. *PLoS One*, 12(1), e0169604. 10.1371/journal.pone.016960428085922

National Center for Education Statistics. (2021). *Digest of Educational Statistics*. NCES. https://nces.ed.gov/programs/digest/d21/tables/dt21_306.20.asp?current=ye

National Center for Education Statistics. (n.d.). *Nontraditional Undergraduates / Definitions and Data.* NCES. https://nces.ed.gov/pubs/web/97578e.asp

National Student Clearinghouse Research Center. (2024). *Current Term Enrollment Estimates: Fall 2023.* NCES. https://nscresearchcenter.org/current-term-enrollment-estimates/

Oakley, B., Felder, R. M., Brent, R., & Elhajj, I. (2004). Turning student groups into effective teams. *Journal of Student Centered Learning,* 2(1), 9–34.

Palioura, M., & Dimoulas, C. (2022). Digital storytelling in education: A transmedia integration approach for non-developers. *Education Sciences,* 12(8), 559. 10.3390/educsci12080559

Prada, E. D., Mareque, M., & Pino-Juste, M. (2022). Teamwork skills in higher education: Is university training contributing to their mastery? *Psicologia: Reflexão e Crítica,* 35(5), 5. 10.1186/s41155-022-00207-135141845

Pratten, R. (2015). *Getting started with transmedia storytelling: A practical guide for beginners.* CreateSpace Independent Publishing Platform.

Robinson, H. A., Kilgore, W., & Warren, S. J. (2017). Care, communication, learner support: Designing meaningful online collaborative learning. *Online Learning : the Official Journal of the Online Learning Consortium,* 21(4), 29–51. 10.24059/olj.v21i4.1240

Saghafian, M., & O'Neill, D. K. (2018). A phenomenological study of teamwork in online and face-to-face student teams. *Higher Education,* 75(1), 57–73. 10.1007/s10734-017-0122-4

Savery, J. R. (2015). Overview of problem-based learning: Definitions and distinctions. *The Interdisciplinary Journal of Problem-Based Learning,* 1(1), 9–20.

Scolari, C. A., Masanet, M.-J., Guerrero-Pico, M., & Establés, M.-J. (2018). Transmedia literacy in the new media ecology: Teens' transmedia skills and informal learning strategies. *El Profesional de la Información,* 27(4), 801–812. 10.3145/epi.2018.jul.09

Squire, K., & Dikkers, S. (2016). *Amplifying Learning with Digital Games: A Multifaceted Approach to Increasing Engagement.* Information Age Publishing.

Thrower, A. C., Danawi, H., & Lockett, C. (2013). Determinants of High Pre-pregnancy BMI of U.S. Puerto Rican WIC Participants. *The International Journal of Childbirth Education,* 28(4), 55–61.

Thrower, A. C., Evangelista, A. A., Baker-Garder, R., & Mogaji, H. (2024). *Autoethnographic Tactics to Closing the Gap on Educational Attainment*. IGI Global., 10.4018/979-8-3693-1074-8

Chapter 7
Media Literacy:
A Study on Media Consumption Habits and Perceptions of Addiction Among Students

Zeynep Yurtseven Avci
Eskisehir Osmangazi University, Turkey

Özge Misirli
https://orcid.org/0000-0002-6135-6815
Eskisehir Osmangazi University, Turkey

Gözde Tekbaş
Eskisehir Osmangazi University, Turkey

ABSTRACT

Abundance of information, ease of contemporary technologies, and cheapening of technology make it easier to access the media. The influence of the media in shaping behavior and shaping society in this way, brings the importance of drawing attention to the risks in the media. Addiction is one of the common topics in the media. Considering that what is widely revealed in the media will be normalized by society after a while, it is possible to say that media literacy plays an important role in recognizing these risks and minimizing them. The aim of this study is to determine the media consumption habits of the participants and the types of addiction they noticed in the media, and to determine their perceptions of an addiction they chose with the help of metaphors. The study was conducted with 176 students who took the Media Literacy course and voluntarily participated in the study. According to the findings, although the participants came across many types of addiction in media content, the addictions they noticed the most were technology-related addictions and substance addiction.

DOI: 10.4018/979-8-3693-3302-0.ch007

INTRODUCTION

Throughout the process of social development, it is evident that the role of the media and its influence on society cannot be ignored. In the context of societal development, it is important to recognise the reciprocal relationship between media and society. The media serve as both a reflection of and an instrument for societal change and, as such, their impact on the behaviours, attitudes and perceptions of individuals and communities is significant. It can be argued that societal change progresses from the individual to the community. However, as this transformation unfolds, the influence of society on the behaviour of individuals becomes increasingly important. This dynamic interplay between the individual and society, while seemingly losing sight of its origins, is heavily influenced by the media. Media shape not only the perceptions and behaviours of individuals, but also the collective norms, values and attitudes of society as a whole. It is therefore essential to recognise the powerful influence of the media in the process of societal development and change. The media play a crucial role in shaping social discourse and promoting the spread of new ideas, beliefs and values. It has the capacity to both reflect and transform society, and its impact on the trajectory of societal development cannot be underestimated.

As technology advances, it has become easier for people to navigate their daily lives and find quick solutions to various problems. However, while people are becoming more connected in a technological sense, they are also becoming more disconnected from themselves and others at a psychological level (Buss, 2000). This phenomenon, reinforced by the influence of the media, has led to a redefinition of previously well-understood concepts

One such concept that has been affected by the influence of the media is addiction. As the media has become more widespread and diverse in terms of accessibility, the way in which addiction is perceived has also evolved. It is now important to examine the impact of the media on the concept of addiction in contemporary times. In order to examine the impact of the media on addiction, it is first necessary to define the concept of addiction. It is therefore crucial to examine how the media have redefined this concept and what the implications are for society as a whole.

Addiction

Rapid progress in many aspect of our lives has also accelerated thought processes, leading to an increase in individual stressors. Coping with these stressors has become more difficult, resulting in the use of dysfunctional coping strategies. Dysfunctional coping strategies, which have a significant impact on individual and societal life, are associated with addictive behaviours. Addictive behaviors are characterized by continuity, repetition, and the potential to promote other diseases (Eryılmaz & Deniz, 2019). Although addictive behaviours provide short-term satisfaction, they eventually lead to a loss of personal control and functionality. Consequently, addiction is a challenging dysfunctional coping mechanism that has been the focus of expert attention for years, with frequent relapses despite intensive efforts (Marlatt et al., 1988).

Addiction has existed in many forms for many years. In particular, smoking, alcohol and drug addiction are among the types that disrupt the functioning of individuals. Although we are more familiar with drug or substance addiction, non-substance addiction has become a new emerging problem in modern society. Non-substance addiction has a reward system mechanism like substance addiction. Although they are all essentially addictions, the diagnosis of different types of addiction is often complex because they differ from each other (Chassin et al., 2007). Among non-substance addictions, gambling disorder, internet addiction, food addiction and telephone addiction are among the most common types we encounter today. However, only gambling disorder is included in the DSM-V as a non-substance addiction, suggesting that the understanding and severity of non-substance addiction is rare. When defining drug or substance dependence, 'loss of control' and 'despite negative consequences' are the main characteristics. Drug addiction is the result of continuous drug use and can be seen as a type of brain disease caused by repeated drug use. Although non-substance addictions do not involve the taking of substances, the symptoms and brain mechanisms are very similar to those of substance addiction. Therefore, researchers have often used the substance addiction model to define and diagnose it (Zou et al., 2017).

The view that addiction is a neurobiological compulsion disease emerged in response to the perception of addiction as a sin or a moral failing in the twentieth century. The addiction model has two parts. The first part claims that drug use is a choice even for addicts, while the second part involves the moral condemnation of this choice. However, this model has proven inadequate in defining addiction psychologically after receiving controversial responses (Pickard, 2020). Addiction is fundamentally based on substance use behavior and is included in the criteria for substance use disorders in the American Psychiatric Association's Diagnostic and Statistical Manual (DSM-IV, APA, 1994). Addiction, which is seen as a compulsive behavior in the face of negative consequences, has been expanded over time to encompass addiction types beyond alcohol and illegal drug use. In 1986, the US Surgeon General's Report first classified smoking as an addictive behavior, and experts began to consider a wider range of compulsive behaviors, including gambling, overeating, and overplaying video games, as "addiction" in later years (Holden, 2001). Therefore, the concept of addiction is no longer limited to substance use behaviors alone.

Attachment Theory, which is one of the fundamental frameworks in explaining development, is an approach that emphasizes the emotional relationships and bonds underlying addiction. This theoretical perspective argues that individuals' emotional experiences from childhood influence their tendencies towards addiction in adulthood. Particularly, it is suggested that individuals who have not experienced secure and healthy attachment are more prone to various types of addiction. In the examination of modern addictions such as media addiction, for many individuals, spending time on social media platforms or online gaming has become a means of emotional attachment and satisfaction. Interacting through the internet has gradually transformed the ways in which individuals establish social relationships and fulfill their emotional needs. However, in these forms of attachment, situations can arise where individuals may indulge excessively or their daily functionality may be affected due to unhealthy attachment patterns. This situation can lead to a problem referred to as media addiction. Research, especially among young people, indicates that intense use of social media is associated with the fulfillment of emotional needs in the online environment. This demonstrates that the emotional attachments and relationships underlying addiction may play a significant role in understanding modern phenomena such as media addiction.

Addiction is a complex phenomenon studied and explored in the psychology literature. Various approaches are offered by addiction theories to understand the mechanisms underlying this phenomenon. From a behavioral perspective, addiction is often associated with the concepts of reward and punishment. Reward represents the positive outcomes obtained as a result of desired behavior, while punishment represents the negative outcomes that arise from undesired behavior. According to the behavioral explanation of addiction, addictive behavior emerges as a result of an individual consistently displaying a positive response to a rewarding stimulus. For example, if an individual feels a positive effect after using a drug, they may be inclined to repeat this behavior and consequently develop an addiction. Therefore there are differences in the definition of addiction between young people and adults. For adolescents to consider a situation as an addiction, in addition to negative aspects such as tolerance and withdrawal, it is also necessary that the situation provides pleasure to the individual. However, it has been observed that for adults the presence of negative aspects is sufficient to consider a behaviour as addictive (Chassin et al., 2007). The current findings reveal both the multifaceted nature of perceived 'addiction' and the diversity in how adults and adolescents conceptualise this construct. However, the meaning of addiction is being reshaped in contemporary society. It can be argued that individual perceptions and different interpretations of addiction contribute to the confusion surrounding the concept of addiction. Given the pervasiveness and accessibility of the media in today's world, the media have a significant impact on shaping these different interpretations. Therefore, the role of the media is crucial in this reframing process and it is useful to examine how addiction is portrayed in the media.

Addiction in Media

It is known that the media has been influential in shaping societies from past to present. While traditional media such as television, radio and newspapers, which were frequently referred to as media in the past, continue to exist, today the influence of different sources such as social media and film/TV platforms on individuals cannot be underestimated. Although the effects of different media sources on individuals differ from each other, it is possible to say that the media plays an important role in shaping the decisions made by individuals and society in general.

All citizens of consumer society are at risk of developing a habit that is generally considered and defined as a problem. How we classify this behavior as a problem and how we perceive it as big and dangerous depends on the social and cultural understanding of problems in the media. Through media channels, examples are publicly expressed and circulated about addiction problems such as movies about shopping addicts and people trying to quit smoking, news about new problematic repetitive behavior types, and video games that contribute to the nature of addiction by presenting complementary, sometimes labeling images (Hellman, 2011).

Media texts about addiction can be reflected in newspapers, the internet, and celebrity magazines. The concept of addiction includes the idea of a force that separates life from a common need hierarchy by drawing boundaries between normal and excessive behavior. In addition, symbolic language, in this case media texts that create addiction images, can be presented beyond boundaries. In addition, media products not only become a part of the process of interpreting social reality but also serve as part of an addiction order that introduces and normalizes addiction objects (Hellman, 2011). The images mediated by the media are constantly involved in redrawing cultural boundaries between things that have gone out of control and things that are thought to act within reasonable limits, and they provide us with information about how problems develop, how they appear, how they can be addressed, etc. Discourses and significant changes related to such popular representations continue to be a part of larger social and cultural processes of change related to the concept of addiction.

The power of the media is effective in directing individuals' decisions. According to the framing effect, which is especially highlighted in public opinion research, asking the same question in different perspectives affects people's opinions and answers (Chong & Druckman, 2007; Scheufele & Tewskbury, 2007). It is clear that media is no longer just limited to radio, television, or newspapers, and with the development and cheapening of technology, people have become able to access media sources at any time. According to McGinty et al. (2019), the topics that receive excessive attention in the media are perceived by the public as significant and urgent issues, and this perception also affects the development of policies and laws regarding such issues. Considering all this, it is possible to say that the media is of great importance in the perception and change of both the individual and the society.

Individual Perceptions and Societal Change

Australian researchers have released a worldwide addiction report which presents "about 240 million people around the world are dependent on alcohol, more than a billion people smoke, and about 15 million people use injection drugs" (Salmassi, 2015). Salmassi (2015) points out that people dependent on alcohol die younger, and have poor health over a long period of time according to the report. At the same time, addiction affects their work and relationships while reducing quality of life. In the report, addictive behaviors are labeled among the primary causes of morbidity and premature death globally, while significant societal and individual costs of gambling and other addictive behaviors on society through health-care costs, public safety, crime and lost productivity, as well as other social costs (Gowing et al., 2015). In this sense, fighting against addiction is among the essential global issues of our world. Wilterdink and Form (2024) highlight the emphasis of some evolutionary theories on the cumulative nature of human knowledge, because of the innovative nature of humans in terms of adding to existing knowledge, replacing insufficient ideas and practices with better ones. That means change is possible.

'Diffusion of Innovation Theory' by Rogers (1962) is a theory applied to explain how new ideas, lifestyles and technologies spread. The theory classifies people according to the criterion of adopting innovations in their relationship with innovations over a certain time series. Rogers suggests that innovation may be a technological development or a new product, such as a mobile phone, a computer, or a hybrid seed, or it may be a concept or way of life. On the other hand, Sellman (2011) suggests that even while ending an addiction, recovery should be thought of in terms of life-style change. The treatment process starts with picking up the pieces of a failed life-style, then rehabilitation (assembling a new life-style) starts. Third stage is practicing the new life-style and the fourth stage is self-management (living the new life-style. In this sense both preventing addiction and recovery from addiction could be thought as lifestyles that should be practiced by groups of people. Wilterdink and Form (2024) argue that most early adopters of innovations are young, urban, and highly educated people. On the other hand, according to several theories that were influenced by diffusion of innovation, behavioral change of an individual starts with perceptions. In this sense, it is very crucial to do research on

Media Literacy

perceptions of young adults about addiction to make a difference on fighting against addiction and having a diffusion of positive behavioral change.

Figure 1. Types of addiction noticed by students in media content

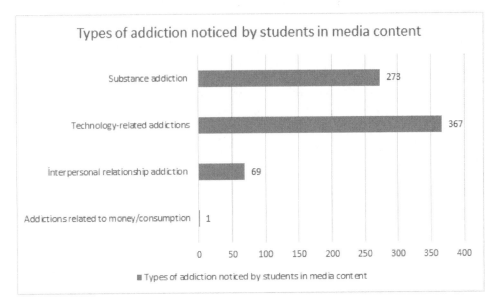

Figure 2. Types of addiction that students notice the most in the content they watch

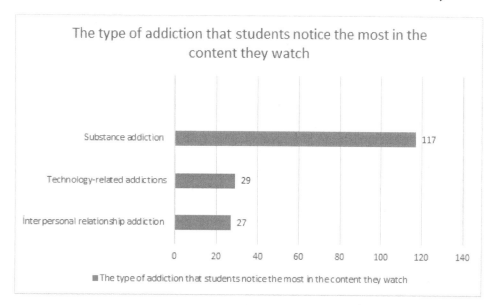

Purpose of Study

It is observed that the concept of addiction has become more widespread and appears in different fields compared to the past. The multifaceted nature of "addiction" causes adults and adolescents to understand and conceptualize this structure in various ways. Considering the intensity of young people among the consumers of different contents in the media, it can be said that young people will also be the ones who frequently encounter the concept of addiction. In this respect, determining young people's conceptualizations and perceptions regarding addiction is considered to have an important impact on changing addiction. In addition, revealing how young people perceive the concept of addiction and their perspectives on addiction in the media and clarifying the concept confusion related to addiction are also important in shedding light on the media from the young people's point of view.

Media is influential both individually and socially. When it is considered that individuals are exposed to intense media content, making conscious decisions becomes quite difficult. Being media literate individuals is an important factor in consuming media content more consciously. It can be said that the media literacy course taught as an elective course in universities is in a critical position to contribute to individuals' understanding of perceived addiction comments and becoming conscious individuals. The aim of this study is to examine the experiences of university students who have taken Media Literacy courses in encountering the concept of addiction in the media, as well as their explanation for the type of addiction they have expressed through a metaphor. Within this scope, the study was conducted in two stages. In the first stage of the study, students' media consumption habits and the types of addiction they noticed in the media were determined. In the second stage, the participants' perceptions regarding a chosen addiction were tried to be determined with the help of metaphors. In this regard, the following questions were sought to be answered:

- What are the addiction types that the participants encounter/noticed the most in the media?
- On which addiction types did the participants produce metaphors?
- According to the metaphors used, what are the participants' perceptions regarding addiction in the media?

METHOD

This study, which aims to reveal students' perceptions of addiction through metaphors reached within the scope of the media literacy course, was designed using the qualitative research design of "phenomenology". Phenomenological research aims to reach a common meaning of the experiences of multiple individuals related to a phenomenon (concept/fact) (Aydın, 2013). Here, the concept of "experience" is used in the sense of "the apprehension of an object, thought, or feeling through the senses or the mind" (Çilesiz, 2011). The focus of this study is how the participants who observed various types of addiction in media content interpreted their observation-based experiences related to addiction. In this context, the phenomenon addressed in the study is the phenomenon of addiction in the media. This section includes information on the participants, instruments, data collection, and data analysis processes.

Participants

The study group of this research consists of students who took the Media Literacy and Critical Media Literacy courses in the Spring semester of the 2021-2022 academic year. Criterion sampling was used in data collection, and students who were taking these courses were determined as the criterion for inclusion in the data collection process. 143 students who took the Media Literacy course and 91 students who took Critical Media Literacy course were reached. The research presents findings related to university students' media consumption habits and types of addiction they notice in the media. Table 1 shows the field of study of the students participating in the study.

Table 1. Distribution of participating students according to field of study

		N	f
Student Distribution by Faculties	Faculty of Health Sciences	81	46.02%
	Faculty of Education	95	53.98%
Total		176	100%

Instruments and Data Collection

This study aimed to reveal how students perceive addiction. Within the scope of the research, the participating students were asked to conduct research on the types of addiction they frequently see in the media and that catch their attention, and then fill out a survey that includes their demographic information as well as various opinions on addiction they have seen in the media based on their experiences. Afterwards, an incomplete metaphor sentence was given to the students to complete about the addiction type they chose based on their own experiences. The structured sentence "Addiction is like...... because......" was used to ask participants to describe addiction using metaphors. Because metaphors provide a strong, rich picture and visual image when describing a situation in qualitative data collection (Yıldırım and Şimşek, 2006). Some participants produced more than one metaphor. These metaphors were accepted on a participant basis and evaluated under the same participant code during coding. The difference between the number of participants and the number of metaphors arises from this.

As part of the study, participants were asked to explain why they chose the respective metaphor. The reason for asking participants to provide an explanation while completing the semi-structured sentence was that the metaphor used alone is often not sufficient to describe the phenomenon and it is important to know why the metaphors were created and to ensure that there is a valid reason for the comparisons made. During the coding process, not only the words (metaphors) used by the participants, but also the statements explaining why the respective metaphor was chosen were taken into account. For instance, in the example given below, the metaphor of "burning candle" could not be initially classified under a specific code by the researchers, but upon review, it was placed under the code of "danger" based on the statement provided.

Media Literacy

Alcohol addiction is similar to the melting of a burning candle. Because alcohol does not show its harmful effects in the early stages of use. With continuous use, it brings the individual to a state of physical and mental decline. And the individual melts away over time, like a burning candle, losing their sense of self. In advanced stages, the result is death, that is, they disappear like a candle.

In this way, all metaphors were examined and through this detailed examination, the metaphors that could not be categorized were given under the "other" section. Thus, the aim was to minimize the loss of data from the results obtained.

Data Analysis

Although the study was designed according to qualitative research methodology, in order to obtain more reliable data from students, survey questions were asked during the research and the data obtained from these questions were made more understandable with percentage distributions, tables, and graphs. In analyzing the data obtained from metaphors, the number of metaphors was taken as the basis while conducting content analysis. First, the types of addiction and the frequency of themes were visualized in table form as percentages and frequencies, and direct quotations from participants were included during interpretation. In data analysis, categories were first created from raw data, categories and data were classified, categories were named, and themes were identified. In reaching the themes, three researchers independently created the codes and themes, and then common themes and codes were determined through meetings. Addiction types selected by participants were named using literature review, and themes were created by researchers using literature review.

The qualitative data in this study was interpreted by asking participants to elaborate on their own metaphors. By doing so, the researchers were able to gain a deeper understanding of the participants' intended meanings and avoid oversimplification. The analysis of the data was conducted with a holistic approach, taking into account both reliability and transferability of the study. To ensure the reliability of the research, the researchers were transparent about their roles in the process, the development of data collection tools, and the procedures used for data collection and analysis. The data collection tool was created based on the experiences of four researchers from different fields of study, who used a combination of quantitative and qualitative techniques to collect data. Reliability was considered the primary criterion for validity in this study, in line with the principles outlined by Lincoln and Guba (1985). By using variation techniques and multiple methods of data collection, the researchers were able to enhance the credibility and transferability of their findings. The data collection tool has been developed based on the literature review and the experiences of three researchers, two of them are in the Department of Computer and Instructional Technology Education and who are also instructors of the Media Literacy course, and one of them is in the Department of Guidance and Psychological Counseling. The fact that the researchers have different expertises that have contributed to approaching the research from different perspectives. Variation techniques (Lincoln & Guba, 1985) have been applied to collect data using multiple methods of quantitative and qualitative approaches, including multiple-choice and open-ended questions. Tables and graphs have been utilized to enhance the comprehensibility of quantitative data. Themes generated in the qualitative data have been supported by participants' direct expressions. To ensure the transferability of the research, all processes have been described in detail.

FINDINGS

Types of Addiction Observed in Media Content

The types and percentages of addiction that attract students' attention in the media content they encounter and consume vary. The responses of the participants regarding the types of addiction they generally notice in media content and the type of addiction that attracts their attention the most in the content they regularly watch are presented in Graph 1 and Graph 2.

The subtopics and their percentages related to the titles presented in Graph 1: substance addiction includes addictive substance addiction; tobacco/cigarette addiction (f:108, 22.2%), alcohol addiction (f:92, 52.3%), and drug addiction (f:73, 41.5%). In the category of technology-related addictions, computer games (f:220, 62.5%), social media (f:153, 86.9%), and screen addiction (f:104, 59.1%) are included. The category of interpersonal relationship addiction (f:69, 39.2%) is defined as being dependent on individuals on a relational basis and shopping addiction is included in the scope of addictions related to money/consumption (f:1; 0.6%).

Regarding the titles presented in Graph 2, for which 176 participants expressed their opinions, the subtopics and their percentages are as follows: The category of substance addiction includes addictive substance addiction; tobacco/cigarette addiction (f:39, 22.2%), alcohol addiction (f:49, 27.8%), and drug addiction (f:29, 16.5%). In the category of technology-related addictions, computer games (f:3, 1.7%), social media (f:24, 13.6%), and screen addiction (f:5, 2.8%) are included. The category of interpersonal relationship addiction (f:27, 15.3%) is defined as being dependent on individuals on a relational basis.

Media Literacy

Metaphors

As part of the study, participants were asked to explain their views by using metaphors. The findings related to this topic are presented in this section. Participants' chosen addiction types to express using a metaphor were grouped into five main themes: Substance and drug addiction (105 metaphors), Technology-related addictions (64 metaphors), Interpersonal relationship addiction (8 metaphors), Money/consumption-related addictions (8 metaphors), and Food and drink addiction (6 metaphors). Under the Substance and drug addiction theme, there were four subtopics: drug addiction (44 metaphors), tobacco addiction (28 metaphors), alcohol addiction (25 metaphors), and gambling addiction (7 metaphors). Technology-related addictions were expressed by participants through the subtopics of technology and internet addiction (38 metaphors), social media addiction (13 metaphors), game and computer addiction (6 metaphors), screen addiction (4 metaphors), and phone addiction (3 metaphors). Under the Interpersonal relationship addiction theme, there were three subtopics: interpersonal relationship addiction (4 metaphors), relationship addiction (3 metaphors), and love addiction (1 metaphor). Money/consumption-related addictions were expressed through the subtopics of shopping addiction (6 metaphors), crypto addiction (1 metaphor), and fame and money addiction (1 metaphor). Food and drink addiction theme included subtopics of food addiction (4 metaphors), coffee addiction (1 metaphor), and chocolate addiction (1 metaphor).

According to the coding conducted by the researchers, it was observed that regardless of the selected addiction type, the used metaphors were clustered around certain concepts which were identified as themes. As shown in Table 2, a total of 193 metaphors included in the study were categorized into nine themes, which are captivity/helplessness (45), danger (27), deception (24), food/drink (20), other addictions (18), illness/deficiency (15), basic needs (10), human relationships (9), and admitting defeat (7). The distributions of these themes under the five main addiction types are presented in Table 2.

Table 2. Distribution of participants' selected metaphors by addiction types and themes

Theme	Addiction Type				
	Substance addiction	Technology-related addictions	Person-related addiction	Money/consumption addiction	Food addiction
Captivity/helplessness	20 (%20)	20 (%34)	1 (%13)	1 (%14)	2 (%67)
Danger	25 (%26)	3 (%5)	1 (%13)	-	-

continued on following page

Table 2. Continued

Theme	Addiction Type				
	Substance addiction	Technology-related addictions	Person-related addiction	Money/consumption addiction	Food addiction
Deception	11 (%11)	9 (%16)	1 (%13)	2 (%29)	1 (%33)
Food and Drink	9 (%9)	7 (%12)	1 (%13)	2 (%29)	-
Other addictions	4 (%4)	12 (%21)	1 (%13)	1 (%14)	-
Illness/deficiency	11 (%11)	3 (%5)	1 (%13)	-	-
Basic Needs	7 (%7)	2 (%3)	1 (%13)	-	-
Human Relationships	6 (%6)	2 (%3)	1 (%13)	-	-
Don't tempt fate	6 (%6)	-	-	1 (%14)	-

*The percentage in the table were calculated by taking into account the distribution of themes for each addiction type. For example, the 25 metaphors gathered under the *danger* theme, which is the most used for *addiction to addictive substances*, constitute 26% of the total number of metaphors used for this addiction type. There were also some metaphors that could not be classified under a specific theme are presented in the table such as wearing a white t-shirt, vacuum cleaner, the tape inside the cassettes.

Metaphor Contents

In this section, examples from different addiction types are given under each theme, with direct quotes from the participants.

Captivity/Helplessness

It is observed that the participants use metaphors such as captivity, swamp, prisoner, handcuffs, bottomless pit, etc. to express captivity and/or helplessness. Under this theme, the most commonly used concepts by the participants were found to be captivity, prison, and similar terms that imply losing one's freedom, not being able to do what one wants, or being compelled to do the same behaviors repeatedly (such as sharing posts on social media). Below are the expressions from the participants regarding these types of metaphors.

"*Alcohol addiction is like being imprisoned in jail. You cannot hold onto your own freedom. The mere thought of having control over it is already a fallacy. From beginning to end, you are under the captivity of financial, social, and economic responsibilities.*"*P16*

"*Phone addiction is similar to enslavement because it controls our brain and emotions. ...Young people try to get the attention they cannot see in real life through likes and comments on social media...unfortunately, by trying to share something new every day, they continue their enslavement.*" *P33*

Media Literacy

"Internet addiction is like being in prison. If internet addiction catches a person, it traps them between four walls, breaks off communication, distances them from the real world, restricts their lives in every field and makes them unhappy." P90

"Interpersonal relationship addiction is similar to being in prison because imprisoned individuals are referred to as convicts, and in interpersonal relationship addiction, you are a captive to the person you are addicted to." P114

"Social media addiction is similar to a handcuff. Because like a handcuff, it binds a person's hand and arm and restricts their life." P27

Some other metaphors that are gathered under the theme of captivity/helplessness are black hole, bottomless pit, and suicide. For example, P54, the black hole metaphor expresses the aspect of drug addiction that destroys the beauty around a person and leaves only darkness: *"Drug addiction is like a black hole because just as a black hole sucks in and destroys the shiny things around it, leaving only darkness behind, drug addiction destroys the good things around people and leaves extinguished lives."* Similarly, P38, the ivy metaphor expresses how drug addiction gradually makes a person helpless with the following statement: *"Drug addiction is like ivy because just as ivy wraps around a tree trunk and gradually withers its body, drugs also kill a person's body and soul over time."*

In P110, the bottomless pit metaphor is used to explain how food addiction is actually an attempt to fulfill some of a person's psychological needs: *"Food addiction is like a bottomless pit because no matter how much you eat, you can't fill the void inside you."* On the other hand, in P80, the same metaphor is used to explain how social media, with its appealing aspects, can lure people in and become an addiction: *"I think social media addiction is like a bottomless pit. Having content that appeals to every taste and thought affects people and draws them into its infinite depth like a bottomless well."* P80

P112 argues that the factor that increases addiction in gaming addiction is the desire to win, using the metaphor of *a swamp* that expresses helplessness:

"Gaming addiction is similar to a swamp. Because a swamp pulls people in and the more people struggle to get out, the more they sink. Games also draw people in, and as people get ambitious to win in games, they lose more and more, and may cause them to disconnect from social life."

P89 uses the metaphor of *a ball rolling downhill* to emphasize the importance of seeking professional help in ending the helplessness felt in addiction. In the following statement, he states:

"Alcohol addiction is similar to a ball rolling downhill. Just as an obstacle is needed to stop the ball, treatment is necessary to stop alcohol addiction."

Danger

Under the theme of danger, expressions using natural disaster metaphors for various addictions, such as *"alcohol addiction being like an earthquake because it always has destructive consequences and leaves behind sadness and damage"* P75, *"substance addiction being like a forest fire because it starts with a small spark and then burns down one's entire life"* P113, and *"technology addiction being like a forest fire because it slowly progresses and causes many long-term damages"* P43 are examined. Additionally, metaphors such as *black cloud, killer, thief, bomb,* and *runaway vehicle* are also explored under this theme. For instance, P103 uses *the thief* metaphor to describe the potential dangers for a substance addict as follows: *"Substance addiction is like a thief. Just as a thief who enters our home steals our material and spiritual values, substance addiction steals our health, time, and all beautiful and potentially beautiful things from our lives"*. Similarly, P75 uses the *virus* metaphor to discuss the potential dangers for a cigarette addict: *"Cigarette addiction is like a virus. The substances we take into our bodies with cigarettes spread to our brains and other organs. Over time, they kill the organs they reach. Just as a virus spreads in our body and harms other organs, smoking also harms our body"*. Similarly, P66 discusses the danger of smoking addiction and emphasizes that:

"Smoking addiction is like a bomb. Because both are harmful and lethal. At the same time, a bomb does not only harm a single person, it causes damage to more than one person when it is used.... Those in the immediate vicinity of the smoker become passive smokers.".

Furthermore, under the theme of *danger*, P79 states that *"substance addiction is like a double-edged sword; the more you use, the more harm you cause to yourself and those around you."* Using the parasite metaphor under the same theme, P145 describes the dangers of addiction as follows:

"Addiction is like a parasite because when the feelings and emotions towards others get out of control, it causes a person to lose their sense of self and self-esteem, leading to addiction."

Substance and Other Addictions

Some participants, when expressing different types of addiction, have chosen another type of addiction as a metaphor. For instance, participant P104, while describing *substance addiction*, used the following statements: *"Substance addiction is similar to food addiction because both result in an increase in dopamine secretion in the body upon consumption, which leads to a feeling of pleasure, and subsequently directs us towards substance consumption with the desire for more pleasure"*. According to the statements of participant P51: *"Technology addiction is similar to gambling because at first, you spend little time and enjoy it, thinking you are winning...You will not want to give up your technological devices, and even if you want to, you will not be able to, just like in gambling, where you will continuously lose with the hope of winning"*. Similarly: "Internet addiction is similar to alcohol. It intoxicates people like alcohol. Long hours spent on the internet can lock the brain like alcohol and can cause death" P75. In addition to these P71 expresses that the similarities between technology addiction and drug addiction are as follows:

"Technology addiction is similar to drugs because it causes individuals to lose consciousness, experience changes in behavior, and also leads to psychological and emotional changes, just like drugs... Individuals are slow to react to events around them and behave as if they were under the influence of drugs...When individuals are away from their devices or not online for a few hours, they need the happiness hormone, and if they cannot find it, they start to feel unhappy and aggressive."

Deception

Under the theme of deception, some metaphors examined include lying, burying one's head in the sand like an ostrich, and wearing a mask. According to P13, *"Gambling addiction is similar to the promises of a liar. It always contains a promise, but the guarantee of these promises is never certain."* P106 uses the same metaphor, stating that *"Alcohol addiction is like lying. Because lying and alcohol are ways for many people to escape reality."* P81 expresses the same situation with a different metaphor, stating that *"Alcohol addiction is similar to ostriches burying their heads in the sand when they sense danger. Because people start drinking alcohol when they see their troubles and problems as danger. In this way, they think they are hiding from their problems and getting away from them."* P65 uses the metaphor of ignorance to express that addiction is once again a deception against oneself with the following statement: *"Technology addiction is similar to ignorance because you think you know everything, but you don't know anything about what's around you."*

Another metaphor examined under the theme of deception is as follows: *"Social media addiction is like a needle injected into the mind. Although it seems to make you feel good, it constantly reminds people of their sense of worthlessness."* P15. Similarly, in the following statement where P17 uses *the metaphor of antidepressants*, emphasis is placed on the deceptive quality of addiction: *"Shopping addiction is similar to antidepressants. It seems good and beautiful, but its effect is temporary. Antidepressants affect emotions such as serotonin. Shopping addiction also affects these emotions, but it is not permanent in the long run and repeats itself like taking medication, leading to a cycle."*

P35 expresses the deceptive effect of addiction, likening it to hypnotic tools with the following statement:

"Technology addiction is similar to hypnotic tools because people enter a period of absent-mindedness and trance when they fall under its influence. In addition, they cannot consciously adapt to the flow of life."

According to P8, using the metaphor of *a climbing rose,* the deception of addiction can last longer and have more dangerous consequences:

"Love addiction is similar to a climbing rose. Just as people are deceived by the beauty and fragrance of a rose, they are deceived by the beauty of love, constantly feeling an infinite need for it and unable to let go. They want to constantly smell the rose, but eventually the thorns go deeper. It causes wounds that do not heal and eventually suffocates people."

According to P47, social media addiction contains deception towards those around us: *"Social Media Addiction is also similar to a mask. Because people are always happy in photos shared on social media. They put on a mask of happiness. There is an impression that everything is going well in life. But in reality, nobody has a perfect, flawless or happy life as people think."*

Disease

Under the metaphor of "disease," various metaphors such as tumor, rotten tooth, cancer, and OCD have been used. For example, the statement of P12 is, *"Alcohol addiction is similar to a tumor in the brain. Because even if it is difficult to realize, it will gradually start to kill the person."* P102 compares substance addiction to a rotten tooth, stating, *"Substance addiction is similar to a rotten tooth... if an*

Media Literacy

individual does not receive treatment before losing their mental health, they are doomed to lose their health, identity, and loved ones." P45 uses the same metaphor for tobacco addiction, saying, *"Tobacco addiction is like unbrushed teeth, because just as unbrushed teeth eventually darken and rot to the point of losing them, tobacco gradually darkens and rots our lungs from smoke, and ultimately we lose our lungs and then our lives."*

Regarding technology use, P9 states that it can be beneficial when used in a healthy manner, but it can have negative effects when it becomes an addiction, saying, *"Technology addiction is similar to unconscious antibiotic use. Because while the antibiotic is beneficial when used consciously and when necessary, it can have bad consequences when used excessively and unconsciously."*

Food and Drink

Some participants used food and drink-related metaphors such as fast food, seeds, and obesity to express different types of addictions. For example, P42 and P115 used different metaphors to describe similar situations related to internet and social media addiction. P115 said that *"internet addiction is like fast food because fast food is a food that makes you want to consume more and more as you eat it, and it creates addiction. Similarly, the more you use the internet, the more you want to use it."*. P42: *"Social media addiction is like a bowl of seeds... We always say that we're watching the last post, photo, or video, but we can't put our phone down."* Another participant used the seed metaphor to describe shopping addiction. P39 said that *"shopping addiction is like eating seeds because even though it may hurt your lips to keep eating seeds, you still find it hard to stop. Similarly, once you start shopping, it becomes difficult to stop, no matter how much financial damage it may cause"*.

Basic Needs

Under the theme of basic needs, metaphors related to breathing, oxygen, and withered trees were used. P46 and P67 used similar expressions for *oxygen* and *breathing* metaphors. P46 said that *"phone addiction is like oxygen because just as a person feels incomplete without their phone and searches for it everywhere, their breath is taken away until they find their phone, and they feel relieved once they have it"*. P67 compared social media addiction to breathing, saying that *"just as a person cannot live without breathing, social media addicts cannot live without using social media."*.

P31 used the *withered tree* metaphor to describe drug addiction, saying that a *"drug addict is like a withered tree because when a tree can't get the nutrients it needs, it eventually withers away. Similarly, when a person doesn't get what they need and instead takes something else, they start to lose their life functions and begin to wither away or die".*

Interpersonal relation addiction

The theme of interpersonal relationship addiction includes metaphors that are associated with various types of interpersonal relationship addictions, such as love, heartbreak, and toxic friendships. For example, in P19, *"smoking addiction is compared to a toxic friendship because, even though you are aware of the harm, you cannot quit immediately."*. In P55, the author uses the following expressions to describe heroin addiction: *"Heroin addiction is similar to heartbreak because when we are in love, we can find ourselves careless and devoid of judgment, ignoring our problems.*

Don't Tempt Fate

Some participants have used metaphors to express that individuals continue addiction, regardless of the type of addiction, by entering a negative cycle, sometimes even risking their harm. P69: *"Drug addiction is like a burning lifebuoy in the middle of an angry sea. The easiest way to escape is to cling to it, but even after being rescued, the burn scars will remain for a lifetime."*

"Drug addiction is similar to the death circle of ants, as ants follow the pheromones left behind by the ant in front of them. If the ant in front takes the wrong path and causes a circle, they will enter a cycle that only leads to death. Here, the ant in front represents the drug that is addictive, the ant behind represents the addicted person, the pheromone represents the reason for the person's attachment, and the resulting death circle represents the ruined life that the addicted person does not notice." P109.

"Crypto addiction is similar to cutting the branch one sits on. They put their money at stake for an uncertain job, and spend their invaluable time on it..." P60

DISCUSSION

The undeniable power of the media has become even more pronounced and difficult to control with the advent of the internet, particularly social media. The heavy participation of young people in social media channels can manifest in various difficulties related to their psychological well-being, social circles, family, and educational experiences (Wesner and Miller, 2008). The effects of media on individuals' direction and the excessive use of social media driven by young people's natural need for friendship result in health and addiction-related problems among children,

Media Literacy

adolescents, and emerging adults (O'Keeffe & Clarke-Pearson, 2011). Studies on media content have revealed that high school and university-level students have a high level of interest in video content containing tobacco, alcohol, and e-cigarettes (Cranwell et al., 2016; Huang et al., 2016).

Media platforms that allow individuals to participate online, such as Facebook, YouTube, and Instagram, provide rapid and uncontrolled access to personal social environments, and exposure to elements of addiction in their content, which brings the importance of media addiction to the agenda (Raacke & Bonds-Raacke, 2008). The need for internet use and satisfaction is one of the alleged causes of online addiction (Chou & Hsiao, 2000). For viewers of media channels and users of other entertainment environments, these platforms can be inclusive in terms of providing passive access to addictions such as sex, shopping, eating and drinking, substance abuse, and tobacco use, in addition to providing entertainment. Both content creation and viewing activities can reveal psychological and interpersonal satisfaction associated with addiction that can lead to addiction for a small minority (Balakrishnan & Griffiths, 2017). Participants did not directly provide metaphors regarding online addiction. Although online internet addiction is not classified directly in the ICD-10 or DSM-5 classifications of mental disorders, games and social media applications where online conversations are frequently conducted reveal addiction risks. It is known that the criteria for game addiction were first established in DSM-5 and ICD-11, and it is now accepted as an addiction group. Similarly, the definition and criteria of social network addiction are also included in scientific publications (Carbonell & Panova, 2017; Dalvi-Esfahani et al., 2019). In studies, it has been observed that the percentage of participants who spend more than 3.5 hours on social media is quite high among young people who are prone to online relationship addiction and addiction. Some of the content in the media is observed through online channels. Therefore, it can be said that participants use indirect observations and metaphors regarding online relationship and communication addiction. Given the increasing online interactions, expanding the scope of media literacy courses is an important need.

Upon examining the metaphors provided by the participants in this study, it is notable that there were addiction types not mentioned by the students despite being present in the literature. The lack of attention given by the participants to these addiction types could be attributed to their relatively low prevalence in the media, absence from the media content followed by the participants, or the fact that certain addiction types were more salient in the media content consumed by the participants. It is also possible that the participants' potential lack of knowledge about addiction could have influenced this observation.

In addition to the addiction types mentioned in the literature and specified in the DSM diagnostic criteria, it is observed that the participants in the study have defined different addiction types (such as ambition addiction, interpersonal relationship addiction, custom addiction, fame addiction, etc.). This situation suggests that there are some misconceptions about addiction concepts. Although some concepts are not an addiction in themselves, they can play an important role in various addictions. For example, while ambition is not an addiction, studies show that individuals with substance abuse experience loss of energy and ambition (Şener et al., 2018). Gaming addiction is also a type of addiction that includes feelings of ambition and anger, and the belief that the person must win constantly (Yücel & Şan, 2018). It is emphasized that in individuals diagnosed with eating disorders and with addictions related to food, their ambitious behavior and feelings are higher compared to non-addicted individuals (Hamulu, 1999). These examples explain the behaviors that students observe under the name of ambition addiction in media channels to a significant extent. Another concept misconception in addiction types is seen in the expressions of person or relationship addiction. In the literature, the criteria for interpersonal relationship addiction explain these person and relationship addictions (Kupfer et al., 2008). In this case, students actually observe visual or auditory stimuli associated with interpersonal relationship addiction in the media.

One of the important points of the study is that all types of addiction, which are defined in the literature and whose diagnostic criteria are determined by international standards, have been observed by students in the media. This indicates that we are exposed to the concept of addiction and addiction types much more than we think. One of the most important things to be done to avoid the negative effects of this exposure is awareness-raising activities. Although the definition and boundaries of media literacy are specific, the concept is prone to misunderstandings and misconceptions. Media literacy aims not to separate or denigrate media and/or media content as good or bad, but to have a critical perspective on consumed media content and to direct individuals towards being conscious media consumers (Şahin, 2014). Therefore, it is important for educational institutions to offer media literacy courses. The inclusion of media literacy courses in universities highlights the necessity for developing digital literacy and promoting social awareness (Okela, 2022). Media channels can create infollution through various written and auditory stimuli, where addiction types can be intertwined. Media literacy is important both for increasing awareness about addiction and for consuming media consciously. Therefore, media literacy courses are considered important for teaching addiction types to students and enabling them to recognize misconceptions about addiction in the media.

LIMITATIONS AND RECOMMENDATIONS

This study was designed to reveal the perspectives of students who took media literacy courses on addiction types in the media. Since media literacy is not a compulsory course, the study was conducted with students who chose to take this course as an elective. To gain a broader perspective, similar studies could be conducted with students at different levels, faculties, and those who do not take this course. Given the frame effect, it is important to draw attention to the impact of the media on societal change. Therefore, in addition to this study, studies that relate students' perspectives on addiction to the media, taking into account the frame effect, will shed more light on the influence of the media.

Declaration of generative AI and AI-assisted technologies in the writing process

During the preparation of this work the author(s) used Deepl (https://www.deepl.com/tr/translator) in order to proof reeding. After using this tool/service, the author(s) reviewed and edited the content as needed and take(s) full responsibility for the content of the publication.

DECLARATION OF INTERESTS

The authors declare that they have no known competing financial interests or personal relationships that could have appeared to influence the work reported in this paper.

REFERENCES

Aydın, M. (2013). Beş yaklaşıma göre nitel araştırma ve araştırma deseni. In Bütün, M., & Demir, S. B. (Eds.), *Nitel araştırma yöntemleri- Beş Yaklaşıma Göre Nitel Araştırma ve Araştırma Deseni* (pp. 69–110). Siyasal Yayınevi.

Balakrishnan, J., & Griffiths, M. D. (2017). Social media addiction: What is the role of content in YouTube? *Journal of Behavioral Addictions*, 6(3), 364–377. 10.1556/2006.6.2017.05828914072

Buss, D. M. (2000). The evolution of happiness. *The American Psychologist*, 55(1), 15–23. 10.1037/0003-066X.55.1.1511392858

Carbonell, X., & Panova, T. A. (2017). Critical consideration of social networking sites' addiction potential. *Addiction Research and Theory*, 25(1), 48–57. 10.1080/16066359.2016.1197915

Chassin, L., Presson, C. C., Rose, J., & Sherman, S. J. (2007). What is addiction? Age-related differences in the meaning of addiction. *Drug and Alcohol Dependence*, 87(1), 30–38. 10.1016/j.drugalcdep.2006.07.00616930860

Chong, D., & Druckman, J. N. (2007). Framing theory. *Annual Review of Political Science*, 10(1), 103–126. 10.1146/annurev.polisci.10.072805.103054

Chou, C., & Hsiao, M. C. (2000). Internet addiction, usage, gratification, and pleasure experience: The Taiwan college students' case. *Computers & Education*, 35(1), 65–80. 10.1016/S0360-1315(00)00019-1

Cilesiz, S. (2011). A phenomenological approach to experiences with technology: Current state, promise, and future directions for research. *Educational Technology Research and Development*, 59(4), 487–510. 10.1007/s11423-010-9173-2

Cranwell, J., Opazo-Breton, M., & Britton, J. (2016). Adult and adolescent exposure to tobacco and alcohol content in contemporary YouTube music videos in Great Britain: A population estimate. *Journal of Epidemiology and Community Health*, 70(5), 488–492. 10.1136/jech-2015-20640226767404

Dalvi-Esfahani, M., Niknafs, A., Kuss, D. J., Nilashi, M., & Afrough, S. (2019). Social media addiction: Applying the DEMATEL approach. *Telematics and Informatics*, 43, 101250. 10.1016/j.tele.2019.101250

Eryılmaz, A., & Deniz, M. E. (2019). *Tüm yönleriyle bağımlılık* [Addiction in all its aspects]. Pegem Akademi. 10.14527/9786052418154

Gowing, L. R., Ali, R. L., Allsop, S., Marsden, J., Turf, E. E., West, R., & Witton, J. (2015). Global statistics on addictive behaviours: 2014 status report. *Addiction (Abingdon, England)*, 110(6), 904–919. 10.1111/add.1289925963869

Hamulu, F. (1999). Obezite komplikasyonları. [Complications of obesity] In Yılmaz, C. (Ed.), *Obezite ve tedavisi* [Obesity and treatment]. (pp. 152–157). Mart Matbaacılık.

Hellman, M. (2010). *Construing and defining the out of control. Addiction in the media 1968–2008*. Yliopistopaino.

Holden, C. (2001). 'Behavioral' addictions: Do they exist? *Science*, 294(5544), 980–982. 10.1126/science.294.5544.98011691967

Huang, J., Kornfield, R., & Emery, S. L. (2016). 100 million views of electronic cigarette YouTube videos and counting: Quantification, content evaluation, and engagement levels of videos. *Journal of Medical Internet Research*, 18(3), e67. 10.2196/jmir.426526993213

Kupfer, D. J., First, M. B., & Regier, D. E. (2002). *A research agenda for DSM–V*. American Psychiatric Association.

Lincoln, Y. S., & Guba, E. G. (1985). Naturalistic inquiry. *Sage (Atlanta, Ga.)*.

Marlatt, G. A., Curry, S., & Gordon, J. R. (1988). A longitudinal analysis of unaided smoking cessation. *Journal of Consulting and Clinical Psychology*, 56(5), 715–720. 10.1037/0022-006X.56.5.7153192787

McGinty, E. E., Kennedy-Hendricks, A., & Barry, C. L. (2019). Stigma of addiction in the media. *The stigma of addiction: An essential guide*, 201-214.

O'Keeffe, G. S., & Clarke-Pearson, K. (2011). The impact of social media on children, adolescents, and families. *Pediatrics*, 127(4), 800–804. 10.1542/peds.2011-005421444588

Okela, A. H. (2022). Egyptian University Students' Smartphone Addiction and their Digital Media Literacy Level. *The Journal of Media Literacy Education*, 15(1), 44–57. 10.23860/JMLE-2023-15-1-4

Pickard, H. (2020). Addiction and the self. *Noûs (Detroit, Mich.)*, 55(4), 737–761. 10.1111/nous.12328

Raacke, J., & Bonds-Raacke, J. (2008). MySpace and Facebook: Applying the uses and gratifications theory to exploring friend-networking sites. *Cyberpsychology & Behavior*, 11(2), 169–174. 10.1089/cpb.2007.005618422409

Şahin, A. (2014). *Eleştirel Medya Okuryazarlığı [Critical Media Literacy]*. Anı yayıncılık.

Salmassi, M. (2015, June). *Researchers Release First Report on Worldwide Addiction Statistics.* Partnership to End Addiction. https://drugfree.org/drug-and-alcohol-news/researchers-release-first-report-worldwide-addiction-statistics/

Scheufele, D. A., & Tewksbury, D. (2007). Framing, Agenda Setting, And Priming: The Evolution Of Three Media Effects Models. *Journal of Communication*, 57(1), 9–20. 10.1111/j.0021-9916.2007.00326.x

Sellman, D. (2010). The 10 most important things known about addiction. *Addiction (Abingdon, England)*, 105(1), 6–13. 10.1111/j.1360-0443.2009.02673.x19712126

Şener, D. K., Akkuş, D., Karaca, A., & Cangür, Ş. (2018). Lise öğrencilerinin madde kullanmama davranışlarını etkileyen faktörler [Factors Affecting Substance Non-Use Behaviors of High School Students]. *Addicta : the Turkish Journal on Addictions*, 5(3), 405–429.

Wesner, M. S., & Miller, T. (2008). Boomers and millennials have much in common. *Organization Development Journal*, 26(3), 89.

Wilterdink, N., & Form, W. (2024, May 18). *Social Change*. Britannica. https://www.britannica.com/topic/social-change/Patterns-of-social-change

Yıldırım, A. ve Şimşek H. (2006). *Sosyal bilimlerde nitel araştırma yöntemleri [Qualitative research methods in social sciences]*. Seçkin Yayıncılık.

Yücel, G., & Şan, Ş. (2018). Dijital Oyunlarda Bağımlılık ve Şiddet: Blue Whale Oyunu Üzerinde Bir İnceleme [Addiction and Violence in Digital Games: A Review on the Blue Whale Game]. *AJIT-e: Academic Journal of Information Technology*, 9(32), 87–100. 10.5824/1309-1581.2018.2.006.x

Zou, Z., Wang, H., d'Oleire Uquillas, F., Wang, X., Ding, J., & Chen, H. (2017). Definition of substance and non-substance addiction. *Substance and non-substance addiction*, 21-41. .10.1007/978-981-10-5562-1_2

Chapter 8
(Re)Imagining Worlds and Reality in Media

Jason D. DeHart
The University of Tennessee, Knoxville, USA

ABSTRACT

This chapter makes use of textual examples and description, as well as autoethnographic case study, to examine media storytelling and envisioning reality through storytelling. Attention is given to concepts of social justice, as well as implications for practice and further research. These implications include considerations of both text and readership, as well as explorations of criticality and notions of representation. A continued call for this kind of close reading of multiple texts and types of texts is central to the chapter.

INTRODUCTION

Imagining stories across media can allow for reconceiving notions of narration across ways of creating. This is certainly a fixture in form for fandom, as Jenkins (2017) has noted, and holds implications that will be explored in this chapter for readers and viewers. However, transmedia can have greater implications for social change and communicating ideas of social justice. This transmedial view of communicating and narrative practices links with students' daily lives as they engage with meaning-making across a variety of forms and modes of utterance (Scolari et al., 2019). Because of the links of both the textual and individual, the center of this chapter focuses on two examples from transmedia content, along with a case study example that draws from the author's experience. This use of autoethnographic case study links both the experience of the individual, as well as the constraints of a particular concept in keeping with the boundedness of case study methodology.

DOI: 10.4018/979-8-3693-3302-0.ch008

The merging of these methodological paradigms has a precedence in educational research (Kinchin & Francis, 2017). Njie and Asimiran (2014) have noted the role of boundedness, including the contextual nature of case study and the specificity of the focus of the case study. In this example, the author uses their first-hand experiences as a member of fandom since childhood to discuss the ways in which transmedia can be practiced, even in an environment where linking to a variety of texts was geographically and economically prohibited.

In terms of positionality, the author notes their identity as a White male from the Appalachian region, and this lens is useful in thinking about what is seen and unseen, as well as what is discovered, as media narratives come to be realized and experienced over time. The limitations of this view include the first-hand and emic perspective of the comments, stemming from a reader point of view.

This work focuses on the socially-framed and focused work that is done across media adaptations, and I draw upon Verrone's (2013) focus on adaptation theory to think about what is present and absent, as well as changed, in the adaptation process. The concept of social justice is hardly new, with President Franklin Delano Roosevelt using the term in one of his fireside chats from 1933. At this period in time, Roosevelt was addressing the need for social improvements – specifically, for encouraging economy stimulating measures that would increase prosperity for individuals in the United States. Given the time period, the reader can deduce that the intended audience for this address was much more limited. In more recent times, the concept of social justice has been applied to the rights of minoritized populations and to representations in media of a range of people and a host of experiences.

Duffy (2014) has foundationally noted the complications within the act of reading, marking the literacy process as one that is sophisticated and one which has many components. Uniting this idea of reading and viewing links with the work of authors like Sadoski and Paivio (2013), who note the presence of both logogens and imogens – word and image forms – as part of critical reading in a dual process. These notions of reading and interpretation of images are first steps in positioning encounters with text from a theoretical stance.

In a text I have used in my instruction with middle grades pre-service educators, Jewell and Durand (2020) noted how the use of "minority" can be reframed as "global majority," a term that denotes that more world-wide representation of individuals whose intersections of identity lead to their being labeled as on the margins of culture. Jewell and Durand (2020) used this term to further illustrate the sense of autonomy and empowerment that individuals and groups of people can and should feel, reducing any sense of shame in their being and cultural/social practices. In alignment with the textual perspective in this chapter, this book is presented in a multimodal fashion, with design elements, color/shade, illustrations, print, and guiding questions. It is both a theoretical and textual example of the probing I have in mind.

(Re)Imagining Worlds and Reality in Media

In keeping with the transmediality of this work, I adopt textual analysis from a young adult graphic novel, an adult graphic novel rendered in the dystopian genre, an autoethnographic case study (Franklin, 2019; Muncey, 2005), and theological/philosophical reflections to act as an ethical sense of underpinning.

REVIEW OF THE LITERATURE

Fairclough (2013) has considered the ways that relationships of power have been explored in language and the use of text, and Hobbs (2020) has examined the role of the reader in making sense of media. Both of these scholars point to the necessity of evaluating texts and the primary role of close reading and analysis for navigating a range of texts with a focus that extends beyond surface details and probes the deeper elements of meaning-making, like embedded messages and interactions.

Bezemer and Kress (2015) have further noted the ways that multimodal texts reposition relationships of power in classroom dynamics, allowing students to take the role of teacher as new types of texts are introduced and navigated. Adding to this sense of criticality, Banks (2006) has explored notions of representation, pointing to the use of accuracy and authenticity in media, and the value that emic voices bring to telling stories of communities and individuals, as well as larger social groups. These explorations include those which are conceived and shared problematically, as when a character is typecast as a villain or negative figure based on race, ethnicity, or some other aspect of identity. Tobin (2000) noted this view of film culture in study of the perceptions of young children. The question at heart here is how to critically engage with storytelling when exposure to problematic concepts begins at a young age – and what do educators do in order to problematize these limiting views of individuals and communities?

An aspect of the criticality and analysis that can be applied to texts includes the ways that characters and ideas are depicted and centered or decentralized in the narrative. Cover (2016) has explored this notion of representation in relation to video games, while Kirkpatrick and Scott (2015) examined representation in comics texts.

CULTURAL MARKERS WITH MULTIMODAL TEXTS

One of the most salient emphases in my courses has been the influence of multiculturalism on texts that can be read and shared in a classroom. I have only a limited framework, but texts support a means of peering into the lives of people who are not like me. I have grown in my ability to question texts and note authentic authorship from emic perspectives. Noting a reliance on both traditional texts and voices from

(Re)Imagining Worlds and Reality in Media

white male groups, I have worked with students to begin thinking about the ways in which texts act in conjunction with one another. Taking this approach meant that students could begin to see the aligned and oppositional, as well as complimentary and confrontational, ways in which texts related together (Ciecierski & Bintz, 2018). As a classroom teacher, I have also existed in this social and political dynamic of recognizing that there are not enough voices available and made accessible, and I have noted the ways even this level of accessibility is challenged at times by policies that seek to limit access to some books and, consequently, some experiences for young learners.

As film and graphic novels are major components of both my work and reading life, conversation began early in this course around how film can be used to disrupt bias and stereotypes, as well as share voices from minoritized communities (Champoux, 1999B). This was a new thread for me in terms of critical literacy, and one which I have hearkened to with more attention since then. The work stems from the writings of Hall (2020), including the ways in which words and signs are used to convey expressions of culture and identity across forms. The visual and verbal combination of films and comics can be rich sources for interrogating the presentation of individuals and communities, including questions of what is left out and what is accurate or inaccurate. From film exploration, I worked with students to examine multicultural examinations of additional types of texts, including graphic novels (Sun, 2017) and infographic responses (Bedard & Fuhrken, 2019). There is always the question, in addition to presence and absence, of how characters are portrayed in dramatic foil relationships, and how information is presented. Much can be linked between the use of informational text and fiction by means of critical literacy, even if these two ways of exploring ideas might seem completely disparate, depending on the approach and epistemology of the researcher and/or educator.

This work with texts and engagements was an extension of my continued linking of theory and practice, and an opportunity to expose students to a range of texts that they could use in instruction. From there, the next in the course was to hand this process over for further practice. This focus on what is relevant and possible in a classroom, or in dialogue with others, is a reverberating thread in my work.

I next connect these ideas through two examples of the ways that texts can link to world-building and critical approaches to reality/definitions of reality.

LINKED TEXT REALITIES ACROSS MEDIA

In the graphic novel *In Real Life* by Cory Doctorow and Jen Wang, the author and illustrator team use science fiction and the visual/verbal space of the graphic novel to imagine a world in which gaming is utilized as a means of enslaving child

(Re)Imagining Worlds and Reality in Media

workers for capital. In the story, the main character engages in gaming and fashions an alternative identity/avatar – this avatar, however, has a real-world connection.

In this case, the main character befriends a fellow player/avatar who is engaged in mining precious materials to be consumed in the game. In the introduction to the work, Doctorow (2014) notes the ways in which audiences take up games as trivial texts, but speaks to the economic considerations of gaming: "When you put economics and games together, you suddenly find yourself in the middle of a bunch of sticky, tough questions about politics and labor" (vii). Images on the introductory pages illustrate the use of inventory items that can be collected in games, acting as a symbol of what is to come in the story structure.

In the organized classroom space of the comics page, the presence of a monitor speaks to the notion of interlinking and networking (Doctorow & Wang, 2014, p. 6), and a subjective narrative view of the screen indicates the items being stored and added within a game space. The class is then interrupted by a speaker from a gaming company who identifies them as an organizer, stating: "I organize a guild online and I'm looking for a few of you chickens to join me" (p. 8). In wordless panels, the character/speaker, appropriately dressed in a shirt that reads "Game Over," turns on a monitor (Panel B, inset), turns out the lights (Panel C, inset), to the screen-washed faces of three youths in the class (Panel D, bottom).

In the next panel introducing the new page, the organizer/speaker is standing in front a projection with a colorful character in the center, and is noting the number of subscribers the game holds. On the same page, the speaker introduces their avatar (Panel B), and then invites responses from the audience to engage in a survey of those who are female and game, as well as those that play against other females. This contrasting result, illustrated through a series of ellipses in a word bubble, points to the perceived gender differences in gaming.

While the presentation of the gaming world to the class has overtones of positive goals, the resulting engagement the game leaves other problems for the main character to unpack. This element of the narrative points to the need for criticality across media, including the ways that groups are disenfranchised, and the ways that narratives can be framed to include certain aspects of information, while leaving others out.

By unpacking a text like this one, educators can invite students to imagine worlds and to consider issues and problems in contemporary society, including long-standing disparities, without adopting a confrontational or negative approach. This is work centered around text and is critical in nature, with the idea of positive dialogue and co-construction in mind. Such a dialogical approach is essential for quality literacy instruction (Stewart et al., 2019). For the meaningful nature of texts to be opened up, educators can engage in moments of conversation around characters and topics.

ENVISIONING A BETTER/DIFFERENT WORLD

At the same time that realities may bend and blend in some textual examples, I further note the ways that dystopian worlds are sometimes crafted and explored in prose, as well as in comics. Attention to literature that focuses on problems with society reached a highpoint of popularity in the early 2010s, following a readership engagement I noted with the *Twilight* series. To the time of this writing, my students have continually and readily engaged with dystopian stories and some of them continue to be fascinated with thinking about possibilities for the future.

In a recent class debate about Artificial Intelligence (AI), a group of students in my class discussed the possibilities and perils with advancing technology, noting elements of Asimov's *I, Robot*, and exploring the implications of these developments for society at large. Students pointed back to the implications of human involvement in technology, and further noted boundaries that could be established and questioned as part of the process. It might be worth noting that this class was composed on approximately twenty high school students.\

Pope explored a dystopian reality in which illicit activities were an essential part of much of daily life in *Heavy Liquid*. Pope uses reds and blacks to convey the nature of this world, and his main character operates in a sense of delirium. The linking of dystopian stories across both print and film-based media can be seen in *The Hunger Games* series, the *Divergent* series, and more. These transmedia stories continue to engage my students – one student recently commented that the 2014 film adaptation of *Divergent* is their study background sound, noting an affinity for one of the actors in the franchise.

While utopian ideals can be located in texts, there are often less positive explorations of what does not work in society, with characters caught in the crux of these systems and conflicting powers. Sometimes, the result is beneficial for the main character, and there are also instances where the consequences are experienced more heavily. In some cases not all visions of the future are positive, and Ames (2013) noted that these visions of reality have potential for engaging students who would otherwise not readily engage with political conversations and topics.

As a final source of analysis, I note the affordances of autoethnographic case study and comment on my use of transmedia as a reader. This close look at self is both an long-established research method (Muncey, 2005), and a source of data and analysis that can be useful for exploration and comparative/creative analysis (Franklin, 2019).

CASE STUDY: RETURNING TO A SENSE OF SELF

In previous work, I have noted my reluctance to line up my home reading practices with those I found in school, and how barriers sometimes arose. On this front, I note my fourth-grade math teacher who took up my "superhero city" drawing and told me I needed to do more math. Most of my storytelling life was relegated to hidden moments in the classroom, and of course to my reading and writing at home. It is no small wonder I wanted to stay home as much as possible and engage in this kind of interaction with text whenever I could.

Years later, I would find that my love of comics made its way into my teaching practices, alongside the tension I felt within school spaces. I made sure to put new comics on my shelf when I could, and they were frequently read. Now, I only wish I had done more with them, and this sentiment has been echoed by other educators I have interviewed who use graphic novels in the classroom.

So, I teach future teachers how to incorporate comics into the instruction with purpose and meaning, as I do with other texts. I embrace all texts for their possibilities and acknowledge the community, very likely the reader of this book, we share a similar affinity and belief in the complexity of comics.

Comic books were an indelible part of my journey in ways I never recognized in the moment, but continue to reflect on. When I was seven, I got very sick with double pneumonia and had to be hospitalized. My parents bought me my first comics. In conversations with my family, this moment still surfaces, particularly when I share some recent writing about comics and heroes. It was not long after this illness that I began dressing up as popular characters more and more, although some of this interaction with media began before my childhood illness.

It is through my interactions with comic book texts that I first forged a path toward engaged readership, and my responses to the medium took a variety of shapes from the beginning of my experience with the works. I continue to explore poetic and visual responses, as well as taking up parts of the comic book in my identity kit (Gee, 2013). In my work in research, I often turn to analyses of visual literature, as well as investigation of classroom practices revolving around the meaningful and intentional use of visual texts, including film and comic books.

These interests stem from the images and artifacts, the beliefs and practices, that I surrounded myself with as a child and that I continue to engage with. I draw on these stories, to some degree, to make sense of the world. Part of this is fandom, and part of this is the nostalgia of having once been an even more devoted fan. I also use elements of comic book lore to communicate about myself, and have done so since I was young. These are the fragments that form part of who I am, and which continue to shape me.

Popular characters were not only captured in costumed attire for play at home, but were also part of my daily assemblage of meaning and self as I attempted to convey to the outside world what I loved. It was actually, in all honesty, probably less an attempt at communication and more a reifying or meditative lingering on the stories I loved. I will note that this was my chosen clothing for a school picture, the one day a year in which a child has the opportunity to wear something that represents them (unless, of course, a parent or guardian makes the choice for them). In some of my school photographs, I am wearing button-up shirts that do not bear the marks of popular characters, but in cases like the one above, I chose to signify my belonging to fandom culture through this choice.

Because of my affinity, popular characters were part of daily discussion, and I drew them, dressed like them in costume and in spirit, and enacted their stories with toys. The artifacts I have gathered and share in this book attest to this interaction.

I returned again and again to the pages of books I loved and often took in the images first, with returns to reading for taking up individual words and narrative threads. I then viewed and reviewed narratives in animation and popular film, including comic book-related films. I find my own identity mirrored in this interaction; this transmedia story, including comic book adaptation, action figures, film, and clothing, reified and established my identity as a comic book reader.

I would be remiss if I were to leave out the fact that comic books also shaped my interactions in my middle grades classroom, and continue to shape my life as a university professor. When it comes to my use of visual texts, I attempt to illustrate how the medium can be drawn on with purpose, and my interactions in the middle grades classroom were focused on a sense of connection and world-building.

I continue to learn, continue to grow, and always want to point readers to comics as meaningful texts that can be instrumental in thinking about the world around us, as well as the spiritual world that lives in us and through us, and made possible by our community with each other and with systems of personal belief.

From both my textual considerations and autoethnographic reflection, I turn to a number of possible implications from this work.

READERSHIP DEFINITIONS

First, the sense of reader and the ways in which the term reader are defined shift and restructure when considering transmedia. Viewing and considering visual content becomes part of the act of readership, thereby resulting in a reframing of reader

(Re)Imagining Worlds and Reality in Media

as a composite action/interaction, combined with viewing. On the other hand, one might subsume viewing as an aspect of reading.

Divorcing reading from viewing might seem to be a traditional response to this problem, but the presence of hypertext and other forms of multimodal text problematizes this singular approach. Text is not a typographic monolith, nor has it arguably ever been. From cave paintings to illustrated primers for children, the use of images alongside the arrangement of letters has been an aspect of the reading process for some time.

ADAPTATIONS

The notions of adaptation translate into the permutations we find within belief systems, and the ways in which others in culture take them up for personal and/or political ends. Sometimes the flexibility of the narrative might be too much to bear the weight of the application, particularly when the essential message is lost in the name of an external agenda. Not only that, but the ways that the stories are enacted and retold in their original has been the focus of the synoptic problem. We have four accounts – three remarkably similar and one more distinct – of the Christological encounter with human history.

While debates have centered on the existence of a common source for the synoptic gospels, the focus of how these matters shape up for our lived and literacy-oriented perspective on theology has notable ties to the ways in which we encounter other narrative works. The presence of a "favorite" gospel can hardly be thought of in terms that are far-removed from a favorite character or favorite television show, or even an ideal dish of food. Rather than seeing the four gospels as a stream of history to be regarded, they are often treated as separate stories that sometimes contradict one another in the telling. Returning to the original language, there are noticeable differences among the configurations of these texts, with the complicated Koine Greek authorship of Luke and the relatively accessible language of John.

Yet, many see these adaptations to person, place, and audience as acceptable and flexible terms for encountering the documents. Meanwhile, a series of spurious gospels exist in which the character of God or the person of Jesus Christ is so removed from the narrative boundaries of what is acceptable that they have been deemed pseudepigrapha. What counts as canonical text is a question that characterizes the boundaries of faith communities, as well as a question that challenges the work of members of the reading community who seek a wider series of voices, but who are often reminded about the Essentialist voices to popular the reading curriculum.

What constitutes a false writing or record seems to run parallel to the ways in which we accept and decline invitations to engage with some adaptations. To be regarded as canonical, a set of ideas have to be kept in fidelity. In my own readership, I readily engaged with permutations of popular characters in the context of the Batman narrative. Yet, my boundaries were most readily met when it came to considerations of content. The death of the central character, in any permutation, left me with an overall negative experience of the text, even though I knew this was a splintered timeline, an alternative narrative, and that there was a dominant storyline that would continue in the mainstream market.

If the trust of reader/believer and writer/artist is broken, then the chain of communication is damaged and the writings are cast aside in favor of a narratology that more closely adheres to whatever constitutes regula – a set of ideas that may vary, depending on the faith/reading community that have assembled around a given set of texts or textual practices. This is the creed that is endemic to fandom, and the concept also relates the treatment of characters in film. Verrone's (2011) work speaks to the power of the cinematic revelation, and so we again return to the question of what counters as the dominant narrative, or preferred version. The narratives are ideally packaged and conceived for the audience represented by fandom, the insider group, and the flexibility of this narrative must, in some ways, regard the outsider or newcomer to the narrative.

NECESSARY STEPS IN CRITICALITY

In addition to considerations of readership and what reading means, the larger questions of power and political/social implications stem from the ways that issues are presented in texts. In Doctorow and Wang's work, the point is illustrated through the ways that particular games and interactions are marketed as inclusive, and yet are harmful to some vulnerable populations. The presentation of narratives and ideas across texts arguably complicate the need for criticality, as information is considered in multiple ways and can be designed to appear and appeal in particular forms to particular audiences.

On the other hand, further research might reframe and problematize the types of criticality that are necessary for engaging with particular texts. Each mode in a multimodal ensemble might present information with elements of design, but the ways in which readers (and viewers?) attempt to make meaning in these spaces might be a more unified endeavor, consisting of similar types of critical interaction across types of texts.

(Re)Imagining Worlds and Reality in Media

As I often mention to my students, just because a reader questions something that does not mean that the reader cannot at the same time agree with an aspect of the same message. On the other hand, majority agreement does not constitute a sound argument or justification. If an idea is strong enough to believe in, it stands to equal measure that the idea can be tested and questioned, evaluated and discussed, with the intention of building a sense of strength and a deeper understanding of the idea, or the development of a new, more nuanced idea.

This sense of ideological development might lead a reader to consider that their viewpoint is being disregarded, but this is hardly the goal. Telling a story across media can help readers visualize and experience both the history and the current resonance of an idea through a variety of multimodal communication systems. In a sense, this would be like exploring a phenomenon through one speaker as opposed to a surround-sound system of composition and comprehension. Ideological development might not mean discarding an idea; rather, such development might simply mean exploring a deeper nuance or a more complex and inclusive articulation of such an idea.

CONCLUSION

The ways in which realities are conceived of and probed can vary based on the textual application used, and educators might consider multiple types of texts in their instruction as means to share more fully-realized conceptions. Authors can make use of multiple means for communicating ideas, but the criticality which is necessary for readers to take up in considering messages is paramount.

As systems and methods proliferate for ways to share meaning and forge relationships and networks, educators can consider and reconsider the ways that texts are valued and shared, as well as composed. Additional attention can be given, both in terms of classroom practice and system-wide policy, for focusing on how meaning is made and how transformations occur across types of communication in media.

Furthermore, educators and educational systems can work to probe the ways that representation occurs in media and across media. In texts, we have the possibility for thinking about the world in terms of what is and what is possible, drawing on elements of both individual experiences and community interactions to fashion representations that are nuanced and thoughtful. The reader and learner's sense of criticality is always essential in order to maintain a proper alignment of actual and envisioned reality, and this is necessary and ethical work.

REFERENCES

Ames, M. (2013). Engaging" apolitical" adolescents: Analyzing the popularity and educational potential of dystopian literature post-9/11. *High School Journal*, 97(1), 3–20. 10.1353/hsj.2013.0023

Banks, J. A. (2006). *Race, culture, and education: The selected works of James A. Banks*. Routledge. 10.4324/9780203088586

Bedard, C., & Fuhrken, C. (2019). Deepening students' reading, responding, and reflecting on multicultural literature: It all started with" Brown Girl Dreaming. *English in Texas*, 49(1), 25–31.

Bezemer, J., & Kress, G. (2015). *Multimodality, learning and communication: A social semiotic frame*. Routledge. 10.4324/9781315687537

Champoux, J. E. (1999). Film as a teaching resource. *Journal of Management Inquiry*, 8(2), 206–217. 10.1177/105649269982016

Ciecierski, L. M., & Bintz, W. P. (2018). Tri-Texts: A potential next step for paired texts. *The Reading Teacher*, 71(4), 479–483. 10.1002/trtr.1649

Cover, R. (2016). Digital difference: Theorizing frameworks of bodies, representation and stereotypes in digital games. *Asia Pacific Media Educator*, 26(1), 4–16. 10.1177/1326365X16640322

Doctorow, C., & Wang, J. (2014). *In real life*. First Second.

Duffy, G. G. (2014). *Explaining reading: A resource for explicit teaching of the Common Core Standards*. Guilford Publications.

Fairclough, N. (2013). *Language and power*. Routledge. 10.4324/9781315838250

Franklin, J. (2019). The theatrical and the accidental academic: An autoethnographic case study. *Arts and Humanities in Higher Education*, 18(4), 281–295. 10.1177/1474022217731543

Gee, J. P. (2013). *The anti-education era: Creating smarter students through digital learning*. St. Martin's Press.

Hall, S. (2020). The work of representation. In *The applied theatre reader* (pp. 74–76). Routledge. 10.4324/9780429355363-15

Hobbs, R. (2020). *Mind over media: Propaganda education for a digital age*. WW Norton & Company.

Jenkins, H. (2017). Adaptation, extension, transmedia. *Literature. Film Quarterly*, 45(2).

Jewell, T., & Derand, A. (2020). *This book is anti-racist: 20 lessons on how to wake up, take action, and do the work.* Frances Lincoln Children's Books.

Kinchin, I. M., & Francis, R. A. (2017). Mapping pedagogic frailty in geography education: A framed autoethnographic case study. *Journal of Geography in Higher Education*, 41(1), 56–74. 10.1080/03098265.2016.1241988

Kirkpatrick, E., & Scott, S. (2015). Representation and diversity in comics studies. *Cinema Journal*, 55(1), 120–124. 10.1353/cj.2015.0064

Muncey, T. (2005). Doing autoethnography. *International Journal of Qualitative Methods*, 4(1), 69–86. 10.1177/160940690500400105

Njie, B., & Asimiran, S. (2014). Case study as a choice in qualitative methodology. *Journal of Research & Method in Education*, 4(3), 35–40. 10.9790/7388-04313540

Pope, P. (2019). (reprint). *Heavy liquid*. Image.

Sadoski, M., & Paivio, A. (2013). *Imagery and text: A dual coding theory of reading and writing*. Routledge. 10.4324/9780203801932

Scolari, C. A., Rodríguez, N. L., & Masanet, M. J. (2019). Transmedia Education. From the contents generated by the users to the contents generated by the students. *Revista Latina de Comunicación Social*, (74), 116–132. 10.4185/RLCS-2019-1324

Stewart, T. T., Coombs, D., Fecho, B., & Hawley, T. (2019). Embracing wobble: Exploring novice teachers' efforts to enact dialogic literacy instruction. *Journal of Adolescent & Adult Literacy*, 63(3), 289–297. 10.1002/jaal.978

Sun, L. (2017). Critical Encounters in a Middle School English Language Arts Classroom: Using Graphic Novels to Teach Critical Thinking & Reading for Peace Education. *Multicultural Education*, 25(1), 22–28.

Tobin, J. (2000). *Good guys don't wear gats": Children's talk about the media*. Teachers College Press.

Verrone, W. (2013). *Adaptation and avant-garde: Alternative perspectives on adaptation theory and practice*. Bloomsbury Academic.

KEY TERMS AND DEFINITIONS

Comic: A form which uses images and words in juxtaposition to tell a story, as well as grammatical features like word balloons, panels, and thought bubbles.

Film: In this case, any visual text which makes use of digital or tradition film technology, whether for entertainment or instructive purposes, and whether short or feature-length.

Multimodality: The use of multiple ways of communicating (modes, such as gestures, audio, image, and more) in combination to convey ideas.

Reading: A process of engaging with visual and verbal material to make meaning.

Representation: A term which is used in this chapter to catch ideas of identity as they are presented in media, as well as larger constructs of reality that are represented.

Text: In this chapter and author's work, any documented or published/disseminated means of communicating ideas, including but not limited to visual, auditory, or traditional print communications.

Transmedia: A term which is owed to Jenkins's research and which describes the phenomenon of stories, ideas, and/or characters that are shared across types of media and brands.

Chapter 9
"What Is Your Real Name?":
A Vignette on Malcolm X's 1963 City Desk Interview

Dennis Matt Stevenson
https://orcid.org/0009-0002-9581-7154
The University of Tennessee, Knoxville, USA

Joshua L. Kenna
The University of Tennessee, Knoxville, USA

ABSTRACT

The purpose of this chapter is to provide a vignette classroom discussion of the primary source YouTube video of Malcolm X's City Desk interview March 1963 with student reactions and teacher commentary taken from classroom experience. Malcolm X is a lynchpin for introducing divisions in Black activism concerning race, policing, and education occurring in 1963, continuing in legacy movements after 1963, and reemerging in the modern push for social justice. Malcolm X holds a place in our collective historical memory that is at the same time recognizable and often misrepresented. This goal for analyzing this specific source is to provide lesson planning of the Long Civil Rights Movement focusing on Malcolm X and his legacy through a detailed sample lesson based on the digital primary source interview of Malcolm X. The larger significance is to ensure secondary classrooms keep pace with history scholarship to illustrate distinct civil rights goals rather than presenting a monolithic Civil Rights Movement.

DOI: 10.4018/979-8-3693-3302-0.ch009

Copyright © 2024, IGI Global. Copying or distributing in print or electronic forms without written permission of IGI Global is prohibited.

"What Is Your Real Name?"

INTRODUCTION

During my sixteen years teaching United States History courses at both the undergraduate and secondary level, I would end class discussions of the Civil Rights Era with a question: "Whose legacy has had the more lasting impact on modern America, Martin Luther King Jr. (MLK) or Malcolm X?" Student responses typically were something like the following:

* MLK. because we have a MLK Holiday.
* MLK because, a simple search on Google or Wikipedia yields 21 national and several international memorials, statues, and parks named for him. This doesn't begin to scratch the surface on the number of streets and schools named for King.

- MLK because his message is one of hope, equality, and the dream of a better future for American race relations. This is just a better message than what Malcolm X offered.
- MLK because until this class, I really didn't know much about Malcolm X. Why didn't we learn this earlier?

This article seeks to address this last response and in so doing, confront the other student responses that consistently see MLK as the messianic figure for Civil Rights and Malcolm X as his opposite. This is done through a classroom vignette with teacher and student responses to the YouTube footage of Malcolm X's *City Desk* interview circa 1963 as an example for disrupting the monolithic view of a singular Civil Rights Movement (CRM). There are four rationales for selecting this interview from the dozens of interviews, speeches, and primary writings of Malcolm X. First, the timing of this interview demonstrates Malcolm X as a pioneer for the Black Power Movement (BPM) in America at a time that is typically discussed as the height of MLK's Non-Violence campaign. Second, this interview is conducted by White correspondents' which somewhat tempers the language and aggressive nature by which Malcolm X presents his case. Third, despite Malcolm modulating his revolutionary tenor, his message is consistent and clear in supporting a self-defense approach to civil activism. Finally, the topics addressed and the interactions in this video offer clear points for guided classroom analysis that encourage students to actively participate in critical media analysis.

Malcolm X appears as antithetical to MLK in mainstream media as well as primary and secondary classrooms, that is if he appears at all (NPR, Joseph, 2020). This misinterpretation stems from both Malcolm X's geographic focus, the North as opposed to the Jim Crow South, and philosophical messaging that called for separatism and self-defense for Black Americans. Whereas MLK has ascended into the collective historical memory of Americans forever frozen in time proclaiming,

"What Is Your Real Name?"

"I have a dream" (Hall, 2005; Rounds, 2020), Malcolm X is given relatively little contextualization beyond the statement "by any means necessary", particularly in early introductions to CRM (Bickford, 2015). This is a common narrative perpetuated in history classrooms where predominantly White teachers may be unfamiliar or uninterested in nuanced discussions of ongoing Civil Rights activism (Grace, 2023). Bettina Love (2019) echoes this sentiment in *We Want to Do More Than Survive* when she states, "In class we did not learn about Black people who resisted oppression outside of Dr. Martin Luther King Jr. and Rosa Parks. Their stories were diluted of any ideas of Black Power" (pp. 48). Princeton scholar Cornel West has referred to this as the "Santa-Clausification" of MLK, and by extension, a Civil Rights movement (West, 1999 and Rounds, 2022).

This issue is echoed in state social studies standards across the United States. Malcolm X is identified in the standards for thirteen states, all of which are at the secondary level and many using Malcolm X as a suggested topic, not a requirement. Meanwhile, twenty-three states standards as well as Washington D.C. explicitly list MLK, including many at the elementary level. The National Council for the Social Studies Standards (NCSS), Advanced Placement (AP) and International Baccalaureate (IB) curriculum ask students to "compare and contrast" Malcolm X and MLK's philosophies (National History Standards); however, this rarely translates to non-college level courses. The suggestion is that Malcolm X, and by extension classroom engagement with diverse and divided Civil Rights activism, is too advanced for the average student and perhaps even the average general educator.

Traditional interpretations place CRM in the mid-1950s to mid-1960s as distinct from BPM of the late 1960s through mid-1970s (Lawson, 1991). CRM pedagogy typically matches top-down reform with grassroots activism such as the dual events of the Supreme Court decision *Brown v. Board of Education* in 1954 and the Montgomery Bus Boycott that began in 1955, the March on Washington in August 1963 that rallied support for the 1964 Civil Rights Act, and the 1965 March on Selma links to the 1965 Voting Rights Act. This back-and-forth interplay between organized activism and federal action places MLK and Rosa Parks as the central figures of the CRM. There is acknowledgement that many figures and organizations supported the national struggle with local civil rights activism throughout that period; however, this is overshadowed by the hero-worship of individual leaders confined to activism in the South inspiring federal legislation with explicitly civic over economic objectives (Hall, 2005, pp. 1234). CRM ends with the assassination of MLK in 1968, giving way to BPM as a distinct and therefore reactionary historical development lumped in with discussions on the Vietnam War and student rebellions.

The argument for BPM as historically distinct from the CRM is based on the more revolutionary rhetoric and actions of the BPM that center around racial pride, economic empowerment, and political and cultural institutions more associated to the urban North and West (Hall, 2005, pp. 1251). Like earlier CRM, BPM is taught via examination of specific leaders in the movement such as Stokely Carmichael, Huey Newton, and Louis Farrakhan. The assertion is that the CRM transformed into BPM because of perceived failures for national legislative initiatives to address cultural and economic racism (see Hall, 2005, Theoharis & Woodward, 2003). Critics of this framework emerge in recent scholarship as historians have been more apt to link these eras as conjoined parts of the Long Civil Rights Movement or simply the Long Movement (LM) (Rounds, 2020; West, 1999). LM consists of four propositions of reevaluation: *Locality*, *Reperiodization*, *Continuity*, and *The South* (Cha-Jua & Lang, 2007). First, *Locality*, CRM and BPM are not singular, national movements; rather, they are a collection of local struggles. Second, *Reperiodization*, CRM and BPM both emerge well before 1954 and continue well after 1975. Third, *Continuity*, CRM and BPM are connected as part of a historical process for black freedom, liberation, and the global human rights movements.

Finally, *The South*, LM creates a framework to view racial oppression as a nationwide issue and The South is not a distinct area for activism. Moreover, LM advocates argue that the South's *de jure* and the North's *de facto* racial oppression are a continuity of race-based policy that emerging in tandem in the decades following emancipation. This contrasts with traditional interpretations that see the North being distinct from the South. Although not every scholar adheres to the LM (see Cha-Jua & Lang, 2007), there has been a growing trend to interweave the CRM and the BPM in academic discussions. Exhibits at the National Civil Rights Museum in Memphis weaves the Black Power and Black Pride movement into the CRM; however, within the traditional K-12 school curriculum there is relatively little attention given to BPM at all when compared to attention given to MLK and the early CRM, let alone a discussion of an LM alternative to traditional CRM pedagogy. One of the key breaking points with traditional CRM teaching is the failure to sufficiently address the importance of Malcolm X to BPM prior to his death in 1965 (Clabough & Bickell, Feb 2020 pp. 320; NARA; NMAM Smithsonian).

Historiography has shifted toward LM interpretations; therefore, secondary classrooms must keep pace. By highlighting early divisions in the civil rights leadership, we bring much needed attention to the human centered experiences to social justice movements. Malcolm X is a lynchpin in classroom discussions for introducing division in the goals of Black activism concerning race, policing, and education up to 1963, continuing in legacy movements after 1963, and reemerging in the modern push for social justice. Malcolm X holds a place in our collective historical memory that is at the same time recognizable, yet misrepresented. The goal is for teachers to address this issue by including a greater set of lessons around and about Malcolm X and his ideologies. This requires an evaluation of state standards and the gaps that exist in national education initiatives.

"What Is Your Real Name?"

Civil Rights Social Studies in the Hands of States

The United States public education system is a convoluted web of state bureaucracies constantly struggling with national initiatives and with each other. This is made clear when examining state standards for social studies education. The reason is that no national curriculum required by law is enforceable in state-level departments of education; therefore, social studies standards are determined by state legislatures. The National Council for the Social Studies (NCSS) provides the following recommendation:

The introduction of standards-based instruction ushered in a movement to clearly articulate the academic outcomes for students across the curriculum.... Adopted standards have become the driving force of instructional programs by informing instructional practices in the classroom, curriculum frameworks, textbooks and other instructional materials, and assessment items and protocols. Therefore, the development of standards should be treated as a serious matter by engaging a collective audience of educational stakeholders in a deliberate, transparent process of development, revision, and adoption (NCSS Position Statement – State and Local Standards https://www.socialstudies.org/position-statements/developing-state-and-local-social-studies-standardsaccessed3/4/2024).

This statement encourages more regulation and standardization that involves education stakeholders (teachers, administrators, parents, and students); however, the language is couched in a tone that is intended to convince, not dictate. The result of this pleading becomes clear when comparing state standards adopted for social studies.

Some of the most extensive social studies standards in terms of specific detail and length exist in Washington D.C. (158 pages) and Massachusetts (217 pages). They include detailed instructions for content to be included at each grade level with specific course topics, names, and analytical concepts. These standards come closest to matching the NCSS purpose statement to provide diverse perspectives and foster awareness for citizenship (https://osse.dc.gov/sites/default/files/dc/sites/osse/page_content/attachments/Adopted%20Standards.pdf and https://www.doe.mass.edu/frameworks/hss/2018-12.pdf accessed 3/4/2024). By comparison, Alaska devotes only ten pages to history content, two pages to geography, and three to government and civics (https://education.alaska.gov/standards accessed 3/4/2024). Is this to say that Alaska, as a state, does not value social studies education or does this suggest that Alaska has more faith in educators and that the state does not feel the need to dictate instruction through extensive regulation?

Examining state standards for social studies becomes more peculiar when regional intricacies are noted. For example, Hawaii is the only state, with the exception of Washington D.C., that specifically mentioned Queen Liliuokalani (http://165.248.107.74/hcpsv3/files/final_hcpsiii_socialstudies_librarydocs_1.pdf, pp. 97). Is this to suggest that the overthrow of the Hawaiian monarchy by American colonizers should be considered local history? Wyoming, in much the same way, has a much more extensive list of Lakota activists than any other state, yet this comes by sacrificing a broader view on the American Civil Rights era. The only reference to CRM in the Wyoming state standards comes at the end of 5th grade in which MLK, Sacagawea, and Helen Keller are inexplicably lumped together in a single standard (https://edu.wyoming.gov/downloads/standards/2018/Social-Studies-Standards.pdf, pp. 16).

Some of the most extensive state standards on the Civil Rights Era are in the Deep South. Tennessee, Mississippi, Florida, and Alabama all require some form of Civil Rights education starting in elementary grades and growing in complexity through middle and high schools. Tennessee brings up Civil Rights education in 5th grade directly referencing MLK, Freedom Rides, and the Civil Rights Act of 1964 (Tennessee Social Standard 5.24 and 5.25 https://www.tn.gov/content/dam/tn/education/standards/ss/Social_Studies_Standards.pdf.) Tennessee state standards appear to recognize the importance the NCSS places on elementary social studies:

The purpose of elementary school social studies is to enable students to understand, participate in, and make informed decisions about their world. Social studies content allows young learners to explain relationships with other people, to institutions, and to the environment, and equips them with knowledge and understanding of the past... The "expanding horizons" curriculum model of self, family, community, state, and nation is insufficient for today's young learners. Elementary social studies should include civic engagement, as well as knowledge from the core content areas of civics, economics, geography, and history (NCSS Positionality Statement pg. 1 https://www.socialstudies.org/system/files/publications/articles/yl_220131.pdf accessed 3/4/2024)

An argument could be made that the purpose of such extensive attention to Civil Rights topics in the social studies standards of Deep South states is because of the regional impact of the 1950s and 1960s Civil Rights Era. An alternative interpretation is that the standards exist to combat ongoing resistance, either through commission or omission, to equitable education from White educators in Southern public-school systems. This perspective is gaining strength among researchers of teacher preparation programs at Primarily White Institutions (PWIs) and their lack of race-based equity instruction. This suggestion is backed by education research. Kristen Duncan (2021) conducted a qualitative research project in the Deep South involving black social studies teacher experiences in utilizing Critical Race pedagogy in secondary classrooms. This narrative study focused on connecting life experiences with teacher practices. The findings consistently demonstrated a failure of teacher training programs to highlight the need for racial justice education; therefore, Black teachers drew on lived experiences rather than their teacher education program for course content; moreover, Black teacher participants commented that their motivations for entering the education field were partially based in the lack of Black representation in the classroom. The cases discussed in Duncan's article show a disconnect in the attitudes of race topics between these Black teachers and the system of teacher education experienced in PWIs. Duncan states:

> *There is very little research focusing on how Black teachers come to engage in racial justice-oriented teaching, and even less that provides insight into how Black teachers perceive teacher education programs at predominantly White institutions (PWIs). This study sheds light on when, where and how Black teachers learn to teach with racial justice aims, and it also illuminates the experiences of Black teachers in PWI teacher education programs. (pp. 201)*

This gap in research and the accompanying discourse in academic circles surrounding teacher preparation programs flies in the face of the NCSS stated position on racial literacy:

> *It is a process of learning to understand how race is a function of power in the United States and that race, while central, remains interdependent with other sociopolitical elements such as gender, class, sexuality, and geography. Within educational contexts, racial literacy has been explored through literacy education to examine how students learn about race and racism and how teachers make pedagogical choices about curriculum and discussion topics based on their racial literacy skills. (NCSS Position Statement – Racial Literacy https://www.socialstudies.org/position-statements/racial-literacy)*

Using Video as a Primary Source: Strategies and Preparation Using the Russell Method

There is an imbalance of state standards and PWI teacher training programs to address ongoing CRM or to contextualize BPM of the 1950s and 1960s. As a small step in correcting these issues, I offer the following primary source analysis of a Malcolm X interview. This is based on a classroom lesson I utilized that demonstrates BPM prior to the 1964 Civil Rights Act and in conjunction with, rather than in opposition to, the works of MLK and CRM in the South. This primary source discussion is not a comprehensive look at the career of Malcolm X, the importance or overall legacy of the Nation of Islam (NOI), nor is this intended as a demonstration of LM historiography; rather, analysis of a visual and audio document from 1963, a year most associated with MLK's leadership in Birmingham and the March on Washington, is a starting point for recognizing diversity of LM language, goals, and audiences.

The focus of this lesson utilizes a primary source interview that took place March 17, 1963 on the Chicago television show City Desk. The full interview was 28 minutes (link - https://www.youtube.com/watch?v=yq-Q-omi3U8); however, for the purpose of this lesson we will use a truncated version that is 9 minutes and 42 seconds (link - https://www.youtube.com/watch?v=9yn0HKPmXhA) The important theme that emerges from this video is the focus on various civil rights issues as they pertain to the North and West rather than the South. Moreover, keep in mind that the intended audience for Malcolm X is mostly lower-socio economic class black men, particularly in urban areas. Even in this interview, where the interviewees are all White, Malcolm X's message consistently addresses issues of poor urban Black Americans. This demographic would experience much higher rates of police violence, food and housing insecurity, and long terms incarceration rates than the middle-class audiences targeted by MLK in his speech 5 months later in Washington D.C.

Video clips of primary sources such as this Malcolm X interview can be utilized as an aid to develop interpretive skills, demonstrate historiography, provide multiple perspectives on a particular historical topic, depict historical atmosphere, or create empathy for a historical period and characters (Marcus, 2010). Regardless of how a film is used as a tool for instruction, there needs to be intentionality and clear purpose. Just like any lesson planning in a social studies classroom, there needs to be explicit methods by which film will facilitate engagement and stimulate academic discourse (Russell, 2017). It is worth taking a brief aside to address the use of video clips as primary sources in the classroom. The Russell method is a simple, yet effective method of planning for lessons based on video clips and ensuring their effective use (Russell, 2017). The four stages of the Russell Method are:

1. The Preparation Stage: This is laying out what exactly needs to be done with this primary interview video clip. Teachers must consider questions: What are the curriculum and lesson standards to which this is contributing? What instructional methods will be utilized ahead of time before we get to the video interview? Much of the preparation stage is going to be more traditional lectures, class discussions, or projects culminating in the use of this clip to supplement existing knowledge. Alternatively, this short clip can be a potential "hook" for introducing content.

"What Is Your Real Name?"

2. The Previewing Stage: Here the teacher views the interview clip outside of the classroom to assess what exactly is wanted from this exercise. The next step is discussing expectations with students in the class before the interview is shown. Questions teachers must consider and pose to their students include: What are students looking for in this clip? What might they expect from this clip? What course content or specific learning goals are supplemented. Teachers should not show a video clip in class, even a primary source, that has not been previewed first.
3. The Watching Stage: During the watching stage, teachers again consider practical questions: When is the viewing of this clip going to take place - in class or asynchronously? How will students have access to this clip? Watching the clip needs to be an active process. Putting on the interview and expecting it to speak for itself without analysis is equivalent to expecting students to read the textbook quietly, a practice that is rarely effective for learning gains in a survey-level classroom (Monte-Sano, 2008. Also see https://teachwithmovies.org/copyright-for-using-movies-in-the-classroom/).
4. The Post Viewing Stage: This is the discussion and assessment of what was seen. A guideline is to prepare a post-viewing discussion equal to the time spent watching a film. During the preparation stage, teachers consider the amount of time that can be devoted to a particular topic. The watching stage may be just as effective when utilizing short clips rather than an entire film. For this lesson we are utilizing a clip that is just short of 10 minutes, which is potentially the basis of a discussion that may take a full 50-minute class period.

Historical Context

Like all history lessons, a discussion of context is necessary prior to introducing the primary source video clip. Below are some key questions and points to provide to students. Teachers could provide a brief lecture or handout. Note that it is not a comprehensive list, but rather highlights to contextualizing this interview. This is part of the pre-viewing phase of analysis.

- At what stage is Malcolm X's career at the time of this interview (March 1963)?

    o The Nation of Islam has gained national recognition. Malcolm X as a spokesperson has been successful in bringing awareness to the need for BPM in Northern America urban centers.

"What Is Your Real Name?"

- o Malcolm X has not yet founded his own Organization for Afro-American Unity, nor has his public break with Elijah Muhammad occurred. At this point, he is firmly Muhammad's disciple.

- What CRM events had occurred by the time of this interview?

    - o Brown v. Board (1954)
    - o Emmett Till lynching (1955)
    - o Rosa Parks arrest and the Montgomery Bus Boycott (1955)
    - o Johnson X assault (1957)
    - o Little Rock Nine integrate Central High School (1957)
    - o Greensboro Woolworths sit-in (1960)
    - o Muhammad Ali (still known as Cassius Clay), accepts Malcolm X as his spiritual mentor (1962)

- What has not yet occurred?

    - o MLK Birmingham campaign (April 1963)
    - o MLK "I Have a Dream" speech (August 1963)
    - o 16th Street Baptist Church bombing by KKK in Birmingham (September 1963)
    - o Assassination of John F. Kennedy and the ascendance of Lyndon Johnson (November 1963)
    - o Muhammad Ali publicizes his membership in NOI (1964).
    - o 1964 Civil Rights Act and the 1965 Voting Rights Act
    - o American full military intervention into Vietnam (1965)
    - o Watts Riots/Protests (1965)
    - o Formation of the Black Panther Party (1966)

Analyzing the Primary Source Interview Video Clip

Next, a teacher should move to the viewing phase of the interview. Below is a vignette to showcase how a teacher might choose to handle the analysis of the primary source video clip. This includes brief descriptions of select timeframes of the video clip with timestamps in parentheses. Under each description is a selected

"What Is Your Real Name?"

transcript of the video clip; again, with time stamps, before offering sample questions and example responses received from students. Note that the student response examples are meant to illustrate interpretive intent rather than direct quotations. At times these interpretations are contradictory or even misinterpretations. It is up to the teacher to determine the direction of this lesson and be ready to respond to student reactions to Malcolm X's messaging.

Opening of the Interview (0:00 to 3:40): The opening portion of this video begins with a series of questions about Malcolm X's name. The main interviewer is Len O'Connor, the longtime host of City Desk. O'Connor attempts multiple times to get Malcolm X to say the name that is on record, which is the family name Little, as well as identify Elijah Muhammad's legal name, Poole. Malcolm will not comply. The first eight second play out as such:

- **O'Connor**: "What is your real name?"
- **Malcolm**: "Malcolm. Malcolm X."
- **O'Connor**: "Is that your legal name?"
- **Malcolm**: "As far as I'm concerned it's my legal name."

Immediately we have the set up for a break between interviewer and interviewee. O'Connor is asking for a name recorded on legal documents and monitored by state authority. By rejecting that name, Malcolm rejects the premise that state actors have the authority to make that determination. This questioning continues as O'Connor asks what is essentially the same question in multiple ways. Malcolm refuses to play along. Moreover, he clearly and definitively explains his logic that the family name that is on record is associated with slavery because it is a White or Caucasian name. At the 1:18 mark O'Connor shifts his approach, but in a way that in Malcolm's view is the same question.

- **O'Connor**: Would you mind telling me what your father's last name was?
- **Malcolm**: My father didn't know his last name. My father got his last name from his grandfather who got it from his grandfather who got it from the slave master. The real names of our people were destroyed during slavery.

This questioning about Malcolm's family name continues to the 2:01 mark. Already, it is becoming clear that this interview, despite the polite language and respectful demeanor, is one of opposing worldviews. Students often pick up on this form of questioning as a mechanism to bait Malcolm X into saying something that would discredit his stance like acknowledging that he made up his new name or that his family name had legitimacy before he made the arbitrary decision to abandon it; however, Malcolm is not taking this bait. This section ends when Malcolm states

"We refuse, we reject that name.... I never acknowledge it whatsoever" (1:50-2:01). At this point, the interview turns to a discussion of Elijah Muhammad. After briefly asking on Muhammad's health and its impact on recent NOI activities, interviewer O'Connor returns to the question of names.

- **O'Connor**: It is a matter of record that Muhammad's last name was Poole, Elijah Poole (There is a brief back and forth before the reply).
- **Malcolm**: That's not his name (2:48-3:40).

For three and a half minutes, this interview focuses on names. This is a good point to stop and consider what has happened. Again, we provide some example questions and a vignette of student responses. This is not a comprehensive list of what can be expected; rather it is a guideline for preparing a more in-depth discussion.

- **Teacher:** Why does O'Connor keep asking about last names?

    o **Student 1:** He is ignorant of the importance of names in this context and is genuinely confused. He keeps asking to better understand where Malcolm is coming from.
    o **Student 2:** He is trying to clarify for the audience how important names are to the NOI (both to Malcolm X and Elijah Muhammad) and keeps asking to get this point across to White America.
    o **Student 3:** He thinks Malcolm is being stubborn and this form of questioning is meant to illustrate that to the audience. By repeatedly interrogating his name as an untruth, he is tacitly framing a different interpretation as fact and painting Malcolm as untrustworthy
    o **Student 4:** He is trying to trap Malcolm into saying something that shows he does not really believe his adopted name is truly valid and instead is making a show of abandoning his family name.
    o **Student 5:** By not only referencing family names rejected by the NOI, but also the matter of record, O'Connor is demonstrating his connection and faith in the system. In his view, the court and government records supersede personal whims when it comes to names. The questions then are about defending this worldview which is in opposition to the NOI stance.

- **Teacher:** What do you make of Malcolm's initial response in which he says that his family name is a "White" or "Caucasian" name that he rejects?

"What Is Your Real Name?"

- o **Student 1:** He has a point and gives plausible reasoning by saying Murphy, Jones, Smith, Powell, and Bunch (therefore also his name "Little" which remains unsaid by either party) are names associated with Irish or British backgrounds and therefore he is right to want a name that more accurately reflects his identity.
- o **Student 2:** His explanation is something he has clearly given multiple times and he was prepared to launch into this soliloquy (tirade?) when the predictable provocation occurred. Everything that happens over the next few minutes is nullified and shows that O'Connor is the one being stubborn.
- o **Student 3:** His perspective and bias become clear with these statements, particularly when he compares this to a "Chinese" or a "Yellow man" having an Irish name. This is an intentionally aggressive response that matches the hostile tone set by the interviewer.
- o **Student 4:** Malcolm is racist in his own right in not considering the possibility of consensual relationships or marriages that may occur and result in inter-ethnic exchange of names.

- **Teacher:** What is the significance of Malcolm's use of specific racial language such as "White" and "Caucasian", "Chinese" and "Yellow" in connection to his use of the phrase "so-called Negro"?

- o **Student 1:** Malcolm and the NOI are working to redefine what Black means in the 1960s context. The term "African American" or even "Afro-American" is not yet in common use; however, the use of Negro or even more derogatory terms is no longer acceptable according to the NOI.
- o **Student 2:** Malcolm is a hypocrite in rejecting "Negro" yet using the term "Yellow", an equally offensive term even by 1960s standards. The terms "White" and "Caucasian" are used mostly in pejorative terms.
- o **Student 3:** Malcolm sees the world purely in racial terms at least in this portion of the interview. Words are a battleground of identity in defining racial pride.

Elijah Muhammad Discussion (3:40-7:31): This section shifts the questioning to the role of Elijah Muhammad as a leader of the NOI. There is a brief interchange in which O'Connor refers to Muhammad by the wrong religious title multiple times. Malcolm corrects the record, but again, only on his terms (3:40 to 4:30)

- **O'Connor**: When did he [Muhammad] become, what he proports to be in your literature, the son of Allah?
- **Malcolm**: I've never heard the honorable Elijah Muhammad referred to as the "son of Allah".
- **O'Connor**: The prophet of Allah.
- **Malcolm**: I've never heard of him referred to as the "prophet of Allah."
- **O'Connor**: What do you refer to him as.
- **Malcolm**: Messenger of Allah…. A prophet is someone who is predicting the future, he is not predicting the future, whereas a messenger carries a message…. And he's to deliver that message of truth and righteousness to the 20 million American so-called Negros.

O'Connor is visibly frustrated following this back in forth about Muhammad's role. He shifts uncomfortably, he puts his hand to his forehead, and while remaining calm in his voice, seems to recognize antagonization in this discussion. With this clarification in place and Malcolm firmly stating that the goal of his organization is to spread a religious message, O'Connor shifts the conversation to an explanation of this religious zeal in action (4:47-5:00).

- **O'Connor**: You took a very moderate position of wanting independence without having any hatred for the whites. Is that correct, do I understand you correctly?
- **Malcolm**: Hatred is not involved in it whatsoever.

O'Connor then questions Malcolm about his comments concerning a plane crash in which mostly White Americans, many from Georgia, were killed. The goal, once again, is to trap Malcolm into saying something that will reveal him as a radical who can and should be dismissed. Malcolm retorts by clarifying his statement and the context in which it was made. Most significant is that he links his comments on the plane crash to an act of police violence that had taken place in Los Angeles (5:45-6:36).

- **Malcolm**: When the plane crashed in France, I pointed out to the crowd at this rally that this was an act of God showing his wrath or complete resentment over the brutal form of injustice that had been inflicted upon our poor unarmed brothers [by the Los Angeles Police].

"What Is Your Real Name?"

Malcolm ends his explanation by comparing his comments to statements made by Dr. Billy Graham, a national white religious leader, to the Chicago newspapers that also claimed the crash was an act of God, yet only Malcolm and the NOI are seen as outrageous (7:15-7:31).

- **Malcolm**: We did not think it was a coincidence that 120 of these whites on this plane came from the state of Georgia, a state that has the worst record in the history of America for the mistreatment of black people in this country.
- **O'Connor**: Worse than Mississippi?

This is an impactful question that deserves significant attention on the brutality of Civil Rights repression in Mississippi leading up to this point. Note that four months after this interview, NAACP representative Medger Evers will be assassinated by the KKK in Mississippi. Therefore, this is a stopping point to consider the following questions.

- **Teacher:** Why do you suppose Malcolm did not correct O'Connor immediately by suggesting he meant the "Messenger of Allah" rather than the "Son of Allah", but instead allowed O'Connor to make a second incorrect statement about the "prophet of Allah"?

  - **Student 1:** Malcolm was genuinely surprised someone could be so off about Elijah Muhammad's religious role and it took him a few moments to collect his thoughts before making the correction.
  - **Student 2:** Malcolm could be reveling in O'Connor's demonstration of ignorance. He is not going to help O'Connor come to the correct conclusion unless he explicitly asks for clarification, which O'Connor eventually does.

- **Teacher:** What does each side's body language, tone of voice, and non-verbal cues suggest about how this interview is going?

  - **Student 1:** O'Connor, despite being an experienced professional, at times cannot hide his frustration or confusion with the situation. This suggests that he is not getting the answers he wants or expects.

- o **Student 2:** Malcolm looks very focused and determined most of the time. This likely suggests he sees this as a battle of words from the beginning.
- o **Student 3:** Malcolm makes the point that he has been misquoted and misrepresented in the press before. He is very careful and focused with his words because he knows the white media will look for reasons to discredit him if he says the wrong thing.
- o **Student 4:** It is possible that O'Connor is genuine in his reactions because he really is interested in what Malcolm has to say. Some things may be unexpected, but that does not mean O'Connor is hostile.
- o **Student 5:** It is possible that O'Connor is a racist or at least an elitist who assumes Malcolm is a radical who should not be platformed like this. He is trying to make Malcolm look foolish and failing in that attempt.

- **Teacher:** What do you think was O'Connor intent for bringing up the plane crash in the first place?

- o **Student 1:** His intent was to try once again to trap Malcolm in saying something that would make him look radical, hypocritical, or possibly just crazy.
- o **Student 2:** He was genuinely curious about how Malcolm would respond to a situation he did not fully understand. He wanted clarification.
- o **Student 3:** He had already made up his mind that Malcolm was a bad person. This was a way to confront him.
- o **Student 4:** He intentionally had the details of Malcolm's response incorrect to better make his case that Malcolm was being unreasonable.
- o **Student 5:** He had been misled by various newspaper accounts of Malcolm's response and is only now hearing what really happened.

- **Teacher:** Is Malcolm outrageous in his statements concerning the plane crash?

- o **Student 1:** Not at all. This seems to be a reasonable explanation. He was misquoted by news outlets and so is understandably frustrated; however, the situation makes sense given his beliefs and the audience

"What Is Your Real Name?"

he was addressing when the comments were made. Moreover, he makes an excellent point that the nation mourns a plane crash, an accident, yet ignores acts of overt violence by the state such as a police shooting. That is the true hypocrisy.

- o **Student 2:** Totally! He is happy that Whites from Georgia died regardless of his attempts to make excuses now. If you are familiar with other speeches or writings of his, he clearly wants to kill "crackers." He is just putting his best face forward while on tv in front of what could be a mostly a White audience.
- o **Student 3:** No, but only in that he is a religious zealot and his attributions of the plane crash to "God's wrath" makes sense. Moreover, Malcolm has clearly bought into the rhetoric of Muhammad and the NOI so does not really have any place to form an opinion of his own. This might be different in another year when Malcolm will make his break with Elijah Muhammad.

- **Teacher:** Why would O'Connor suggest Mississippi instead of Georgia as an alternative for the "worst state in the history of America for the treatment of black people in this country"?

- o **Student 1:** Mississippi is known for high profile cases of violence such as Emmit Till and the continued existence of Parchman Farm. Georgia on the other hand is relatively passive under a governor (Vandiver) who supports segregation, but not of mass arrests and police brutality.
- o **Student 2:** The South confuses people in the North; however, Mississippi is a shorthand for racism in this era. A Northern journalist may be congratulating himself on knowing that Mississippi is a hotbed of racism.
- o **Student 3:** It is too early for MLK's Birmingham campaign which will begin the following month, April 1963. Had this interview occurred later, Alabama might have replaced Mississippi.

Bitten with a Smile or Bitten with a Growl (7:35-9:42). Malcolm addresses O'Connor's question about Mississippi. Moreover, another member of the panel, Floyd Kalber, another Chicago news personality mainstay and future mentor to Tom Brokaw, jumps in with a question concerning the enrollment of the first African American student James Meredith into the University of Mississippi. The conversation then turns to Malcolm's position and the NOI's stance on integrated education in America. Keep in mind that Brown versus the Board of Education decision had occurred 9 years earlier, and yet it is estimated that by the time president John F. Kennedy took office in 1961, less than 6% of Southern schools had been integrated. When asked his view on the "James Meredith incident" referring to this enrollment (7:35-7:48).

- **Malcolm**: Mississippi is a little less hypocritical today than Georgia, but both of them are still practicing the same thing. Now whites in Georgia bites Negros with a smile whereas they used to bite them with a growl, but we are still being bitten.

(7:55 to 9:42)

- **Kalber**: What is your organization's position on what has happened there recently [referring to James Meredith]?
- **Malcolm**: Well, the honorable Elijah Muhammad was justice for every one of the 20 million so-called Negros, and to take just one negro and stick him in college... is a disgrace! It's a waste of taxpayer's money. It's a farce. It's hypocrisy because if it's right for one negro to be forced into that university, then every negro in that state who is qualified has the same right to go to that university.

This is a moment when Malcolm's perspective is made very clear. By identifying the enrollment of Meredith as hypocrisy rather than progress, Malcolm is calling out much of the so-called gains of the civil rights era as being likewise hypocritical. This point should be emphasized repeatedly during this lesson. The key question concerns what has been gained by the legal battles in courtrooms and via legislation. King would say that this is progress; however, Malcolm says this is a farce. The interview ends with the statement that was mentioned at the beginning of this article concerning the desire for Black Americans to have their own schools to avoid the controlling elements of white authorities and what he sees as the pandering of civil rights legislation initiatives. Before ending the lesson, a teacher may ask some additional questions and offer some final discussion points for students to consider.

- **Teacher**: How does Malcolm X and the NOI's messaging differ from King and the SCLC as of 1963?

    o   North v South experiences with racism
    o   Upper and middle class versus lower class audiences
    o   Reconciliation versus separation

"What Is Your Real Name?"

- **Teacher:** What factors help to explain the differences identified above?

    o   South versus North in terms of race laws
    o   Views on authority – King up to 1963 as a reformer and Malcolm as a revolutionary
    o   The role of religion - King as Baptist versus Malcolm as a Muslim
    o   The legacy of Garveyism
    o   Experiences with police and legal systems
    o   Education – "Dr." MLK versus Malcolm's education in prison

Implication-Next Steps for a Comparison Between Malcolm X And Post-1965 King

So often secondary social studies classrooms fall into the trap of oversimplifying discussion of civil rights. This article has focused on one small step in expanding and complicating our vision of that era, but it cannot stop there. Peniel Joseph's seminal work *The Sword and The Shield* (2020) continues the conversation for academic scholars, which this classroom discussion should initiate. As he describes it, 1963 is only the beginning. More aggressive federal civil rights legislation and the hope to hold accountable these promises of change brough Malcolm more into the mainstream of politics while pushing King toward more radical action and rhetoric. By the time of his assassination, Malcolm had given voice to an emerging Black Power ideology, forcing it into mainstream discourse.

This sample lesson is a gateway into a more responsive and aggressive teaching of CRM with BPM in the 1960s and continuing through to modern events. In the future, similar lessons should be formulated around the unique and often divergent views of human rights activists such as Marcus Garvey, Elijah Muhammad, John Lewis, Ella Baker, Stokely Carmichael, Eldridge Cleaver, Bobby Seale, Assata Shakur, Muhammad Ali, Colin Kaepernick and a multitude of organizations and individuals who contribute to the ongoing struggle for dignity in America. As significant is the need to recognize that King was a radical who took inspiration from Malcolm X. As Joseph describes:

Malcolm inspired blacks to unapologetically love themselves. He set a fearless example in this regard, offering his story of individual triumph against racism and poverty as a chance at collective redemption for the entire black community. Malcom's death arrived before the public acknowledgment of Black Power – a movement

"What Is Your Real Name?"

birthed from his activism and which would spur King to greater radicalism, more forceful political rhetoric, and an embrace of radical black dignity.

REFERENCES

Ahmed, A. (2020). Islam and Black America: The religious life of Malcolm X. *Journal of African American Studies*, 24(3), 456–481. 10.1007/s12111-020-09492-5

Boyd, H. (1993). 1992: Year of the X. *The Black Scholar*, 23(1), 22–26. 10.1080/00064246.1993.11413073

Busey, C.L., Duncan, K.E., & Dowie-Chin, T. (2022) *Critical What What? A theoretical systematic review of 15 years of Critical Race Theory.* Research in Social Studies Education, 2004–2019.

Byrd, D., & Miri, S. J. (2016). *Malcolm X: From political eschatology to religious revolutionary* (1st ed.). Brill. 10.1163/9789004308688

Cha-Jua, S. K., & Lang, C. (1999). Strategies for Black Liberation in the Era of Globalism: Retronouveau Civil Rights, Militant Black Conservatism, and Radicalism. *The Black Scholar*, 29(4), 25–47. 10.1080/00064246.1999.11430982

Cleaver, E. (1968). *Soul on Ice*. Ramparts Press.

Combs, B. H., Dellinger, K., Jackson, J. T., Johnson, K. A., Johnson, W. M., Skipper, J., Sonnett, J., & Thomas, J. M. (2016). The Symbolic Lynching of James Meredith: A Visual Analysis and Collective Counter Narrative to Racial Domination. *Sociology of Race and Ethnicity (Thousand Oaks, Calif.)*, 2(3), 338–353. https://doi-org.utk.idm.oclc.org/10.1177/2332649215626937. 10.1177/2332649215626937

Davis, D. W., & Davenport, C. (1997). The Political and Social Relevancy of Malcolm X: The Stability of African American Political Attitudes. *The Journal of Politics*, 59(2), 550–564. 10.1017/S0022381600053573

Duncan, K. (2021). *"They Act Like they went to hell!": Black Techers, Racial Justice, and Teacher Education.* Racial Justice and Teacher Education.

Duncan, K. E. (2020). What Better Tool Do I Have?: A Critical Race Approach to Teaching Civics. *High School Journal*, 103(3), 176–189. 10.1353/hsj.2020.0011

Gibson, D.-M. (2012). *A History of the Nation of Islam: Race, Islam, and the Quest for Freedom.* Praeger. http://www.abc-clio.com/product.aspx?isbn=9780313398070

Grace, J., & Aming-Attai, R. (2023). 'This is so white': examining black and Brown pre-service teachers' sense of belonging in a predominantly White educator preparation program. *Whiteness and Education (Print)*, 1–18. 10.1080/23793406.2023.2277789

JAH. (1993). Movie reviews - A note on Malcolm X. *The Journal of American History (Bloomington, Ind.)*, 80(3), 1179-.

Joseph, P. E. (2020). *The Sword and the Shield: The Revolutionary Lives of Malcolm X and MLK* (1st ed.). Basic Books.

Laughter, J. (2021). *Critiquing inequities in scripted curricula.*

Lee, S. (1992). *MALCOLM X* (Film). Spin (New York, N.Y.).

Love, B. (2020). *WE WANT TO DO MORE THAN SURVIVE: Abolitionist Teaching and the Pursuit of Educational Freedom.* BEACON.

Love, B. L. (2021). Empty Promises of Equity: Whether White People are Ready or not, Policies Have to Change. *Education Week*, 40(18), 24–24.

Lyden, J. C. (2018). King in the Wilderness. *Journal of Religion and Film*, 22(1). Gale Academic OneFile. link.gale.com/apps/doc/A537719928/AONE?u=tel_oweb&sid=googleScholar&xid=f285fcb4

Meredith, J. (1966). *Three Years in Mississippi.* Indiana University Press.

Rapoport, A. (2005). *Teaching in a comfort zone: Practitioners' views and rationale for teaching global citizenship.*

Rapoport, A. (2009). A Forgotten Concept: Global Citizenship education and State Social Studies Standards. *Journal of Social Studies Research.*

Rosiek, J., & Kinslow, K. (2016). Resegregation as Curriculum: The Meaning of the New Segregation in U.S. Public Schools. Taylor & Francis Group.

Rounds, C. (2020). "Dead Men Make Such Convenient Heroes": The Use and Misuse of MLK's Legacy as Political Propaganda. *Journal of Black Studies*, 51(4), 315–331. 10.1177/0021934720908489

Sanders, R., Stovall, D., & White, T. (2018). *Twenty-first-century Jim Crow schools: the impact of charters on public education.* Beacon Press. https://www.socialstudies.org/position-statements

Theoharis, J.., & Woodard, K. (2005). *Groundwork local black freedom movements in America.* New York University.

Valtonen, T., Tedre, M., Mäkitalo, K., & Vartiainen, H. (2019). Media Literacy Education in the Age of Machine Learning. *The Journal of Media Literacy Education*, 11(2), 20–36. 10.23860/JMLE-2019-11-2-2

West, C. (1999). *The Cornel West reader.* Basic Books.

X, M., & Haley, Alex. (1992). *The Autobiography of Malcolm X* (1st Ballantine books hardcover ed.). Ballantine Books.

Chapter 10
Emotional Literacy through Tea Objects:
A Literary Rendition

Ran Xiang
The University of British Columbia, Canada

ABSTRACT

As an unconventional and alternative way of doing qualitative research, arts-based methodology has gained growing interest from scholars. ABR harbors a great variety of approaches, including visual arts (photography, painting), performance art (music, ethno-drama), and literary genres (fiction, creative non-fiction, autobiography). Creative non-fiction is a genre of writing that uses literary techniques to create factually accurate narratives. It differs from fiction in that writers cannot make up or alter facts, but they can capture them in much more dramatic ways. In this chapter, the author employs literary writing techniques in the creative non-fiction writeup of her experience visiting three rare tea objects exhibitions in Japan. This chapter serves as a literary application in the field of emotional literacy, exploring how objects can elicit affective responses from human beings and the knowledge produced in the body.

PROLOGUE

Research in the field of literacy has been influenced by different waves of epistemological developments, including positivism, post-positivism, post-structuralism, interpretive, social constructivism, and critical frames. The corresponding methodologies have evolved from experimental, correlational, and quantitative to mixed methods, participatory, and qualitative. Recent developments in chaos and

DOI: 10.4018/979-8-3693-3302-0.ch010

complexity theory have informed a post-humanist/new materialist orientation to the world, conceiving matter as agentic and lively, moving away from a Cartesian and Newtonian view of seeing matter as inert and uniform (Coole & Frost, 2010). If the world is a messy entanglement between human beings and other forces, the methodologies that social science researchers use need to adapt accordingly. Jerry Rosiek (2018) points out the alignment of New Materialism and arts-based research: "[ABR] requires imaginative portrayal and performances that invite us to appreciate multiple formations of ourselves as subjects and agents, multiple relations with other human and non-human agents, and a collective of individual and futurities" (p. 44). As an unconventional and alternative way of doing qualitative research, arts-based methodology has gained growing interest from scholars (Leavy, 2018; Cahnmann-Taylor & Siegsmund, 2018). ABR harbors a great variety of approaches, including visual arts (photography, painting), performance art (music, ethno-drama), and literary genres (fiction, creative non-fiction, autobiography). Creative non-fiction is a genre of writing that uses literary techniques to create factually accurate narratives. It differs from fiction in that writers cannot make up or alter facts, but they can capture them in much more dramatic ways (Gutkind, 1997). A good creative non-fiction writing has the power to attract and capture readers who do not have prior interest in or connection to the subject.

In this paper, I propose to employ literary writing techniques in the creative non-fiction writeup of my experience visiting three rare tea objects exhibitions in Japan. It seems that the tea objects, as Kathleen Stewart suggests in her book Ordinary Affect (2007), exert a pull, an impact on me. The non-human-human-affective-assemblage is "not the kind of analytic object that can be laid out on a single, static plane of analysis… (p. 4). Their significance lies in the intensities they build and in what thoughts and feelings they make possible. The question they beg… [lies in] where they might go and what potential modes of knowing, relating, and attending to things are already somehow present in them in a state of potentiality and resonance (p. 3)." This paper serves as a literary application in the field of emotional literacy, exploring how objects can elicit affective responses from human beings and the knowledge produced in the body.

TENMOKO

Tenmoko (also known as Jian ware) was considered the highest-ranking tea bowl in the world of chanoyu. It was first brought to Japan by Japanese monks who studied at the Zen temples in Zhejiang Tianmu Mountain during South Song Dynasty (1127-1279), therefore known as Tenmoku. Whisked tea ( ) and "tea fights" ( ) were popular in Song, so the dark glazed Jian ware with its wider opening was the

Emotional Literacy through Tea Objects

most suited type of tea bowl for whisking and color display. The rarest type of Jian ware is yohen tenmoku ( ), because the iron element in the clay starts to crystalize at high temperatures, causing the tea bowl to exhibit iridescent color patterns. Contemporary artisans still cannot fully decipher the techniques to duplicate the yohen tenmoku at the same level of delicacy. There are only three existing yohen temenku tea bowls, all of which are kept in Japan and deemed national treasures. One of them is owned by the Zen temple Daitoku-ji ( ); one is owned by the Fujita Family; and the other is owned by the president of Mitsubishi company. In spring 2019, these yohen tenmoku tea bowls were exhibited in three Japanese cities roughly around the same time. With proper planning, viewers would be able to see all of them in one trip. My visits to the yohen tenmoku exhibitions lead to subsequent visits to a tea shop, Zen temples, and a tea caddy store. I had strong yet different affective responses to each of the yohen tenmoku tea bowls in my transient encounters. Each of them possesses a personality of its own.

THE SIBLING RIVALRY

A strolling deer was grazing the grassland, raising her head up from time to time, looking at us. I glimpsed the beautiful silhouette of the deer, strode forward to the Nara National Museum.

A few minutes after 9am, I lined up outside the second floor, brochures in my hand:

"This particular tenmoku was owned by Takugawa Leyasu ( ) and his successors. In 1918, Hitaro Fujita auctioned this piece at 53000 Japanese yen, which was worth 40 kilograms of gold at the time. This tea bowl becomes a private collection of the Fujita Museum of Art."

I moved forward slowly along the shell-shaped separators into the special display room.

Emotional Literacy through Tea Objects

Figure 1.

She (figure 1) sat on top of a dark velvet surface inside a transparent box, bathed in yellow lights from the four top corners and a white central beam from above. Numerous round bubbles exploded inside her; iridescent color clouds connected the round bubbles. Visible scratches and signs of usage covered the inside skin, yet she exhibited captivating neon yellowish and greenish sheen. It was indeed a starry night projected into a tea bowl.

As I ambled back and forth, I spotted some vague color circles on the outside skin. I stepped back from the crowd, kneeled on the ground, tilted my body, trying to catch a glimpse of the lighting on the outside: dimmer and smaller color spots grew rampant, like dark spots on the hands of an old lady. The bubbles inside burst from the bottom to the opening, as if in the Danish fairytale *The Mermaid*, the little mermaid disappeared into ascending bubbles to the sky. I barely saw the outside, no view of the foot at all. I wish I had the chance to hold her in my hand, touch her skin, make tea in it.

I stood so close to her and yet she was so distant. How much does it take to understand a historical tea object? I was grateful to be in her presence and only wish I could spend more time with her.

Emotional Literacy through Tea Objects

Figure 2.

Another member of the tenmoku family, yoteki tenmoku (   ), also a national treasure, sat inside a box in the main exhibition room. The only difference between these two types of tenmoku is that yoteki tenmoku (figure 2) does not change color under light. The numerous oil spots that cover her entire body, inside and outside, remain shiny and bright. No special room, no artistic lighting. She was there, alone. Few admirers. For a while, I was the only viewer in front of the box.

Do they, like human beings, have sibling rivalry? Is yohen tenmoku the overshadowing sister? Yoteki tenmoku was otherwise stunning, just not in front of her sister.

I wanted to say goodbye to yohen tenmoku before I left, yet I could not find my way back into the display room—the lineup was too long. Parting was always a difficult emotion for me, moving in and out of cities, getting acquainted and getting estranged from friends, seeing people off……. Parting with a rare tea object was not any easier.

As I walked out, my eyes started to water and the stairs beneath my feet became blurry.

THE CAGED PRINCESS

The second yohen tenmoku exhibition was held at Miho Museum ( ) in Shiga prefecture. The museum was designed by the late Chinese American architect IM Pei ( ), whose works include the glass pyramids of the Louvre Museum and the East Wing of the National Gallery. This yohen tenmoku has been guarded by Ryokoin ( ), one sub-temple of the Daitoku-ji, for 400 years and was the most rarely exhibited among the three, only previously shown three times. Even NHK was unable to obtain permission to videotape this yohen tenmoku for their documentary. I was intrigued before I went.

I took the train from Kyoto and transferred to a direct bus in Shiga prefecture. The bus took us on a winding path into the mountain, different shades of green, blasting sunlight. My body was swaying from side to side and my head was getting heavy. Suddenly the swaying stopped.

Emotional Literacy through Tea Objects

Figure 3.

I smelled some airy fragrance right after I got off the bus. A narrow path led to a tunnel (figure 3); pink cherry blossom trees lined both sides. The blossoms started to wither. A gentle wind blew off the petals, some falling on the ground, some falling on me. Echoing sound of people's chatter and footsteps inside the tunnel magnified. Towards the end of the S-shaped tunnel, the pleasant smell of cherry blossom became unnoticeable. An open space and the museum's front door jumped into view. I walked across the open space, stepped up the stairs and looked back: the museum was harbored by the green mountain, only connected to the outside through one narrow tunnel.

How I arrived at the museum embodied the opening lines of Tao Yuanming's ( ) essay *The Peach Blossom Spring* ( ), when a fisherman of Wuling wanders along a stream to a grove of blossoming peach trees. Pedals of fragrant blossoms were falling on the ground. The fishman is greatly surprised and follows the stream further, only to find a small opening inside a mountain. At the beginning, it is so narrow that he can barely pass, but after a few steps, he reaches an open land.

The front door of the Miho Museum was a full moon-shaped glass door. Through the atrium, I could see visitors walking, an old pine extending his limbs out on the terrace, and the never-ending greens. The lineup to the exhibition started right beside the reception desk, winding all the way to the end of the hall and up to the second floor. Staff members handed out candy bars to us.

Two and a half hours after I left my hotel, I arrived at the entrance of the exhibition.

Emotional Literacy through Tea Objects

Figure 4.

Figure 5.

Emotional Literacy through Tea Objects

Figure 6.

Figure 7.

On the walls outside the entrance were photos of the everyday life of the Zen monks: the back shadow of an abbot walking into the temple (figure 4), a dog sitting by the door (figure 5), miso sauce sprayed over cucumber chunks (figure 6) and baskets of pickled plum (figure 7) with the inscription "very sour indeed". They were ordinary yet lively. The preface to the show was written by the Director of Miho Museum, Mr. Kumakura Isao. He explained that the tenmoku tea bowl was a national treasure and the worn-out sandal was the symbol of the Zen spirit. A price cannot be put on either of them, which is the intention behind the title *Shining Tea Bowl and Worn-out Sandals: Living in Zen and the Daitoku-ji Ryokoin Heritage*.

Emotional Literacy through Tea Objects

Figure 8.

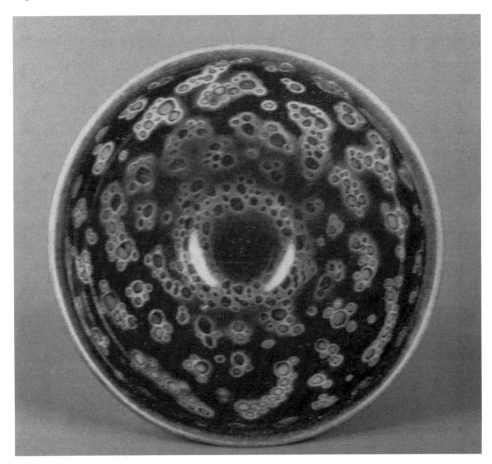

She was so blue (figure 8).

Under the central white beam inside the dark exhibition hall, she exhibited blue-purplish aura. She seemed melancholy and mysterious. Tiny clusters of white spots covered the inside of her dark glazed skin, all the way from the bottom to the opening, denser at the bottom, scarcer towards the opening.

She was different from the first one, different colors and glistening patterns. She was humble and quiet. I walked around the display box slowly, trying to catch a glimpse of her from different angles, visible scratches covered the inside. I walked to the back, a bit further away from the tea bowl. Smouldering blue purplish light emitted from the center of the tea bowl, like an opening to an alternative universe. I kneeled on the floor to see the outside, smooth dark skin without glistening spots.

I recalled a scene in Louis Cha's chivalric novel where people were astounded by the beauty of the veiled princess from afar. She was just like the veiled princess. I was captivated. I could not help but wonder what she would look like with matcha in it. Would it be different to drink from her than to drink from our practice piece tea bowl? Was she still being used every day or was she only enshrined and adored? Has she become a caged princess? Is that why she seemed so blue?

Emotional Literacy through Tea Objects

Figure 9.

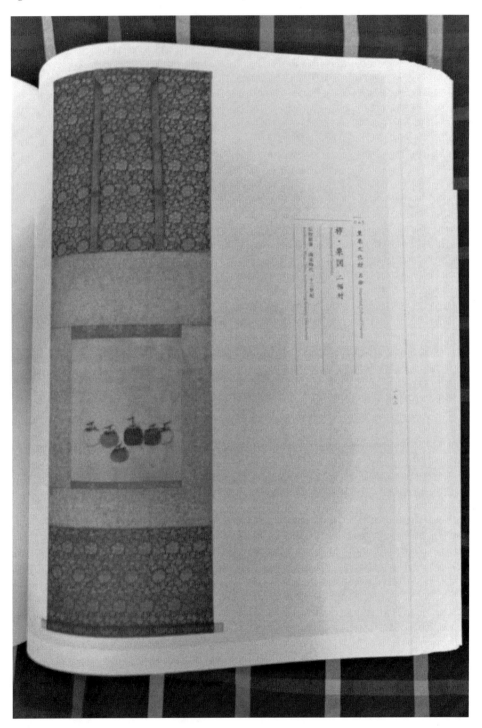

There were over 200 pieces being exhibited, from tea utensils to paintings and sutra calligraphy. Yet other than the blue yohen tenmoku, there was only one other object that was equally captivating to me: *Six Persimmons ( )*, a painting by a Chinese Zen monk Muqi ( )(figure 9).

They looked so ordinary, six persimmons lined up, nothing else. There was no calligraphy, no stamps nor signature on the scroll, only six persimmons in various shapes and colors, achieved by playing with darker or lighter ink tonality. The persimmon in the center was the darkest, two other adjacent persimmons were lighter, and the two on the furthest side were almost opaque.

What makes this painting so highly acclaimed? I didn't understand.

It was empty and full at the same time. When I looked at it, I felt the same way as when I was in the tearoom. I liked looking at them a lot. I liked the way I felt. I stood a few meters away and stared at the painting until my stomach was growling. It's time.

In Tao's essay, the fisherman enters Shangri-la by chance and he is never able to find his way back. Will I be able to see these valuable pieces again? Will I come back to Miho Museum? Parting was a difficult emotion for me. Tears rolled down my cheeks, fell on the ground.

*

"Can we sit a bit more? Do you have to go through security now? You have lots of time." I grabbed his arm.

"It is 12 now, one hour left. I need to go."

"Ok... Can you visit me during the summer months next year? We can go hiking and do all the outdoor stuff that people in Vancouver love to do. And Wreck beach. You always wanted to see that."

"Summer months are usually the busiest, might be difficult. Cannot make promises now.

We will see each other in a few months. Will happen before you know it. Be well."

We stood up and walked towards the security lineup. He lowered his lips, quickly brushed against my cheek, walked ahead. Tears rolled down my cheeks, fell on the ground. I leaned my torso against the entrance door: he waited in line, went through the security machine, picked up his stuff, and disappeared.

*

Five days after my visit to the Miho Museum, the architect IM Pei passed away.

Six months later, a small organism invisible to the human eye started to turn the world topsy-turvy.

Can we ever go back?

Emotional Literacy through Tea Objects

TEA AND ZEN ARE OF ONE TASTE

Both the tea seeds and the yohen tenmoku tea bowls were brought to Japan by the Zen monks. They were the first to plant tea gardens, as they drank tea to stay alert during meditative practices. Some of the best tea, whether green tea or oolong, was first cultivated by the Zen monks. The well-circulated phrase "Zen and tea are of one taste" was coined by the early developer of wabi-cha Murata Juko ( ) (1423-1502). After seeing the Daitoku-ji exhibition, I grew more curious about Zen.

I walked across the Shijo bridge and turned right into an alley to get to Kennin-ji ( ). Before I reached my destination, I saw a sign on the side of the road: "Shoden-Eigen-in Temple Special Spring Opening" and "Spring tea served with yokan". I went in without a second thought.

I sat on the tatami in seiza, looking at the garden within reach. A small, full and well-maintained garden, more greens than colors. Gentle drafts brought in more afternoon heat. Cicadas were singing. It was different from Ichibo'an in Vancouver, when even in summer, sitting inside the tearoom was cool and sometimes chilly. While I waited for my sweets, two ladies in kimono walked in and sat down beside me. They bowed and smiled at me.

As usual, sweets were served first. Two slices of strawberry and three pieces of orange on top of one layer of pink jelly. Never had a yokan like this before: fresh, sweet and creamy with a tinge of tartness. The best so far. I did not savor the matcha carefully because I was hung up on the aftertaste of yokan and thinking about where I could get it to bring home. When I finished my tea, I moved my legs to a cross-legged position. I sat comfortably for a while, looking at the garden. The two ladies finished their tea and left. Some other guests came in.

I felt energized after tea and went on to visit Kennin-ji.

Figure 10.

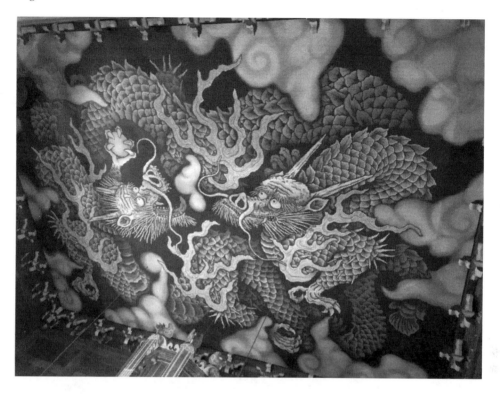

Kennin-ji Temple was founded by Yousai (1141-1215) in 1202. The Zen master Yousai ( ) was considered the pioneer of the Japanese tea ceremony for his effort of bringing the green tea seeds back to Japan and promoting tea consumption. He also wrote the book *Kissa Yokoshi* ( ). The unique Wind and Thunder Gods Board was housed in the back hall, connected to the Cho-on-tei garden. The Daiouen and the Hojo were in the middle, facing kara sensui garden on both sides. A long corridor connected the Main Hall to the Twin Dragon Dharma Hall (figure 10). The layout of Kennin-ji was similar to the traditional residential housing of siheyuan. Both have various foldings, connected by a corridor and occupy a large space.

I lived in a siheyuan ( ) when I was a kid and felt an affinity to the space in Kennin-ji. The Toyo-bo Teahouse at the far corner was not open to the public. I walked across the corridor to the Dharma Hall. The large ink painting covered the entire ceiling: one dragon held the ball in his paws, with a smug smile on his face; the other dragon looked pissed. They were similar to the dragon images in Chinese cartoons, except that their horns were sharp and pointed.

Emotional Literacy through Tea Objects

Figure 11.

I walked across the corridor back to the Hojo again. The entire hall was surrounded by a kara sensui garden on the front and the side (figure 11). Visitors cannot enter the Hojo, but only stroll on the porch. Two standing rocks and one lying rock gathered in the left corner of the front garden. Rippling lines float across the entire garden; circled line surrounded the rocks. I only got the sea metaphor; not sure what the rocks represented. I walked beside one pillar, sat on the porch like other visitors. I took down my backpack, leaned against the pillar, stretched my legs. My body was relaxed as I admired the dry landscape garden—I wished I could pause time.

TWO FOR ONE

My chanoyu teacher Keith sensei always ordered matcha from Ippodo tea shop ( ). After seeing the Zen gardens in Kennin-ji, I went to check out its Kyoto main store. Established in 1717, Ippodo was a Japanese family-owned tea company known for producing the highest quality green tea. As soon as I stepped into the tea shop, a salesman greeted me.

"Good afternoon. How can I help you?" He bowed slightly.
"I want to have some tea."
"Ah, the Kakobu tearoom is on your right. This way please and someone there will assist you."

The aroma of green tea permeated the tearoom, so familiar and comforting. I slouched onto the chair by the bar. The customers at the nearby table were having sencha. Other tables were having Matcha. A young lady handed me the menu.

So much to choose from. Ippodo carries four types of green tea: matcha, gyokuro, sencha and bancha. Matcha and gyokuro are both made from shaded leaves that have *umami* flavor. Matcha is powdered tea; gyokuro is leafed tea. Sencha and bancha are made from open-field tea leaves. With more sun exposure, they have a sharper taste. Larger and courser tea leaves are roasted to make hojicha. From matcha to bancha, the sweet umami taste is gradually replaced by the rich and pungent taste. Different names of each type of tea are arranged according to quality and price point.

"Are you ready?"
"Hmm, yeah, koicha. Ummon-no-mukashi (*The finest matcha on the menu*)."
"Great choice."

A young lady carrying a tray of tea bowl, chasan and a small can of matcha stopped at the preparation table opposite me. She picked up the kishaku and opened the kettle to get hot water. She poured some hot water into the tea bowl, briskly warmed the chasan and dumped the water into the kensui. These steps were similar

Emotional Literacy through Tea Objects

to Chanoyu practices, but she did not follow the strict procedures. Two scoops of matcha in the dark tea bowl, the lady poured a bit of hot water and slowly mixed the powder into a paste. A gush of warm matcha scent. She poured more water onto the paste and started whisking gently. A thick jade green paste dissolved into a smooth creamy texture of koicha.

"Dozo." She put the tea bowl in front of me.
"Thank you."

A small sip into the mouth. Rich, layered, full of umami. The bitterness is soon replaced by the sweet aftertaste. It's better than the koicha I tasted in okeiko, probably because this is freshly made spring tea. An even layer of koicha got stuck on the inside of the tea bowl—a good indicator of consistency and whisking skill. I put the tea bowl back.

"Did you like it?"
"I do. Very nice, rich and subtle."
"I am glad you like it. The tea left inside the tea bowl is enough to make usucha. Let me make that for you."
"Great! Two for one. Thanks so much!"

She poured more hot water into the tea bowl and whisked forcefully. Jade green changed into light frothy green.

In chanoyu, the host is always expected to prepare the best tea for the guests, so turning leftover koicha into usucha will never happen. Yet in a casual setting like this, it is acceptable. It saves the matcha and makes cleaning easier.

Two bowls of matcha in my tummy, I was revitalized. I walked around to look for some tea to take home. A tea caddy engraved with Ippodo deal caught my eye. It is in the shape of a natsumei, only it is made of metal, a nice rose gold color, quite weighty in my hand.

"Excuse me? Do you carry a different size of this tea caddy?"
"Sorry, we don't. This engraved tea caddy only comes in one size, but the caddies are made locally, by a shop called Kaikado. You can check them out."

AGING AND AGED: KAIKADO CHAZUSTU

The shop is supposed to be either right I am standing or in the air. I don't get Google Maps. I walked into the alley, and looked around. A white banner sticking out from the wall read " ".

Figure 12.

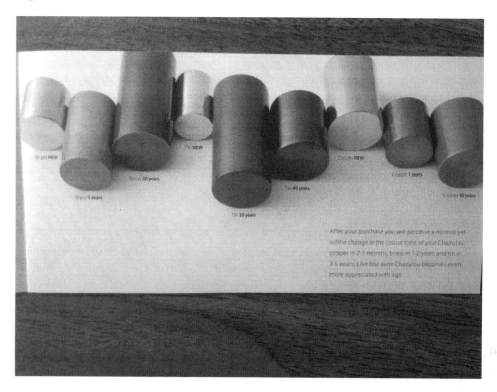

Inside the shop, tea caddies made of tin, brass and copper in various sizes were displayed separately on the shelves, alongside the aged tea caddies (figure 12). The new tea caddy made of brass had a lemon color, with a natural sheen; the brightness was lost after five years of use. The thirty-year-old brass had an earthy color. The new tin caddy looked similar to stainless steel; a twenty-year-old tin caddy had a dark mossy green color. A forty-year-old tin caddy looked like it was made of a different material, perhaps lead. The new copper tea caddy had the most appealing color to me, a bright amberish color. After one year of aging, it became caramel. Ten years of usage gave it a toffee candy color—looked delicious. I picked up a small copper tea caddy, opened the lid. When the lid and the body lined up, the lid descended slowly and expelled the air out of the container. It was so delicate, durable and versatile.

Aging is a similar process for objects and for people. The magic ingredient of time always takes something away and adds more back. I love the delicious caramel color of aged copper. I picked up the smaller one, put it down and picked up the bigger one again.

Emotional Literacy through Tea Objects

"I had the same problem when I bought my first chazustu." A lady with curly hair said to me.

"Yeah? I think I will go for a small copper. Nice and sweet, the right size for me."

"I got that one for myself too. I am picking up a wedding gift for a friend today. I want the chazustu to be engraved. I hope they use it often, enjoy the beautiful aging process and maybe pass it on to their kids. The growing of a family, an heirloom. We dispose things too easily now. You know you can get a tea scoop with your purchase and they engrave it for free?" She pointed to the small stand in the corner, "They do it right there."

"Oh, I didn't know that. Thanks. Are you…"

"Christy, you are here already. It will be ready in a moment. How are you doing?" A middle-aged man came out from the back.

"I am alright. Work is still busy back home—this vacation has done good for me. I am leaving in a few days."

"Good to catch up with you. Will hand it out in a few minutes." He went back in.

"Were you saying something to me just now?" Christy turned to me again.

"Ah, I was going to ask if you are a traveller, like me."

"I came back to Japan every year. As my Japanese got a bit better, I got to know more people, like the owner of this shop. Is this your first time? How do you like it?"

"Yeah, I came to see the yohen tenmoku exhibitions. One thing led to another, I visited Zen temples, tea shops and will leave tomorrow to see the third exhibition in Tokyo. Tea is my interest and my research topic."

"Tea, did you go to Uji, the nearby city known for matcha plantation."

"Not yet, got delayed at the beginning, cannot fit Uji into my schedule. Will come back though. There is a lot of tea stuff in Kyoto; did not have the chance to see all of them. Tea has magic powers."

"I'd agree. I have a simple tea set at my office. I pour tea to myself every day. Whenever I know I will be having a difficult meeting, I always bring my tea with me. It is like a place of sanctuary, makes me feel better."

"Interesting."

"Christy, your chazustu is ready. Sorry about the wait."

"No worries. Thanks so much." Christy turned around, "Nice chatting with you. Good luck with your research and safe trips."

"You too."

When Christy left. I bought my copper chazustu and wrote my given name in kenji. Ten minutes later, the owner came back with the tea scoop engraved " ".

Emotional Literacy through Tea Objects

THE FLAMBOYANT ONE

The last stop before I left Japan was to visit the third yohen tenmoko exhibition at the Seikado Bunko Museum (   ) in Tokyo. The exhibition featured inaba tenmoku (   ), the most precious type of yohen tenmoku because of its vivid luster and finely chiselled foot. The Inaba tenmoku came to the possession of Iwasaki family, president of Mitsubishi, in 1930s. Although Iwasaki Koyota owned this rare object, he never used it to drink tea. He thought of yohen tenmoku as the national treasure that an ordinary man like him did not deserve to use it.

Figure 13.

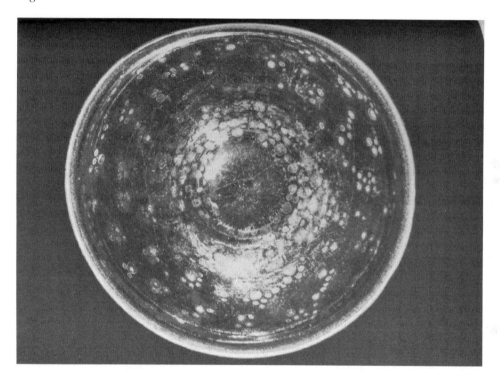

He was tied by fish lines to the four corners of the box, like a martyr (figure 13). The box was set in the middle of the atrium, surrounded by natural sunlight from the front and the side. No staff members keeping order, no artificial lighting, no special setup. Everything was so normal. Several viewers were resting on the chairs opposite the box. A few were standing in front of the box.

Emotional Literacy through Tea Objects

I walked around the box slowly in full circles. The glistening spots were in the shape of bear claws, yellow-neon-ish color on the top, blue-purple-ish color on the bottom. He has the most exuberant and flamboyant color spots, almost covering his entire skin. When viewing from different angles under natural light, he exhibited rainbow-like shines. I stepped back and sat on the chair. I saw some smoldering light from the opening of the tea bowl, as if an epiphany was about to take place.

The subdued light of a cloudy day did not obscure his prowess, yet he reminded me of something with an evil spirit, some poisonous fungi or flowers that devour the prey who fall for their unearthly attractive appearance. This tea bowl would be perfect for the emperor to order death of his subordinates. The poison started to seep out of the skin of the tea bowl as soon as tea was poured in. A savory and a quick death. How joyful!

I wanted to part from him, the sooner the better. He was handsome, yet I felt repulsed.

EPILOGUE: AN EARLY SUMMER AFTERNOON'S DAYDREAM

I called a cab to my hotel and sat on the stairs outside while I waited.

Why do I feel so different about the yohen tenmoku tea bowls? Why do I feel sad parting with the blue tenmoku and repulsed by the most colorful one? The feeling of being captivated by the potency of some ancient tea objects is so strong. I never doubted the magic of materials and I have many times been surprised and charmed, but yohen tenmoku was special. Perhaps people who have come into possession of the tea bowls have imbued them with different energy. Zen monks making tea in it made the yohen tenmoku a Zen object, humbling and quiet. Ibana tenmoku was never owned by a Zen temple, only by warlords and art collectors. I suppose in the interchange between the owner and the yohen tenmoku, both become anew.

The Miho trip was so exhausting. Many things came to mind, too much too soon, like flooding.

I was reminded by the memory of parting with loved ones. I started chanoyu lessons in 2017, about two years ago. Keith sensei rarely talked about the "one time one meeting" ( ) principle, but bowing at the beginning of class, during practices and end of the class embodied and reiterated the idea. Perhaps this heightened awareness of the transient nature of all encounters intensifies my feelings. The wabi-sabi ( ) principle that emphasizes the imperfect and incomplete; the mono-no-aware ( ), the bittersweet sentiment of impermanent things; the spirit of Zen; the particular object-people-place-time assemblage; the atmospheric of the curatorial……

The impact and significance of certain things can only be felt rather than analyzed. People need to come to them repeatedly to be able to articulate. Perhaps certain knowledge can only be felt in the body.

Practicing chanoyu at Nitobe, admiring the kara sensui garden at Kennin-ji, and staring at the six persimmons are moments that I enjoy immensely. Those moments are simple yet extraordinary. I forgot about myself in those specific time/space. Those might just be moments of Zen.

A professional Japanese tea person Senxia (2013) writes that there are two categories of things in the world, one that can be understood immediately and one that cannot. Chanoyu belongs to the second. After years of practice, people start to think that they have mastered it, only to realize that they only understand a fraction of it. Is this what Rikyu meant when he says chanoyu is nothing but boiling water and drinking tea?

My cab arrived and I hopped in.

I long for a return.

REFERENCES

Cahnmann-Taylor, M., & Siegesmund, R. (2018). *Arts-based research in education: Foundations for practice*. Routledge.

Coole, D. H., & Frost, S. (Eds.). (2010). *New materialisms: Ontology, agency, and politics*. Duke University Press.

Gutkind, L. (1997). *The art of creative nonfiction: Writing and selling the literature of reality*. Wiley.

Leavy, P. (2018). *Handbook of arts-based research* (1st ed.). The Guilford Press.

Rosiek, J. (2018). Art, agency and inquiry: Making connections between new materialism and contemporary pragmaticism in arts-based research. In Cahnmann &Siegesmund (Eds.) *Arts-based research in education: Foundations for practice*. Routledge.

Senxia, D. (2013). *Ri ri shi hao ri: Chadao dailai de shiwu zhong xingfu. [Everyday is a good day: Fifteen kinds of happiness brought by Chado]*. Printing Industry Publication.

Stewart, K. (2007). *Ordinary affects*. Duke University Press.

Chapter 11
On These Haunted Streets:
A Photopoetic Process of Transmedia Storytelling as Critical Multimodal Literacy

Lalenja Harrington
University of North Carolina at Greensboro, USA

Karen Cox
Independent Researcher, USA

ABSTRACT

This chapter outlines the development of a collaborative transmedia storytelling process by the authors, whose visual and poetic work is articulated here within the framework of critical multimodal literacy (CML). The authors were tasked to help bring forward the stories of black musicians involved in the opera Omar, and in doing so discovered an artistic process that was strengthened by the intersection of their critical approaches. Chronicling their engagement with Omar provided them with a uniquely situated opportunity to describe their individual meaning making processes, and then discuss how consideration of each other's process impacted our storytelling. The authors do this through sharing specific story examples from the oral history project. Engagement with black artistic presence in opera also allowed them to explore our shared focus on anchoring this work within a socio-political context that supports the naming/transformation of inequities; helping to illustrate how this work is situated within the framework of CML and reflects a transmedia process of layered storytelling.

DOI: 10.4018/979-8-3693-3302-0.ch011

INTRODUCTION

Figure 1. Omar production photo

Photo credit: Karen Cox; poem: Lalenja Harrington

In May of 2022, the Spoleto Music Festival premiered *Omar* at the Sottile Theater in Charleston, SC. The opera was a labor of love born from the minds and hands of Rhiannon Giddens and Michael Abels, to honor the life of Omar Ibn Said, a Muslim-African man who was enslaved in that very same city in 1807 (Cooper, 2019). On a beautiful summer day, as visitors, festival goers and residents shopped, ate and recreated outside of the doors of the theatre, a story of systematic dehumanization that this country has yet to reckon with, unfolded on the stage inside - a dissonance that was not lost on the black musicians telling Said's story. It is the reconciling of this tension that we, the authors of this article, were tasked to chronicle as an oral history project through visual portraits and poetry. It is our process of visual and poetic storytelling that will be the focus of this chapter.

Omar, which has since been recognized by the 2022 Pulitzer Prize in music, is significant for a number of reasons. As stated by co-composer Giddens, "This is a story that hasn't been represented in the operatic world — or in any world (Cooper, 2019, para 3)." Ibn Said wrote his autobiography in 1831, and it is the

...only known extant memoir of a slave that was written in Arabic in America... [recounting]...his youth and studies in West Africa, his enslavement in Charleston, and his escape, recapture, jailing and eventual sale to a brother of North Carolina's governor. The Library of Congress recently digitized it and put the manuscript and a trove of related documents on its website (Cooper, 2019, para 4).

In this way, the production offered not only a telling of history that has been largely ignored, but it also became a vehicle for black artists to embody experiences beyond predictably stereotypical operatic standards like *Porgy and Bess*. There was a shared desire to disrupt how black stories have been told in classical settings, to center black voices in said telling, and to nurture an artistic process that attended to the spirit of the black folks involved. The care with which Giddens, Abels, and director Kaneza Schaal, as well as the entire creative team gave this story, and their commitment to the disruption of opera's problematic history of representation was evident in all aspects of the production.

A part of this disruption involved viewing the production as an opportunity to recognize, highlight and visibilize the experiences and stories of the musicians and vocalists involved in the opera, particularly those with black heritage. In an effort to capture those experiences, Giddens invited author/artists, Karen and Lalenja to help gather and share those stories artistically through visual portraiture and the poetic, resulting in an artistic collaboration that the authors view as a critical literacy (CL) project; a way of "reading the word and the world" with the understanding that all texts are biased and informed by the ideology of the creator (Gisselson, 2020), and in a manner that encourages people to transform inequities in their social and political worlds (Zaino & Bell, 2022, 32).

For the purposes of this chapter, we further define CL as practice that challenges more traditional definitions of literacy that focus on technical skills and the valuing of writing over orality and embodied expression, and disrupts hegemonic reading practices by recognizing "the ways in which minoritized people, particularly racialized people, leverage literacies to effect change" (Zaino & Bell, 2022, 32). As an artist team composed of a black, southern American woman and an Irish woman, both of whom have specific relationships to ancestral trauma and experiences of oppression, it was our collective goal to "leverage" those lenses and our areas of literacy to help capture the complex stories of Omar and the artists telling his story.

With that in mind, we acknowledge that the project brought us both an unexpected chance to not only explore the criticality of *Omar's* storytelling through the lens of each author's own area of expertise, but also to explore the impact of intersecting those areas of expression as a process of critical *multimodal* literacy (CML). We resonate with Ajayi (2015)'s framing of CML as the intersection of multiple modes and media for meaning making where multimodality is defined as the "intercon-

On These Haunted Streets

nections and interrelations among differing modes of representation that coexist in a multimodal text and how the different modes provide differing affordances for interpreting texts" (218). We would argue that in the hands of Giddens, Schaal and Abels, Omar is in and of itself such an example of CML. This chapter is designed to explore that assertion and highlight our process of artistic co-creation- an emerging transmedia storytelling process that has developed/continues to develop. In the following section we provide historical context for the opera to help anchor that discussion.

CONTEXTUALIZING *OMAR*

Omar Ibn Said's autobiography offers "a voice from the time of slavery" that gives us a different way to understand history than what we have known before (CBS Sunday, 2022). The opera was inspired by his writings, and indeed as one can see from the first image, his words were ever present as a part of the very foundation of the set. Said's story is reflective of the twenty to thirty per cent of enslaved Africans who were of Muslim descent (La Opera, 2022)- perspectives that we are not generally able to experience through the contemporary media landscape, outside of dehumanizing narratives that perpetuate violent, essentialized stereotypes

After studying Islam for 25 years, Said was stolen from his home country of Senegal and in 1807 he was forcibly brought to South Carolina. He was likely on one of the last "legal" ships to do so before the act prohibiting the importation of slaves went into effect that same year. His story includes an escape from a cruel South Carolina owner, and then a 200 mile trek to Fayetteville NC where he was captured, jailed, and then released to a planter who was impressed by the charcoal writings in Arabic he'd made on the walls of his jail cell. Said died in 1864 at the age of 93 and was never freed (Rhiannon Giddens, personal communication, June 10, 2024). As tempting as it might be to frame his life as a tragedy, although there were certainly tragic events that shaped it, his story is ultimately one of triumph, as Giddens and Abels stressed in their creation of this opera (CBS Sunday, 2022). "What we hope folks remember," Giddens has said, "is not the middle passage, not the bad master, but how he remained connected to his God" (LA Opera, 2022).

In this way, *Omar* is a powerful counternarrative, written and directed by black artists working to reclaim history and offer a different experience for black musicians on the operatic stage in the process. In the NY Times article *Opera Can No Longer Ignore Its Race Problem*, black artists speak to their frustration with the state of representation in this artform. One of the interviewed artists, Morris Robinson, illustrates this clearly with his statement,

In 20 years, I've never been hired by a Black person; I've never been directed by a Black person; I've never had a Black C.E.O. of a company; I've never had a Black president of the board; I've never had a Black conductor," Mr. Robinson said. *"I don't even have Black stage managers. None, not ever, for 20 years (Barone, 2020, para, 3).*

The actual demographics provided in the article reflect Robinson's experience, highlighting facts like The Met's track record of not having one black composer for any of the 306 operas that it has produced in its 137-year history up through 2020 (Barone, 2020). Fellow artist Russell Thomas spoke to his desire to see work created by and for black audiences, saying, "Stop allowing white people to tell Black people about the Black experience…that, to me, is outrageous. Don't tell me about how I should feel to be Black and how I should move" (Barone, 2020, para 3). The Met finally addressed this absence in 2021, by commissioning *Fire Shut up in My Bones* by Terrance Blanchard (*Fire Shut Up in my Bones*, n.d.).

Given this landscape, *Omar*, *Fire* and the limited number of other works like it (i.e *X and Central Park 5* by Anthony Davis) take on a significance for musician and audience goer alike by providing opportunities to hear black stories, told by black creators, and performed by black artists who "move" as Thomas says, in ways that are rooted in the black experience. Giddens postulates that the moments of rootedness in the black church tradition might explain why black musicians resonate with *Porgy and Bess*, with Gershwin's "representation of his faith through black church scenes" (Rhiannon Giddens, personal communication, June 7, 2024). "Because black people who sing that opera, I mean, people wouldn't do it if it didn't speak to them," she says, affirming her own powerful experience of "making church on stage every night" when she sang the role of Bess in 2023 (Rhiannon Giddens, personal communication, June 7, 2024). Witnessing the same moments of spiritual connection from the musicians in Omar, across multiple productions, was significant for Giddens, and an important part of her and Abel's vision for the opera, as well as making space to nurture spirit and care for the processing of generational trauma. Again, a departure from the status quo of opera's traditional modus operandi that Giddens knew it would be significant to capture.

Giddens has also identified the Muslim story in the American context as an important distinguishing feature of Omar. "It is really important in that arena… representing the black Muslim experience, which has been…just so invisible" she says. With so few balanced historical representations of the Muslim experience in the media (outside of perhaps *Daughters of the Dust* by Julie Dash), Omar plays an important cultural role, particularly in the classical world. Giddens affirmed,

On These Haunted Streets

...what I wanted to do with Omar was not only represent, of course, the invisible, the black Muslim as invisible, made visible, but also pulling deeply from American folk traditions in a way that was immediately accessible to people while still being interesting enough to merit, you know, an entire 64 piece of orchestra and classical singers, you know? Which is kind of a tall order...I'm so deeply rooted in both of the traditions that I could, I feel like married those two traditions in a way that felt very, you know, I feel like this actually is the black folk, American folk opera opera, you know (Rhiannon Giddens, personal communication, June 7, 2024).

The "marriage" that Giddens references, which she believes is so essential for understanding the wholeness of Omar's life, is what situates Omar as an example of CML and what we describe later as transmedia storytelling. Ultimately, her call to create was anchored in her desire to engage a similar multimodal process of documentation, in a way that was organic and authentic to all of the artists involved.

I wasn't interested in documentation in the old way of like, here are the facts, here is a picture, a Polaroid of the facts. It's like you have a lens. Karen has a lens, obviously, apart from her camera lens, 'cause you're both artists. So, and then of course they're artists in the show. So this idea of making a, not document, but... where you have a record of it that was still artistic. Like coming from an artistic place. I mean, that's kind of how I operate in general... like whoever I wanna involve in it, I want them to have their own perspective, because they're gonna have their own perspective anyway (Rhiannon Giddens, personal communication, June 7, 2024).

Although Giddens has stated that "[she] often doesn't know what [her] intent is [with documentation] until after the project is over" she did know that she didn't want the "usual" press photos, "polaroids of facts," that would focus on Omar as simply as stage presentation.

Outside of the historical and cultural significance of Omar's story that Giddens has articulated, she also noticed that artists were sharing deep experiences about the significance of their engagement as black folk telling and connecting to his story. She reached out to us as artistic collaborators, to help her "vision" how documentation of these complexities might occur, to help her create "art for art's sake" that also told the important stories of this production.

There is a lot of truth in a stanza, you know, in a rhymed couplet. You can find like two pages worth of prose in that sometimes... It was like, you know, I could do an essay on each person, or, you know, we could distill it to a photo... a poem. So I'd rather have somebody who owns their perspective and are thinking about it in an artistic way..because then I knew that some sort of truth would still come through (Rhiannon Giddens, personal communication, June 7, 2024).

Although she doesn't use the same language, Giddens describes a critical multimodal literacy approach here, one that not only describes the work of Schaal and her other collaborators, but also the opera itself, which uses elements of visual literacy through its brilliant set, a combination of musical literacies through the blend of classical and folk music structures, as well as embodied, cultural and place-specific literacies that inform Omar's story. As black creators and artists, Giddens, along with Schaal and Abels, also see this production as a vehicle for change, a place to consider

…what space is being held for the people doing this work? You know, which has not generally been part of the operatic process. You know, it's like, you're an actress, you're an actor, you're a singer. Get with, get on with it, do the thing and go home. Like, take your check and go home (Rhiannon Giddens, personal communication, June 7, 2024).

For she and her team, it was necessary to tell Omar's story in a creative environment that actively challenged the white supremacist principles that undergird western classical traditions. Omar was an opportunity to reclaim and lift the fullness and nuance of black stories by engaging in cultural and artistic practices that are reflective of the community in which the stories are situated, rather than a blind adherence to "canon." Omar was also an opportunity to approach storytelling from what researcher Stephanie Tolliver describes below as an "endarkened" practice, shaped by black culture,

My mother was my first storyteller. Through story, I learned about who she was, and I began to understand the deep-rooted communal connections cultivated by my grandmother and grandfather as well as those who came before them. These stories preserved my family history and ensured that I began my life with the foundation of my people. They helped me locate myself amongst the legacy of my family, enhancing my view of self, others and the world. They helped me bond with my family, those I had met and those I had not. Sometimes they validated my experiences or provided a level of catharsis when I had a bad day. Other times, stories were an educational tool that helped me learn to read and tell my own stories. (Toliver, 2021, xiv)

Like Toliver, we view storytelling as an important vehicle for building literacy skills that is also connected to intergenerational knowing and expression/witness of lived experience, and we value the power of combining media, in this case image and poem, to create accurate representations of those lived experiences (Boylorn, 2013); a process of transmedia storytelling that we frame in the next section.

ROOTED IN STORYTELLING

We view the intersection of our approaches to story as "transmedia storytelling" which Slota et al (2016) describe as a narrative process that is "dispersed across multiple delivery channels [and] multiple media" (643). This approach is different from "crossmedia delivery" in that it involves a synthesis of different aspects of a story across different modes of media, rather than the telling of the same story across multiple delivery channels (Slota, et al, 2016). The intersection of our individual literacies come together to create a "whole" story, in much the same way that Giddens instinctively knew that multiple modes would be necessary to tell the larger story of *Omar*.

To tell *our* story of process, we will highlight our individual approaches and areas of literacy and then discuss how our approaches intersect. We will highlight the steps that we took both individually and collectively, identify the elements that we have come to understand as our photopoetic process, and we will also provide examples from the Omar project of this collective process through three co-constructed stories.

ANSWERING THE CALL

Giddens initially called on Cox to create photographic portraits of all cast members who chose to participate, inspired by her 1) critical documentary work, 2) commitment to storytelling and 3) her outsider status as a person with Irish heritage. This was an intentional decision made by Giddens, who felt that Cox's outsider status, but also her connection to the Irish history of activism against oppression, would encourage folks to respond in a way that they might not with her. "It was important that Karen was in control of those sessions" Giddens said, because "she's an outsider… they could talk to her in a way they wouldn't talk to me… but she's also a sympathetic outsider because Irish folks… are usually for the oppressed." That lens would also prove to be an important cultural connector for the artistic collaboration with Harrington as well.

The entire cast was invited to schedule portrait sessions with Cox during the production. After a really strong response, time allowed for the completion of 27 sessions with singers, dancers, orchestral musicians who responded to the invitation. The respondents represented varying levels of experience in the opera world, some with professional status and some without. During each session, Cox interviewed participants using a set of questions developed by Giddens, as their portraits were taken. Interviews were recorded- again, not with any particular end-product in mind, Giddens just knew that this moment was an important one to catch.

As Cox engaged in portrait sessions, Giddens considered other creative storytelling possibilities as a part of her intent to capture the intricacies of Omar's story. She invited collaborator and poet Harrington to explore the potential of the poetic as a part of the storytelling process. Harrington's positionality as a black, southern artist/scholar with experience using poetry to capture life stories was a significant part of her call to engage. The combination of Harrington's and Cox's cultural backgrounds made for a powerful intersection of analytical lenses. They were also encouraged by Giddens to collaborate without expectation or imposed structure, and after a few artist/creator brainstorming sessions, bringing their different areas of literacy to bear, the photopoetic creative process that we discuss later in the chapter was developed.

Storytelling through portraiture (Karen's voice)

Every image sheds light on the assumptions of the day. Every image reveals, as well as defines, events. Every image must be read, must be interpreted. This is a perilous act, one that often leads us far away from the safe ground sought by most historians. Yet reading the image, like reading any text, is a way to engage the past and connect it to our lives. – Louis Masur, Historian (Rockenbach & Fabian, 2008)

My process of visual image making involves being aware of the contextual, cultural and emotional landscape (the "assumptions of the day to which Masur refers above); what needs to be communicated and how that needs to be implemented. Creative observation is a fundamental part of this. In an increasingly visual world, imagery is not always supplemented with additional information meaning that an image alone can provide layers of information. The creation of images can result in new knowledge or added emphasis on existent knowledge with the potential to elicit psychological and emotional responses from the viewer. Processes of visual literacy combined with context can produce intense imagery - some of the tools I engaged with included:

Figure 2. Elements of Karen's process

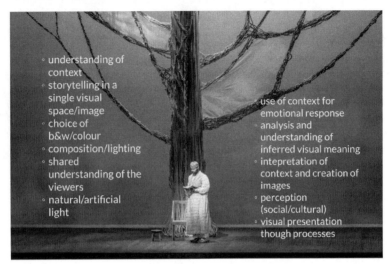

Photo Credit: Karen Cox

John Debes first used the term visual literacy (VL) in 1969 to describe "a group of vision-competencies [like those above] a human being can develop by seeing and at the same time having and integrating other sensory experiences" (visual literacy today, n.d, para 2). VL involves the discrimination and interpretation of "actions, objects, symbols, natural or man-made" that one encounters in the environment (visual literacy today, n.d, para 2). For Messaris (1995), VL can be defined as "the gaining of knowledge and experience" about visual media, combined with a "heightened conscious awareness of those workings" (as cited in Bamford, 2013). Said knowledge is used to creatively decode and interpret what is "seen with the eye and what is 'seen' with the mind" and to encode and compose meaningful communication (VL today, n.d, para 2).

In *Omar*, the visual component of the project consisted of a number of these "seen" elements engaged simultaneously. Each visual depiction started with a brief initial interview with the subject of each individual portrait. The location and time was chosen by the individual. On meeting each subject/artist, I chose the best area of light and most suitable background for the image. The interview consisted of a series of questions and I found that conducting the interview first put the subject more at ease for the portrait shots. The process of making the image was a combination of ensuring the subject was in a comfortable physical position, judging the surrounding light and background, building an image composition relating to both inferred and volunteered information together with a sensitive approach to the image making.

An additional layer to my process involves an intuitive cognizance and recognition of all or any emotion expressed by the individual in tandem with an awareness of the final image possibilities. The context of the project (the making of an opera and portraits of the cast) was at the forefront of decisions made on final images. I felt that the use of black and white for all of the visual portraits of the *Omar* artists was appropriate for the tone and layering of the images in addition to the context of the project. The use of black and white was also more impactful for the final visual of the text/image relationship, a decision drawing on a "system of representation and signification that allows us to produce and communicate thoughts and images about reality.' (Kazmierczak, 2001, 181). The true representation of the individual in a visual image involves the many components of visual literacy. The application of these methods was intrinsic to the visual portrayal of the *Omar* artists.

Storytelling through found poetry (Lalenja's voice)

I have a clear memory of standing in front of my mamma's floor to ceiling book "wall" as a teenager, and selecting For Colored Girls who have Considered Suicide When the Rainbow is enuf by Ntozake Shange. Finding myself in those pages shifted my world. I didn't have formal words for that shift at the time, but it happened nonetheless, as I began a lifelong engagement with the world through the poetic employing what I now understand to be poetic literacy (PL) skills.

In his writing from 1925, I.A. Richards offers us a rich description of what poetic literacy can look and feel like, beginning, he says,

> *...by reading it [a poem] very slowly, preferably aloud, giving every syllable time to make its full effect upon us. And let us read it experimentally, repeating it, varying our tone of voice until we are satisfied that we have caught its rhythm as well as we are able and, whether our reading is such as to please other people or not, we ourselves at least are clear as to how it should 'go' (484).*

This reading, Richards (1925) says, should include a noticing of the " sound of the word 'in the mind's ear' and the feel of the word imaginarily spoken...[which] together give the full body as it were, to the words, and it is with the full bodies of words that the poet works..." (484). The next step involves raising images in the mind, "not of words, but of things for which the words stand; perhaps of ships, perhaps of hills; and together with them, it may be, other images of various sorts (484)." Richards' description resonates with me deeply because of the focus on embodied reading practices to take in the "full bodies of words."

As a process of relational meaning-making, I also resonate with Zaino and Bell (2022)'s description of poetry as

On These Haunted Streets

A uniquely useful method for expressing the ambiguity and inconmmensurability of 'affective encounters' [Lenters, 2016]... [that] allows for thematic and narrative coherence as well as sudden shifts in tone, juxtapositions of imagery, and a refusal of narrative sense, thus allowing us to 'work with complexity rather than seeing to order it through linear accounts [Burnett & Merchant, 2018, 18] (Zaino & Bell, 2022, 29).

Along with being a way of knowing and affective evocation described above, poetry is for me, ontologically, a critical way of being in the world. Living poetically, as Weibe (2015) describes it, requires engaging with poetry on multiple levels- as a form of critical literacy, meaning making, inquiry, storytelling and aesthetic expression. Poetry is also a cultural anchor that holds me as I move through, amongst, alongside, throughout each of these spaces with a Black feminist sensibility committed to naming "socio political inequities by centering minoritized and acting as a counter-narrative to dominant discourse within and beyond the academy" (Zaino & Bell, 2022, 35).

Omar provided a perfect platform to put said sensibilities, reading practices and storytelling into action through the use of found poetry. Found poetry has been described as a process of selecting "words, phrases, and details from existing texts" and reordering them (as one might do to images in a collage) as a complete poem (Roessing, 2019, 43). In its most basic form, it is an "ekphrastic" process that exclusively uses the selected text- verbatim- to construct the new poem (Weibe, 2015). Poetic tools that shaped my "finding" of poetic stories for this project include:

> **Ephemeral listening** (Armos, 2024)
> close attention
> to what is expressed
>   and what is missing
> transcribing
> the silences
>
> alongside
>   what is vocalized
>   held in the body
>
> **Feelin it in my bones** (Richards, 1925; Weibe, 2015; Judd, 2023)
>   senses on full alert
>   saying
>   yes body
>   speak to mind and spirit
>   help me find the words
>   that cannot be
>   spoken
>   yes poet's soul
>   do your work
>
> **Ekphrastic choices** (Weibe, 2015)
> dialogic response
>   to storied text
>   honoring the knowing
>   of chosen words
>   expressed
>   by those who are too often
>   expected
>   demanded
>   to be silent
>
> **Translation through conventions of theory and form** (Weibe, 2015)
> literary
> poetic
> like
>   the breaking
>   of lines
>   and
>   assiduous application of assonance
>   consonance
>   rhythm
>   phrasing
>
> **The unsettling of truth/boundless unknowing** (Zaino & Bell, 2022; Rackley, Bradford & Peairs, 2022)
>   conscious permission
>   to tangle
>   with the unknown
>   be true to what makes us
>   uncomfortable
>   making space
>   capturing
>   all of the
>   unspeakable things
>   that have the power
>   to transform us

Ultimately for me, operating from a place of poetic literacy anchored in Black feminist praxis means understanding how body/mind/spirit engages with word to evoke and/or accept feeling as knowledge, create otherwise worlds through literary convention, and creatively use the limited/limiting mode of written language to capture the impossibilities of the unknown/unspeakable (Evans-Winters, 2019; Judd, 2023). Found poetry, an "experience of knowing [that is] tinkered with in the process of creation" (Judd, 2023, 9) and that lives in the minds, hands, bodies, and hearts of both the storyteller and poet, was an integral method for bringing the stories of *Omar* artists forward. That process was further complexified by my engagement with Karen's portraits, which we will describe in the next section.

Photopoetic storytelling as critical multimodal literacy (Our voice)

Originally, we came to this project as individual artists with the intent of "creating separately" and then bringing image and word together as final stories. We found however, that richer and fuller stories developed when we moved through the process iteratively and collaboratively- as Lalenja incorporated the visual into her poetry, and Karen drew on the poetic to inform her visual stories. In so doing, we stumbled upon a collective multimodal process, that we describe here as the photopoetic.

The intersection of photography and poetry represent a critical multimodal literacy (CML) that acknowledges the "sophisticated, interconnected skills learners need to receive and process multiple media, navigate cultural codes and interpersonal interactions, and re/act accordingly" (Rhoades, Dallacqua, Kersten, Merryfield, & Miller, 2015 as cited in Rhoades, 2020, 178-179). Such an approach asks creators and readers to use multiple modes of meaning making to consider power and identity, promote critical consciousness, and think more expansively and inclusively in general. (Rhoades, 2020). Given the socio-political emphasis that we have in our work both individually and together, this literacy framework feels particularly appropriate.

For this project, we also particularly resonate with what Abas (2023) has identified as integral elements as CML:

- Disrupting the commonplace by using new, varied texts/sources, frames, language, forms of analysis
- Considering multiple viewpoints
- Interrogation of socio-political systems and power relationships
- Taking action service of social justice (Abas, 2023, 164)

We embrace the potential for this multimodal process to disrupt not only our thinking and interpretation, but also for the viewer/reader-inviting them to pause and make space for what they might not have known. We hope that our poetic and visual viewpoints work in tandem to tell fuller stories that encourage viewers/readers to ask critical questions about history, power and identity in this country. We hope that highlighting counternarratives/stories offers an alternate "reading" of what art forms like opera can generate for artists and audiences alike.

The intersection - our photopoetic process and reading practices

On These Haunted Streets

We present our collective "steps" in figure 2. Although this list still feels relatively "individualized", these steps did not happen in a vacuum as we began intentionally sharing our processes with each other and discovering how the final stories were impacted by the collaboration. It was in the space of our multiple chats and check-ins with each other that we began to see how the intersection of our processes expanded our meaning-making, and that we both centered embodied response as an important "reading

Figure 3. Steps of emerging photopoetic process

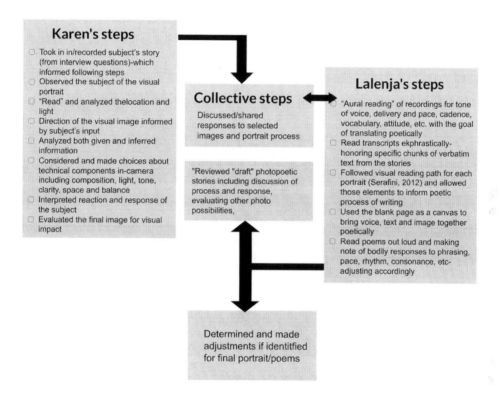

path" for both visuals and text. Karen would describe how her emotional responses to each subject played out in the execution and selection of final images, and hearing about those responses to her process would then become another source of information for Lalenja's writing, ultimately providing more contextual information to the images themselves.

For Lalenja, who initially planned to stay true to the more ekphrastic approach of found poetry, engagement with the visual required a shift in approach, including the addition of some of her own poetic language beyond what was lifted from the

On These Haunted Streets

transcripts. There was an opportunity here, to bring the visual into the poetic, to align the mood and tone of the poem with the visual story- to expand the story beyond what came forward through textual and aural readings. To do so, Lalenja paid close attention to her visual reading path with each image, and how each poem was informed by this reading (see figures 3-5 for examples of process).

Of the number of portraits taken, we chose to include the following three because they 1) reflect 3 different thematic elements related to the black experience, 2) allowed us to clearly discuss process and 3) perhaps most importantly, were the first three that resonated in our bodies-that felt instinctively right to include. The examples include a description of each author's engagement with the creative process. Lalenja's include the visual reading path that impacted her poetic process, represented by the bold text.

Examples of photopoetic process
Chantal's Story.

Figure 4. Chantal's story

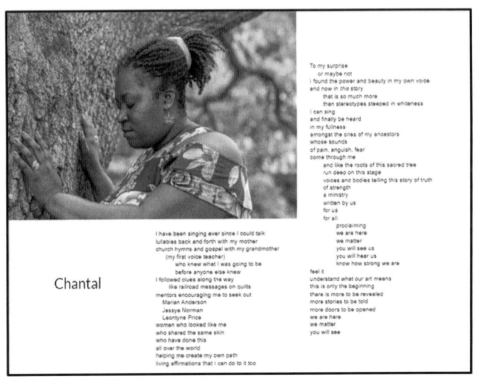

Photo Credit: Karen Cox; Poem: Lalenja Harrington

Karen's process. A deeply emotional person, Chantal used the interview time to reflect on past experiences and hopes for the future. I felt that this depth of feeling and connection to the past and awareness of the present was essential to illustrate in her visual portrait. Our meeting took place in a quiet park full of statuesque trees. We made portraits in different parts of the location; however, as Chantal stood beside a particular tree in a momentary state of silent reflection, I asked her to place her hands on the trunk of the tree. As she did this, she closed her eyes, the connection she seemed to forge felt almost palpable and I immediately hit the shutter release button.

Lalenja's process. Visual reading path:*The look of groundedness on Chantal's face, the presence of the tree in the frame, her hands on the tree, the textural interplay of her clothing as a cultural marker.* Upon seeing the image, my bodymindspirit responded to the visual connection to the tree as a metaphor for ancestral legacy (***amongst the cries of my ancestors***). Chantal displays such a deep connection- I could feel her spirit communicating with the tree, which made certain aspects of her interview take center stage (***like the roots of this sacred tree***)- her emphasis on that connection through the portrait helped guide me as I made decisions on what elements of her story to bring forward through THIS poetic iteration of her story- the portrait visually exhibits the sense of peace that Chantal describes in finally being heard and seen (***I found the power and beauty in my own voice***), as well as the ways in which she feels like she channels the spirit of her ancestors with her hands as literal points of transfer (***my ancestors…whose sounds of pain, anguish fear come through me***) The location of this tree, in Charleston, rooted in the very earth where so many enslaved folks were displaced, survived and died was an important element of this "reading"- an embodiment of Chantal's affirmation of presence and futurity (***we are here, we matter, you will see***). Chantal's story, as a cast member of Omar, is one of ancestral lineage and self-actualization.

Scott's Story.

On These Haunted Streets

Figure 5. Scott's Story

Scott

This story needs to be told
  to unearth
what has been hidden
to show that we are not monolithic
and that our narrative is bigger
than what has been peddled back to us
  to justify
all the ways that they have tried
to make us feel less than
like we're not worth shit
it's up to us
  to celebrate
the reality of what was
and what is
to bring these truths to our community
  to correct the story

Nobody ever forgets about the Holocaust
but slavery,
they want to sweep it under the rug
there is a difference
in how these two stories
are being told
We hold great power in *this* telling
this reckoning
  here on these haunted streets
I want to be a part of it
it's different
helping to tell a story
instead of just watching
all the fucked up shit they have been
doing to us foreva
I can put all of my energy into this
to make it do what it do
so we can be free
to be what we be

Photo Credit: Karen Cox; Poem: Lalenja Harrington

Karen's process. Scott was verbally expressive from the offset and this energy could be seen mirrored very clearly in his body language. As he gathered his thoughts after each interview question, he tended to look towards the water. Our meeting took place in a small park near the water but I wanted to base his portrait shots at the water's edge as he was so clearly drawn to it. Scott is a dancer in the Omar cast and I asked him to crouch down to get that sense of movement but he naturally drifted into a sitting pose which immediately felt like the most natural one for his visual portrait. The natural light was bright with distinct afternoon shadows which feature in the image to reflect his strength of spirit.

Lalenja's process. Visual reading path: *Scott's posture and placement in the frame, the location at the water's edge, the look of determination on Scott's face, the forward-looking gaze and sense of coiled energy.* I see this image as a visual counternarrative (***to unearth what has been hidden***). Scott unapologetically locates himself in a setting (at the water's edge) that has been both a place of nourishment and oppression/displacement for folks of African heritage (***it is up to us to celebrate the reality of what was and what is***). He speaks to the reclaiming of our story and how he wants to be at the center of the re-telling- in much the same way that he has centered himself in this scene (***to bring these truths to our community, to correct the story***). His expression and body language all evoke that feeling of determination

On These Haunted Streets

and agency, and were of great impact for me as the poet- it was important to me that the words highlighted in the poem and the overall tone of his story were reflective of the spirit he displayed in the photo. Although he is seated, I can still feel his potential for movement- he feels engaged (*I want to be a part of it, its different, helping to tell a story instead of just watching*). Scott's story is an affirmation of the power of "for us, by us", the power of art in the hands of the people who have lived that identity and experience.

Michael's Story.

Figure 6. Michael's story. Photo Credit: Karen Cox; Poem: Lalenja Harrington

Michael

Music
moving
through my hands
like the pieces of a puzzle
    complicated
    contours
    of expression
interlocking
and creating
new shapes of understanding
as I draw up a blueprint
for artists
to share connections
with something greater
than themselves
than
    ourselves

architect's joy
such composing of life
and building of images
that tell this story
(his) story
of the power of faith
to transcend
and find joy
in the midst of pain and tragedy
a disquieting dissonance
that,
like the city on whose streets
we present our song
is beautiful
and disturbing
at the same time

Karen's Process. On meeting Michael, he is a gentle, softly-spoken individual with a sense of calm in the way he presents himself. This sense of serenity and wisdom was pervasive and it seemed fundamental to capture this in his visual portrait. We met in a green area next to the Sottile theatre in Charleston; a fittingly calm space. We spoke for quite a while and he expressed his feelings on the opera and what it meant to him. Each answer was answered carefully and meaningfully. Michael's portrait was of simple design – he was in a naturally tranquil space and with the evening light (illumination) breaking through the tree canopy cover overhead, the composition and image took shape intuitively and using elements of light plus personal and conceptual contexts.

On These Haunted Streets

Lalenja's Process. Visual Reading path: *the serene look on Michael's face, the direction of his gaze, the light coming down from above, the composition and location in nature*

I was immediately connected to a sense of spirituality when I saw this image (**to share connections with something greater than themselves**). The light, the composition, his posture and his facial expression all drew that forward in my body. I deeply resonated with his description of himself as architect and creator, (**architect's joy such composing of life**) and as I was transcribing and writing, the image stayed present in my mind. That visual anchor impacted the very words that stood out to me, and took on importance in THIS telling of his story. He speaks to the power of faith in his interview (**the power of faith to transcend and find joy**)- and for me, this image is a visual representation of that. Michael' s story is one of faith and co-creation.

Process from here…

Giddens hopes to include these *portrait stories* and others in a "Making of Omar" book that illustrates the significance of the Charleston production. The next stage of process for the portraits included in this chapter as well as the other 24, will include the gathering of feedback from the participants themselves to ensure that they are in agreement with their final stories Any feedback provided will be integrated into the work, through another layer of adjusting/revising/reimagining of the final portrait story. It is important for us and for Giddens, that artists feel that their stories are represented well by our collaboration. We also anticipate that this added layer will continue to deepen and enlighten our process.

Feelin into the impossibility

Academics have a long history of claiming and defending the superiority of verbal over visual for representing knowledge … however, in the last decade, digital technologies have broken down the barriers between words and pictures, and many of these same academics are now willing to acknowledge that melding text with image constructs new meaning." (Metros & Woolsey, 2006, 80)

This chapter describes a reciprocal coming together of literacies who challenge the hierarchy that Metros & Woolsey (2006) describe, and whose CML, transmedia intersection ultimately serves to tell fuller, richer, and more complete stories. As educators in each of our different realms, we hope that this work will inspire an expanded understanding of how folks can engage in/integrate different modes of literacy to better show what they know- to de-center written word alone as the preferred expression of knowledge. As artists, each of us entered the project with a box of tools reflective of our specific areas of visual and poetic literacy, and unexpectedly discovered a powerful intersection that allowed us to more fully represent the multi-layered stories of the artists in this production. All of these stories speak to a complex engagement with Omar and the history that "his story" represents. They help us understand the lived experiences of the black artists entrusted to represent this history, and how this production differs from other experiences within this very traditionally Western form. As oral histories and works of art, they are significant in and of themselves. They also help us to tell our photopoetic story.

As our artistic collaboration grows, we expect the process to evolve as well. We liken our process to the stone walls in Ireland that use the same materials but are designed and build differently based on what is needed in that moment/location. With new projects, it becomes more and more of an iterative process that we engage in intentionally as we make new discoveries about how this multimodal approach works to tell stories more fully. We anticipate that future work will allow us to continue exploring elements that we have found to be present in our process, such as the following,

- A CML focus on the socio-political- understanding the social purpose and cultural context through text and image
- Process as a vehicle for Witness - deep listening/viewing without the need to collect, categorize or acquire (Wong, 2021)
- Process with an emphasis on embodied knowledge making/literacies
- Process that centers bodymindspirit connection
- Process that promotes an understanding of place

as well as others that are likely to arise as we work together– a potential for continued scholarship.

We also both share a curiosity around what the process would look and feel like if the direction was reversed and/or unfolded organically without a designated order of steps, with Karen using Lalenja's poems to inform her visual engagement. With that in mind, we give a nod to this evolution with this final photo/poem. The photo offered here by Karen, was chosen based on her "feel" about our process. The photo was taken in Epecuén, Argentina, and represents the literal "unearthing" of an old town that was underwater for more than a century. Lalenja's accompanying poem, which is inspired by text from this chapter, was informed by the image, the legacy of the trees and uncovering of history, as well as Karen's feelings about it. It is our process: our story.

On These Haunted Streets

Figure 7. Trees of Epecuén

Photo credit: Karen Cox; Poem: Lalenja Harrington

REFERENCES

Abas, S. (2023). Critical multimodal literacy practices in student-created comics. *Literacy*, 57(2), 161–170. https://doi-org.libproxy.uncg.edu/10.1111/lit.12324. 10.1111/lit.12324

Ajayi, L. (2015). Critical Multimodal Literacy: How Nigerian Female Students Critique Texts and Reconstruct Unequal Social Structures. *Journal of Literacy Research*, 47(2), 216–244. 10.1177/1086296X15618478

Bamford, A. (2013). *The Visual Literacy White Paper* [White paper]. Adobe Systems Pty Ltd Australia. https://aperture.org/wp-content/uploads/2013/05/visual-literacy-wp.pdf

Barone, J. (2020). Opera can no longer ignore its race problem. *NY Times*. https://www.nytimes.com/2020/07/16/arts/music/opera-race-representation.html

Boylorn, R. (2013). *Sweetwater: Black women and narratives of resilience*. Peter Lang.

CBS Sunday Morning. (2022, August 14). *The opera "Omar," on a Muslim slave in America* [Video]. YouTube. https://www.youtube.com/watch?v=lZ0L8qbhea0

Cooper, M. (2019, June 19). *Rhiannon Giddens is writing an opera*. New York Times.

Evans-Winters, V. (yr). *Black feminism in qualitative inquiry: A Mosaic for writing our daughter's body*. Routledge.

Fire shut up in my bones. (n.d.). Metropolitan Opera: Fire Shut up in my Bones. https://www.metopera.org/season/2023-24-season/fire-shut-up-in-my-bones/

Giselsson, K. (2020). Critical Thinking and Critical Literacy: Mutually Exclusive? *International Journal for the Scholarship of Teaching and Learning*, 14(1), 5. 10.20429/ijsotl.2020.140105

Kazmierczak, E. T. (2001). A semiotic perspective on aesthetic preferences, visual literacy, and information design. *Information Design Journal*, 10(2), 176–187. 10.1075/idj.10.2.15kaz

Metros, S. E., & Woolsey, K. (2006). Visual Literacy: An institutional imperative. *Educational Review*, 41(3), 80–81. https://eric.ed.gov/?id=EJ745830

Opera, L. A. (2022, October 13). *Omar: Behind the story* [Video]. YouTube. https://www.youtube.com/watch?v=xgYuwXR9TMk

Rackley, L., Bradford, T., & Peairs, D. (2022). Love and poetics: Black life beyond literacy research as we know it. *International Studies in Sociology of Education*, 31(1–2), 67–79. https://doi-org.libproxy.uncg.edu/10.1080/09620214.2021.1882871

Rhoades, M. (2020). A Contemporary Arts-Based Approach to Critical Multimodal Literacy. *Language Arts*, 97(3), 178–185. https://www.jstor.org/stable/26873330. 10.58680/la202030417

Richards, I. A. (1925). Science and Poetry. *Atlantic (Boston, Mass.)*, (Oct), 481–491.

Rockenbach, B., & Fabian, C. A. (2008). Visual literacy in the age of participation. *Art Documentation*, 27(2), 26–31. 10.1086/adx.27.2.27949492

Roessing, L. (2019). After-reading response: Using found poetry for synthesizing text. *AMLE Magazine*, 7(1), 43-46. https://login.libproxy.uncg.edu/login?url=https://www.proquest.com/trade-journals/after-reading-response-using-found-poetry/docview/2184342339/se-2

Serafini, F. (2012). Expanding the four resources model: Reading visual and multi-modal texts. *Pedagogies*, 7(2), 150–164. 10.1080/1554480X.2012.656347

Slota, S., & Young, M. (2016). A New Hope: Negotiating the Integration of Transmedia Storytelling and Literacy Instruction. *Journal of Adolescent & Adult Literacy*, 59(6), 642-646. https://www.jstor.org/stable/44011325

Toliver, S. R. (2021). *Recovering Black storytelling in qualitative research*. Taylor & Francis. 10.4324/9781003159285

What is Visual Literacy? (n.d.). Visual Literacy Today. https://visualliteracytoday.org/what-is-visual-literacy/

Wiebe, S. (2015). Poetic Inquiry: A Fierce, Tender, and Mischievous Relationship with Lived Experience. *Language and Literature*, 17(3), 152. 10.20360/G2VP4N

Wong, D. (2021). Witnessing. In Diamond, B., & Castelo-Branco, S. (Eds.), *Transforming Ethnomusicology* (pp. 187–201). Oxford University Press. 10.1093/oso/9780197517604.003.0012

Zaino, K., & Bell, J. (2022). We are each other's breath: Tracing interdependency through critical poetic inquiry. *Studies in Sociology of Education*, 31(2), 27–48.

Appendix

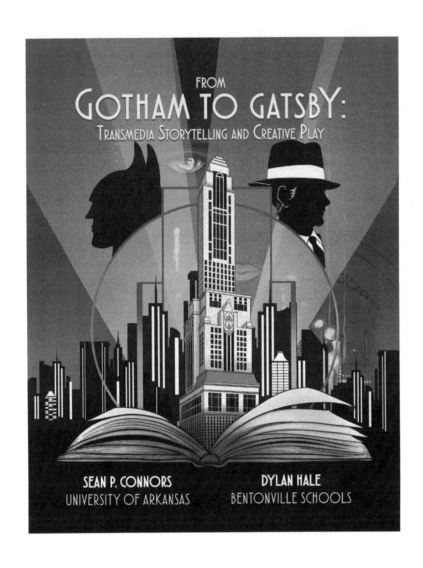

TITLE: From Gotham to Gatsby: Transmedia Storytelling and Creative Play
AUTHORS: Sean P. Connors, University of Arkansas; Dylan Hale, Bentonville Schools

As defined by Jenkins (2013), this involves attending to "elements that were systematically excluded from the narrative with ideological consequences" (p. 143).

References

Alper, M., & Herr-Stephenson, R. (2013). Transmedia play: Literacy across media. Journal of Media Literacy Education, 5(2), 366-369.

Brownell, C. J. Writing as a minecrafter: Exploring how children blur world of play in the elementary English language arts classroom. Teachers College Record: The Voice of Scholarship in Education, 123(3), 1-19.

Cantor, J. (2022). Beautiful little fools. Harper Perennial.

Dyson, A. H. (2018). From Superman play to singing the blues: On the trail of child writing and popular culture. Language Arts, 96(1), 37-46.

Fitzgerald, F. S. (1925/2004). The Great Gatsby. Scribner.

Herr-Stephenson, B., Alper, M., Reilly, E., & Jenkins, H. (2013). T Is for transmedia: Learning through transmedia play. USC Annenberg Innovation Lab and The Joan Ganz Cooney Center at Sesame Workshop.

Hirsch Jr., E. D. (1988). Cultural literacy: What every American needs to know. Vintage.

Jenkins, H. (2013). Reading critically and reading creatively. In Jenkins, H., Kelley, W., Clinton, K., McWilliams, J., Pitts-Wiley, R., & Reilly, E. (Eds.), Reading in a participatory culture : Remixing Moby-Dick in the English classroom (pp. 137-149). Teachers College Press and National Writing Project.

Leitch, T. (2007). Film adaptation and its discontents: From Gone with the Wind to The Passion of Christ. The Johns Hopkins University Press.

Smith, M. F. (2021). Nick. Little Brown and Company.

Compilation of References

Abad-Santos, A. (2016, March 7). The biggest drama in comic books right now is over Spider-Man and race. *Vox*.https://www.vox.com/2016/3/7/11173456/spider-man-miles-morales

Abas, S. (2023). Critical multimodal literacy practices in student-created comics. *Literacy*, 57(2), 161–170. https://doi-org.libproxy.uncg.edu/10.1111/lit.12324. 10.1111/lit.12324

Abercrombie, D. (2017, August 2). Miles Morales: A Spider-Man novel – An interview with Jason Reynolds. *Redital*.https://www.redital.com/2017/miles-morales-a-spider-man-novel-an-interview-with-jason-reynolds/

Ahmed, A. (2020). Islam and Black America: The religious life of Malcolm X. *Journal of African American Studies*, 24(3), 456–481. 10.1007/s12111-020-09492-5

Ajayi, L. (2015). Critical Multimodal Literacy: How Nigerian Female Students Critique Texts and Reconstruct Unequal Social Structures. *Journal of Literacy Research*, 47(2), 216–244. 10.1177/1086296X15618478

Aldama, F. L. (2017). *Latinx superheroes in mainstream comics*. University of Arizona Press.

Aldama, F. L. (2020). Gender and sexuality in comics. In Aldama, F. L. (Ed.), *The Routledge Companion to Gender and Sexuality in Comic Book Studies* (1st ed., pp. 1–12). Routledge. 10.4324/9780429264276-1

Alfonseca, K. (2020). This Afro-Latina comic book artist uses her characters as a voice for outsiders. *HuffPost*. https://www.huffpost.com/entry/latinx-comic-book-artist-natacha-bustos-marvel_n_5f696408c5b655acbc6ee48d

Ames, M. (2013). Engaging" apolitical" adolescents: Analyzing the popularity and educational potential of dystopian literature post-9/11. *High School Journal*, 97(1), 3–20. 10.1353/hsj.2013.0023

Amon, B. T. (2019). Transmedia narratives in education: The potentials of multisensory emotional arousal in teaching and learning contexts. *Narrative Transmedia*, 1-26.

Arizpe, E., & Styles, M. (2016). *Children reading picturebooks: Interpreting visual texts* (2nd ed.). Routledge.

Ash, K., & Kellner, D. (2016). *Teaching in the Multimodal World: Digital Tools for New Literacies*. Routledge.

Atari, M., Haidt, J., Graham, J., Koleva, S., Stevens, S. T., & Dehghani, M. (2023). Morality beyond the WEIRD: How the nomological network of morality varies across cultures. *Journal of Personality and Social Psychology*, 125(5), 1157–1188. 10.1037/pspp000047037589704

Aydın, M. (2013). Beş yaklaşıma göre nitel araştırma ve araştırma deseni. In Bütün, M., & Demir, S. B. (Eds.), *Nitel araştırma yöntemleri- Beş Yaklaşıma Göre Nitel Araştırma ve Araştırma Deseni* (pp. 69–110). Siyasal Yayınevi.

Bainbridge, J. (2020). "This land is mine!:" Understanding the function of supervillains. In Burke, L., Gordon, I., & Ndalianis, A. (Eds.), *The superhero symbol: Media, culture, and politics* (pp. 63–78). Rutgers University Press.

Bakhtin, M. (1965). *Rabelais and His World*. Indiana University Press, 15-16.

Balakrishnan, J., & Griffiths, M. D. (2017). Social media addiction: What is the role of content in YouTube? *Journal of Behavioral Addictions*, 6(3), 364–377. 10.1556/2006.6.2017.05828914072

Bamford, A. (2013). *The Visual Literacy White Paper* [White paper]. Adobe Systems Pty Ltd Australia. https://aperture.org/wp-content/uploads/2013/05/visual-literacy-wp.pdf

Banks, J. A. (2006). *Race, culture, and education: The selected works of James A. Banks*. Routledge. 10.4324/9780203088586

Barone, J. (2020). Opera can no longer ignore its race problem. *NY Times*. https://www.nytimes.com/2020/07/16/arts/music/opera-race-representation.html

Barry, L. (2019). *Making comics*. Drawn Quarterly.

Beach, R., Anson, C. M., Breuch, L. K., & Swiss, T. (2016). *Teaching writing using blogs, wikis, and other digital tools*. Teachers College Press.

Beach, R., Castek, J., & Scott, J. (2017). Acquiring Processes for Responding to and Creating Multimodal Digital Productions. In Hinchman, K. A., & Appleman, D. A. (Eds.), *Adolescent literacies: A handbook of practice-based research* (pp. 292–309). Guilford Publications.

Bedard, C., & Fuhrken, C. (2019). Deepening students' reading, responding, and reflecting on multicultural literature: It all started with" Brown Girl Dreaming. *English in Texas*, 49(1), 25–31.

Bein, S., & Lewis, D. (2022). Transforming Wakanda: Justice (or not?) in Black Panther. In Pérez, E., & Brown, T. E. (Eds.), *Black Panther and philosophy: What can Wakanda offer the world?* (pp. 14–21). John Wiley & Sons. 10.1002/9781119635871.ch2

Bellah, R., Madsen, R., Sullivan, W. M., Swidler, A., & Tipton, S. M. (1985). *Habits of the Heart: Individualism and Commitment in American Life*. University of California Press, 14.

Bendis, B. M. (Writer), & Pichelli, S. (Illustrator). (2011). *Ultimate Comics Spider-Man* #1. Marvel Comics.

Compilation of References

Bendis, B. M. (Writer), & Pichelli, S. (Illustrator). (2016). *Spider-Man #2*. Marvel Comics.

Berger, P. L., & Luckmann, T. (1966). *The Social Construction of Reality: A Treatise in the Sociology of Knowledge*. Anchor Books, 118-119.

Betancourt, D. (2018, December 13). Miles Morales is a Spider-Man who's biracial like me. So why wasn't I more excited for his movie? *The Washington Post.*https://www.washingtonpost.com/arts-entertainment/2018/12/13/miles-morales-is-spider-man-whos-biracial-like-me-so-why-wasnt-i-more-excited-his-movie/

Bezemer, J., & Kress, G. (2015). *Multimodality, learning and communication: A social semiotic frame*. Routledge. 10.4324/9781315687537

Bishop, R., & Counihan, E. (2018). Beyond the page: New literacies in the twenty first century. *Voices from the Middle*, 25(4), 39–44. 10.58680/vm201829628

Black Panther #11 (2017). "A nation under our feet, part 10." Script: T. Coates. Art: C. Sprouse.

Black Panther #12 (2017). "A nation under our feet, part 10." Script: T. Coates. Art: B. Stelfreeze.

Black, R. W. (2009). Online fan fiction and critical media literacy. *Journal of Computing in Teacher Education*, 26(2), 75–80.

Bolling, B. (2020). Transmedia superheroes, multimodal composition, and digital literacy. In Kirtley, S. E., Garcia, A., & Carlson, P. E. (Eds.), *With Great Power Comes Great Pedagogy* (pp. 117–134). University of Mississippi Press. 10.2307/j.ctvx5w9g0.14

Booker, M. K. (Ed.). (2010). *Encyclopedia of comic books and graphic novels* [2 volumes]. Bloomsbury Publishing USA.

Botelho, M. J., & Rudman, M. K. (2009). *Critical multicultural analysis of children's literature: Mirrors, windows, and doors*. Routledge. 10.4324/9780203885208

Botzakis, S., Savitz, R., & Low, D. E. (2017). Adolescents reading graphic novels and comics: What we know from research. In Hinchman, K. A., & Appleman, D. A. (Eds.), *Adolescent Literacies: A Handbook of Practice-based Research* (pp. 310–322). The Guilford Press.

Botzakis, S., Savitz, R., & Low, D. E. (2017). Adolescents reading graphic novels and comics: What we know from research. In Hinchman, K. A., & Applemann, D. A. (Eds.), *Adolescent Literacies: A Handbook of Practice-Based Research* (pp. 310–322). The Guilford Press.

Boyd, H. (1993). 1992: Year of the X. *The Black Scholar*, 23(1), 22–26. 10.1080/00064246.1993.11413073

Boylorn, R. (2013). *Sweetwater: Black women and narratives of resilience*. Peter Lang.

Brown, J. A. (2013). Panthers and vixens: Black superheroines, sexuality, and stereotypes in contemporary comic books. In Howard, S. C., & Jackson, R. L.II, (Eds.), *Black Comics: Politics of Race and Representation* (pp. 133–150). Bloomsbury.

Brubaker, E. (2005). *Batman: The Man Who Laughs*. DC Comics.

Bruner, J. (1986). *Actual Minds, Possible Worlds*. Harvard University Press, 88. 10.4159/9780674029019

Burdett, J. (2003). Overcoming challenges in collaborative learning. *Educational Leadership*, 61(1), 64–68.

Burke, L. (2020). Introduction: "Everlasting symbols.". In *L. Burke, I. Gordon, & A. Ndalianis* (pp. 1–22). Rutgers University Press.

Busey, C.L., Duncan, K.E., & Dowie-Chin, T. (2022) *Critical What What? A theoretical systematic review of 15 years of Critical Race Theory*. Research in Social Studies Education, 2004–2019.

Buss, D. M. (2000). The evolution of happiness. *The American Psychologist*, 55(1), 15–23. 10.1037/0003-066X.55.1.1511392858

Byrd, D., & Miri, S. J. (2016). *Malcolm X: From political eschatology to religious revolutionary* (1st ed.). Brill. 10.1163/9789004308688

Cahnmann-Taylor, M., & Siegesmund, R. (2018). *Arts-based research in education: Foundations for practice*. Routledge.

Campbell, E. (2021). In conversation…*Miles Morales: Spider-Man* and *Miles Morales: Shock waves*. Journal of Children's Literature, 47(2), 92–94.

Campbell, J. (2008). *The hero with a thousand faces*. New World Library.

Camus, A. (1942). *The Myth of Sisyphus*. Gallimard, 108.

Carbonell, X., & Panova, T. A. (2017). Critical consideration of social networking sites' addiction potential. *Addiction Research and Theory*, 25(1), 48–57. 10.1080/16066359.2016.1197915

Carless, D., & Liu, N. F. (2006). Peer feedback: The learning element of peer assessment. *Teaching in Higher Education*, 11(3), 279–290. 10.1080/13562510600680582

Casale-Hardin, M. A. (2015, Jun 15). "Mejorar la raza": An example of racism in Latino culture. *Huffpost*. https://www.huffpost.com/entry/mejorar-la-raza-an-exampl_b_7558892

Cavna, M. (2011, August 4). Miles Morales and me: Why the new biracial Spider-Man matters. *The Washington Post*. www.washingtonpost.com/blogs/comic-riffs/post/miles-morales-and-me-why-the-new-biracial-spider-man-matters/2011/08/04/gIQABzlGuI_blog.html

CBS Sunday Morning. (2022, August 14). *The opera "Omar," on a Muslim slave in America* [Video]. YouTube. https://www.youtube.com/watch?v=lZ0L8qbhea0

Centeno, A. (2023, October 6). What *Spider-Man: Miles Morales* gets right about cultura and the authentic Puerto Rican experience. *IGN*. https://www.ign.com/articles/spider-man-miles-morales-cultura-authentic-puerto-rican-experience

Compilation of References

Center for Disease Control and Prevention. (2012). *Higher education and income levels keys to better health, according to annual report on nation's health*. CDC. https://www.cdc.gov/media/releases/2012/p0516_higher_education.html

Center for Disease Control and Prevention. (2024a). *Minority Health*. CDC. https://www.cdc.gov/minorityhealth/index.html

Center for Disease Control and Prevention. (2024b). *Racism and Health*. CDC. https://www.cdc.gov/minorityhealth/racism-disparities/index.html

Center for Disease Control and Prevention. (2024c). *Health Disparities*. CDC. https://www.cdc.gov/healthyyouth/disparities/index.htm

Cha-Jua, S. K., & Lang, C. (1999). Strategies for Black Liberation in the Era of Globalism: Retronouveau Civil Rights, Militant Black Conservatism, and Radicalism. *The Black Scholar*, 29(4), 25–47. 10.1080/00064246.1999.11430982

Champoux, J. E. (1999). Film as a teaching resource. *Journal of Management Inquiry*, 8(2), 206–217. 10.1177/105649269982016

Chan, G. (2022, November 7). Jumping into multiple story worlds with author and illustrator Pablo Leon. *Forbes*. https://www.forbes.com/sites/goldiechan/2022/11/07/jumping-into-multiple-story-worlds-with-pablo-leon/?sh=78cf7f1d6b18

Chassin, L., Presson, C. C., Rose, J., & Sherman, S. J. (2007). What is addiction? Age-related differences in the meaning of addiction. *Drug and Alcohol Dependence*, 87(1), 30–38. 10.1016/j.drugalcdep.2006.07.00616930860

Chisolm, J. S., & Whitmore, K. F. (2018). Visual learning analysis: Using digital photography to analyze middle level students' social-emotional learning and engagement. *Voices from the Middle*, 25(4), 34–38. 10.58680/vm201829627

Chong, D., & Druckman, J. N. (2007). Framing theory. *Annual Review of Political Science*, 10(1), 103–126. 10.1146/annurev.polisci.10.072805.103054

Chou, C., & Hsiao, M. C. (2000). Internet addiction, usage, gratification, and pleasure experience: The Taiwan college students' case. *Computers & Education*, 35(1), 65–80. 10.1016/S0360-1315(00)00019-1

Christmas [Cartoon short]. In H. Wilcox (Executive Producer), *Spidey and his Amazing Friends*. Disney Junior; Marvel Studios Animation.

Ciecierski, L. M., & Bintz, W. P. (2018). Tri-Texts: A potential next step for paired texts. *The Reading Teacher*, 71(4), 479–483. 10.1002/trtr.1649

Cilesiz, S. (2011). A phenomenological approach to experiences with technology: Current state, promise, and future directions for research. *Educational Technology Research and Development*, 59(4), 487–510. 10.1007/s11423-010-9173-2

Civil War #1-7 (2006-2007). Script: M. Millar. Art: S. McNiven.

Civil War #3 (2006). Script: M. Millar. Art: S. McNiven.

Civil War #4 (2006). Script: M. Millar. Art: S. McNiven.

Civil War #5 (2006). Script: M. Millar. Art: S. McNiven.

Civil War: X-Men #1 (2006). Script: D. Hine. Art: Y. Paquette.

Civil War: X-Men #2 (2006). Script: D. Hine. Art: Y. Paquette.

Civil War: X-Men #3 (2006). Script: D. Hine. Art: Y. Paquette.

Civil War: X-Men #4 (2006). Script: D. Hine. Art: Y. Paquette.

Clark, D. D. (2019). Matt Murdock's ill-fitting Catholic faith in Netflix's *Daredevil*. In Stevenson, G. (Ed.), *Theology and the marvel universe* (pp. 139–156).

Cleaver, E. (1968). *Soul on Ice*. Ramparts Press.

Coker, C. H. (2016). *"Just to Get a Rep." Luke Cage. Season 1, episode 5*. Marvel. Netflix.

Coker, C. H. (2016). *"Soliloquy of Chaos." Luke Cage. Season 1, episode 12*. Marvel. Netflix.

Coker, C. H. (2016). *"Suckas Need Bodyguards." Luke Cage. Season 1, episode 6*. Marvel. Netflix.

Coker, C. H. (2016). *"You Know My Steez." Luke Cage. Season 1, episode 13*. Marvel. Netflix.

Coker, C. H. (2018). *"Can't Front on Me." Luke Cage. Season 2, episode 12*. Marvel. Netflix.

Coker, C. H. (2018). *"The Creator." Luke Cage. Season 2, episode 11*. Marvel. Netflix.

Coker, C. H. (2018). *"They Reminisce Over You." Luke Cage. Season 2, episode 13*. Marvel. Netflix.

Colbry, S., Hurwitz, M., & Adair, R. (2014). Collaboration theory. *Journal of Leadership Education*, 13(4), 63–75. https://www.emerald.com/insight/content/doi/10.12806/V13/I4/C8/full/html. 10.12806/V13/I4/C8

Collins, K. H., Joseph, N. M., & Ford, D. Y. (2020). Missing in action: Gifted Black girls in science, technology, engineering, and mathematics. *Gifted Child Today*, 43(1), 55–63. 10.1177/1076217519880593

Combs, B. H., Dellinger, K., Jackson, J. T., Johnson, K. A., Johnson, W. M., Skipper, J., Sonnett, J., & Thomas, J. M. (2016). The Symbolic Lynching of James Meredith: A Visual Analysis and Collective Counter Narrative to Racial Domination. *Sociology of Race and Ethnicity (Thousand Oaks, Calif.)*, 2(3), 338–353. https://doi-org.utk.idm.oclc.org/10.1177/2332649215626937. 10.1177/2332649215626937

Coogan, P. (2006). *Superhero: The secret origin of a genre*. MonkeyBrain Books.

Coogler, R. (Director). (2018). *Black panther* [Film]. Marvel Pictures.

Compilation of References

Cook, M. P., & Frey, R. (2017). Using superheroes to visually and critically analyze comics, stereotypes, and society. *SANE Journal: Sequential Art Narrative in Education*, 2(2), 1.

Coole, D. H., & Frost, S. (Eds.). (2010). *New materialisms: Ontology, agency, and politics*. Duke University Press.

Cooper, M. (2019, June 19). *Rhiannon Giddens is writing an opera.* New York Times.

Cover, R. (2016). Digital difference: Theorizing frameworks of bodies, representation and stereotypes in digital games. *Asia Pacific Media Educator*, 26(1), 4–16. 10.1177/1326365X16640322

Cranwell, J., Opazo-Breton, M., & Britton, J. (2016). Adult and adolescent exposure to tobacco and alcohol content in contemporary YouTube music videos in Great Britain: A population estimate. *Journal of Epidemiology and Community Health*, 70(5), 488–492. 10.1136/jech-2015-20640226767404

Curtis, N. (2016). *Sovereignty and superheroes*. Manchester University Press.

Curtis, N. (2021). Two paths to the future: Radical cosmopolitanism and counter-colonial dignity in Black Panther. In White, R. T., & Ritzenhoff, K. A. (Eds.), *Afrofuturism in Black Panther: Gender, identity, and the remaking of blackness* (pp. 299–314).

Curtis, N. (2023). Superhero storytelling: The law, sovereignty and time. *Law, Culture and the Humanities*, 17438721231169162. 10.1177/17438721231169162

Dallacqua, A. K., & Low, D. E. (2019). I never think of the girls": Critical gender inquiry with superheroes. *English Journal*, 108(5), 76–84. 10.58680/ej201930128

Dallacqua, A. K., & Low, D. E. (2021). Cupcakes and beefcakes: Students' readings of gender in superhero texts. *Gender and Education*, 33(1), 68–85. 10.1080/09540253.2019.1633460

Dalvi-Esfahani, M., Niknafs, A., Kuss, D. J., Nilashi, M., & Afrough, S. (2019). Social media addiction: Applying the DEMATEL approach. *Telematics and Informatics*, 43, 101250. 10.1016/j.tele.2019.101250

Davis, D. W., & Davenport, C. (1997). The Political and Social Relevancy of Malcolm X: The Stability of African American Political Attitudes. *The Journal of Politics*, 59(2), 550–564. 10.1017/S0022381600053573

Dawson, C. M. (2018). Visual thinking strategies in the English classroom: Empowering students to interpret unfamiliar texts. *Voices from the Middle*, 26(1), 44–48. 10.58680/vm201829774

DeHart, J. D. (2024b). *Words, images, & worlds* [podcast]. https://www.youtube.com/@WordsImagesWorlds/videos

DeHart, J. D. (2018). Strategies for a safe literacy space for English language learners. *Kappa Delta Pi Record*, 54(2), 90–92. 10.1080/00228958.2018.1443681

DeHart, J. D. (2024). *Building critical literacy and empathy with graphic novels*. NCTE.

Deloitte. (2023). *Delivering on the promise of Digital Collaboration*. Deloitte. https://www.deloitte.com/au/en/services/consulting/blogs/delivering-on-promise-digital-collaboration.html

Deman, J. A. (2023). *The Claremont run: Subverting gender in the X-Men*. University of Texas Press.

DePrada, J. (2022). Teamwork skills in higher education: Is university training contributing to their mastery? *The Journal of Higher Education*, 47(3), 321–336.

Derry, K. (2017). Bulletproof love: *Luke Cage* (2016) and religion. *Journal for Religion* [JRFM]. *Film and Media*, 3(1), 123–155.

Diaz, V. (2023). Chris Miller & Phil Lord chat about Puerto Rican culture in *Spider-Man: Across the Spider-Verse! Brite & Bubbly.*https://briteandbubbly.com/chris-miller-phil-lord-interview-spider-man/#:~:text=This%20film%20actively%20shows%20more,characters%20in%20a%20superhero%20film

Dixon, C. (1997). *Batman/Wildcat*. DC Comics.

Doctorow, C., & Wang, J. (2014). *In real life*. First Second.

Dollar Bin Bandits. (2023). *Interview with Geoff Johns.*https://www.youtube.com/watch?v=KluvNlmNI0o

Dos Santos, J., Powers, K., & Thompson, J. K. (Directors). (2023). *Spider-Man: Across the Spider-Verse* [Film]. Columbia Pictures, Marvel Entertainment, & Sony Pictures Animation.

Du Bois, W. E. B. (2014). *The souls of Black folk*. (Unabridged Edition). Dover Publications Incorporated.

Duffy, G. G. (2014). *Explaining reading: A resource for explicit teaching of the Common Core Standards*. Guilford Publications.

Duncan, K. (2021). *"They Act Like they went to hell!": Black Techers, Racial Justice, and Teacher Education*. Racial Justice and Teacher Education.

Duncan, K. E. (2020). What Better Tool Do I Have?: A Critical Race Approach to Teaching Civics. *High School Journal*, 103(3), 176–189. 10.1353/hsj.2020.0011

Eason, B. (2008). *DARK KNIGHT FLASHBACK: THE JOKER, PART 1*. Comic Book Resources. https://www.cbr.com/dark-knight-flashback-the-joker-part-i/.

Eason, B. (2008). *DARK KNIGHT FLASHBACK: THE JOKER, PART 2*. Comic Book Resources. https://www.cbr.com/dark-knight-flashback-the-joker-pt-ii/

Eason, R. (2008). The Birth of the Joker: The Men Behind the Clown. *Gotham Chronicles*, 12(3), 45–59.

Compilation of References

Echevarria, R. (2023). *Treatment of the differently abled: Representations of disability from Victorian periodicals to contemporary graphic narratives*. [Undergraduate Honors Thesis, The University of Central Florida].

Eco, U., & Chilton, N. (1972). The Myth of Superman. *Diacritics*, 2(1), 14–22. 10.2307/464920

El Nuevo Dia. (2011) Tras la muerte de Peter Parker, el heredero del traje de Spiderman, será Miles Morales, un joven de origen hispano. [Link to news article by El Nuevo Día] [Status Post]. *El Nuevo Dia*. https://www.facebook.com/100064912923247/posts/226486017394289/

Epstein, R., Blake, J., & González, T. (2017). Girlhood interrupted: The erasure of Black girls' childhood. SSRN *Electronic Journal*. Crossref, 10.2139/ssrn.3000695

Eryılmaz, A., & Deniz, M. E. (2019). *Tüm yönleriyle bağımlılık* [Addiction in all its aspects]. Pegem Akademi. 10.14527/9786052418154

Espinoza-Zemlicka, L. (2020). Fans in the gutter: People of color in comics fandom. *Pathways (Chestnut Hill, Mass.)*, 1(2), 1–12.

Eury, M. (2005). *The justice league companion*. TwoMorrows Publishing.

Evangelista, A., & Thrower, A. (2022). Collaborative Online Learning Experiences Among Health Educators. *NERA Conference Proceedings 2022*. Digital Commons. https://digitalcommons.lib.uconn.edu/nera-2022/8

Evangelista, A., & Thrower, A. (2023a). Online Collaboration: The influence of faculty characteristics, training & presentation mode. *Journal of Education & Practice*. https://www.iiste.org/Journals/index.php/JEP/article/viewFile/61775/63764

Evangelista, A., & Thrower, A. (2023b). Rethinking the online environment through collaborative learning. *Open Scholarship of Teaching and Learning*, 2(3). 10.56230/osotl.70

Evans-Winters, V. (yr). *Black feminism in qualitative inquiry: A Mosaic for writing our daughter's body*. Routledge.

Evans-Winters, V. E., & Esposito, J. (2010). Other people's daughters: Critical race feminism and Black girls education. *Educational Foundations*, (Winter-Spring), 11–24.

Fairclough, N. (2013). *Language and power*. Routledge. 10.4324/9781315838250

Feige, K. (Producer), & Coogler, R. (2018). *Black Panther* [Motion Picture]. USA. Marvel.

Feige, K. (Producer), & Coogler, R. (2022). *Black Panther: Wakanda Forever* [Motion Picture]. USA. Marvel.

Feige, K. (Producer), Russo, A., & Russo, J. (2016). *Captain America: Civil War* [Motion Picture]. USA. Marvel.

Fhlainn, S. N. (2011). The Dark Knight: Heath Ledger's Joker, Anarchy, and Chaos in Gotham. *The Journal of Popular Film and Television*, 39(2), 82–83.

Filippi, N. (2009). *"Future X." Wolverine and the X-Men. Season 1, episode 9. Nicktoons.* Television.

Fire shut up in my bones. (n.d.). Metropolitan Opera: Fire Shut up in my Bones. https://www.metopera.org/season/2023-24-season/fire-shut-up-in-my-bones/

Fleming, L. (2015). *Worlds of Making: Best Practices for Establishing a Makerspace for Your School.* Corwin Press.

Fordham, S. (1993). "Those loud Black girls": (Black) women, silence, and gender "passing" in the academy. *Anthropology & Education Quarterly*, 24(1), 3–32. 10.1525/aeq.1993.24.1.05x1736t

Foucault, M. (1978). *The History of Sexuality: An Introduction* (Vol. I). Random House.

Fox, G. A., & Giella, J. (1961). *The Flash* (Vol. 123). DC Comics.

Franklin, J. (2019). The theatrical and the accidental academic: An autoethnographic case study. *Arts and Humanities in Higher Education*, 18(4), 281–295. 10.1177/1474022217731543

Franzese, T. (2020, December 15). Why we love *Spider-Man: Miles Morales*. *Inverse*. https://www.inverse.com/gaming/spider-man-miles-morales-ps5-harlem-diversity-inclusion

Freeman, M., & Taylor-Ashfield, C. (2017). 'I read comics from a feministic point of view': Conceptualizing the transmedia ethos of the Captain Marvel fan community. *Journal of Fandom Studies*, 5(3), 317–335. 10.1386/jfs.5.3.317_1

Freeman, S., Eddy, S. L., McDonough, M., Smith, M. K., Okoroafor, N., Jordt, H., & Wenderoth, M. P. (2017). Active learning increases student performance in science, engineering, and mathematics. *Proceedings of the National Academy of Sciences of the United States of America*, 111(23), 8410–8415. 10.1073/pnas.1319030111124821756

Freire, P. (1983). The importance of the act of reading. *Journal of Education*, 165(1), 5–11. 10.1177/002205748316500103

Freud, S. (1919). *The Uncanny.* Imago Publishing.

Fu, A. (2015). Fear of a black Spider-Man: Racebending and the colour-line in superhero (re)casting. *Journal of Graphic Novels & Comics*, 6(3), 269–283. 10.1080/21504857.2014.994647

Gao, F., Luo, T., & Zhang, K. (2013). Tweeting for learning: A critical analysis of research on microblogging in education published in 2008-2011. *British Journal of Educational Technology*, 44(3), 783–801.

Gavaler, C., & Goldberg, N. (2019). *Superhero thought experiments: Comic book philosophy.* University of Iowa Press. 10.2307/j.ctvn5twvb

Gee, J. P. (2013). *The anti-education era: Creating smarter students through digital learning.* St. Martin's Press.

Ghiso, M. P., & Low, D. E. (2013). Students using multimodal literacies to surface micronarratives of United States immigration. *Literacy*, 47(1), 26–34. 10.1111/j.1741-4369.2012.00678.x

Compilation of References

Ghodsi, S. M., & Laal, M. (2012). Benefits of collaborative learning. *Procedia: Social and Behavioral Sciences*, 31, 486–490. 10.1016/j.sbspro.2011.12.091

Gibson, D.-M. (2012). *A History of the Nation of Islam: Race, Islam, and the Quest for Freedom*. Praeger. http://www.abc-clio.com/product.aspx?isbn=9780313398070

Gibson, M. (2018). Let's hear it for the girls! Representation of girlhood, feminism, and activism in comics and graphic novels. *Mai, Feminism and Visual Culture*, 1(1), 1–13.

Gill, V. S. (2016). "Everybody else gets to be normal": Using intersectionality and Ms. Marvel to challenge "normal" identity. *The ALAN Review*, 44(1), 68–78.

Giselsson, K. (2020). Critical Thinking and Critical Literacy: Mutually Exclusive? *International Journal for the Scholarship of Teaching and Learning*, 14(1), 5. 10.20429/ijsotl.2020.140105

Gomez, J. (2018, December 12). Miles Morales in 'Into The Spider-Verse' is the Afro-Latinx representation we were missing — and not just because he's a superhero. *Bustle*.https://www.bustle.com/p/miles-morales-in-into-the-spider-verse-is-the-afro-latinx-representation-we-were-missing-not-just-because-hes-a-superhero-14947742

Gowing, L. R., Ali, R. L., Allsop, S., Marsden, J., Turf, E. E., West, R., & Witton, J. (2015). Global statistics on addictive behaviours: 2014 status report. *Addiction (Abingdon, England)*, 110(6), 904–919. 10.1111/add.1289925963869

Grabowski-Górniak, P., & Polska, W. (2019). The death of the (super) hero: The duality in depictions of death in superhero narratives. *Symbolae Europaeae*, 14, 61–73.

Grace, J., & Aming-Attai, R. (2023). 'This is so white': examining black and Brown pre-service teachers' sense of belonging in a predominantly White educator preparation program. *Whiteness and Education (Print)*, 1–18. 10.1080/23793406.2023.2277789

Graham, C., & Jones, N. (2019). Impact of a social network messaging app on team cohesiveness and quality of completed team projects in an undergraduate team project. *Journal of Educational Technology Systems*, 47(4), 539–553. 10.1177/0047239518821937

Graham, J., Haidt, J., Koleva, S., Motyl, M., Iyer, R., Wojcik, S. P., & Ditto, P. H. (2013). Moral foundations theory: The pragmatic validity of moral pluralism. In Devine, P., & Plant, A. (Eds.), Vol. 47, pp. 55–130). Advances in experimental social psychology. Academic Press.

Guschwan, M. (2012). Fandom, brandom and the limits of participatory culture. *Journal of Consumer Culture*, 12(1), 19–40. 10.1177/1469540512438154

Gutkind, L. (1997). *The art of creative nonfiction: Writing and selling the literature of reality*. Wiley.

Haidt, J., & Joseph, C. (2007). The moral mind: How five sets of innate intuitions guide the development of many culture-specific virtues, and perhaps even modules. In Carruthers, P., Laurence, S., & Stich, S. (Eds.), *The innate mind* (Vol. 3, pp. 367–391).

Hall, S. (1997). *Representation: Cultural Representations and Signifying Practices.* Sage Publications.

Hall, S. (2020). The work of representation. In *The applied theatre reader* (pp. 74–76). Routledge. 10.4324/9780429355363-15

Hamulu, F. (1999). Obezite komplikasyonları. [Complications of obesity] In Yılmaz, C. (Ed.), *Obezite ve tedavisi* [Obesity and treatment]. (pp. 152–157). Mart Matbaacılık.

Harzan, A. (Writer), & Bachynski, D. (Director). (2022). Halted holiday / Merry Spidey.

Hellman, M. (2010). *Construing and defining the out of control. Addiction in the media 1968–2008.* Yliopistopaino.

Helwig, C. C. (2006). Rights, civil liberties, and democracy across cultures. In Killen, M., & Smetana, J. G. (Eds.), *Handbook of moral development* (1st ed., pp. 185–210). Psychology Press.

Helwig, C. C., & Jasiobedzka, U. (2001). The relation between law and morality: Children's reasoning about socially beneficial and unjust laws. *Child Development*, 72(5), 1382–1393. 10.1111/1467-8624.00354 11699676

Helwig, C. C., & Kim, S. (1999). Children's evaluations of decision-making procedures in peer, family, and school contexts. *Child Development*, 70(2), 502–512. 10.1111/1467-8624.00036

Henderson, S. E. (2017). Daredevil: Legal (and moral?) vigilante. *Ohio State Journal of Criminal Law*, 15, 133–182.

Hicks, V. (2019). Stages of minority identity development: A juxtaposition of T'Challa and Erik Killmonger. In Langley, T., & Simmons, A. (Eds.), *Black Panther psychology: Hidden kingdoms* (pp. 36–51). Sterling Press.

Hines, C. (2021). My brain is all the super-power I need': Examining Black girls in STEM and schooling spaces in Marvel comics. *Research on Diversity in Youth Literature*, 4(1), 9.

Hines, C. M., & Menefee, D. L. (2022). #BlackGirlLiteratureMatters: Exploring the multiplicities of Black girlhood. *English Journal*, 111(3), 67–74. 10.58680/ej202231570

Hobbs, R. (2020). *Mind over media: Propaganda education for a digital age.* WW Norton & Company.

Holden, C. (2001). 'Behavioral' addictions: Do they exist? *Science*, 294(5544), 980–982. 10.1126/science.294.5544.980 11691967

Hosein, S., & Clement, R. (2017). The proverbial and image hangover: A discussion between Comics Researchers. *The Word Hoard*, 6, 35–43.

Houston, L. (1993). "Days of Future Past: Part I." X-Men: The Animated Series. Season 1, episode 11. Fox Kids. Television.

Compilation of References

Houston, L. (1993). *"Days of Future Past: Part II." X-Men: The Animated Series. Season 1, episode 12. Fox Kids*. Television.

Houston, L. (1995). *"One Man's Worth: Part I." X-Men: The Animated Series. Season 4, episode 1. Fox Kids*. Television.

Houston, L. (1995). *"One Man's Worth: Part II." X-Men: The Animated Series. Season 4, episode 2. Fox Kids*. Television.

Hovious, A., Shinas, V. H., & Harper, I. (2021). The compelling nature of transmedia storytelling: Empowering twenty-first-century readers and writers through multimodality. Technology. *Knowledge and Learning*, 26(1), 215–229. 10.1007/s10758-020-09437-7

Huang, J., Kornfield, R., & Emery, S. L. (2016). 100 million views of electronic cigarette YouTube videos and counting: Quantification, content evaluation, and engagement levels of videos. *Journal of Medical Internet Research*, 18(3), e67. 10.2196/jmir.426526993213

Huber, P. (2020). Theorizing a Critical Race Content Analysis for Children's Literature about People of Color. *Urban Education*, 1–25.

Hughes-Hassell, S. (2013). Multicultural young adult literature as a form of counter-storytelling. *The Library Quarterly: Information, Community. Policy*, 83(3), 212–228.

Hutcheon, L. A. (2006). *A theory of adaptation*. Routledge. 10.4324/9780203957721

Inside Higher Ed. (2024). *Enrollments Rise After Pandemic-Related Declines*. Inside Higher Ed. https://www.insidehighered.com/news/students/retention/2024/01/24/enrollment-rising-first-time-pandemic

Insomniac Games (2018). *Marvel's Spider-Man* (PlayStation 4 version) [Video game]. Sony Interactive Entertainment.

Insomniac Games (2020). *Spider-Man: Miles Morales* (PlayStation 4 version) [Video game]. Sony Interactive Entertainment.

Insomniac Games (2023). *Marvel's Spider-Man 2* (PlayStation 4 version) [Video game]. Sony Interactive Entertainment.

JAH. (1993). Movie reviews - A note on Malcolm X. *The Journal of American History (Bloomington, Ind.)*, 80(3), 1179-.

Jenkins, H. (2006). Fans, Bloggers, and Gamers: Exploring Participatory Culture. New York University Press.

Jenkins, H., Ito, M., & Boyd, D. (2016). *Participatory Culture in a Networked Era: A Conversation on Youth, Learning, Commerce, and Politics*. Polity Press.

Jenkins, H. (2006). *Convergence Culture: Where Old and New Media Collide*. New York University Press.

Jenkins, H. (2006). *Convergence Culture: Where Old and New Media Collide.* NYU Press, 5-6.

Jenkins, H. (2017). Adaptation, extension, transmedia. *Literature. Film Quarterly*, 45(2).

Jenkins, H. (2020). What else can you do with them? In Burke, L., Gordon, I., & Ndalianis, A. (Eds.), *Superheroes and the civic imagination* (pp. 25–46). Rutgers University Press.

Jewell, T., & Derand, A. (2020). *This book is anti-racist: 20 lessons on how to wake up, take action, and do the work.* Frances Lincoln Children's Books.

Jimenez, A. (2016, April 5). Miles from representation: On needing more from Bendis's Spider-Man. *The Middle Spaces.* https://themiddlespaces.com/2016/04/05/miles-from-representation/

Jiménez, L. M. (2018). PoC, LGBTQ, and Gender: The intersectionality of America Chavez. *Journal of Lesbian Studies*, 22(4), 435–445. 10.1080/10894160.2018.144950129727592

Johnson, D. W., & Johnson, R. T. (2009). An Educational Psychology Success Story: Social Interdependence Theory and Cooperative Learning. *Educational Researcher*, 38(5), 365–379. 10.3102/0013189X09339057

Johnson, H., & Gasiewicz, B. (2017). Examining displaced youth and immigrant status through critical multicultural analysis. In Johnson, H., Mathis, J., & Short, K. G. (Eds.), *Critical content analysis of children's and young adult literature: Reframing perspective* (pp. 28–43). Routledge.

Jolley, D. (2000). *JSA: The liberty files.* DC Comics.

Joseph, P. E. (2020). *The Sword and the Shield: The Revolutionary Lives of Malcolm X and MLK* (1st ed.). Basic Books.

Jung, C. G. (1959). Archetypes and the Collective Unconscious. Princeton University Press. 117.

Kang, J. C. (2023, June 6). The Post-racial vision of "Across the Spider-Verse". *The New Yorker.* https://www.newyorker.com/news/our-columnists/the-post-racial-vision-of-across-the-spider-verse

Kang, M., Yoon, S., Yoo, Y. R., Lim, H., & Kim, M. (2012). Investigating the Predictive Power of Metacognition and Perceived Interaction on Web-Based Collaborative Learning Outcomes. *World Conference on Educational Media and Technology*, Denver, Colorado, USA.

Kazmierczak, E. T. (2001). A semiotic perspective on aesthetic preferences, visual literacy, and information design. *Information Design Journal*, 10(2), 176–187. 10.1075/idj.10.2.15kaz

Kelly, L. L. (2020). Exploring Black girls' subversive literacies as acts of freedom. *Journal of Literacy Research*, 52(4), 456–481. 10.1177/1086296X20966367

Killen, M. (2018). The origins of morality: Social equality, fairness, and justice. *Philosophical Psychology*, 31(5), 767–803. 10.1080/09515089.2018.1486612

Killen, M., & Smetana, J. G. (2015). Origins and development of morality. In Lamb, M. E. (Ed.),.; 7th ed., Vol. 3, pp. 701–749). Handbook of child psychology. Wiley-Blackwell Publishing Ltd.

Compilation of References

Kinchin, I. M., & Francis, R. A. (2017). Mapping pedagogic frailty in geography education: A framed autoethnographic case study. *Journal of Geography in Higher Education*, 41(1), 56–74. 10.1080/03098265.2016.1241988

Kington, C. S. (2015). Con culture: A survey of fans and fandom. *Journal of Fandom Studies*, 3(2), 211–228. 10.1386/jfs.3.2.211_1

Kinney, M. E. (2013). Linda Hutcheon's *a theory of adaptation*. Critical Voices. *The University of Guelph Book Review Project*, 3(3), 7–15.

Kirkpatrick, E., & Scott, S. (2015). Representation and diversity in comics studies. *Cinema Journal*, 55(1), 120–124. 10.1353/cj.2015.0064

Kisner, J. (2024, February 6). The magic of Raina is real. *The Atlantic*. https://www.theatlantic.com/magazine/archive/2024/03/raina-telgemeier-cartoonist-smile-guts-books/677180/

Klepek, P. (2017, July 7). Why Miles Morales, the first Black/Latino Spider-Man, means so much to people. *Vice*. https://www.vice.com/en/article/gybyq3/why-miles-morales-the-first-black-spider-man-means-so-much-to-people

Kohlberg, L. (1971/1981). *The philosophy of moral Development: Moral stages and the idea of justice*. Harper & Row.

Kohlberg, L. (1980). Stages of development as a basis for education. In Munsey, B. (Ed.), *Moral development, moral education, and Kohlberg: Basic issues in philosophy, psychology, religion, and education* (pp. 15–100). Religious Education Press.

Korté, S., & Who, H. Q. (2019). *What is the story of Wonder Woman?* Penguin.

Krippendorff, K. (2003). Content analysis: An introduction to its methodology. *Sage (Atlanta, Ga.)*.

Kupfer, D. J., First, M. B., & Regier, D. E. (2002). *A research agenda for DSM–V*. American Psychiatric Association.

Lai, E. R. (2011). *Collaboration: A literature review*. Pearson. https://images.pearsonassessments.com/images/tmrs/Collaboration-Review.pdf

Laughter, J. (2021). *Critiquing inequities in scripted curricula*.

Laurillard, D. (2013a). *Teaching as a design science: Building pedagogical patterns for learning and technology*. Routledge. 10.4324/9780203125083

Laurillard, D. (2013b). *Rethinking university teaching: A conversational framework for the effective use of learning technologies* (2nd ed.). Routledge. 10.4324/9781315012940

Leavy, P. (2018). *Handbook of arts-based research* (1st ed.). The Guilford Press.

Lecker, M. (2007). *Treacherous, deviant, and submissive: female sexuality represented in the character Catwoman* [Doctoral dissertation, Bowling Green State University].

Lee, S. (1992). *MALCOLM X* (Film). Spin (New York, N.Y.).

Lee, H. J., & Baek, E. (2012). Facilitating deep learning in a learning community. *International Journal of Technology and Human Interaction*, 8(1), 1–13. 10.4018/jthi.2012010101

Letizia, A. (2020). *Graphic novels as pedagogy in social studies: How to draw citizenship*. Palgrave Macmillan. 10.1007/978-3-030-44252-1

Levitz, P., & Liew, S. (2015-2016). *Dr. Fate*. DC Comics.

Lincoln, Y. S., & Guba, E. G. (1985). Naturalistic inquiry. *Sage (Atlanta, Ga.)*.

Love, B. (2019). *We want to do more than survive: Abolitionist teaching and the pursuit of educational freedom*. Beacon Press.

Love, B. (2020). *WE WANT TO DO MORE THAN SURVIVE: Abolitionist Teaching and the Pursuit of Educational Freedom*. BEACON.

Love, B. L. (2021). Empty Promises of Equity: Whether White People are Ready or not, Policies Have to Change. *Education Week*, 40(18), 24–24.

Low, D. E. (2015). *Comics as a medium for inquiry: Urban students (re-)designing critical social worlds*. [Unpublished doctoral dissertation. University of Pennsylvania, Philadelphia, PA].

Low, D. (2012). Spaces invested with content: Crossing the gaps in comics with readers in schools. *Children's Literature in Education*, 43(4), 368–385. 10.1007/s10583-012-9172-5

Low, D. (2017a). Students contesting "colormuteness" through critical inquiries into comics. *English Journal*, 106(4), 19–28. 10.58680/ej201729013

Low, D. (2017b). Waiting for Spider-Man: Representations of urban school 'reform' in Marvel comics' Miles Morales series. In Abate, M. A., & Tarbox, G. A. (Eds.), *Graphic Novels for Children and Young Adults: A Collection of Critical Essays* (pp. 278–297). UP of Mississippi. 10.2307/j.ctv5jxmqd.22

Low, D. E., & Campano, G. (2016). Multiliteracies, the arts, and postcolonial agency. In Campano, G., Ghiso, M. P., & Welch, B. J. (Eds.), *Partnering with immigrant communities: Action through literacy* (pp. 92–102). Teachers College Press.

Low, D. E., Lyngfelt, A., Thomas, A. A., & Vasquez, V. M. (2022). Critical literacy and contemporary literatures. In Pandya, J. Z., Mora, R. A., Alford, J., Golden, N. A., & deRoock, R. S. (Eds.), *The critical literacies handbook* (pp. 308–316). Routledge. 10.4324/9781003023425-36

Lugo, J. (2021). *Puerto Rican culture references in* Marvel's Spider-Man: Miles Morales - JJ's first 20. [Video]. YouTube.https://www.youtube.com/watch?v=ri2mzQWCkIE

Luke Cage #3 (2017). Script: D. Walker. Art: N. Blake II.

Luke Cage #3 (2018). "Everyman, parts 5 & 6." Script: A. Del Col. Art:Lindsay, J..

Luke Cage: Gang War #1 (2023). Script: R. Barnes. Art: R. Bachs.

Luke Cage: Gang War #2 (2023). Script: R. Barnes. Art: R. Bachs.

Compilation of References

Luke Cage: Gang War #3 (2024). Script: R. Barnes. Art: R. Bachs.

Luke Cage: Gang War #4 (2024). Script: R. Barnes. Art: R. Bachs.

Lund, M. (2015). "X Marks the Spot:" Urban dystopia, slum voyeurism and failures of identity in *District X. Journal of Urban Cultural Studies*, 2(1-2), 35–55. 10.1386/jucs.2.1-2.35_1

Lyden, J. C. (2018). King in the Wilderness. *Journal of Religion and Film*, 22(1). Gale Academic OneFile. link.gale.com/apps/doc/A537719928/AONE?u=tel_oweb&sid=googleScholar&xid=f285fcb4

Lyotard, J.-F. (1984). The Postmodern Condition: A Report on Knowledge. University of Minnesota Press, 36.

Mack, A. D. (2020). Afrosurrealism, aristotle, and racial presence in Netflix's *Luke Cage. Dialogue. The Interdisciplinary Journal of Popular Culture and Pedagogy*, 7(2), 26–37.

Magoon, K. (2020, June 17). Our modern minstrelsy. *The Horn Book*. https://www.hbook.com/story/our-modern-minstrelsy

Manning, M. K., Wiacek, S., Scott, M., Jones, N., & Walker, L. Q. (2021). *The DC Comics Encyclopedia New Edition*. Penguin.

Manovich, L. (2001). *The Language of New Media*. MIT Press, 91.

Marlatt, G. A., Curry, S., & Gordon, J. R. (1988). A longitudinal analysis of unaided smoking cessation. *Journal of Consulting and Clinical Psychology*, 56(5), 715–720. 10.1037/0022-006X.56.5.7153192787

Marmot, M., Ryff, C. D., Bumpass, L. L., Shipley, M., & Marks, N. F. (1997). Social inequalities in health: Next questions and converging evidence. *Social Science & Medicine (1982)*, 44(6), 901–910. 10.1016/S0277-9536(96)00194-3

Marmot, M. G., & Shipley, M. J. (1996). Do socioeconomic differences in mortality persist after retirement? 25-year follow-up of civil servants from the first Whitehall study. *BMJ (Clinical Research Ed.)*, 313(7066), 1177–1180. 10.1136/bmj.313.7066.11778916748

Martinez, M. J. (2022). Aspiration and the violence of gentrification in Marvel's *Luke Cage. Cultural Studies Critical Methodologies*, 22(2), 163-172.

Martínez-Roldán, C. M. (2013). The representation of Latinos and the use of Spanish: A critical content analysis of Skippyjon Jones. *Journal of Children's Literature*, 39(1), 5–14.

Martin, J. (2023b). Superhero media as a potential context for investigating children's understanding of morally relevant events. *Libri & Liberi: Journal of Research on Children's Literature*, 12(1), 11–35. 10.21066/carcl.libri.12.1.1

Martin, J. (2024). Time-travel and teleology: Morality, society, and the life of Lucas Bishop. *REDEN. Revista Española De Estudios Norteamericanos*, 5(2), 128–153. 10.37536/reden.2024.5.2414

Martin, J. F. (2021). The many ways of Wakanda: Viewpoint diversity in Black Panther and its implications for civics education. *Dialogue: The Interdisciplinary Journal of Popular Culture and Pedagogy*, 8(1), 24–36.

Martin, J. F. (2023a). Harlem's superhero: Social interaction, heterogeneity of thought, and the superhero mission in Marvel's *Luke Cage. Popular Culture Review*, 34(2), 43–89. 10.1002/j.2831-865X.2023.tb00798.x

Martin, J. F., Killian, M., & Letizia, A. (2023). Comics and community: Exploring the relationship between society, education, and citizenship. In DeHart, J. D. (Ed.), *Exploring comics and graphic novels in the classroom* (pp. 203–228). IGI Global.

McArthur, S. A. (2016). Black girls and critical media literacy for social activism. *English Education*, 48(4), 362–379. 10.58680/ee201628672

McCloud, S. (1993). *Understanding Comics: The Invisible Art*. Harper Perennial.

McCloud, S. (1994). *Understanding comics: The invisible art*. William Morrow.

McEwan, D., Ruissen, G. R., Eys, M. A., Zumbo, B. D., & Beauchamp, M. R. (2017). The effectiveness of teamwork training on teamwork behaviors and team performance: A systematic review and meta-analysis of controlled interventions. *PLoS One*, 12(1), e0169604. 10.1371/journal.pone.016960428085922

McGinty, E. E., Kennedy-Hendricks, A., & Barry, C. L. (2019). Stigma of addiction in the media. *The stigma of addiction: An essential guide*, 201-214.

McGrath, K. (2007). Gender, race, and Latina identity: An examination of Marvel Comics' amazing fantasy and arana. *Atlantic Journal of Communication*, 15(4), 268–283. 10.1080/15456870701483599

McLuhan, M. (1964). *Understanding Media: The Extensions of Man*. McGraw-Hill, 19–20.

McMillen, S. M. (2020). Re-envisioning black masculinity in *Luke Cage*: From blaxploitation and comic books to Netflix. *Journal of Popular Culture*, 53(2), 484–472. 10.1111/jpcu.12905

McWilliams, O. C. (2013). Who is afraid of a Black Spider(-Man)?" *Transformative Works and Cultures,* 13. https://journal.transformativeworks.org/index.php/twc/article/view/455/355

Meredith, J. (1966). *Three Years in Mississippi*. Indiana University Press.

Metros, S. E., & Woolsey, K. (2006). Visual Literacy: An institutional imperative. *Educational Review*, 41(3), 80–81. https://eric.ed.gov/?id=EJ745830

Micheline, J. A. [@elevenafter]. (2016). [Tweet]. Twitter.

Miczo, N. (2016). *How Superheroes Model Community: Philosophically, Communicatively. Relationally.*

Compilation of References

Miller, H. C., Hines, C. M., & Rodríguez-Astacio, R. M. (2022). *Teaching Miles Morales: Suspended* to resist erasure in a time of book bans. *English Journal*.

Miller, H. C., Hines, C. M., & Rodríguez-Astacio, R. M. (2022). With great power comes… youth empowerment? A critical content analysis of Marvel's superhero young adult literature. *The ALAN Review*, 50(1), 33–44.

Millner, D., & Rodríguez, M. P. (2023). *Miles Morales Spider-Man: Through a Hero's Eyes*. Disney Books.

Mills, R. M. (2023, June 1). 'Across the Spider-Verse' and the Latino legacy of Spider-Man. *The Conversation.* https://theconversation.com/across-the-spider-verse-and-the-latino-legacy-of-spider-man-205892

Mills, R. M. (2022). A post-soul Spider-Man: The remixed heroics of Miles Morales. *The Black Scholar*, 1(52), 41–52. 10.1080/00064246.2022.2007345

Moeller, R. A., & Becnel, K. (2018). Drawing diversity: Representations of race in graphic novels for young adults. *School Library Research*, 21, 1–17.

Molina-Guzmán, I. (2021). *Into the Spider-Verse* and the commodified (re)imagining of Afro-Rican visibility. In Dagbovie-Mullins, S. A., & Berlatsky, E. L. (Eds.), *Mixed-race superheroes*. Rutgers University Press. 10.36019/9781978814639-012

Moore, B.C. (2013). *JSA Liberty Files: The whistling skull*. DC Comics. *Stargirl*.

Moore, A. (1988). *The Killing Joke*. DC Comics.

Moore, A., & Begoray, D. (2017). "The last block of ice": Trauma literature in the high school classroom. *Journal of Adolescent & Adult Literacy*, 61(2), 173–181. 10.1002/jaal.674

Morris, B. (2020). *Marvel's Spider-Man Miles Morales: Wings of fury*. Titan Books.

Morris, B. (2021). YA author: The Black duality sandwich. *Voices from the Middle*, 28(3), 12–13. 10.58680/vm202131173

Morris, E. (2007). "Ladies" or "loudies"? Perceptions and experiences of Black girls in classrooms. *Youth & Society*, 38(4), 490–515. 10.1177/0044118X06296778

Morris, M. (2018). *Pushout: The criminalization of Black girls in schools*. New Press.

Morrison, G. (1989). *Arkham Asylum: A Serious House on Serious Earth*. DC Comics.

Muhammad, G., & Haddix, M. (2016). Centering Black girl literacies: A review of literature on the multiple ways of knowing Black girls. *English Education*, 48(4), 229–336. 10.58680/ee201628670

Muncey, T. (2005). Doing autoethnography. *International Journal of Qualitative Methods*, 4(1), 69–86. 10.1177/160940690500400105

Murray, J. H. (1997). *Hamlet on the Holodeck: The Future of Narrative in Cyberspace*. The Free Press, 55.

Muscio, A. (2023). The ambiguous role of science and technology in Marvel superhero comics: From their 'Golden Age'to the present-day. *Technological Forecasting and Social Change*, 186, 122149. 10.1016/j.techfore.2022.122149

Myers, W. (2014, March15). Where Are the People of Color in Children's Books? *New York Times*. https://www.nytimes.com/2014/03/16/opinion/sunday/where-are-the-people-of-color-in-childrens-books.html

National Center for Education Statistics. (2021). *Digest of Educational Statistics*. NCES. https://nces.ed.gov/programs/digest/d21/tables/dt21_306.20.asp?current=ye

National Center for Education Statistics. (n.d.). *Nontraditional Undergraduates / Definitions and Data*. NCES. https://nces.ed.gov/pubs/web/97578e.asp

National Student Clearinghouse Research Center. (2024). *Current Term Enrollment Estimates: Fall 2023*. NCES. https://nscresearchcenter.org/current-term-enrollment-estimates/

New Avengers #18. (2014). Script: J. Hickman. Art: V. Schiti

New Avengers #21. (2014). Script: J. Hickman. Art: V. Schiti

Newby, R. (2018, December 12). 'Into the Spider-Verse' and the importance of a biracial Spider-Man. *The Hollywood Reporter*. https://www.hollywoodreporter.com/movies/movie-news/why-spider-man-spider-verse-is-important-fans-color-1168367/

Newton, M. (2011, August 4). How the media reacted to news of a non-white Spider-Man. *Forbes*. https://www.forbes.com/sites/matthewnewton/2011/08/04/how-the-media-reacted-to-news-of-a-non-white-spider-man/?sh=9dcb94a4f612

Nietzsche, F. (1883). *Thus Spoke Zarathustra*. Ernst Schmeitzner, 26.

Nietzsche, F. (1886). Beyond Good and Evil. Random House.

Njie, B., & Asimiran, S. (2014). Case study as a choice in qualitative methodology. *Journal of Research & Method in Education*, 4(3), 35–40. 10.9790/7388-04313540

Nolan, C. (Director). (2008). *The Dark Knight*. Warner Bros. Pictures.

Nucci, L., & Ilten-Gee, R. (2021). *Moral Education for Social Justice*. Teachers College Press.

Nucci, L., Turiel, E., & Roded, A. D. (2017). Continuities and discontinuities in the development of moral judgments. *Human Development*, 60(6), 279–341. 10.1159/000484067

O'Keeffe, G. S., & Clarke-Pearson, K. (2011). The impact of social media on children, adolescents, and families. *Pediatrics*, 127(4), 800–804. 10.1542/peds.2011-005421444588

Oakley, B., Felder, R. M., Brent, R., & Elhajj, I. (2004). Turning student groups into effective teams. *Journal of Student Centered Learning*, 2(1), 9–34.

Compilation of References

Okela, A. H. (2022). Egyptian University Students' Smartphone Addiction and their Digital Media Literacy Level. *The Journal of Media Literacy Education*, 15(1), 44–57. 10.23860/JMLE-2023-15-1-4

Opera, L. A. (2022, October 13). *Omar: Behind the story* [Video]. YouTube. https://www.youtube.com/watch?v=xgYuwXR9TMk

Palioura, M., & Dimoulas, C. (2022). Digital storytelling in education: A transmedia integration approach for non-developers. *Education Sciences*, 12(8), 559. 10.3390/educsci12080559

Parker, M. (2021). *Teaching Artfully*. Clover Press.

Peacock, S. (2019). Joker: A Serious Study of the Clown Prince of Crime. University of Mississippi Press.

Peeples, D., Yen, J., & Weigle, P. (2018). Geeks, fandoms, and social engagement. *Child and Adolescent Psychiatric Clinics of North America*, 27(2), 247–267. 10.1016/j.chc.2017.11.00829502750

Persichetti, B., Ramsey, P., & Rothman, R. (Directors). (2018). *Spider-Man: Into the Spider-Verse* [Film]. Columbia Pictures, Marvel Entertainment, & Sony Pictures Animation.

Peters, T. D. (2020). Daredevil as legal emblem. *Law. Technology and Humans*, 2(2), 198–226. 10.5204/lthj.1656

Philips, M. (2022). Violence in the American imaginary: Gender, race, and the politics of superheroes. *The American Political Science Review*, 116(2), 470–483. 10.1017/S0003055421000952

Phillips, T. (Director). (2019). *Joker*. Warner Bros. Pictures.

Phillips, N. D., & Strobl, S. (2013). *Comic book crime: Truth, justice, and the American way*. New York University Press.

Pickard, H. (2020). Addiction and the self. *Noûs (Detroit, Mich.)*, 55(4), 737–761. 10.1111/nous.12328

Pope, P. (2019). (reprint). *Heavy liquid*. Image.

Prada, E. D., Mareque, M., & Pino-Juste, M. (2022). Teamwork skills in higher education: Is university training contributing to their mastery? *Psicologia: Reflexão e Crítica*, 35(5), 5. 10.1186/s41155-022-00207-135141845

Pratten, R. (2015). *Getting started with transmedia storytelling: A practical guide for beginners*. CreateSpace Independent Publishing Platform.

Price-Dennis, D. (2016). Developing Curriculum to Support Black Girls' Literacies in Digital Spaces. *English Education*, 48(4), 337–361. 10.58680/ee201628671

Quattro, K., & Schelly, B. (2004). *The New Ages: Rethinking Comic Book History*. Comicartville Library.

Raacke, J., & Bonds-Raacke, J. (2008). MySpace and Facebook: Applying the uses and gratifications theory to exploring friend-networking sites. *Cyberpsychology & Behavior*, 11(2), 169–174. 10.1089/cpb.2007.005618422409

Rackley, L., Bradford, T., & Peairs, D. (2022). Love and poetics: Black life beyond literacy research as we know it. *International Studies in Sociology of Education*, 31(1–2), 67–79. https://doi-org.libproxy.uncg.edu/10.1080/09620214.2021.1882871

Rapoport, A. (2005). *Teaching in a comfort zone: Practitioners' views and rationale for teaching global citizenship.*

Rapoport, A. (2009). A Forgotten Concept: Global Citizenship education and State Social Studies Standards. *Journal of Social Studies Research*.

Reynolds, J. (2017). *Miles Morales: Spider-Man*. Marvel.

Reynolds, J. (2023). *Miles Morales: Suspended*. Atheneum.

Reynolds, J. A., & Leon, P. (2021). *Miles Morales: Shock waves*. Marvel/Graphix.

Reynolds, J. A., & Leon, P. (2022). *Miles Morales: Stranger tides*. Marvel/Graphix.

Rhoades, M. (2020). A Contemporary Arts-Based Approach to Critical Multimodal Literacy. *Language Arts*, 97(3), 178–185. https://www.jstor.org/stable/26873330. 10.58680/la202030417

Richards, I. A. (1925). Science and Poetry. *Atlantic (Boston, Mass.)*, (Oct), 481–491.

Riesman, A. (2014, May 1). Comics Legend Brian Michael Bendis on *Guardians of the Galaxy*, Sexism, and Making a Nonwhite Spider-Man. *Vulture*. https://www.vulture.com/2014/04/comics-brian-michael-bendis-spider-man-guardians-x-men.html

Riesman, A. (2018, December 14). Is Miles Morales finally getting his due as Spider-Man? *Vulture*. https://www.vulture.com/2018/12/miles-morales-of-into-the-spider-verse-the-race-problem.html

Robinson, H. A., Kilgore, W., & Warren, S. J. (2017). Care, communication, learner support: Designing meaningful online collaborative learning. *Online Learning : the Official Journal of the Online Learning Consortium*, 21(4), 29–51. 10.24059/olj.v21i4.1240

Rockenbach, B., & Fabian, C. A. (2008). Visual literacy in the age of participation. *Art Documentation*, 27(2), 26–31. 10.1086/adx.27.2.27949492

Rocksteady Studios. (2009-2016). *Batman: Arkham series*. Warner Bros. Interactive Entertainment.

Rodríguez de Tió, L. (1893). A Cuba. *Ciudad Seva*. https://ciudadseva.com/texto/cuba-y-puerto-rico-son-de-un-pajaro-las-dos-alas/

Rodríguez-Astacio, R. M., Hines, C. M., & Miller, H. C. (2024). Criticality and the cowl: Teaching Black superhero narratives with DC graphic novels for young adults. *The ALAN Review*, 51(2), 11–19.

Compilation of References

Rodríguez-Astacio, R. M., & Low, D. E. (2023). Using superhero graphic novels to foreground transitions in our teaching with upper elementary and middle grades readers. *The Reading Teacher*, 76(5), 640–645. 10.1002/trtr.2189

Rodríguez, N. N., & Vickery, A. E. (2020). Much bigger than a hamburger: Disrupting problematic picturebook depictions of the Civil Rights movement. *International Journal of Multicultural Education*, 21(2), 109–128. https://ijme-journal.org/index.php/ijme/article/view/2243/1371. 10.18251/ijme.v22i2.2243

Roessing, L. (2019). After-reading response: Using found poetry for synthesizing text. *AMLE Magazine,7*(1), 43-46. https://login.libproxy.uncg.edu/login?url=https://www.proquest.com/trade-journals/after-reading-response-using-found-poetry/docview/2184342339/se-2

Rosenblatt, L. (1978). *The reader the text the poem: The transactional theory of the literary work*. Southern Illinois Press.

Rosiek, J. (2018). Art, agency and inquiry: Making connections between new materialism and contemporary pragmaticism in arts-based research. In Cahnmann & Siegesmund (Eds.) *Arts-based research in education: Foundations for practice*. Routledge.

Rosiek, J., & Kinslow, K. (2016). Resegregation as Curriculum: The Meaning of the New Segregation in U.S. Public Schools. Taylor & Francis Group.

Rounds, C. (2020). "Dead Men Make Such Convenient Heroes": The Use and Misuse of MLK's Legacy as Political Propaganda. *Journal of Black Studies*, 51(4), 315–331. 10.1177/0021934720908489

Rowsell, J., McLean, C., & Hamilton, M. (2012). Visual literacy as a classroom approach. *Journal of Adolescent & Adult Literacy*, 55(5), 444–447. 10.1002/JAAL.00053

Sabin, R. (1996). *Comics, Comix & Graphic Novels: A History of Comic Art*. Phaidon Press, 61.

Sadoski, M., & Paivio, A. (2013). *Imagery and text: A dual coding theory of reading and writing*. Routledge. 10.4324/9780203801932

Saghafian, M., & O'Neill, D. K. (2018). A phenomenological study of teamwork in online and face-to-face student teams. *Higher Education*, 75(1), 57–73. 10.1007/s10734-017-0122-4

Şahin, A. (2014). *Eleştirel Medya Okuryazarlığı [Critical Media Literacy]*. Anı yayıncılık.

Salmassi, M. (2015, June). *Researchers Release First Report on Worldwide Addiction Statistics*. Partnership to End Addiction. https://drugfree.org/drug-and-alcohol-news/researchers-release-first-report-worldwide-addiction-statistics/

Sanders, R., Stovall, D., & White, T. (2018). *Twenty-first-century Jim Crow schools: the impact of charters on public education*. Beacon Press. https://www.socialstudies.org/position-statements

Savery, J. R. (2015). Overview of problem-based learning: Definitions and distinctions. *The Interdisciplinary Journal of Problem-Based Learning*, 1(1), 9–20.

Scheufele, D. A., & Tewksbury, D. (2007). Framing, Agenda Setting, And Priming: The Evolution Of Three Media Effects Models. *Journal of Communication*, 57(1), 9–20. 10.1111/j.002 1-9916.2007.00326.x

Schieble, M. (2012). Critical Conversations on Whiteness With Young Adult Literature. *Journal of Adolescent & Adult Literacy*, 56(3), 212–221. 10.1002/JAAL.00130

Schwarz, H. (2016). Diasporas of the Mind: Jewish and Postcolonial Writing and the Nightmare of History by Bryan Cheyette. *Philip Roth Studies*, 12(2), 105–109. 10.5703/philrothstud.12.2.0105

Scolari, C. A., Masanet, M.-J., Guerrero-Pico, M., & Establés, M.-J. (2018). Transmedia literacy in the new media ecology: Teens' transmedia skills and informal learning strategies. *El Profesional de la Información*, 27(4), 801–812. 10.3145/epi.2018.jul.09

Scolari, C. A., Rodríguez, N. L., & Masanet, M. J. (2019). Transmedia Education. From the contents generated by the users to the contents generated by the students. *Revista Latina de Comunicación Social*, (74), 116–132. 10.4185/RLCS-2019-1324

Sellman, D. (2010). The 10 most important things known about addiction. *Addiction (Abingdon, England)*, 105(1), 6–13. 10.1111/j.1360-0443.2009.02673.x19712126

Şener, D. K., Akkuş, D., Karaca, A., & Cangür, Ş. (2018). Lise öğrencilerinin madde kullanmama davranışlarını etkileyen faktörler [Factors Affecting Substance Non-Use Behaviors of High School Students]. *Addicta : the Turkish Journal on Addictions*, 5(3), 405–429.

Senxia, D. (2013). *Ri ri shi hao ri: Chadao dailai de shiwu zhong xingfu. [Everyday is a good day: Fifteen kinds of happiness brought by Chado]*. Printing Industry Publication.

Serafini, F. (2012). Expanding the four resources model: Reading visual and multi-modal texts. *Pedagogies*, 7(2), 150–164. 10.1080/1554480X.2012.656347

Shadowland #1 (2010). Script: A. Diggle. Art: B. Tan. *Black Panther #12* (2017). "A nation under our feet, part 10." Script: T. Coates. Art: B. Stelfreeze.

Shapira, T. (2019). Wrestling with legacy. In Darowski, J. (Ed.), *The Ages of The Flash: Essays on the Fastest Man Alive* (pp. 91–105). McFarland.

Sheridan, T., et al. (2023-2024). *Alan Scott: Green Lantern*. DC Comics.

Short, K. G. (2019). Critical Content Analysis of Visual Images. In Johnson, H., Mathis, J., & Short, K. G. (Eds.), *Critical Content Analysis of Visual Images in Books for Young People: Reading Images* (1st ed., pp. 3–22). Routledge. 10.4324/9780429426469-1

Singer, M. (2002). "Black Skins" and White Masks: Comic Books and the Secret of Race. *African American Review*, 36(1), 107–118. 10.2307/2903369

Slota, S., & Young, M. (2016). A New Hope: Negotiating the Integration of Transmedia Storytelling and Literacy Instruction. *Journal of Adolescent & Adult Literacy*, 59(6), 642-646. https://www.jstor.org/stable/44011325

Compilation of References

Smetana, J. G. (1983). Social-cognitive development: Domain distinctions and coordinations. *Developmental Review*, 3(2), 131–147. 10.1016/0273-2297(83)90027-8

Smyth, T. (2022). *Teaching with Comics and Graphic Novels*. Taylor & Francis. 10.4324/9781003291671

Snowber, C. N. (2012). Dancing a curriculum of hope: Cultivating passion as an embodied inquiry. *Journal of Curriculum Theorizing*, 28(2).

Solórzano, D. G., & Yosso, T. J. (2002). Critical Race Methodology: Counter-Storytelling as an Analytical Framework for Education Research. *Qualitative Inquiry*, 8(1), 23–44. 10.1177/107780040200800103

Sontag, S. (1964). *Against Interpretation and other Essays*. Farrar, Straus and Giroux.

Soriano, R. N. B. (2021). The World's Hero: God's and Archetypes in the Myth of Superman. *International Journal of Language and Literary Studies*, 3(2), 262–276. 10.36892/ijlls.v3i2.582

Sousanis, N. (2015). *Unflattening*. Harvard University Press.

Squire, K., & Dikkers, S. (2016). *Amplifying Learning with Digital Games: A Multifaceted Approach to Increasing Engagement*. Information Age Publishing.

Stewart, K. (2007). *Ordinary affects*. Duke University Press.

Stewart, T. T., Coombs, D., Fecho, B., & Hawley, T. (2019). Embracing wobble: Exploring novice teachers' efforts to enact dialogic literacy instruction. *Journal of Adolescent & Adult Literacy*, 63(3), 289–297. 10.1002/jaal.978

Strong, M. T., Cook, T., Belet, L., & Calarco, P. (2023). Changing the world: How comics and graphic novels can shift teaching. *Humanity & Society*, 47(2), 245–257. 10.1177/01605976231158969

Strong, M. T., Greenidge, G., & Chaplin, K. S. (2023). Afrofuturism as an instructional method. In Chin, J., & Kozimor, M. L. (Eds.), *Emerging stronger: Pedagogical lessons from the pandemic* (pp. 86–101). Routledge. 10.4324/9781003316336-12

Sun, L. (2017). Critical Encounters in a Middle School English Language Arts Classroom: Using Graphic Novels to Teach Critical Thinking & Reading for Peace Education. *Multicultural Education*, 25(1), 22–28.

Šuvaković, M. (2005). *Pojmovnik suvremene umetnosti*. Horetzky, Zagreb, Vlees & Beton.

The Lives and Times of Lucas Bishop #1 (2009). Script: D. Swierczynski. Art: L. Stroman.

The Lives and Times of Lucas Bishop #2 (2009). Script: D. Swierczynski. Art: L. Stroman.

Thein, A. H., Beach, R., & Parks, D. (2007). Perspective-taking as transformative practice in teaching multicultural literature to white students. *English Journal*, 97(2), 54–60. 10.58680/ej20076247

Theoharis, J.., & Woodard, K. (2005). *Groundwork local black freedom movements in America.* New York University.

Thomsen, J. (2018). Comics, Collage, and Other Things with Crayons: The Power of Composing with Image. *English Journal*, 107(3), 54–61. 10.58680/ej201829467

Thrower, A. C., Danawi, H., & Lockett, C. (2013). Determinants of High Pre-pregnancy BMI of U.S. Puerto Rican WIC Participants. *The International Journal of Childbirth Education*, 28(4), 55–61.

Thrower, A. C., Evangelista, A. A., Baker-Garder, R., & Mogaji, H. (2024). *Autoethnographic Tactics to Closing the Gap on Educational Attainment.* IGI Global., 10.4018/979-8-3693-1074-8

Timm, B., & Radomski, E. (Creators). (1992-1995). *Batman: The Animated Series.* Warner Bros. Animation.

Tobin, J. (2000). *Good guys don't wear gats": Children's talk about the media.* Teachers College Press.

Toliver, S. R. (2021). *Recovering Black storytelling in qualitative research.* Taylor & Francis. 10.4324/9781003159285

Turiel, E. (1983). *The development of social knowledge: Morality and convention.* Cambridge University Press.

Turiel, E. (1998). The development of morality. In Damon, W. (Ed.),; 5th ed., Vol. 3, pp. 863–932). Handbook of child psychology. Wiley.

Turiel, E. (2002). *The culture of morality.* Cambridge University Press.

Turiel, E., & Banas, K. A. (2020). The development of moral and social judgments: Social contexts and processes of coordination. *Eurasian Journal of Educational Research*, 20(85), 23–44. 10.14689/ejer.2020.85.2

Turiel, E., Killen, M., & Helwig, C. C. (1987). Morality: its structure, function, and vagaries. In Kagan, J., & Lamb, S. (Eds.), *The emergence of morality in young children* (pp. 155–243).

Turiel, E., & Nucci, L. (2018). Moral development in context. In Dick, A., & Mueller, U. (Eds.), *Advancing developmental science: Philosophy, theory, and method* (pp. 95–109). Psychology Press.

Uncanny X-Men #282 (1991). Script: W. Portacio. Art: J. Byrne.

Valtonen, T., Tedre, M., Mäkitalo, K., & Vartiainen, H. (2019). Media Literacy Education in the Age of Machine Learning. *The Journal of Media Literacy Education*, 11(2), 20–36. 10.23860/JMLE-2019-11-2-2

Variety Staff. (2018). Post Malone and Swae Lee drop new song 'Sunflower' from 'Spider-Man' soundtrack". *Variety.* https://variety.com/2018/music/news/post-malone-swae-lee-sunflower-spider-man-soundtrack-1202984388/

Compilation of References

Vasquez, V. (2010). *Getting beyond "I like the book": Creating space for critical literacy in K-6 classrooms* (2nd ed.). International Reading Association.

Verrone, W. (2013). *Adaptation and avant-garde: Alternative perspectives on adaptation theory and practice*. Bloomsbury Academic.

Versaci, R. (2001). How comic books can change the way our students see literature: One teacher's perspective. *English Journal*, 91(2), 61–67.

Vin. (n.d.). Spider-Man Miles Morales reading guide. *Cosmic Circus*.https://thecosmiccircus.com/spider-man-miles-morales-reading-guide/

Vygotsky, L. (1978). Mind in Society: The Development of Higher Psychological Processes. Harvard University Press, 80.

Wainryb, C. (2004). 'Is' and 'ought': Moral judgments about the world as understood. *New Directions for Child and Adolescent Development*, 103(103), 3–18. 10.1002/cd.9415112532

Wainryb, C., & Turiel, E. (1993). Conceptual and informational features in moral decision making. *Educational Psychologist*, 28(3), 205–218. 10.1207/s15326985ep2803_2

Wandtke, T. R. (2012). *The meaning of superhero comic books*. McFarland.

Wanzo, R. (2015). It's a Hero? Black Comics and Satirizing Subjection. In Gateward, F., & Jennings, J. (Eds.), *The Blacker the ink: Constructions of black identity in comics and sequential art* (pp. 314–332). Rutgers University Press. 10.2307/j.ctt1hd186b.19

Wesner, M. S., & Miller, T. (2008). Boomers and millennials have much in common. *Organization Development Journal*, 26(3), 89.

West, C. (1999). *The Cornel West reader*. Basic Books.

Whaley, D. (2016). *Black Women in Sequence: Re-inking Comics, Graphic Novels, and Anime*. University of Washington Press.

What is Visual Literacy? (n.d.). Visual Literacy Today. https://visualliteracytoday.org/what-is-visual-literacy/

White, M. D. (2019). *Batman and ethics*. John Wiley & Sons.

Wiebe, S. (2015). Poetic Inquiry: A Fierce, Tender, and Mischievous Relationship with Lived Experience. *Language and Literature*, 17(3), 152. 10.20360/G2VP4N

Williams, A. (2018). The '*Spider-Man: Into The Spider-Verse*' soundtrack is exactly what Black superhero music should be. *Uproxx*. https://uproxx.com/music/spider-man-into-the-spider-verse-soundtrack-review/

Wilson, S. (2011, August 2). Miles Morales: Spider-Man's PC new replacement is half-Black, half-Latino. *LA Weekly*.https://www.laweekly.com/miles-morales-spider-mans-pc-new-replacement-is-half-black-half-latino/

Wilterdink, N., & Form, W. (2024, May 18). *Social Change*. Britannica. https://www.britannica.com/topic/social-change/Patterns-of-social-change

Wissman, K. K., Staples, J. M., Vasudevan, L., & Nichols, R. E. (2015). Cultivating research pedagogies with adolescents: Created spaces, engaged participation, and embodied inquiry. *Anthropology & Education Quarterly*, 46(2), 186–197. 10.1111/aeq.12098

Wolk, D. (2021). *All of the Marvels: A journey to the ends of the biggest story ever told*. Penguin.

Wong, D. (2021). Witnessing. In Diamond, B., & Castelo-Branco, S. (Eds.), *Transforming Ethnomusicology* (pp. 187–201). Oxford University Press. 10.1093/oso/9780197517604.003.0012

Wood, M. (2016). Moral decisions in Marvel's Civil War: Stages of hero development. In Langley, T. (Ed.), *Captain America vs. Iron Man: Freedom, Security, Psychology* (pp. 11–23). Sterling Press.

Worlds, M., & Miller, H. C. (2019). *Miles Morales: Spider-Man* and reimagining the canon for racial justice. *English Journal*, 108(4), 43–50. 10.58680/ej201930049

Wright, B. W. (2003). *Comic book nation: The transformation of youth culture in America*. JHU Press. 10.56021/9780801865145

Wright, J. C. (2021). Morality as a regulator of divergence: Protecting against deviance while promoting diversity. *Social Cognition*, 39(1), 81–98. 10.1521/soco.2021.39.1.81

X, M., & Haley, Alex. (1992). *The Autobiography of Malcolm X* (1st Ballantine books hardcover ed.). Ballantine Books.

X-Factor #26 (2007). "Messiah complex, part 7." Script: P. David. Art: S. Eaton.

X-Men #206 (2007). "Messiah complex, part 9." Script: M. Cary. Art: C. Bachalo.

X-Men: Legends #5 (2023). Script: W. Portacio & B. Haberlin. Art: W. Portacio.

X-Men: Legends #6 (2023). Script: B. Haberlin & W. Portacio. Art: W. Portacio.

Yang, G. (2008). Graphic novels in the classroom. *Language Arts*, 85(3), 185–192. 10.58680/la20086181

Yıldırım, A. ve Şimşek H. (2006). *Sosyal bilimlerde nitel araştırma yöntemleri [Qualitative research methods in social sciences]*. Seçkin Yayıncılık.

Young, J. L., Foster, M. D., & Hines, D. (2018). Even Cinderella is White: (Re)Centering Black girls' voices as literacies of resistance. *English Journal*, 107(6), 102–108. 10.58680/ej201829719

Yücel, G., & Şan, Ş. (2018). Dijital Oyunlarda Bağımlılık ve Şiddet: Blue Whale Oyunu Üzerinde Bir İnceleme [Addiction and Violence in Digital Games: A Review on the Blue Whale Game]. *AJIT-e: Academic Journal of Information Technology*, 9(32), 87–100. 10.5824/1309-1581.2018.2.006.x

Zaino, K., & Bell, J. (2022). We are each other's breath: Tracing interdependency through critical poetic inquiry. *Studies in Sociology of Education*, 31(2), 27–48.

Compilation of References

Zou, Z., Wang, H., d'Oleire Uquillas, F., Wang, X., Ding, J., & Chen, H. (2017). Definition of substance and non-substance addiction. *Substance and non-substance addiction*, 21-41. .10.1007/978-981-10-5562-1_2

About the Contributors

Jason D. DeHart earned his PhD from The University of Tennessee, Knoxville in 2019. DeHart has authored a forthcoming book for NCTE and has edited a number of books for IGI Global and Routledge.

***

Alex Evangelista (EdD) is an Assistant Professor in the BMCC Health Education Department. Professor Evangelista's research considers the impact and training of educators in collaborative online and associated technology-based learning experiences. Professor Evangelista's educational background is in Physical Education, Health, and Educational Leadership. He has taught Physical and Health Education at all levels, K-12 and higher education for over 15 years. Professor Evangelista holds several fitness and first aid certifications, including Certified Strength & Conditioning Specialist (CSCS) and Basic Life Support (BLS). Professor Evangelista also has an interest in health and fitness-related entrepreneurship and has received several grants for his work in this area.

Christian Hines, Ph.D., is an assistant professor of Literacy at Texas State University. She is a comics and young adult literature in education scholar-practitioner. Her research highlights the representation of Black youth and adolescence in literature, particularly their visual narratives in comics and graphic novels. She leans into comics and graphic novels, specifically diverse teen superhero narratives as a way for students and practitioners to understand the intersectional lived experiences of youth and the impact that youth has on society and enacting resistance.

David E. Low is an Associate Professor of Literacy Education at California State University, Fresno. His published work explores intersections among comics, multimodal authorship, pop culture, identity, and social critique.

Justin F. Martin, Ph.D., is an Associate Professor of Psychology at Whitworth University. His research explores the intersection of moral development and superhero and dystopian media. His superhero scholarship highlights superhero media as a context for generating pedagogical and research activities that examine the relationship between moral and nonmoral social concepts. Recent publications explore Black Panther, Luke Cage, Mr. Freeze, Bishop, and The Walking Dead. He is the co-editor of Arkham's Souls: A Multidisciplinary Analysis of Batman's Villains and Villainesses (Lexington, 2023) with Marco Favaro. He teaches courses in statistics, research methods, developmental psychology, moral development, and morality within the Marvel Universe.

Ozge Misirli is a faculty member of Department of Computer Education and Instructional Technology in Eskisehir Osmangazi University. She has an MA in Primary Math Teaching and a Ph.D. in Computer Education and Instructional Technology. She has offered several undergraduate courses such as Information Technologies and media literacy. She conducts researches on social media, effective use of social media by children and families, ICT integration and gender balance in ICT. She is still working as a faculty member at Eskisehir Osmangazi University.

About the Contributors

Vladimir Popov (b. 1982) was born in Zrenjanin, Serbia. He graduated from the Technical Faculty Mihajlo Pupin in Zrenjanin with an MSc in information technologies. He continued his education at the Faculty of Media and Communications in Belgrade, Singidunum University, where he is currently a Ph.D. student at the program of Transdisciplinary Studies of Contemporary Art and Media. During his professional artist career, he worked in the field of commercial illustration and sequential storytelling for various US and European publishers, such as Z2 Comics, Scout Comics, Dark Horse, Vault Comics, Top Cow, Image Comics, IDW Publishing, Boom Studios, Dynamite Entertainment, Stela, DoubleTake, Wired Magazine, Soleil, Glenat, La Feltrinelli, and others on high-profile licensed titles such as Clive Barker's Hellraiser and Next Testament, Robocop, Steed and Mrs. Peel, Noir, Pathfinder, Cartoon Network's Adventure Time and Amazing World of Gumball, Maze Runner and other creator-owned titles, multimedia projects, crypto art, etc.

René M. Rodríguez-Astacio (he/him/his) is an Assistant Professor of Secondary English Studies and Adolescent Literacies at California State University, Fresno. Born and raised in Puerto Rico, his teaching specialties are Children's and Young Adult literature, and adolescent literacies. He researches and advocates for diverse representations of adolescents, and centers his work around Latine and queer representation in literature for adolescents in its many forms. He currently serves on the Lesbian, Gay, Bisexual, Transgender, Queer/Questioning, Intersex, Asexual, + (LGBTQIA+) Advisory Committee of NCTE, as well as Elected Board Member in the Children's Literature Assembly (CLA).

Yamil Sárraga-López is a lecturer in the English Department at the California State University, Fresno. His work explores teaching writing in the classroom including the potentials of children's and young adult literature as well as graphic novels towards the development of writing skills for K-16 students. He is also interested in multicultural literature and it's role in the English classroom.

Gözde Tekbaş completed her undergraduate and graduate studies in psychological counselling and guidance at Hacettepe University. During her undergraduate years, she conducted mental health counselling sessions with 12 clients accompanied by a supervisor, and increased this number to more than 30 during her master's years. In the same years, she conducted short-term career counselling sessions with more than 50 clients within the scope of Career Fair. She prepared her master's thesis on decision and career strategies for adolescents and developed two scales within the scope of her thesis. Since 2021, she has been continuing her doctoral education at Hacettepe University. In the same year, TEKBAŞ started to work as a research assistant in the guidance and psychological counselling programme at Eskişehir Osmangazi University and continues to work in the same institution.

Anika Thrower earned her B.S. in consumer science/nutrition from Norfolk State University and both her MPH and Ph.D. in public health and community health from Walden University. As a health practitioner, Dr. Thrower served in Women, Infants and Children's (WIC) programs around the United States for over 16 years. Her most valued experiences includes serving within a Native American community and within the first WIC program in the state of Connecticut. Because of her background, service, and research, she has expertise in utilizing the transtheoretical behavioral health model in underrepresented populations. Serving as a principle researcher and endorsed by the Connecticut Department of Public Health she completed research within a sample of a WIC clinic investigating health-based variables steeped in VENA. Because of the high quality of her research, she won the Presidential Alumni Research Dissemination Award within her institution of higher learning. Dr. Thrower's has published several peer-reviewed scholarly articles. Appointed by the mayor, she co-chaired the New Haven Food Policy Council. Along with others, Dr. Thrower's expertise led to establishing the city's first Food Action Plan. She serves as an Assistant Professor within the Health Education department at City University of New York-Borough of Manhattan Community College. Before her current position, Dr. Thrower taught at Springfield College and Southern Connecticut State University. She teaches coursework in stress management and community health education rooted in culturally responsive pedagogy. Dr. Thrower's research interests include investigating mental health, stress and food security issues that adversely affect the quality of life of women and other members of underrepresented populations. Long standing she advocates issues around maternal & child health. As exemplified in her book entitled The Art of Dominating the Winner's Circle of the College-Minded Student she seeking ways to close gaps in obtaining higher education attainment.

About the Contributors

Ran Xiang is a PhD candidate in the Department of Curriculum and Pedagogy at UBC, with a focus on Art Education. Before pursuing her current degree, she has finished her first MA in Comparative Literature at University of Alberta and her second MA in Education Studies at UBC. Her dissertation project investigates the educative potential of tea ceremony learning. Her research interests include arts-based methodology, object, and materiality, affect and bodily learning.

Zeynep Yurtseven Avci holds a PhD in 2012 from North Carolina State University, Department of Instructional Technology. She is currently working as an Associate professor in the Department of Computer Education and Instructional Technology at the Faculty of Education and director of Distance Education Center at Eskisehir Osmangazi University. Her areas of expertise include innovative educational technologies, development of instructional materials using technology, contribution of technology use in learning, communication and collaboration tools, and technology professional development. Dr. Avci has national and international articles, book chapters and papers on educational technology.

Index

A

addictions 149, 151, 152, 160, 161, 162, 164, 165, 167, 168, 169, 170, 172, 173, 174
American Civil Rights 194
artistic collaboration 240, 245, 258
Aura 223
autoethnographic case study 175, 177, 180, 186, 187

B

Black girl literacies 1, 7, 8, 9, 22, 26
Black Power 190, 191, 192, 207
Black Power Movement 190
Boricua Identity 39, 57

C

Civil Rights 63, 189, 190, 191, 192, 193, 194, 195, 196, 198, 203, 206, 207, 209
collaborative learning 133, 134, 138, 139, 140, 141, 142, 143, 144, 145, 146, 147
comic books 2, 23, 26, 27, 28, 29, 30, 31, 32, 33, 34, 36, 37, 40, 51, 56, 58, 99, 101, 114, 121, 122, 123, 124, 125, 127, 128, 181, 182
comics 1, 2, 3, 4, 5, 6, 8, 21, 23, 24, 25, 26, 27, 29, 31, 32, 34, 35, 36, 37, 45, 47, 49, 56, 58, 59, 61, 62, 67, 80, 91, 99, 100, 103, 104, 105, 106, 107, 108, 109, 110, 111, 113, 114, 115, 116, 117, 118, 120, 121, 125, 126, 127, 128, 129, 130, 131, 132, 177, 178, 179, 180, 181, 182, 187, 260
critical literacies 2, 61
Critical Multimodal Literacy 238, 240, 244, 251, 260, 261
critical thinking 7, 89, 127, 128, 130, 141, 142, 143, 187, 260
culturally responsive 3, 20

D

DC universe 106, 108, 112
digital literacies 8
Diversity in Comics 187

E

educational experiences 141, 142, 143, 168
educational settings 128, 139, 141
educational spaces 3, 4, 5, 9, 14, 39
education attainment 133, 135
emotional literacy 211, 212
English Education 25, 26
enrollment 133, 134, 135, 137, 141, 143, 145, 147, 205, 206

F

fandom 103, 105, 106, 110, 111, 112, 113, 114, 115, 116, 175, 176, 181, 182, 184

G

Golden Age 104, 108, 111, 115, 121
graphic novels 1, 2, 3, 4, 5, 7, 8, 9, 16, 21, 22, 23, 24, 25, 26, 27, 28, 30, 33, 40, 49, 51, 58, 59, 61, 63, 98, 99, 100, 104, 114, 132, 178, 181, 187

H

higher education 133, 134, 135, 137, 140, 141, 142, 143, 144, 146, 147, 186, 187
higher-order thinking 126, 128
historical memory 189, 190, 192
human psyche 118, 123, 124, 130

L

literacy practices 1, 2, 3, 4, 7, 9, 10, 20, 21, 260

M

Marvel Comics 1, 24, 25, 31, 34, 36, 47, 58, 61, 105

media consumption habits 149, 157
media literacy 7, 8, 21, 25, 114, 126, 128, 142, 149, 156, 157, 160, 169, 170, 171, 173, 174, 210
mental health 127, 129, 167
Miles Morales 17, 25, 28, 29, 30, 31, 32, 33, 34, 35, 36, 37, 39, 40, 41, 42, 44, 45, 46, 47, 49, 50, 51, 53, 55, 56, 57, 58, 59, 60, 61, 62, 63, 64
Morality 66, 67, 68, 69, 75, 77, 82, 89, 90, 91, 95, 97, 98, 99, 100, 101, 120, 123, 124, 125, 130

N

national treasure 215, 222, 234
nontraditional students 133, 134, 137, 139, 141

P

participatory culture 115, 127, 131, 141, 145
Poetic Literacy 248, 250, 257
popular characters 104, 107, 111, 116, 181, 182, 184
Primary Source Analysis 195
psychological complexity 41, 120, 122, 123, 124
psychological depth 126, 129, 130

R

reading experiences 8, 9

S

scholarly attention 65, 72
science fiction 16, 178
sensui garden 228, 230, 236
societal attitudes 128, 129
societal issues 125, 126, 130
societal norms 5, 117, 124, 125, 129
societal order 67, 79
socio-academic variables 140, 141
STEM 18, 24, 110, 181, 184
Superheroes 5, 6, 17, 23, 24, 26, 34, 37, 44, 62, 63, 65, 66, 67, 68, 69, 70, 71, 73, 75, 76, 77, 78, 79, 84, 86, 88, 89, 90, 91, 92, 93, 94, 96, 98, 99, 100, 103, 111, 114, 123
superhero narratives 5, 63, 66, 67, 68, 69, 70, 71, 73, 75, 79, 80, 88, 91, 104, 114

T

Teamwork skills 140, 141, 142, 144, 147
tenmoku tea 213, 222, 227, 235
Transmedia Storytelling 118, 128, 129, 130, 133, 134, 142, 143, 145, 147, 238, 241, 243, 245, 261

V

video games 28, 30, 33, 45, 46, 124, 125, 127, 128, 129, 130, 151, 153, 177
Vignette 189, 190, 198, 200
Visual Literacy 3, 26, 126, 127, 244, 246, 247, 248, 260, 261
visual reading 253, 254, 255, 257
visual storytelling 3, 125

Ensure Quality Research is Introduced to the Academic Community

Become a Reviewer for IGI Global Authored Book Projects

  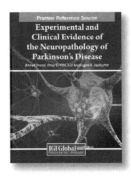 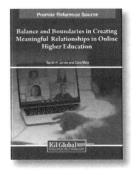

The overall success of an authored book project is dependent on quality and timely manuscript evaluations.

Applications and Inquiries may be sent to:
development@igi-global.com

Applicants must have a doctorate (or equivalent degree) as well as publishing, research, and reviewing experience. Authored Book Evaluators are appointed for one-year terms and are expected to complete at least three evaluations per term. Upon successful completion of this term, evaluators can be considered for an additional term.

If you have a colleague that may be interested in this opportunity, we encourage you to share this information with them.

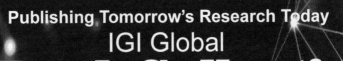

Are You Ready to Publish Your Research?

IGI Global offers book authorship and editorship opportunities across three major subject areas, including Business, STM, and Education.

Benefits of Publishing with IGI Global:

- Free one-on-one editorial and promotional support.
- Expedited publishing timelines that can take your book from start to finish in less than one (1) year.
- Choose from a variety of formats, including Edited and Authored References, Handbooks of Research, Encyclopedias, and Research Insights.
- Utilize IGI Global's eEditorial Discovery® submission system in support of conducting the submission and double-blind peer review process.
- IGI Global maintains a strict adherence to ethical practices due in part to our full membership with the Committee on Publication Ethics (COPE).
- Indexing potential in prestigious indices such as Scopus®, Web of Science™, PsycINFO®, and ERIC – Education Resources Information Center.
- Ability to connect your ORCID iD to your IGI Global publications.
- Earn honorariums and royalties on your full book publications as well as complimentary content and exclusive discounts.

Join Your Colleagues from Prestigious Institutions, Including:

Learn More at: www.igi-global.com/publish
or by Contacting the Acquisitions Department at: acquisition@igi-global.com

Individual Article & Chapter Downloads
US$ 37.50/each

Easily Identify, Acquire, and Utilize Published Peer-Reviewed Findings in Support of Your Current Research

- Browse Over **170,000+ Articles & Chapters**
- **Accurate & Advanced** Search
- Affordably Acquire **International Research**
- **Instantly Access** Your Content
- Benefit from the *InfoSci® Platform Features*

" *It really provides an excellent entry into the research literature of the field. It presents a manageable number of highly relevant sources on topics of interest to a wide range of researchers. The sources are scholarly, but also accessible to 'practitioners'.* "

- Ms. Lisa Stimatz, MLS, University of North Carolina at Chapel Hill, USA